ANTI-GRAVITY & THE WORLD GRID

Edited by David Hatcher Childress

The Lost Science Series:

- •THE ANTI-GRAVITY HANDBOOK
- •ANTI-GRAVITY & THE WORLD GRID
- •ANTI-GRAVITY & THE UNIFIED FIELD
- •VIMANA AIRCRAFT OF ANCIENT INDIA & ATLANTIS
- •THE MANUAL OF FREE ENERGY DEVICES & SYSTEMS
- •TAPPING THE ZERO POINT ENERGY
- •THE BRIDGE TO INFINITY
- •THE ENERGY GRID
- •ETHER TECHNOLOGY
- •THE DEATH OF ROCKETRY

Write for our free catalog of unusual science and travel books.

ANTI-GRAVITY & THE WORLD GRID

Edited by David Hatcher Childress

Adventures Unlimited Press/Publisher's Network
STELLE, ILLINOIS 60919

I dedicate this book to the ***ancients,***
who mapped the world grid many,
many years ago. This lost science is
just now being rediscovered.

ANTI-GRAVITY & THE WORLD GRID

Printed in the United States of America

Fourth Printing, June, 1992

ISBN 0-932813-03-8

Published by
Adventures Unlimited Press
Box 22, Stelle, Illinois 60919-9989 USA

TABLE OF CONTENTS

Special Thanks to Richard Leviton, Bill Donovan, Bethe & Bill, Bruce Cathie, Dave Millman, Ideal Computers, Nadia, Tammy, Jake, Harry, Richard LeFlors Clark, Carole, Thomas Bearden and all the people at the Gaia Conference and the Tesla Society—without their help, this book would never have been made.

There isn't any energy crisis .
It's simply a crisis of ignorance .
-R. Buckminster Fuller

ANTI-GRAVITY & THE WORLD GRID

Edited by David Hatcher Childress

MAPPING THE WORLD GRID
BY
DAVID HATCHER CHILDRESS

What is the World Grid? How can it be it mapped? What does it do? Why should we be concerned about it? What does it have to with anti-gravity?

In my many travels around the world in search of lost cities and ancient mysteries I have often wondered if there was some link connecting many of the ancient megalithic sites. Some years ago I discovered that there was no such thing as a coincidence. If the placement of ancient sites was no coincidence, what then was the overall organizing principle for the carefully laid out world wide pattern?

Are megalithic sites laid out on a grid? What is a grid anyway? According to my large and trusty Webster's dictionary, a grid is " a network of uniformly spaced horizontal and perpendicular line, specifically one used for locating points (as on a map, chart or aerial photograph) by means of a system of coordinates."

In other words, we are speaking about an intelligent geometric pattern into which, theoretically, the Earth and its energies are organized--- and possibly in which the ubiquitous ancient megalithic sites are also positioned.

What we are speaking of is fundamentally different from longitudinal and latitudinal lines that we are so familiar with from conventional geography. Proponents of the Earth Grid theory suggest that the grid lines are actually of a more basic nature than the more arbitrary, later conventions of cartography.

However the familiar image of the Earth as a globe girded in a lattice of longitude and lattitude lines helps us understand what an Earth Grid, based on more primary energy lines, might be like. I say "energy lines" particularly, because one of the most consistent observations readers will encounter in this book is that the geometric pattern of the Earth Grid is *energetic* in nature. And that this Earth energy, organized into a precise web, was once, and can be again, the source of a free and inexhaustible supply of power, once empowering older civilizations of high tehnological achievement. Most Grid theorists state confidently that this Grid technology can be reclaimed again---today.

While UFOs are a very controversial subject, which may contribute to its perennial popularity, some theorists claim that there is a fundamental relation between UFO phenomenon and

Mapping the ***World Grid,*** was popular in the Middle Ages and many techniques are still used by the dowsers of today.

magnetic-vortex-gravity anomalies in the Grid. This subject will be discussed in the book.

Furthermore, gravity is as complex a subject as UFOs and the World Grid. Ask your average man on the street if he knows what gravity is---most likely he will say, "Ofcourse! Everyone knows what gravity is. That's what keeps my feet on the ground!"

Even though gravity is an apparent physical principle defining life on Earth, it is still beyond the understanding of even the most intelligent scientist. No one has yet satisfactorily explained gravity. Is gravity a manifestation of energy from the Earth, connected with the Grid? If so, can we use certain points on the Grid to master gravity? Are UFOs defying the Earth's gravity field, using some sort of anti-gravity? These are all pressing questions. Perhaps by observing UFO phenomena, we can deduce certain engineering principles in operation in the Grid.

Already the Grid seems to implicate two fundamental realities of physical life: gravity and energy. In the pages that follow, you'll be treated to some of the most advanced and exciting theories on the World Grid.

Contributors to this volume approach the Grid from diverse professional and philosophical points of view. The result is a compilation of views (the first, and possibly definitive) of the Grid that spans the poetic to the mathematical.

For example, professional anthropologists Bethe Hagens and William Becker's chapter, "The Planetary Grid System," gives a thorough overview of the geometry and geography of a unique World Grid model they call "EarthStar". Bruce Cathie, author of four books on the harmonics of the World Grid, presents a fascinating mathematical probe into the Grid incorporating Einstein's Unified Field Theory; Cathie comes up with some most surprising conclusions.

Richard LeFlors Clark, Ph.D., discusses gravity vortex areas around the Earth that have been exploited either secretly by governments or by amateur scientists for the purposes of levitation and anti-gravity. He warns that you may become "permanent space debris" if you wander into one of these areas at the wrong time!

Richard Leviton presents the Grid as a interactive spiritual workshop for the purposes of aligning human with planetary energies through the "megalithic temple." The Earth Grid is seen as a living hologram of the organization of the solar system, intricately linked with the life and destiny of human beings.

Harry Osoff discusses the controversial and totally

MARINO SANUDO's map of the world from the beginning of the 14th century. From Bongars, *Gesta Dei per Francos.* Hanoviae 1611. (Diam. of circle in original 330 m. m.)

Creating a grid is essential in any map making.

mysterious U.S. Navy "**Philadelphia Experiment**", and relates it to the Grid structure and governmental research cover-ups. He thereby strengthens tahe view of secret governmental research into the areas of anti-gravity and the World Grid. Then Barbara Hero gives a musician's understanding of the Earth in her chapter, "International Harmony Based Upon A Music Of Planetary Grid Systems."

Other topics in the book include discussions of the electrical genius Nikola Tesla and the "Star Wars" plan, the mysterious Oregon Vortex, acoustic levitation of stones, and more. Nor do we take ourselves so seriously that we can't relax and have a little laugh from time to time. Thus, the back of the book has chapters on anti-gravity patents, Newspaper Headlines, The Anti-Gravity File and even Comix.

What are we to make of all this seemingly wild conjecture? The reports of our Grid theorists certainly go against the grain of modern scientific views. And they draw upon information which is often times subjective at best, and certainly controversial. Grid theories challenge the very basis of our physical world view. Nor do they all agree with each other. However, major innovations in science often come from seemingly "crackpot" speculation. I leave it to the readers to decide which theories fit best into their own reality structure.

Personally, now, as I continue traveling around the world, I regard with a more thoughtful eye the complex of ancient temples, cities and mounds. While I may not agree with, or totally understand, all of the theories presented in this book, each one has illuminated for me in a special way the reality that the Earth is a unified living planet, and that we as humans have a special and responsible place within this total enviroment.

Earth's Magnetic Field

–THE OLD CONCEPTS–

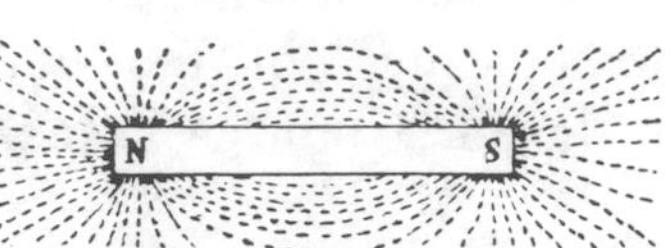

–THE NEW CONCEPTS–

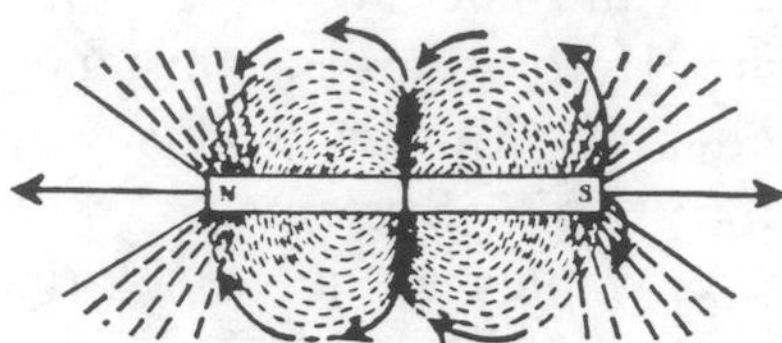

–THE OLD–

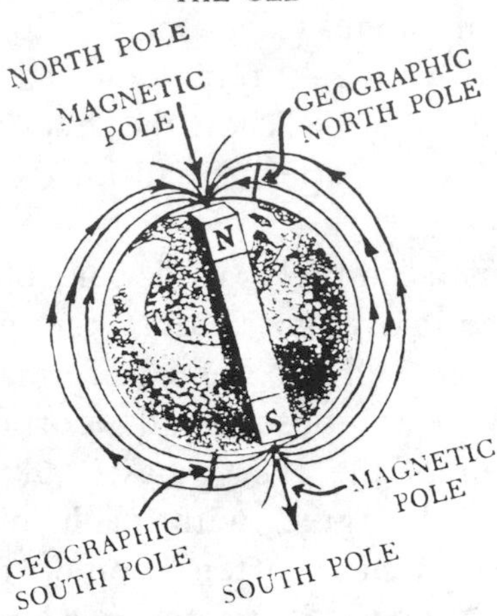

The Old Concepts of the Laws of Magnetism

–THE NEW–

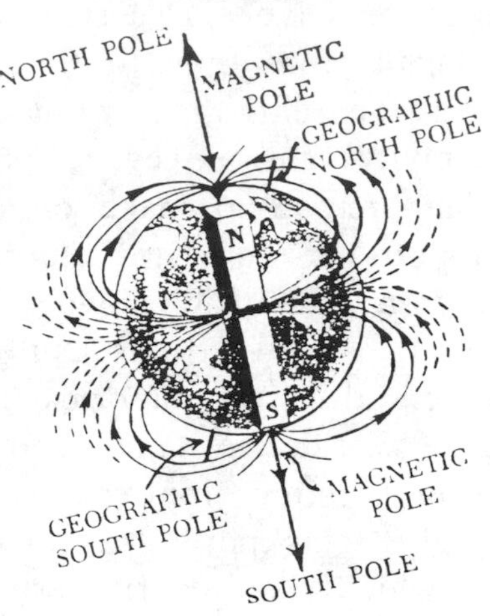

The New Concepts of the Laws of Magnetism

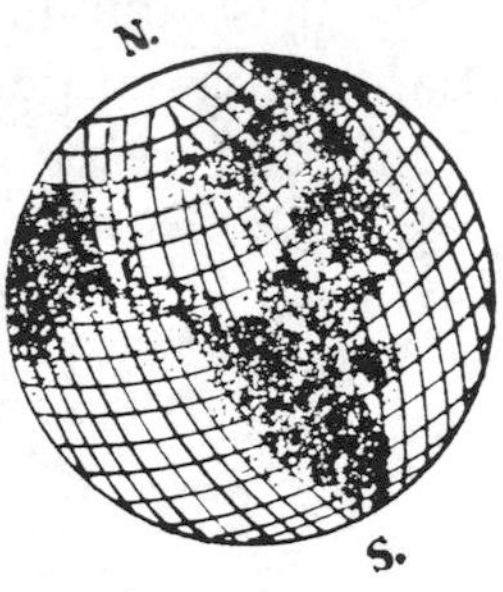

From the book, MAGNETISM AND ITS EFFECTS ON THE LIVING SYSTEM by Albert Davis and Walter Rawls, Jr. Here we see how the Earth's Magnetic Field creates an electro-magnetic grid around the earth. What does this grid have to do with the earth's gravitational field?

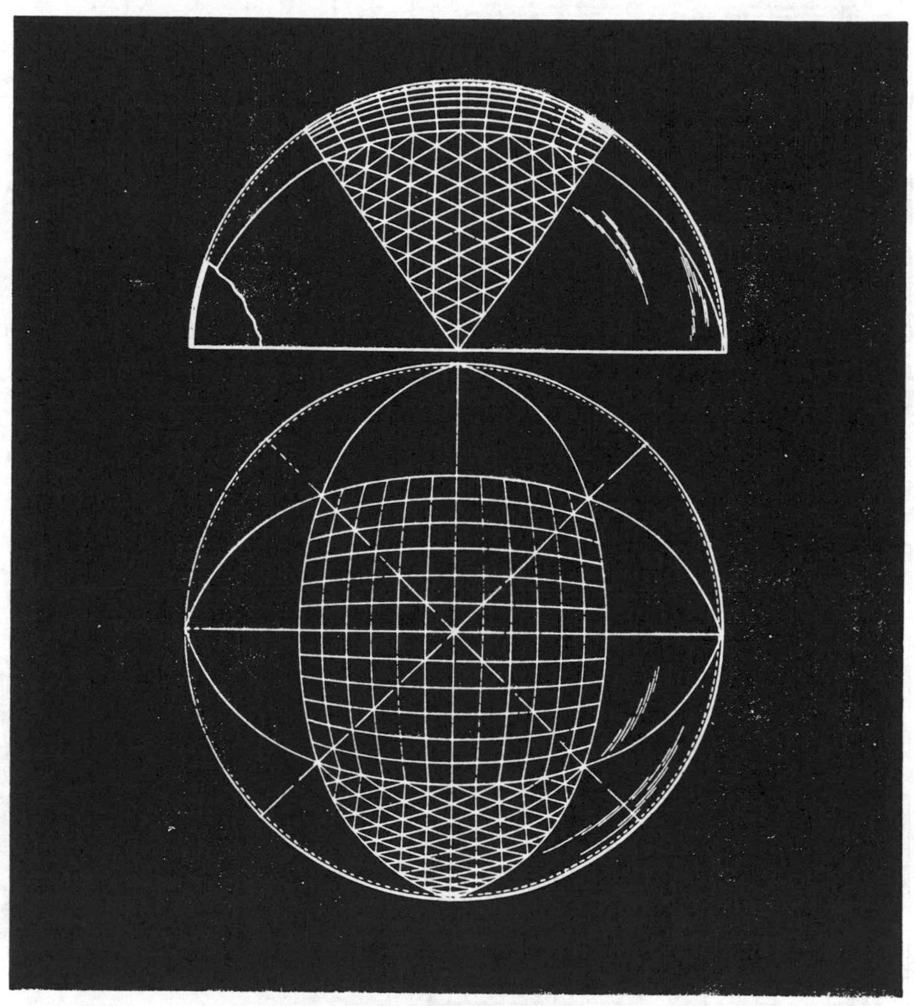

U.S. patent drawing for Dymaxion map

R. Buckminster Fuller did a great deal of work on the world grid. He copyrighted his "dymaxion" map in 1946.

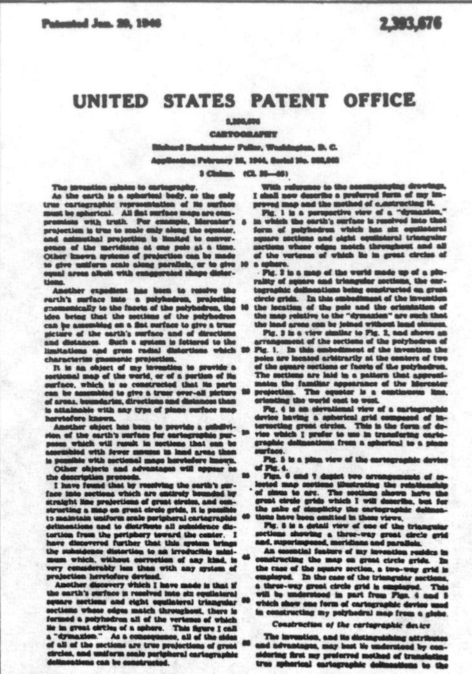

Patented Jan. 29, 1946 2,393,676

UNITED STATES PATENT OFFICE

2,393,676

CARTOGRAPHY

Richard Buckminster Fuller, Washington, D. C.

Application February 25, 1944, Serial No. [illegible]

3 Claims. (Cl. 35—46)

The invention relates to cartography.

As the earth is a spherical body, so the only true cartographic representation of its surface must be spherical. All flat surface maps are compromises with truth. For example, Mercator's projection is true to scale only along the equator, and azimuthal projection is limited to convergence of the meridians at one pole at a time. Other known systems of projection can be made to give uniform scale along parallels, or to give equal areas albeit with exaggerated shape distortions.

Another expedient has been to resolve the earth's surface into a polyhedron, projecting gnomonically to the facets of the polyhedron, the idea being that the sections of the polyhedron can be assembled on a flat surface to give a truer picture of the earth's surface and of directions and distances. Such a system is fettered to the limitations and gross radial distortions which characterize gnomonic projection.

It is an object of my invention to provide a sectional map of the world, or of a portion of its surface, which is so constructed that its parts can be assembled to give a truer over-all picture of areas, boundaries, directions and distances than is attainable with any type of plane surface map heretofore known.

Another object has been to provide a subdivision of the earth's surface for cartographic purposes which will result in sections that can be assembled with fewer seams in land areas than is possible with sectional maps heretofore known.

Other objects and advantages will appear as the description proceeds.

I have found that by resolving the earth's surface into sections which are entirely bounded by straight line projections of great circles, and constructing a map on great circle grids, it is possible to maintain uniform scale peripheral cartographic delineations and to distribute all subsidence distortion from the periphery toward the center. I have discovered further that this system brings the subsidence distortion to an irreducible minimum which, without correction of any kind, is very considerably less than with any system of projection heretofore devised.

Another discovery which I have made is that if the earth's surface is resolved into six equilateral square sections and eight equilateral triangular sections whose edges match throughout, there is formed a polyhedron all of the vertexes of which lie in great circles of a sphere. This figure I call a "dymaxion." As a consequence, all of the sides of all of the sections are true projections of great circles, and uniform scale peripheral cartographic delineations can be constructed.

With reference to the accompanying drawings, I shall now describe a preferred form of my improved map and the method of constructing it.

Fig. 1 is a perspective view of a "dymaxion," in which the earth's surface is resolved into that form of polyhedron which has six equilateral square sections and eight equilateral triangular sections whose edges match throughout and all of the vertexes of which lie in great circles of a sphere.

Fig. 2 is a map of the world made up of a plurality of square and triangular sections, the cartographic delineations being constructed on great circle grids. In this embodiment of the invention the location of the pole and the orientation of the map relative to the "dymaxion" are such that the land areas can be joined without land cleavage.

Fig. 3 is a view similar to Fig. 2, and shows an arrangement of the sections of the polyhedron of Fig. 1. In this embodiment of the invention the poles are located arbitrarily at the centers of two of the square sections or facets of the polyhedron. The sections are laid in a pattern that approximates the familiar appearance of the Mercator projection. The equator is a continuous line, orienting the world east to west.

Fig. 4 is an elevational view of a cartographic device having a spherical grid composed of intersecting great circles. This is the form of device which I prefer to use in transferring cartographic delineations from a spherical to a plane surface.

Fig. 5 is a plan view of the cartographic device of Fig. 4.

Figs. 6 and 7 depict two arrangements of selected map sections illustrating the relationship of chord to arc. The sections shown have the great circle grids which I will describe, but for the sake of simplicity the cartographic delineations have been omitted in these views.

Fig. 8 is a detail view of one of the triangular sections showing a three-way great circle grid and, superimposed, meridians and parallels.

An essential feature of my invention resides in constructing the map on great circle grids. In the case of the square section, a two-way grid is employed. In the case of the triangular sections, a three-way great circle grid is employed. This will be understood in part from Figs. 4 and 5 which show one form of cartographic device used in constructing my polyhedral map from a globe.

Construction of the cartographic device

The invention, and its distinguishing attributes and advantages, may best be understood by considering first my preferred method of translating true spherical cartographic delineations to the

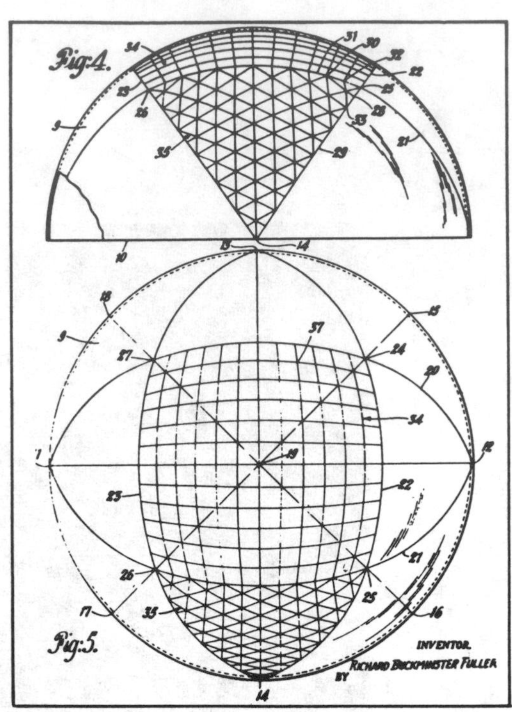

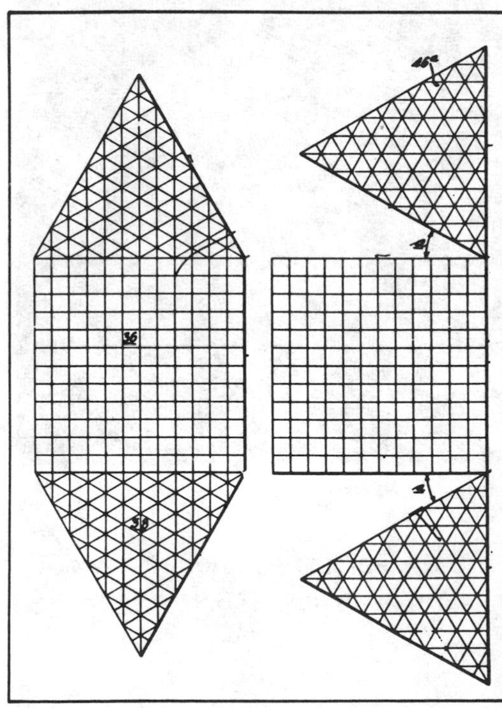

Jan. 29, 1946. R. B. FULLER 2,393,676

CARTOGRAPHY

Filed Feb. 25, 1944 5 Sheets-Sheet 1

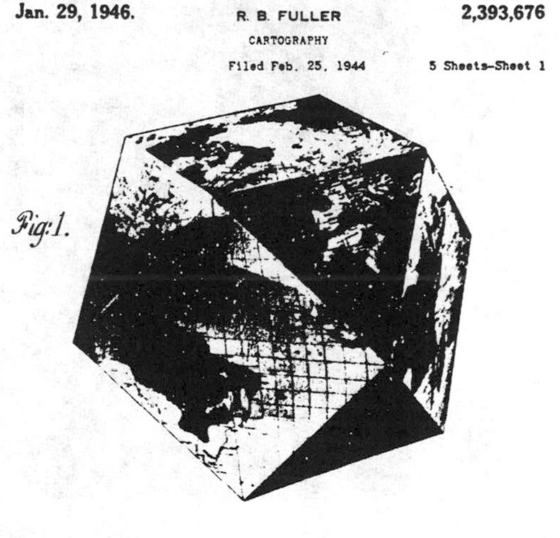

Pages from Fuller's U. S. patent covering the Dymaxion map. Science *referred to this as "the first cartographic patent to issue from the U. S. Patent Office."*

Buckminster Fuller defines a sphere (a) as "a multiplicity of discrete events, approximately equidistant in all directions from a nuclear center." The discrete points of such a system can be inter-triangulated. The tetrahedron (b), the octahedron (c), and icosahedron (d) are the only possible cases of omni-equilateral, omni-triangulated finite systems. Pictured at (e) are the 15 great circles developing from rotation of the icosahedron in respect to the 15 axes inter-connecting opposite midpoints of the icosahedron's 30 edges. The 120 resulting right spherical triangles represent the maximum unitary subdivision of a one-radius-system.

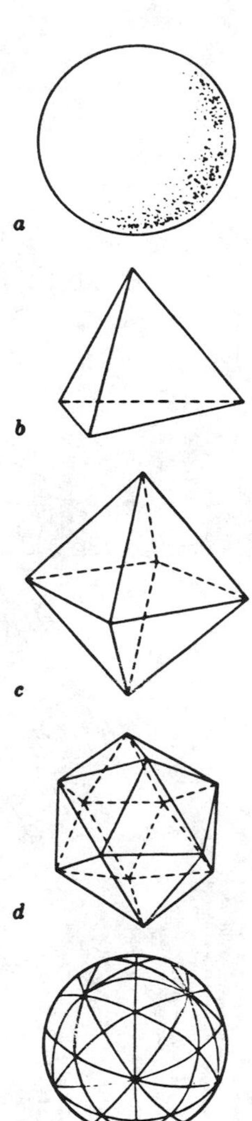

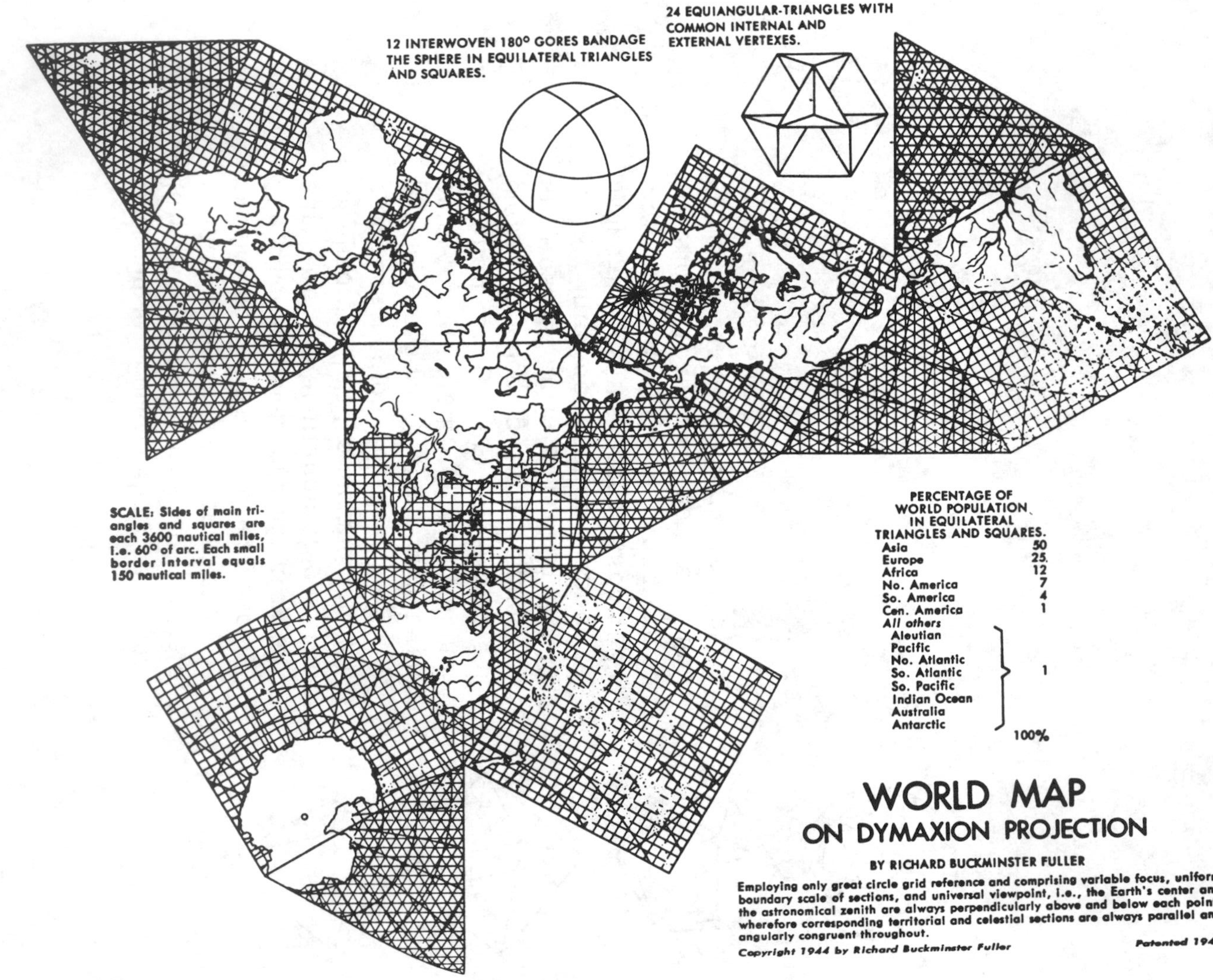
12 INTERWOVEN 180° GORES BANDAGE THE SPHERE IN EQUILATERAL TRIANGLES AND SQUARES.
24 EQUIANGULAR-TRIANGLES WITH COMMON INTERNAL AND EXTERNAL VERTEXES.
SCALE: Sides of main triangles and squares are each 3600 nautical miles, i.e. 60° of arc. Each small border interval equals 150 nautical miles.
PERCENTAGE OF WORLD POPULATION IN EQUILATERAL TRIANGLES AND SQUARES.
Asia 50
Europe 25
Africa 12
No. America 7
So. America 4
Cen. America 1
All others
Aleutian
Pacific
No. Atlantic
So. Atlantic
So. Pacific
Indian Ocean
Australia
Antarctic
1
100%
WORLD MAP
ON DYMAXION PROJECTION
BY RICHARD BUCKMINSTER FULLER
Employing only great circle grid reference and comprising variable focus, uniform boundary scale of sections, and universal viewpoint, i.e., the Earth's center and the astronomical zenith are always perpendicularly above and below each point, wherefore corresponding territorial and celestial sections are always parallel and angularly congruent throughout.
Copyright 1944 by Richard Buckminster Fuller
Patented 1946

Crystalline planet

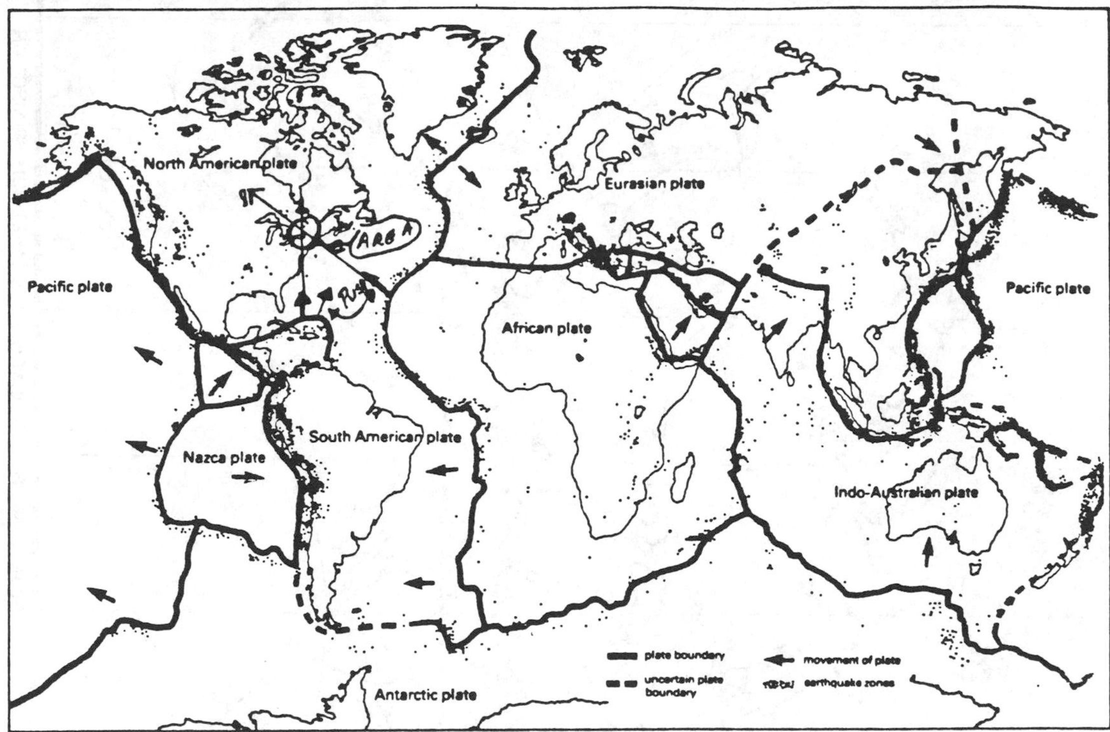

The belief that our Earth has a basic harmonic symmetry is very ancient. Socrates told his pupil Simmias: 'My dear boy, the real earth viewed from above is supposed to look like one of those balls made out of twelve pieces of skin sewn together.' Some 2000 years later, in the 1960s, three Russian scientists had the idea of re-examining the globe to see if any pattern should emerge linking significant places in history; it did. After several years' research in Moscow, they published their findings in *Khimiya i Zhizn*, the popular science journal of the USSR Academy of Sciences, entitled: 'Is the Earth a Large Crystal?'.

Drawing from their combined experience of history, engineering, and electronics, they decided that there was nothing in theory to have prevented a lattice-work pattern – a 'matrix of cosmic energy', as they put it – being built into the structure of the Earth at the time it was formed, whose shape could still be dimly perceived today. *Komsomol's Pravda*, the official Russian journal for the younger generation, followed up the idea with a suggestion that Earth had begun life as a crystal, and that only slowly did it mould itself into the spheroid it is today.

According to their hypothesis, the crystal can still be seen in twelve pentagonal slabs covering the surface of the globe – a dodecahedron. Overlaid on this are 20 equilateral triangles. The entire geometric structure, they claim, can be seen in its influence on the siting of ancient civilizations, on earth faults, magnetic anomalies, and many other otherwise unrelated locations, which are placed either at the intersections of the grid, or along its lines.

'Is the Earth a large crystal?' – the Soviet illustration as it appeared in *Khimya i Zhisn*.

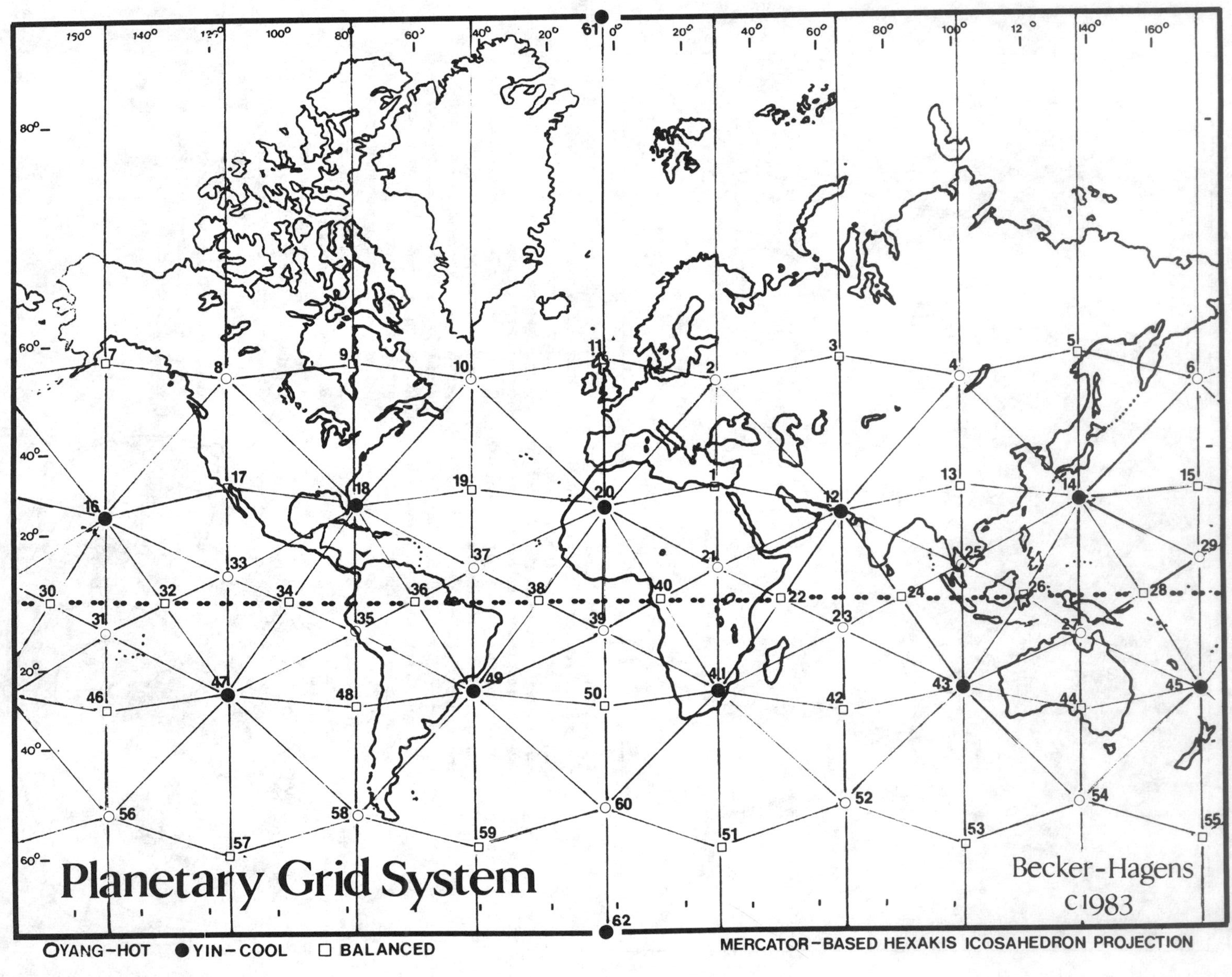
Planetary Grid System
Becker-Hagens
c1983
OYANG-HOT ●YIN-COOL □ BALANCED
MERCATOR-BASED HEXAKIS ICOSAHEDRON PROJECTION

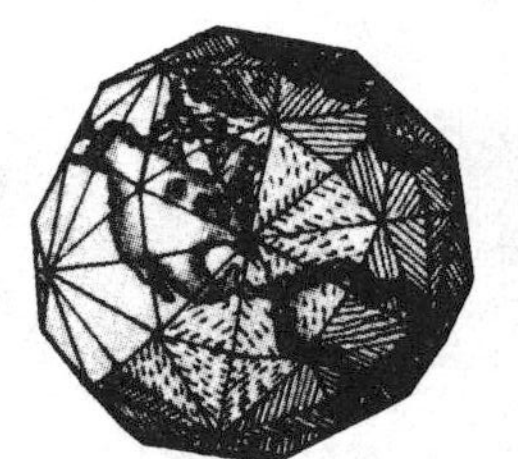

Planetary Grid System

No.	Location	Latitude	Longitude
1	□ EGYPT	31.72°N	31.20°E
2	○ WESTERN RUSSIA	52.62°N	31.20°E
3	□ CENTRAL USSR	58.28°N	67.20°E
4	○ LAKE BAYKAL	52.62°N	103.20°E
5	□ SEA OF OKHOTSK	58.28°N	139.20°E
6	○ BERING SEA (Aleutian Islands)	52.62°N	175.20°E
7	□ GULF OF ALASKA	58.28°N	148.80°W
8	○ ALBERTA	52.62°N	112.80°W
9	□ HUDSON'S BAY	58.28°N	76.80°W
10	○ NORTH ATLANTIC	52.62°N	40.80°W
11	□ SCOTLAND (Findhorn)	58.28°N	4.80°W
12	● KARACHI (Pakistan, Indus River)	26.57°N	67.20°E
13	□ HIMALAYAS	31.72°N	103.20°E
14	● IWO JIMA (Japan)	26.57°N	139.20°E
15	□ MIDWAY ISLAND	31.72°N	175.20°E
16	● HAWAII	26.57°N	148.80°W
17	□ BAJA CALIFORNIA	31.72°N	112.80°W
18	● BAHAMAS	26.57°N	76.80°W
19	□ MID-ATLANTIC NORTH	31.72°N	40.80°W
20	● ALGERIA	26.57°N	4.80°W
21	○ SUDAN	10.81°N	31.20°E
22	□ SOMALIA BASIN	0°	49.20°E
23	○ CHAGOS ARCHIPELAGO	10.81°S	67.20°E
24	□ CEYLON PLAIN (Sri Lanka)	0°	85.20°E
25	○ GULF OF THAILAND	10.81°N	103.20°E
26	□ SULAWESI	0°	121.20°E
27	○ GULF OF CARPENTARIA	10.81°S	139.20°E
28	□ SOLOMON ISLANDS	0°	157.20°E
29	○ MARSHALL ISLANDS	10.81°N	175.20°E
30	□ PHOENIX ISLANDS	0°	166.80°W
31	○ CAROLINE ISLANDS	10.81°S	148.80°W
32	□ MID-SOUTH PACIFIC	0°	130.80°W
33	○ CLIPPERTON ISLANDS	10.81°N	112.80°W
34	□ GALAPAGOS ISLANDS	0°	94.80°W
35	○ PERU	10.81°S	76.80°W
36	□ AMAZON	0°	58.80°W
37	○ GUIANA BASIN	10.81°N	40.80°W
38	□ ROMANCHE GAP	0°	22.80°W
39	○ ASCENSION ISLAND	10.81°S	4.80°W
40	□ GABON	0°	13.20°E
41	● SOUTH AFRICA	26.57°S	31.20°E
42	□ INDIAN OCEAN RIDGE	31.72°S	67.20°E
43	● WHARTON BASIN	26.57°S	103.20°E
44	□ SOUTH AUSTRALIA	31.72°S	139.20°E
45	● LOYALTY ISLANDS	26.57°S	175.20°E
46	□ SOUTH PACIFIC	31.72°S	148.80°W
47	● EASTER ISLAND	26.57°S	112.80°W
48	□ NAZCA PLATE	31.72°S	76.80°W
49	● RIO DE JANEIRO	26.57°S	40.80°W
50	□ ATLANTIC RIDGE	31.72°S	4.80°W
51	□ ATLANTIC-INDIAN OCEAN BASIN	58.28°S	31.20°E
52	○ McDONALD ISLAND (Indian Ocean)	52.62°S	67.20°E
53	□ SOUTH INDIAN BASIN	58.28°S	103.20°E
54	○ KANGAROO FRACTURE	52.62°S	139.20°E
55	□ EMERALD BASIN	58.28°S	175.20°E
56	○ UDINTSEV FRACTURE	52.62°S	148.80°W
57	□ ALBATROSS CORDILLERA	58.28°S	112.80°W
58	○ SOUTH AMERICAN TIP	52.62°S	76.80°W
59	□ EAST SCOTIA BASIN	58.28°S	40.80°W
60	○ SOUTH ATLANTIC RIDGE	52.62°S	4.80°W
61	● NORTH POLE	90.00°N	
62	● SOUTH POLE	90.00°S	

The Planetary Grid System shown on the reverse side was inspired by an original article by Christopher Bird, "Planetary Grid," published in New Age Journal #5, May 1975, pp. 36-41. The hexakis icosahedron grid, coordinate calculations, and point classification system are the original research of Bethe Hagens and William S. Becker. These materials are distributed with permission of the authors by Conservative Technology Intl. in cooperation with Governors State University, Division of Intercultural Studies, University Park, Illinois 60466 312/534-5000 x2455. This map may be reproduced if they are distributed without charge and if acknowledgement is given to Governors State University (address included) and Mr. Bird.

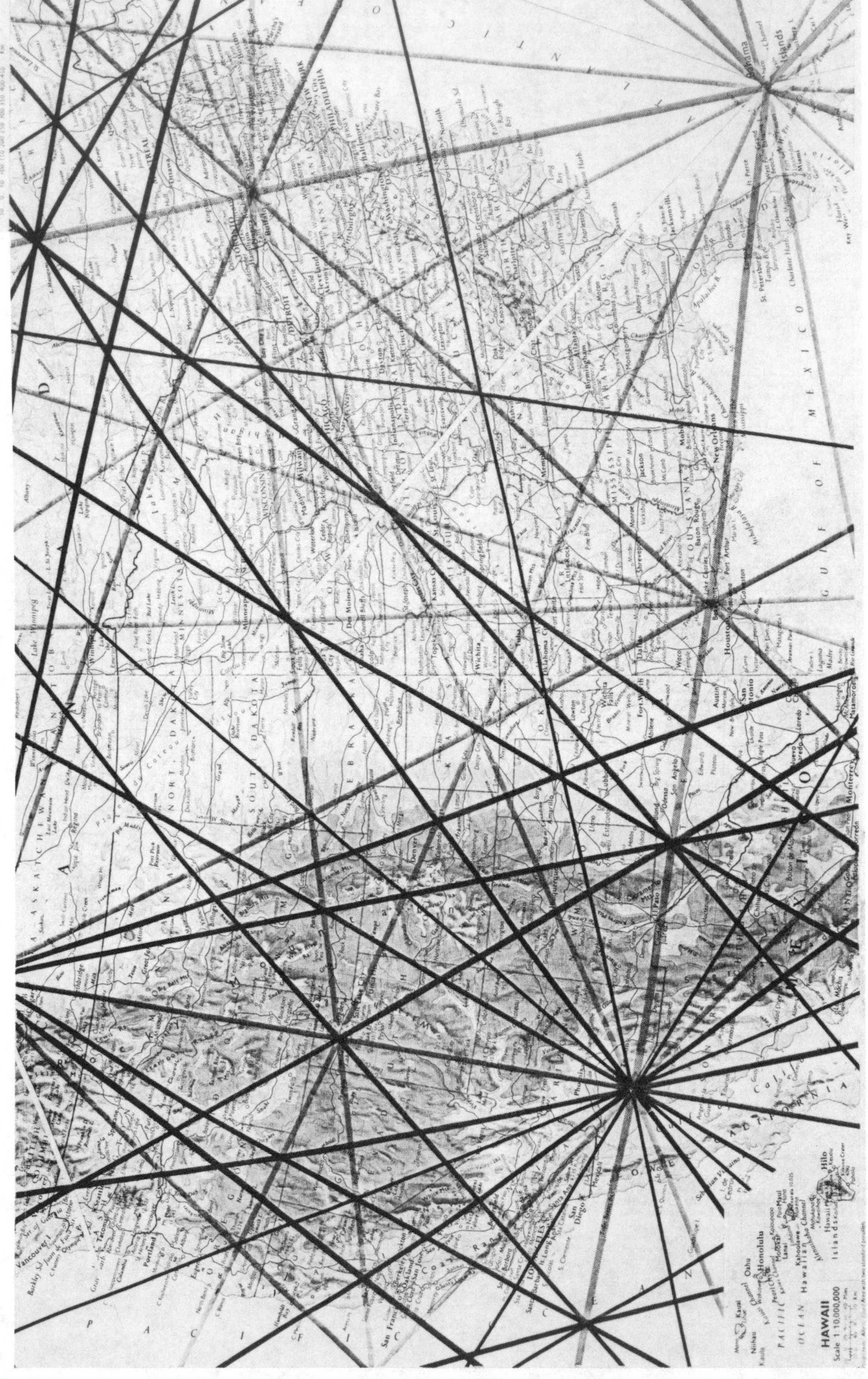
Scale 1:12,000,000
HAWAII
Scale 1:10,000,000
GULF OF MEXICO
PACIFIC

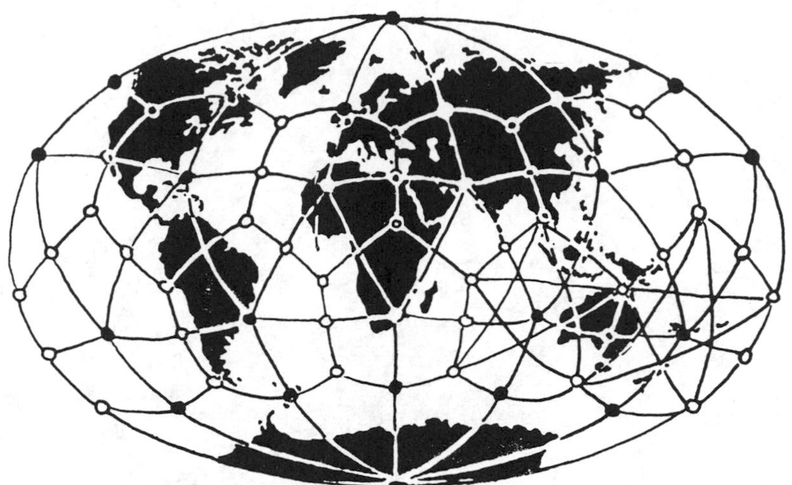

Earth crystalline energy grid

The so-called Russian Grid,
treating the earth as if it were a gigantic crystal.

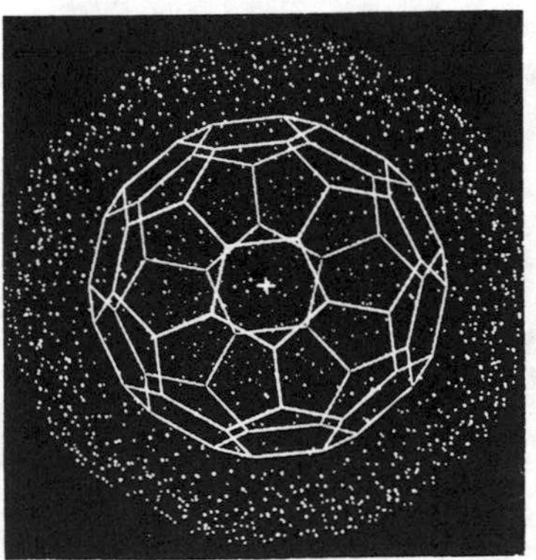

Computer simulation of molecule C_{60}; a hollow sphere, it can hold other atoms.

Note similarities in grid concepts with this computer model of a carbon molecule.

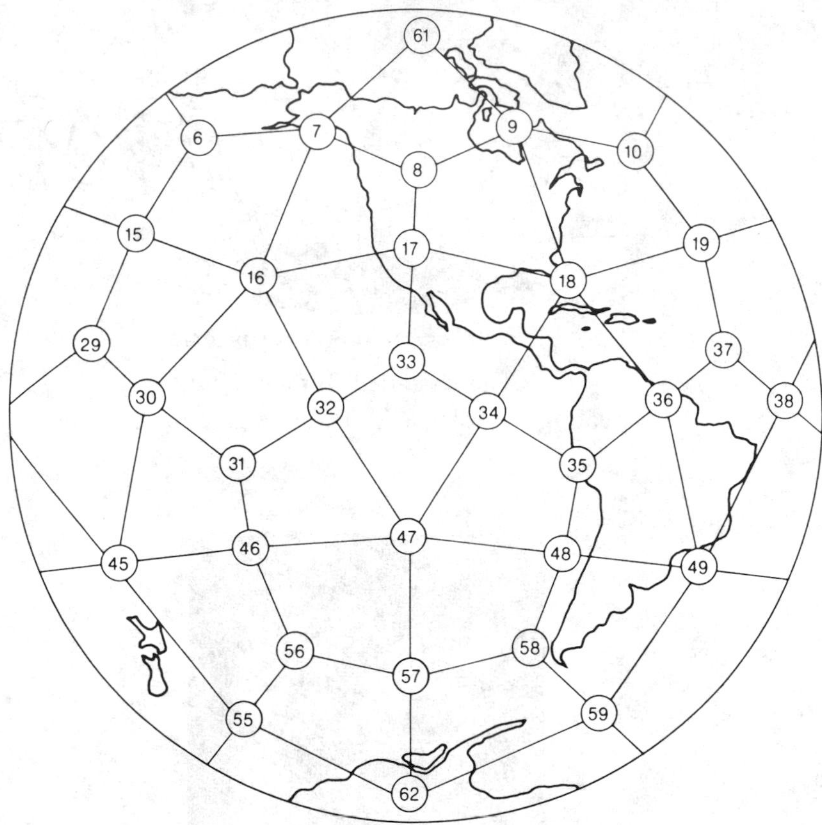

David Zink's map of megalithic sites and other features from his book **The Ancient Stones Speak**, (Dutton, 1979).

The Planetary Grid System:

Some of the significant features of the major grid intersections: (1) Giza, the Great Pyramid; (3)Tyumen oil field, USSR; (4) Lake Baikal, USSR, many unique plants and animals; (9) Hudson Bay, present location of north magnetic pole; (11) northern British Isles, Maes Howe, Ring of Brodgar, Callanish; (12) Mohenjo Daro—Rama Empire culture; (13) Xian Pyramids, largest in the world; (14) southern Japan, "Dragon's Triangle," great seismic activity; (16) Hamakulia, nearby lies Hawaii, scene of high volcanic and earthquake activity; (17) the sophisticated canal civilization of Cibola; (18) Bimini, the site of huge "man-made" walls underwater, discovered in 1969, the date that Edgar Cayce had predicted that evidence of Atlantis would be discovered; (20) Algerian megalithic ruins; (21) megaliths at Axum, the Coptic Christian center in Ethiopia; (25) Bangkok and Ankor Wat; (26) Sarawak, Borneo, site of ancient megalithic structures; (28) Pohnpei Island, Micronesia, site of the megalithic city of Nan Madol; (35) Lima, Peru, boundary of the Nazca Plate, Pisco, the Candlestick of the Andes & the Nazca Lines; (40) Gabon, West Africa, natural atomic reactor in operation about 1.7 million years ago; (41) Zimbabwe with its ancient mines & structures; (44) the Maralinga Atomic Test Site, which also has megalithic ruins; (47) Easter Island and its megaliths; (62) German underground Antarctic base?

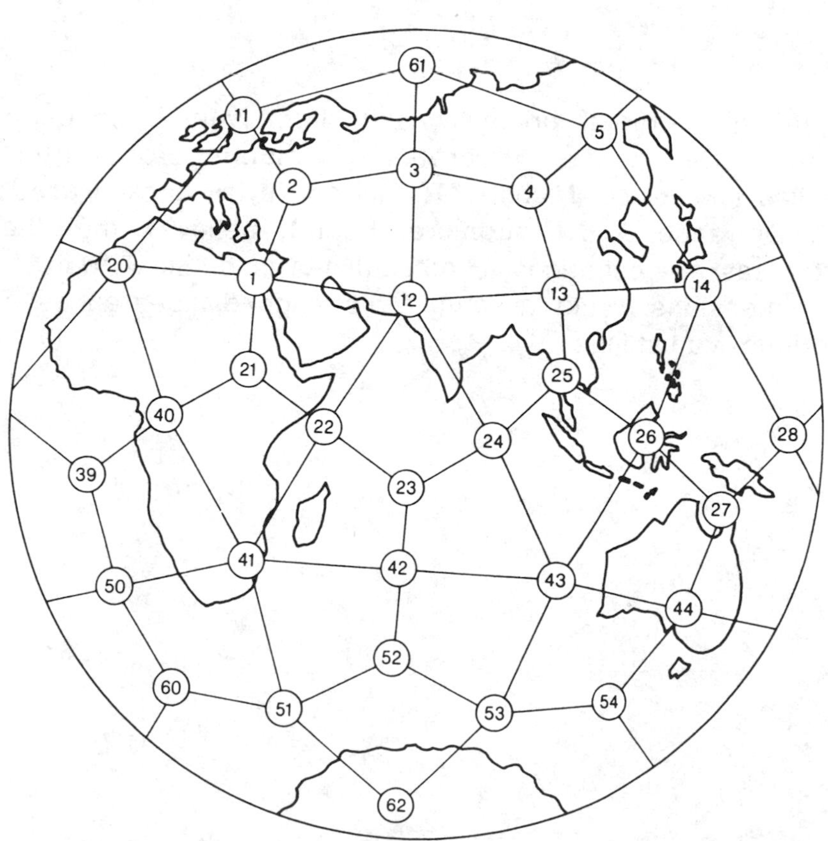

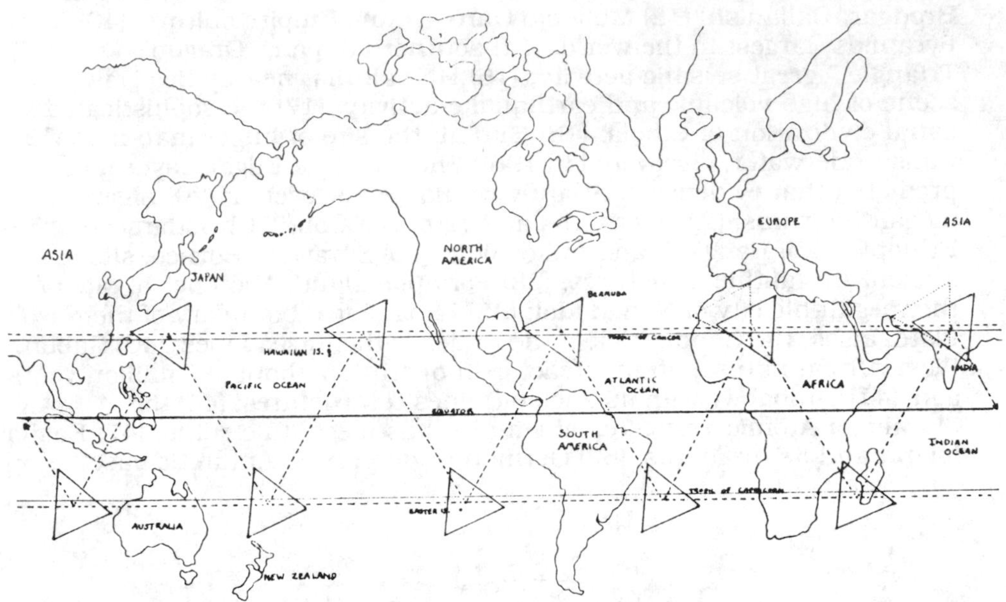

The ten "vile vortices" originally taken from Ivan T. Sanderson. At these ten areas, theoretically, magnetic-gravitational anomalies take place. Nicholas R. Nelson, in his book, **Paradox** (1980, Dorrance & Co. Ardmore, Penn.), believes that these vortex areas are entrances to other dimensions. Such "doors" to other dimensions would account for strange disapearances and mysterious vanishings.

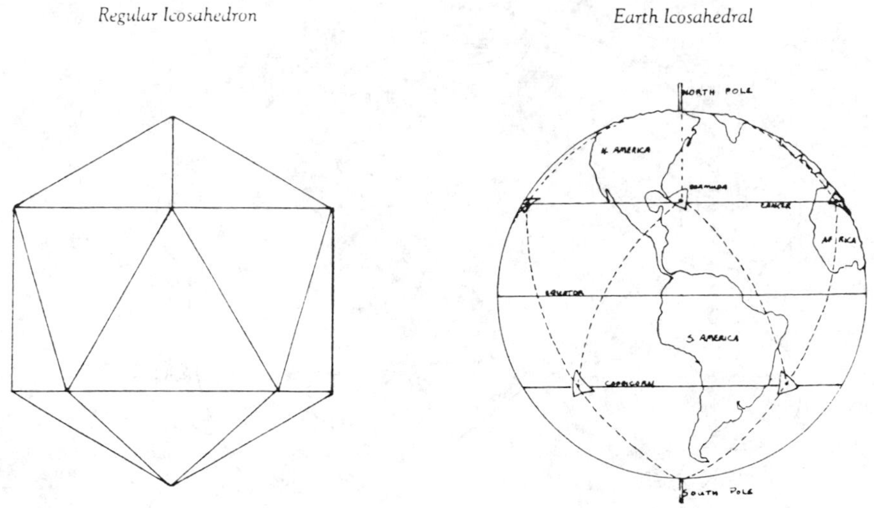

More illustrations from **Paradox,** Nelson sees the earth as an Icosahedron. Below is an enlargement of the Bermuda Triangle vortex area, one of the supposed "vile vortexes".

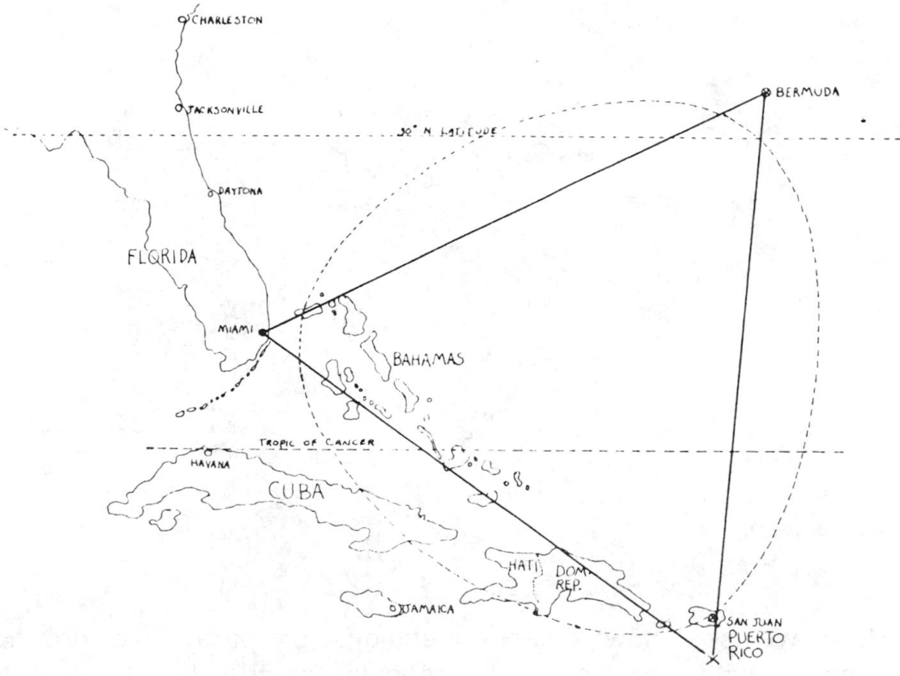

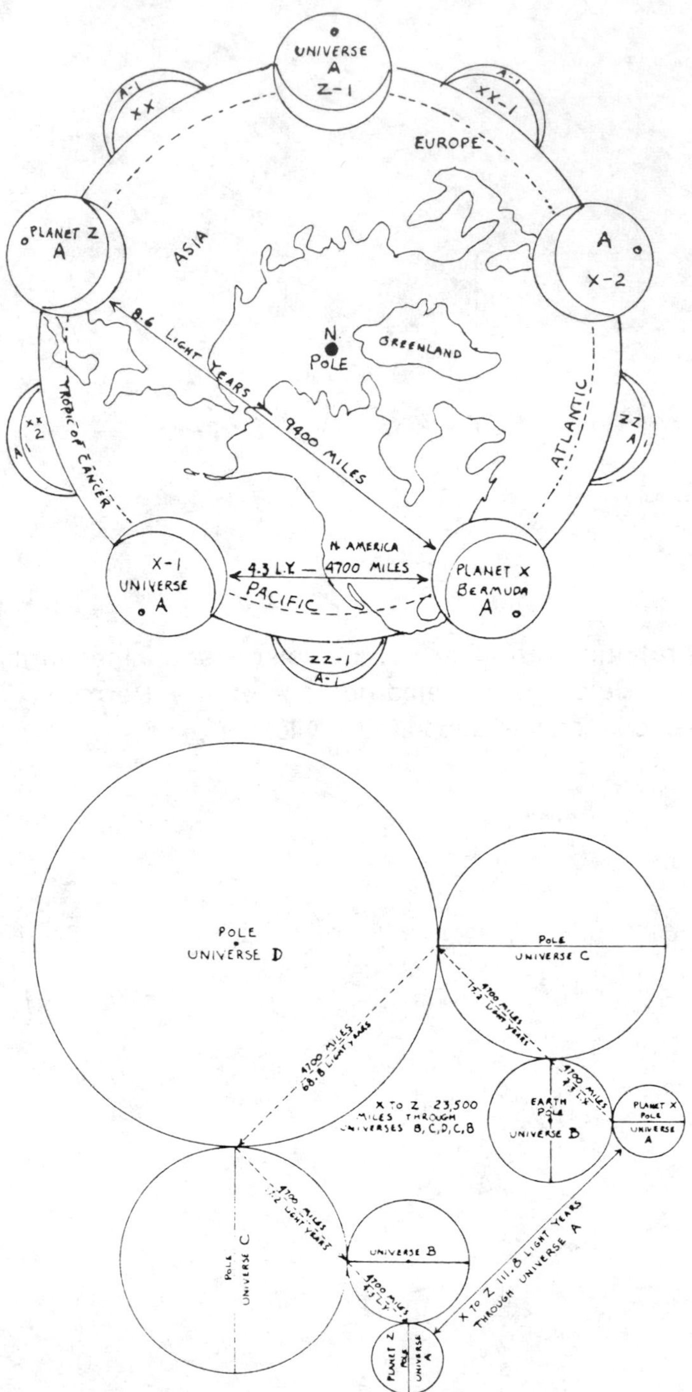

Here we see how other dimensions or parallel worlds can connect with the earth, theoretically at the ten hypothetical vortex areas of the earth.

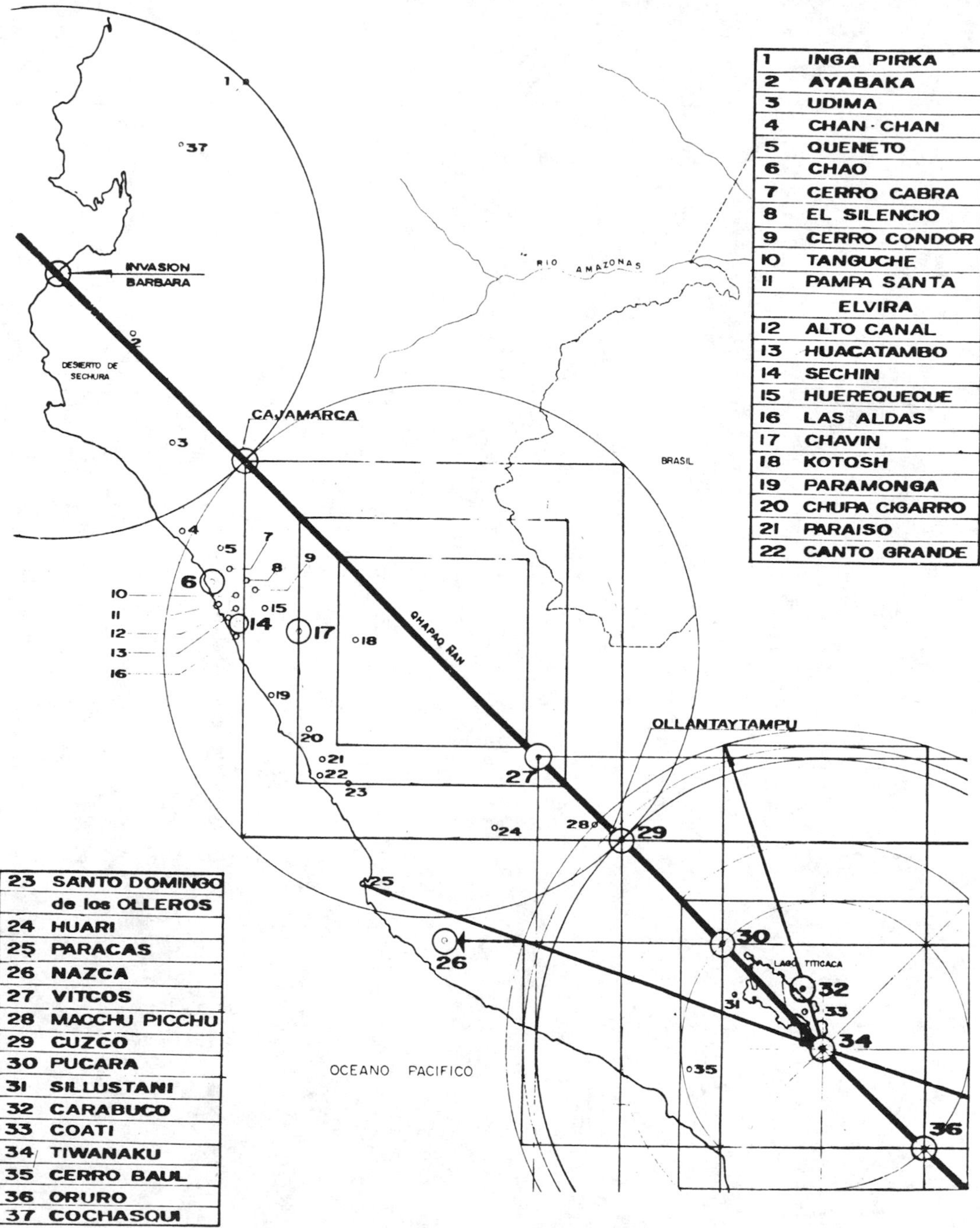

This illustration is from the book **Genesis de la Cultura Andina** (Genesis of the Andean Culture) by Carlos Milla Villena, published in Peru. It shows the "grid line"-mathematical relationship of the megalithic remains of Tiahuanaco in Bolivia, with those in Cuzco, Peru and Vitcos, brief capital of the Incas in exile, as well as the point of entry into Peru that Pizarro and his conquistadors took during their conquest. Also on the grid line is Cajamarca, where the conquistadors captured the Inca Atahualpa and so sealed the fate of the Inca Empire. Were the Incas, or perhaps an earlier culture aware of the world grid?

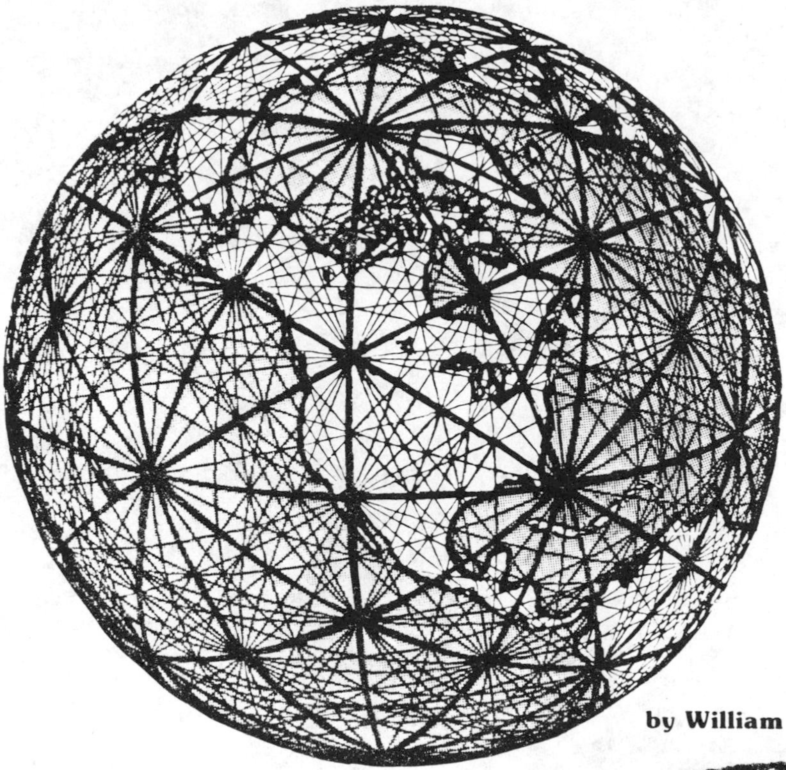

by William Becker and Bethe Hagens

The Planetary Grid: A New Synthesis

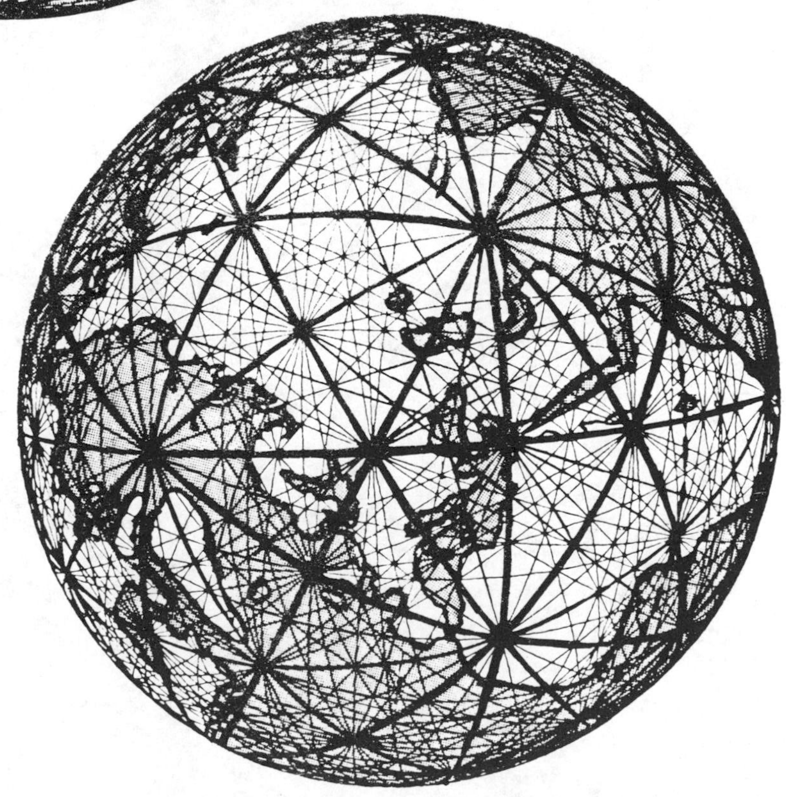

Bill Becker (Professor of Industrial Design at the University of Illinois, Chicago) and Bethe Hagens (Professor of Anthropology at Governors State University) are a husband-wife team. In 1981, they started a product and graphics design partnership, Conservative Technology. Contact them at 105 Wolpers Road, Park Forest, Illinois 60466.

"The experience of life in a finite, limited body is specifically for the purpose of discovering and manifesting supernatural existence within the finite."

Attributed to Pythagoras

Introduction

We've entitled our current exercise in planetary grid research "A New Synthesis" — and indeed we hope it is. All that may be new about our work is that we have simply found a unique blend of the previously "unblended" ideas of others. Those others are true visionaries in the areas of unexplained earth phenomena, human history, discovery, and the art-science of geometry (earth measure). Over the last year and six months, we've received literally hundreds of letters from researchers all over the globe — who are seeking a comprehensive explanation for a continuum of phenomena and events which traditional science emotionally rejects as "impossible," "hallucinatory," and/or "unquanitifiable." Yet the events continue to be catalogued, with many reports suppressed or labelled "fraud" by orthodox scientists. Worldwide networks of questioning theorists persist and grow with each report. We will try to mention as many of our correspondents as we can within the text of this article. Several contributors, listed at the end, have truly transformed our view of this work.

* * * * *

In 1200 A.D., a new energy began to move within the cultures of the West. After centuries of obedient reflection within the established order of Roman Christianity, the spirit of individualism and exploration began to emerge. The 14th century great plagues of Europe, in which one fourth of the Continental population had died — with three out of four persons afflicted, had awakened in the West the archetypal imperative to "control Nature or die!" By the 15th century, Leonardo da Vinci and the multi-disciplined geniuses of the Renaissance had rediscovered the lost scientific principles of pre-Christian Greece and Rome, and had invented the "view point" of the individual within their perspective drawing and painting systems. Paintings and public murals now began to put the individual at the center of a "world view" which, for the first time in centuries, conveyed the notion that through individual effort and analysis, the person — the viewer — could come to order and "control" the often hostile natural environment.

This "individual point of view" (perspective view point on "horizon") required "detached awareness" (standing distant from that which is viewed) and a consummate dedication to visual detail and analysis in order to "render an in-depth perspective." The writing and journalism of today still ring with the Renaissance archetypes.

Now it is 500 years later, and Leonardo's manifest symbol of individual view point and detachment has brought us to viewing video discs of the earth as seen from the moon. It has also brought us to the uneasy conclusion that our pre-Renaissance imperative to control Nature (literally "that which is born") or die has ushered us into a technological malaise where most of our man-made "natural" control systems are in crisis — especially those systems which exploit, pollute, or dramatically disturb the biospheric processes of the earth.

Just as the perspective pictorial systems of the Renaissance artists "brought into focus" the unspoken cultural archetypes of their time, we feel that the current network of planetary grid researchers (of whom we are a part) may be on a similar path toward developing a unifying symbol of a new earth: a paradigm as transcendent over our passing "Iron Age" as the Renaissance was over the Dark Ages. What may make the proposition even more fascinating is the parallel analogy that — just as the driving force behind the creative energies of the Renaissance was the rediscovery of Greco-Roman science/philosophy; so with our planetary grid theorists, the driving force behind most research efforts is the continuing flow of evidence, both physical and metaphysical, that the existence of Pre-Egyptian civilizations — some with highly advanced technologies — is now no longer speculative, but a necessary assumption for developing any comprehensive archaeological treatise.[1] We believe that the planetary grid is an ancient model that brings control through

Illustration #1
These stones on display at the Ashmolean Museum in Oxford, England suggest a life of creative intellectual synthesis for the Neolithic craftsmen who crafted and "wrapped" them with leather thongs.

comprehensive understanding and not through detached myopic analysis/manipulation. The contemporary video artist/philosopher Dan Winter expresses the idea beautifully. "Our destiny is to encounter our embracing collective mind with increasing intimacy and resonance. We awaken to a love life, in which personal love expands to planetary love — through this touching new body of mindfulness. A new body of mind crystallizes among us."[2]

Planetary Grid Researchers: Prehistoric to Present

The oldest evidence of possible planetary grid research rests within the Ashmolean Museum of Oxford, England. On exhibit are several hand-sized stones of such true geometric proportion and precise carving that they startle the casual viewer. Keith Critchlow, in his book *Time Stands Still*, gives convincing evidence linking these leather-thonged stone models (see illustration #1) to the Neolithic peoples of Britain — with a conservative date of construction at least 1000 years (ca. 1400 B.C.) before Plato described his five Platonic solids in the *Timaeus*. And yet, here they are — the octahedron, icosahedron, dodecahedron, tetrahedron, and cube all arrayed for comparison and analysis. Other multi-disciplined archaeological researchers like Jeffrey Goodman[3] and A.M. Davie[4] have dated the stone polyhedra to as early as 20,000 B.C. and believe they were used as projectiles or "bolas" in hunting and warfare. Davie has seen similar stones in northern Scotland which he attributes to the early art of "finishing the form" of crystalline volcanic rocks which exhibit natural geometry. He dates these artifacts to at least 12,000 years before Plato (ca. 12,400 B.C.). Critchlow writes, "What we have are objects clearly indicative of a degree of mathematical ability so far denied to Neolithic man by any archaeologist or mathematical historian." In reference to the stones' possible use in designing Neolithic Britain's great stone circles he says, "The study of the heavens is, after all, a spherical activity, needing an understanding of spherical coordinates. If the Neolithic inhabitants of Scotland had constructed Maes Howe (stone circle) before the pyramids were built by ancient Egyptians, why could they not be studying the laws of three-dimensional coordinates? Is it not more than a coincidence that Plato as well as Ptolemy, Kepler, and Al-Kindi attributed cosmic significance to these figures." Yet another historian, Lucie Lamy, in her new book on the Egyptian system of measure gives proof of the knowledge of these basic geometric solids as early as the Egyptian Old Kingdom, 2500 B.C.

We agree, in general, with all the above researchers that the crafting of sophisticated three-dimensional geometries was well within the capabilities of Pre-Egyptian civilizations. With the concept that knowledge of these geometries was necessary to the building of stone circles and astronomical "henges" — we also agree — and would add that we have evidence that suggests that these hand-held stones were "planning models," not only for charting the heavens and building calendrical monuments, but were also used for meteorological study; to develop and refine terrestrial maps for predicting major ley lines of telluric energy; and, in conjunction with stone circles, were used to construct charts and maps for worldwide travel long before the appearance of the pyramids.

Take another look at the five Neolithic stones. Notice the placement of points on not only completed intersections where thongs connect — but on the "open corners" where thongs might be added. The central figure, the dodecahedron, has all twelve centers of its pentagonal faces marked with points for further "wrapping" — as with the cube figure to the far right. Its corners are defined similarly by marked open points. Now note the tetrahedron, the second figure from the right. Its four vertexes or corners, which traditionally define four triangles, have already been bisected by a second array of thongs defining another tetrahedron overlapping the first at midpoints. It is our contention that these stones were not wrapped and marked with leather to facilitate their use as "bolas" or projectiles. The stones and their varied nets are too delicate and complex to have been used as hunting and warfare shot. Their appearance struck us initially as ritual objects similar to the decorative reed spheres found in Southeast Asia; or as religious symbols such as the mysterious bronze and gold spheres found in France and Vietnam — which some say depict the ancient text of the *Tao Teh Ching*. It may well be that all of these hand-held objects served similar planning and mnemonic functions for the people who treasured and crafted them. (See illustration #2)

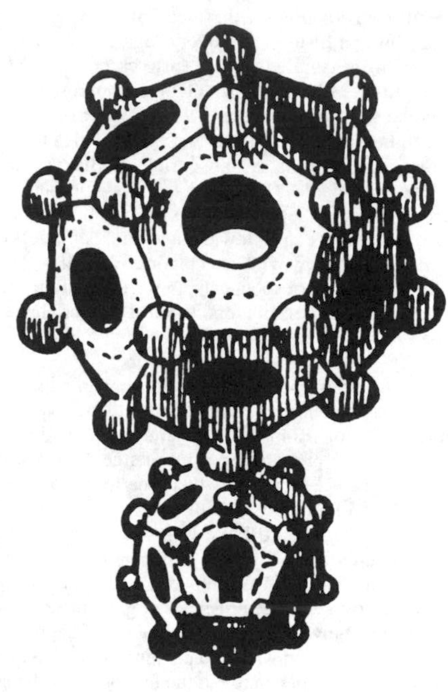

Illustration #2
Gold and bronze figures exhibiting twelve facets and twenty "horns" have been unearthed in France and Vietnam. Vietnamese war veterans recognize them as sacred Taoist objects marking acupuncture points.

Viewing the stone polyhedra together, we can only conclude as Keith Critchlow does — that their intended use was for the study, comparison, and analysis of spherically determined systems of geometry. Given the apparent use of these stones as "planning models," and given the apparent "extra wrap" of thongs on the tetrahedron — consider the result if the Neolithic craftsman of these forms had decided to discover the ultimate in delineated spherical geometry models, a single sphere upon which would be combined all the wrappings and points of all five solids.

The most direct route to such a figure is as follows: Take the icosahedron wrapping pattern and combine it with the existing pattern of points and thongs on the dodecahedron. The combination of figures provides a form composed of 15 "great circles" which intersect at 62 predicted common points.[5] (See illustration #3)

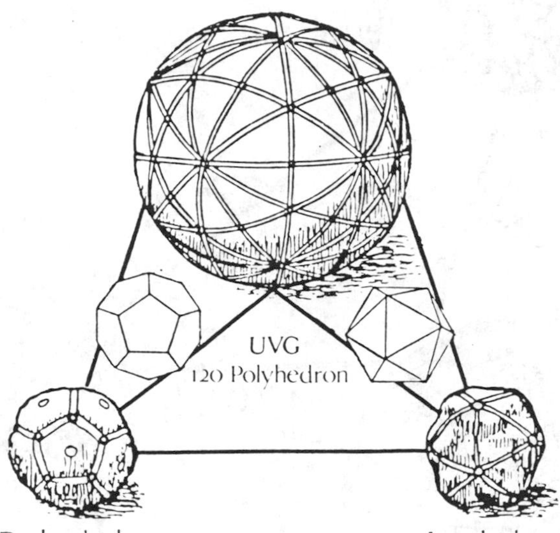

Illustration #3
The Neolithic craftsman could easily have created this beautiful polyhedron — which requires the overlap of a dodec and icosahedron. Fifteen "great circles" or "equators" of leather thong create the 120 Polyhedron.

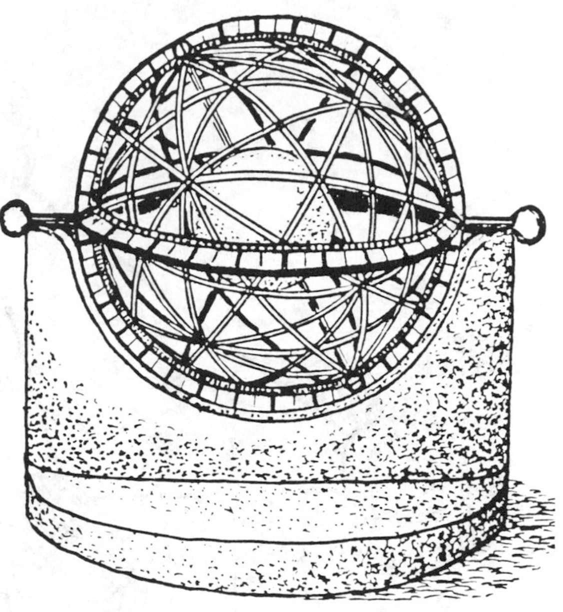

Illustration #4
The Minoan archives in Crete catalog the carved granite figure in which our armillary sphere rests as an unknown object. These were of such importance that archaeologists have cast concrete replicas for their restorations at Knossos. Notches in the top of the stand have led some to suggest that these might have been some sort of spit barbeque device.

This figure, which synthesizes the dodecahedron and icosahedron with its 120 triangles, was not only known to the Greeks but to other civilizations much earlier. We believe that its geometry can be applied in two forms: the "girded sphere" or marked stone used for mapping, dowsing, or geometry (earth measure); and the armillary sphere or "celestial basket" used as an astronomical device to measure time via the solstices and daily sunrises. The armillary sphere casts a shadow on the captured stone within its framework (see illustration #4) — thus echoing the ancient analogy "As above, so below."[6]

Returning to the creation of our ultimate spherical model, the second step would be to take the other figures — cube, tetrahedron, and octahedron — and lay out their line arrays over the existing 62 point pattern. You will find that not only is the 62 point system of vertexes compatible with the icosahedron and dodecahedron — but that all the leather thong patterns of all the polyhedral stones are precisely "mappable" over those same 62 vertexes. In fact, our surprised craftsman would soon discover that all five stone arrays can be overlapped one upon the other with different corner matchings until a beautiful polyhedron with 121 "great circles" and 4,862 points has been developed. This is the ultimate single sphere pattern which houses all five Platonic solids within multiple orientations (see illustration #5). This is the same form that was used by R. Buckminster Fuller for his domes and, in our research, we have called it the Unified Vector Geometry (UVG) 120 Sphere. We consider it the key component in our proposed "new synthesis" of planetary grid research.

Plato's description in the *Timaeus* of a cosmology based on the five regular volumes (tetrahedron, octahedron, cube, icosahedron, and dodecahedron) echoes Pythagorean teaching regarding the manifestation of the infinite within the finite. Plato postulates a metaphysics in which the four elements of Greek science — earth, air, fire, and water — are associated with four of the five solids. He mysteriously reserves his description of that most noble form used by the Creator to fabricate the universe as "a certain fifth composition." Tradition relates the cube to earth, tetrahedron with fire, octahedron with air, icosahedron with water, and the dodecahedron with the universe or "prana/aether." Because he had written that, "The earth viewed from above, resembles a ball sewn together from twelve pieces of skin," we believe he related the dodecahedron to Gaia, the living planet earth. We also propose that Plato's mysterious "fifth composition" is more complex than the dodecahedron — but based upon it. We suggest that Plato's most noble framework for building the universe is a form which unifies and supports all the forces operating simultaneously within the five

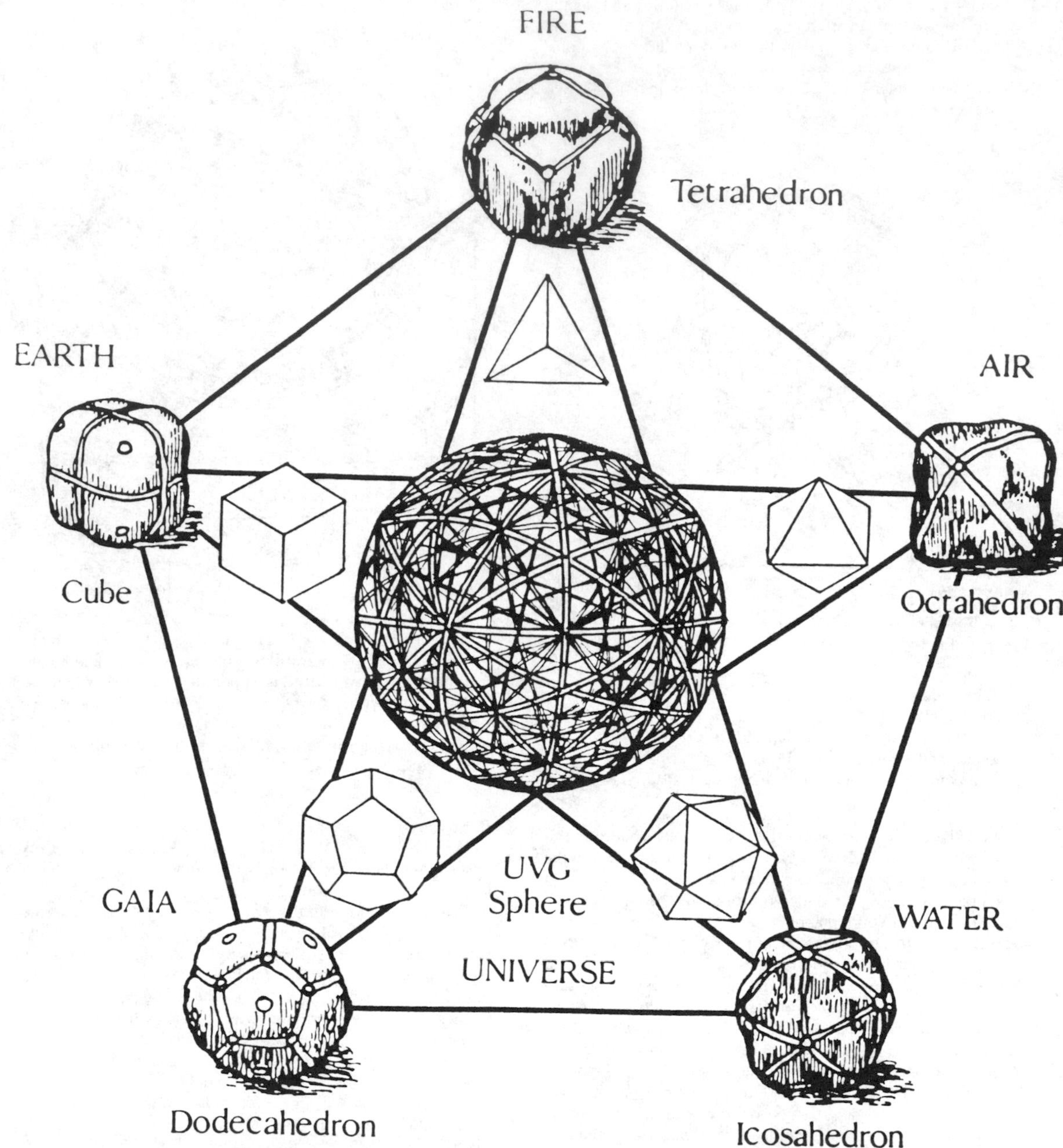

Pythagorean Cosmic Morphology

Illustration #5

©Becker-Hagens 1984

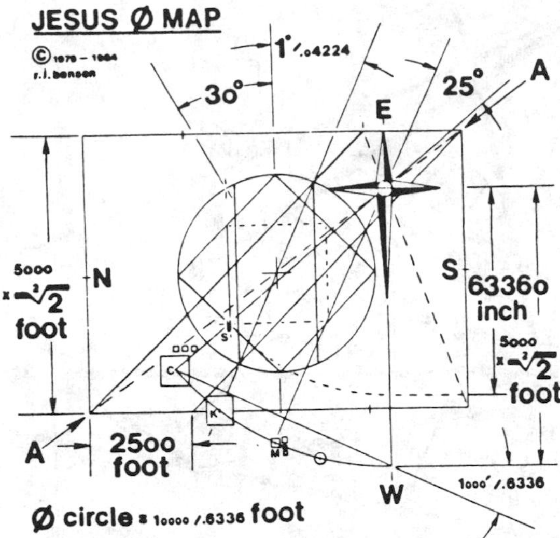

Reprinted with permission of the author from *World's Oldest Ø Map 6018 B.C.*

Illustration #6
The world's oldest map, which Richard J. "Dick" Benson dates to 6018 B.C., depicts the elegant theory of mathematics embodied in the planning of the city of Cairo. The megaliths shown are (C) Cheops, (K) Kephren, (M) Mikerinus, and (S) Sphinx. Benson's work may well provide a helpful, radically new framework for historical linguistics as well as uncover a lost simplicity in the art and numbers of geometry.

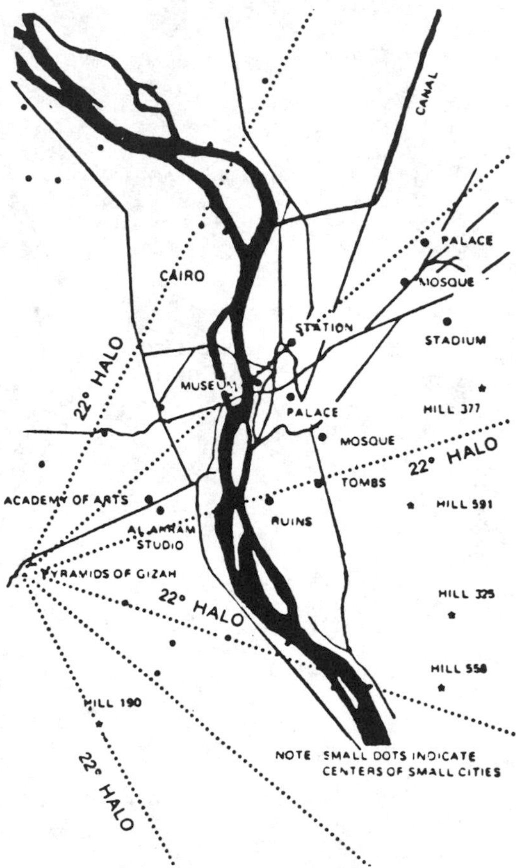

CAIRO ALIGNMENTS FOR "HIDDEN HALOS"

Reprinted with permission of the editor from *Stonehenge Viewpoint*.

Illustration #7
Donald Cyr is encouraging the use of a simple Halo Sighting Template to be superimposed on maps of ancient sites in order to detect alignments that may indicate "hidden halos" — atmospheric events that were almost certainly a part of the daily life of Megalithic man. This sort of research will require the cooperation of compartmentalized scientists in astronomy, geology, archaeology, and other disciplines — but may recreate a holistic approach to Gaia that supported the lifestyle of the ancients.

regular solids, the four primary elements, and the earth (Gaia) itself — the Unified Vector Geometry 120 Sphere. We further contend that this sphere is the pattern upon which the ancients built their armillary spheres, which to this day are used to cast shadows for reading the solstices and equinoxes.

Contemporary researchers like Donald Cyr[7] and Sir J. Norman Lockyer[8], experts in archaeoastronomy, have again and again detected in the site layouts of ancient stone circles and cities, a circular plan of radiating lines diverging from sacred centers at angles of 22 +, 11 +, 46 +, 90, 120 and 180 degrees. These radiating lines, it was found, consistently align with standing stones, stone circles, and sunrise/solstice marking points on mountain peaks and crest "notches" surrounding the site. A related set of angles in the Megalithic landscape, 23½ and 47 degrees, is equally regular but does appear to relate to celestial phenomena of the common variety. In many cases, these and the other angles link one sacred site to another miles distant. The basic triangle in our Unified Vector Geometry (UVG) 120 Sphere exhibits just these angles, at intervals strangely correspondent with those found by Lockyer, and Cyr and others.

Plato had travelled extensively while making notes for the *Timaeus*. His visit to Egypt would have brought him in touch with the historian/planners of the city of Cairo. Engineer/geometer Richard J. "Dick" Benson[9] believes that Cairo is possibly the most ancient surviving example of a precise geometric site plan based not only on the angles discovered by Cyr and others but on angles which connect sites across continents and which — again — are almost eerily similar to those in the UVG 120 Sphere. (See illustrations #6, #7)

Illustration #8
The U.S. Navy has analyzed the Piri Reis map and determined that it is a correct circular grid projection from Cairo. The half diamond (outlined by grid points 37, 19, 20 and 38) which contains the complete construction infill of the original map shows a superficial, though perhaps indicative, resemblance to two Basic Triangles of the UVG system we propose.

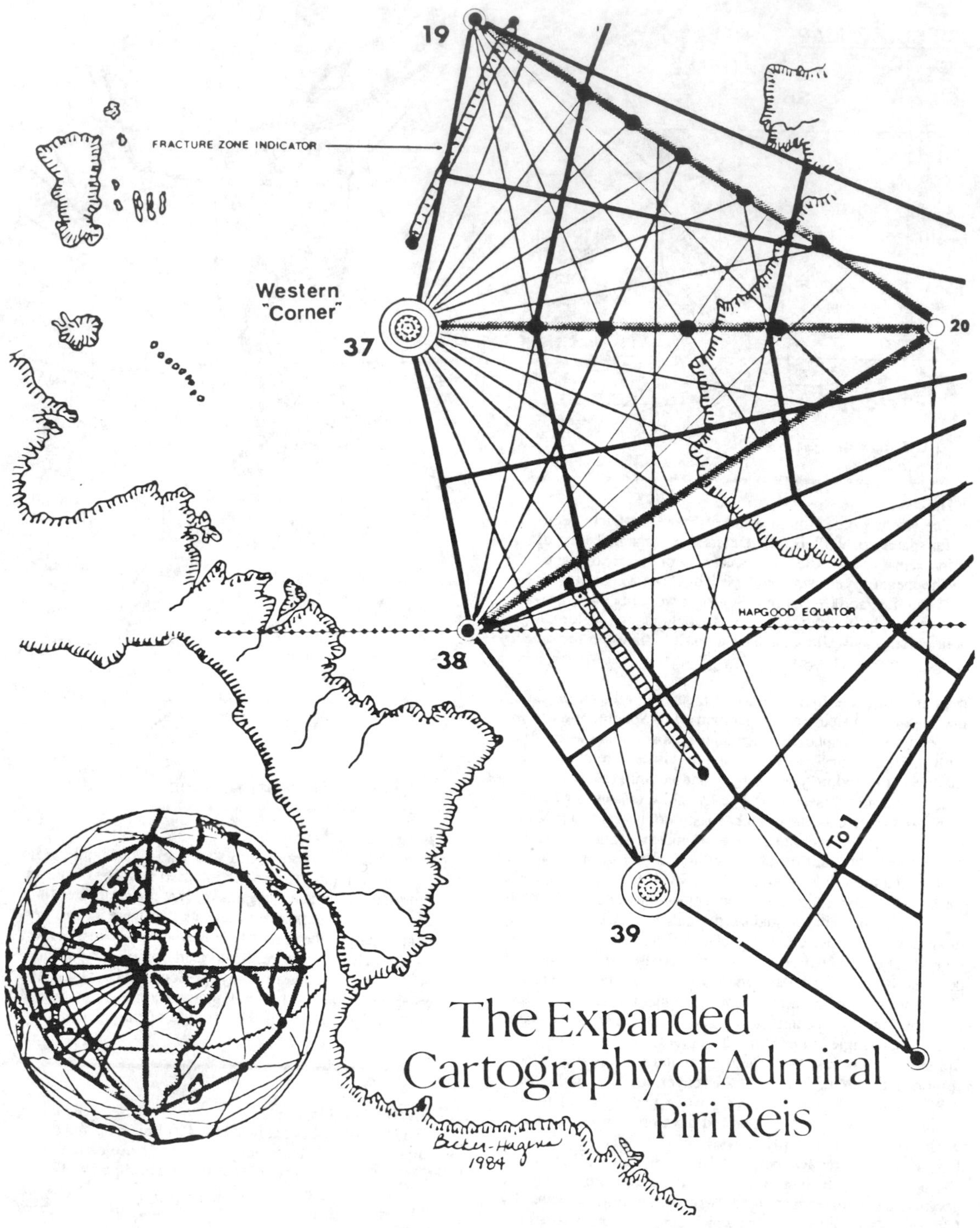

The Expanded Cartography of Admiral Piri Reis

Could Plato have avoided in the *Timaeus* a direct reference to the simple dodecahedron as his framework for universal creation because he was still searching for "a certain fifth composition" which would satisfy the magnificent site plan of Cairo that Benson's map implies? Or was he restricted by a secret vow to the Pythagorean Brotherhood not to reveal to the world the true form of Pythagoras' compound polyhedron, which held all the solids within its form and had been used in the global grid and armillary sphere "planning models" for Cairo and other sacred cities?

Since Plato, history has lightly sketched what seems to have been a *sub rosa* quest for a Cairo-centered mapping system, which would "square the circle" and/or show the way to the Holy Grail. (Interestingly, a 13th century writer named Wolfram described the Grail as a "precious stone fallen from heaven.") Curious artifacts like the Piri Reis map, dated 1523 A.D., but believed to be a copy of an ancient Greek original, show "wind rose" lines converging on Cairo with angular divisions of 22 + and 11 + degrees (see illustration #8). Could this map have been an extension of the site lines and solstice/sunrise markers which encircle ancient Cairo? Viewed "from above," the major points on the Piri Reis map so nearly approximate points on our UVG 120 Sphere that we have included a sketch using our geometry and Piri Reis' lines which attempts to complete the missing portion of the world map the Admiral originally drew.

The Piri Reis map and another unique document, the Buache map of 1737, contribute much toward our contention that early, possibly Pre-Egyptian civilizations possessed mathematical, astronomical, and geophysical skills equal to those in this confused "Iron Age." Both maps possess highly accurate and unique views of the continent of Antarctica not known, supposedly, before the International Geophysical Year of 1958. (See illustration #9) The Piri Reis map was found in Istanbul in 1929

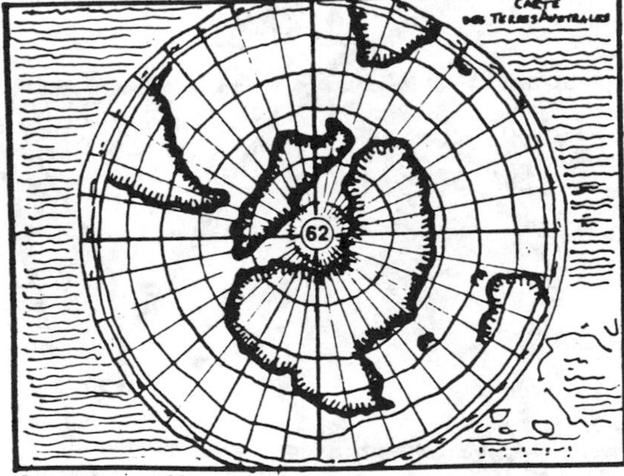

Illustration #9
The Buache Map of 1737 shows Antarctica correctly without its ice cover and may indicate everything from a dramatically different earth climate than today to a technical capacity beyond that generally attributed to human culture 10,000 years ago. The map provides an interesting piece in grid theory: the centers of all UVG 10/12 Pentagons fall at the edges of continents or in oceans.

and is said to have been copied from a map originating in the library in ancient Alexandria. The Buache map of 1737 is said also to be the result of copying ancient Greek maps. Both maps astonishingly depict Antarctica's true land masses through their icy cover — though instruments to detect such land masses were not invented until 1958. Even if the maps are complete frauds, they still predict Antarctica's true profile thirty years early.

The matter of maps which can't exist — but do — is a kind of continuing corollary avenue of research compatible with Unified Vector Geometry. The maps of the so-called mythical continents of Mu and Pan (as described in the channelled *Oahspe, A New Bible in the Words of Jehovih*; in the writings of controversial scientist/philosopher Sir James Churchward; and in revelations of the Lemurian Brotherhood to the Lemurian Fellowship in Ramona, California) were all made long before the geophysical year studies and the contemporary pioneering ocean cartography of Marie Tharp and Bruce Heezen (see illustration #10). Notice the remarkable patterns of mountain ridges running 270° around Hawaii; the flat "plain" to the northeast; the boundary through the western quarter of the United States and Canada which marks the division between the Pacific plate and the North American shield. Whether or not these continents existed is a less important question than how accurately the maps mesh with the best contemporary scientific knowledge. The correspondence is very close.

Returning to the maps of Piri Reis, Buache, and the ancient sea kings, what kind of planning models would an ancient mariner need to construct such maps? Ivan Sanderson, researcher into the unexplained, asked such questions in the 1960s and 70s — and with several associates, he set out to "pattern the mysteries" by taking full advantage of modern communication technology and statistical data analysis. His success was startling. His 1972 article in *Saga* magazine, "The Twelve Devil's Graveyards Around the World," plotted ship and plane disappearances worldwide, focusing attention on 12 areas, equally spaced over the globe, in which magnetic anomalies and other energy aberrations were linked to a full spectrum of strange physical phenomena (see illustration #11).

Highest on Sanderson's statistical priority list was a lozenge-shaped area east of Miami, in the Bahamas, on the western tip of the infamous Bermuda Triangle. This area's "high profile" of strange events, Sanderson concluded, was mostly due to the enormous flow of air/sea traffic in the area. Other zones of anomaly, though less familiar, were equally rich in disappearances and space-time shift occurences. A pilot flying with passengers near the Hawaii zone suddenly found himself in a "dead zone" without instruments and unable to communicate beyond the cockpit. After flying some 350 miles, the "phenomenon" lifted and the pilot found that tower officials could find no measurable time had elapsed between the beginning of his "dead zone" experience and its end.

Another area of continuing disappearances and mysterious time-warps is the Devil's Sea located east of Japan between Iwo Jima and Marcus Island. Here events have become so sinister that the Japanese government has officially designated the area a danger zone. Sanderson theorized that the tremendous hot and cold currents crossing his most active zones might create the electromagnetic gymnastics affecting instruments and vehicles. His theory is now being balanced against several.

These same areas, in the pattern of an icosahedron, have been mapped out in the *Keys of Enoch* (1977) by J. J. Hurtak but

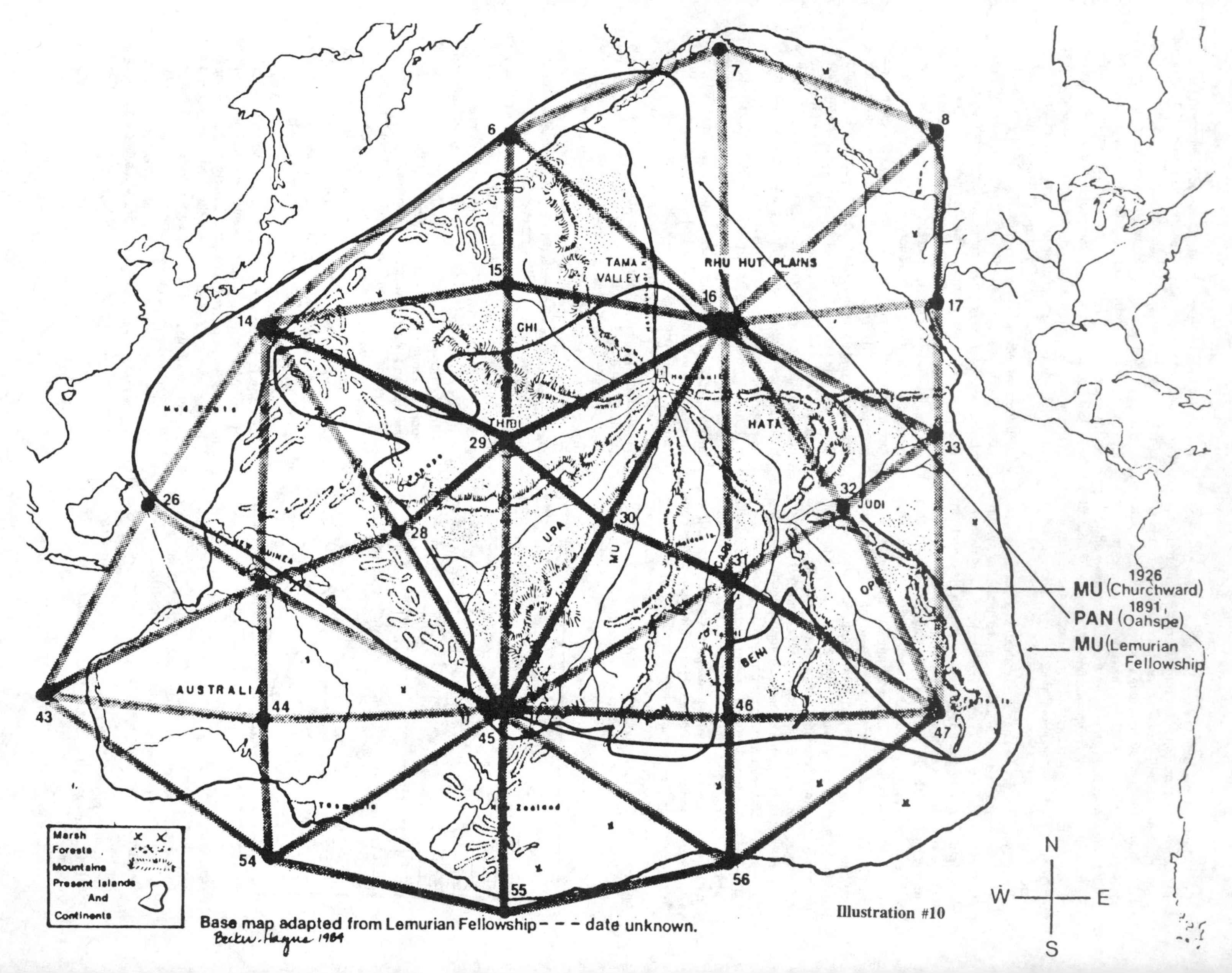

Base map adapted from Lemurian Fellowship - - - date unknown.

Illustration #10

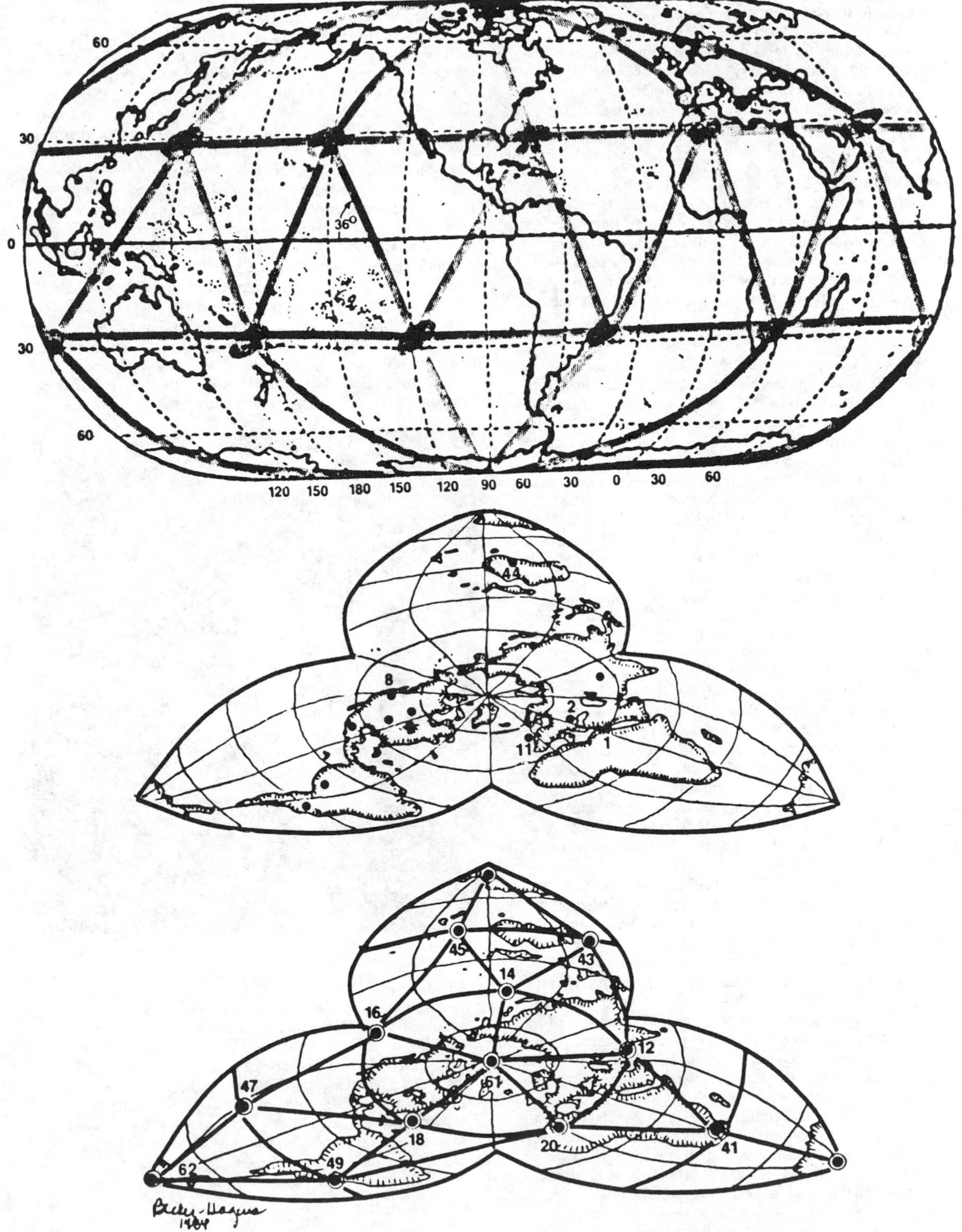
60
30
0
30
60
36°
120 150 180 150 120 90 60 30 0 30 60
44
8
2
11
1
45
43
14
16
12
47
61
18
20
41
62
49

Illustration #11

The lozenge-shaped anomalies of electro-magnetic aberration were identified by Ivan Sanderson in the late '60s and were the impetus for a worldwide reinvestigation of practical whole earth geometry. A source of confusion has been over the location of equally spaced points zig-zagging the globe 36^{0} from the equator. This is not point latitude but rather the angle of incidence with the equator (as shown above).

Illustration #12

In his tour de force *The Book of Knowledge: The Keys of Enoch*, a meta-linguistic code document of linguistic-cybernetic information, Dr. J.J. Hurtak proposes areas of artificial (above) and natural (below) time warp areas used for contact by the Brotherhood. Numbers reflect planetary grid coding points we have adopted that duplicate the original Russian system.

are explained as natural time-warp contact areas used by the Brotherhood. It is not unreasonable metaphysical theory to assume a pulse to the universe, an electromagnetic heartbeat which makes time appear to go backward and ahead — for planes of existence to manifest and disappear. What better spots for contact than Sanderson's? (See illustration #12)

Ivan Sanderson and his energetic colleagues are surely the contemporary rediscoverers of what has come to be called the "Planetary Grid" — so named by Christopher Bird in an article which appeared in the *New Age Journal* of May 1975. Bird's writing brought to light that a truly "morphogenetic"[10] worldwide research effort, involving earth/human origins and grids, had taken off parallel to and as a result of Sanderson's work. Bird wrote about three Russian researchers (Nikolai Goncharov, a Muscovite historian; Vyacheslav Morozov, a construction engineer; and Valery Makarov, an electronics specialist) who had published an article entitled "Is the Earth a Large Crystal?" Their work, supportive of and following immediately upon Sanderson's, had outlined a worldwide grid of points nearly identical to Sanderson's 12 and had added 50 more. These occured where Sanderson's global icosahedron overlapped the Russians proposed combination of icosa and dodecahedron. These new lines and points, in conjunction with Sanderson's, now matched most of the earth's seismic fracture zones and ocean ridge lines as well as outlined worldwide atmospheric highs and lows, paths of migratory animals, gravitational anomalies, and even the sites of ancient cities.[11]

The tradition established by the Russians with the overlapping icosa/dodecahedron grid has been adopted by almost all grid researchers with the exception of New Zealand's Captain Bruce Cathie who is working with the cubeoctahedron (Fuller's vector equilibrium model, briefly discussed in the next section of this article). Among the rest, there are some common themes in the predictive science of the grid and some dramatic divergences. Those involved in what might be thought of as "classic geometrics" use the model to predict physical events and measurable phenomena in the tradition of Ivan Sanderson: Athelstan Spilhaus (faults, seismic activity, continental drift); J.J. Hurtak (time warps, evidence of paraphysical grid line connections among pyramids in the Americas); A.M. Davie (coincident events). Another branch of theory centers in harmonics. Bruce Cathie is meticulously charting the courses of phenomena grouped under the title of "UFO." Michael Helus has undertaken a universal theory of harmonics that he calls "Astrosonics" and is attempting to develop a practical health technology for people to get "in tune" with Gaia by reactivating the harmonics of the cosmic time and place of their birth. He believes that planetary grid harmonics can and will be manipulated if we do not develop a responsible stewardship for this profound and powerful resource. John Sinkiewicz has developed a theory not unlike that of Donald Cyr — that we may be making an enormous mistake if we assume that "Nature" is natural, that it's always been like this — with wild climate swings, tornadoes, pole wobble, and the like. Sinkiewicz believes the earth energy grid is out of alignment, is no longer anchored at the north and south poles, and that New Age spiritual communities around the world are gradually rediscovering the new grid and building their sacred sites in accordance to activate it. Ray Stoner, working with shamans among the Central American and North American Indians, has gone a step further and is searching the museums and ruins for potential pieces of the grid "power system" he believes was once in operation around the world and centered in the pyramids. His is potentially the most politically revolutionary theory since so many key "artifacts" (such as the unusual stone yoke shown in illustration # 13) are found in the museums and collections of the very wealthy.

Photo: Howard Kisor

Illustration #13

Archaeologists hypothesize that "stone yokes" such as this one on display at Chicago's Field Museum were worn by Mayan athletes during their strenuous and violently competitive games. These yokes measure approximately 24" by 18" and are about 4" in width. They appear to be carved from solid granite and weigh perhaps several hundred pounds. Ray Stoner has noticed a resemblance to magnets, even down to carvings of heads facing opposite directions on the two poles. In our opinion, the object is incomplete, perhaps requiring some sort of attractive base plate.

The work of both Stoner and Sinkiewicz provide something of a bridge to the work of the dowsers, notably Christopher Bird (who dowses for information); Terry Ross (former President of the American Society of Dowsers who practices a kind of dowsing of manifestation for needy Third World countries); and the thousands of dowsers here and in Europe who are slowly uncovering a transcontinental network of lines based on a kind of sixth sense of the flow of Gaia and the "ley" of the land. This same type of work has been carried on in China and Japan for thousands of years as Geomancy — the identification of archetypes of the tiger and the dragon in the landscape, and the siting of buildings and their functions with respect to balancing these forces with the flow of underground water and cosmic energy. (See illustration #14) A branch of dowsers in this country (including Tom Bearden, Ken MacNeill, Toby Grotz, and Walter Baumgartner) are pushing the politics of grid research into the development of practical "free energy devices" that will be decentralized, affordable, and supportive of personal freedom.

A New Synthesis: Predictions and Speculations

In 1983, upon first seeing a drawing of the Russian planetary grid in Moira Timms' book *Prophecies and Predictions*, we immediately recognized the work of R. Buckminster Fuller — who had spent a lifetime developing his models and theory of "nature's comprehensive building system." There before us, adapted from Chris Bird's article, was a drawing of an "incomplete" geodesic sphere — in fact, the exact sphere upon which Fuller had based his geodesic domes and much of his theory of synergetic geometry. With the simple addition of 60 lines which connected the vertexes of Sanderson's icosahedron to the vertexes of the added Russian dodecahedron we had duplicated the Neolithic craftsman's model and established Fuller's 15 "great circle" polyhedron as a key link in the chain of grid ideas. After locating Bird's original article and finding the Russian work in *Chemistry and Life*, a USSR science

Illustration #15

Our goal in producing EarthStar was the creation of a map that would be comfortable to an audience oriented to the equatorial linearity and continental positioning of a standard Mercator map. It depicts major river systems, seismic zones, major ocean currents and the lines of the UVG 120 Polyhedron. The map is an excellent tool for distance estimation, as the sides of the Basic Triangle measure 1400, 2200 and 2600 miles respectively. (An interesting numerological coincidence: the sides of the Basic Triangle add up to 6200 miles, or one-quarter of the circumference of the earth). We believe that this map was used by ancient navigators of the seas and skies, who would have found these great circle routes the most convenient and efficient for long-distance travel.

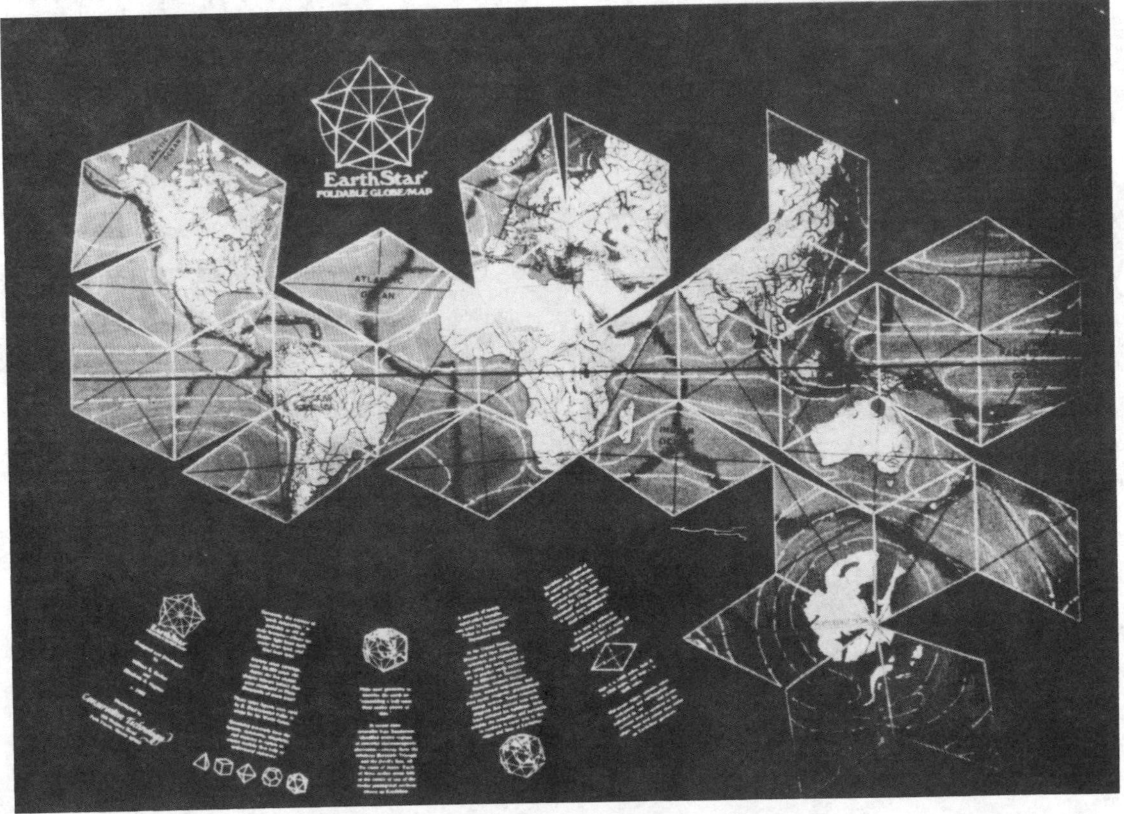

Illustration #16
The UVG 4/30 Diamond centers on EarthStar will provide, we believe, the most fertile zones for research into the ancient history of the earth because they appear to be so geologically stable. In addition, there is a surprisingly full history of advanced cultures in these areas already established: the complex of Alexandria/Cairo/Jerusalem (point 1); a possible nuclear waste storage area postulated by Jalandris in Gabon (point 40); the People of the Four Corners (point 13); the sacred lands of the Hopi (point 17); the sacred lands of the Australian aborigines (point 44); the vast complex of megaliths and stone circles in the British Isles (point 11); the extraordinary Ugansk Bay Eskimo art complex (point 9); the ancient splendor of Amazonian cities now buried in vegetation (point 36); the Argentine Tafi megaliths (point 48); the contemporary site of major Soviet defense research (point 5), and the nearly unmatchable biological splendor of the Galapagos Islands (point 34).

Becker-Hagens EarthStar®

magazine, we went into what many researchers, writers and artists call "curiosity/compulsion syndrome." Everything we seemed to hear, see, read, and even eat related "in some way" to the planetary grid. Three months after glancing at that Russian drawing, our library had totally changed, cardboard and store-bought globes littered our tables, and we were driving to Washington, D.C. to meet with Chris Bird.

Since that time nearly a year ago, a cascade of information from friends, students, co-researchers, and others has brought us to this current presentation.

We propose that the planetary grid map outlined by the Russian team Goncharov, Morozov and Makarov is essentially correct, with its overall organization anchored to the north and south axial poles and the Great Pyramid at Gizeh. The Russian map, however, lacks completeness, in our opinion, which can be accomplished by the overlaying of a complex, icosahedrally-derived, spherical polyhedron developed by R. Buckminster Fuller. In his book *Synergetics 2*, he called it the "Composite of Primary and Secondary Icosahedron Great Circle Sets." We have shortened that to Unified Vector Geometry (UVG) 120 Sphere, because of the form's elegant organization of 121 "great circles" running through its 4,862 points. We use the number 120 due to its easy comprehension as a spherical polyhedron with 120 identical triangles — all approximately 30°, 60° and 90° in composition. All other forms within our Unified Vector Geometry use shape names and numbers which refer to the quantity of smallest UVG Basic Triangles within a given form — and the number of named forms in the UVG 120 Polyhedron or Sphere. Thus, when we refer to our "Pac-Man" pentagons which appeared in our first planetary grid map, you should know that we also call them UVG 10/12 Pentagons, because *ten* of our Basic Triangles create each pentagon and there are *twelve* pentagons in the UVG 120 Sphere and Polyhedron.

In our commercially available EarthStar foldable globe/map,[12] we use the UVG 4/30 Diamond (or rhomb). Within this diamond are 4 Basic Triangles, and there are 30 diamonds in the 120 Polyhedron and Sphere (see illustrations #15, #16). This figure permits not only easier assembly of the UVG 120 Polyhedron (in the form of the rhombic triacontahedron) than our pentagon-based hexakis icosahedron, but also permits easy orientation to the four compass points when working with the globe or map (see illustration #17, and chart).

And now we come to our most fascinating discovery of all — the predictive utilization of the Basic Triangle. It is this figure which we knew to be the result of multiple mappings of all five regular Platonic solids on the surface of a sphere or combined polyhedral form (icosahedron and dodecahedron) like the hexakis icosahedron and/or rhombic triacontahedron. What we hadn't known until recently was that R. Buckminster Fuller had not only drawn and analyzed the Basic Triangle, but had also noted all its internal angles in planar and spherical notation (See illustration #18). Also what we hadn't known until quite recently was that this triangle could predict so many kinds of events and geographic patterns, at so many times and places throughout human history. As mnemonic tools, the UVG Basic Triangle and 120 Sphere store and integrate biology, metaphysics, mythology, astronomy, geology, human struggle — or in the words of Pythagoras, "the supernatural within the finite."

Illustration #17 (See page 63)
The geometry of EarthStar is the rhombic triacontahedron projection method developed by R. Buckminster Fuller. We have continued to use the numbering system originally published by Russian researchers.

Planetary Grid Projection

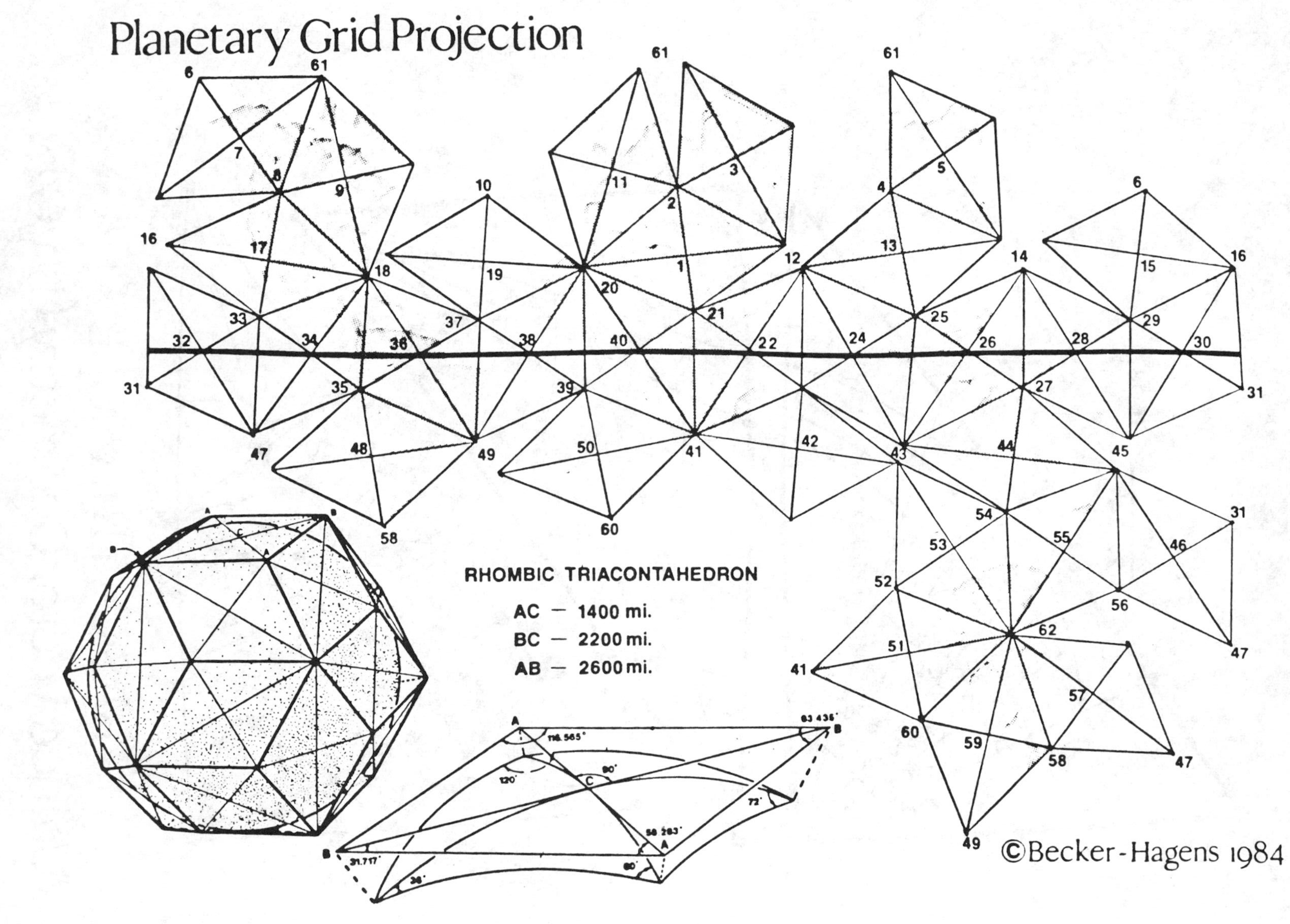

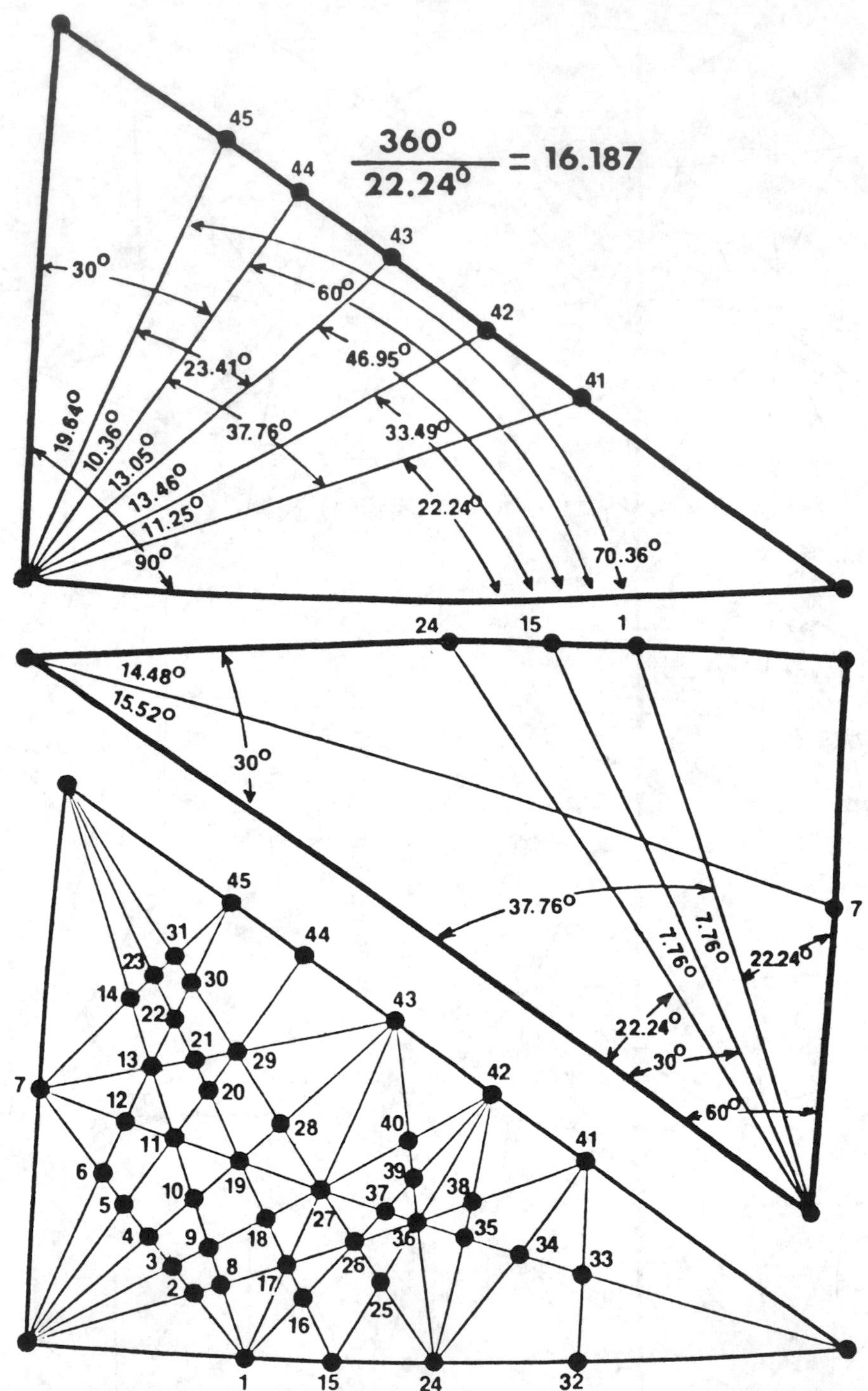

BASIC TRIANGLE
Unified Vector Geometry (UVG)

Illustration #18

Within the Basic Triangle's 30, 60 and 90 degree angles (whose lines and vertexes define 120 of those triangles, 62 major grid points, and 15 major great circles) are arrayed 45 intersection points and 16 lines which manifest 106 minor great circles and 4800 minor points over the face of the globe (UVG total is 4862 points). By noting the three numbers for the Basic UVG Triangle followed by a single number for a minor grid point (example — Oxford, England falls near 2-11-20/2 on our European maps); two numbers for a minor grid line (example — Italy's boot heel is defined by Basic Triangle 2-1-20/43-28 minor line).

* * * * *

On September 1, 1983, in the pre-dawn sky, a 747 jumbo jet is cruising over the last island in the Aleutian chain. The Korean pilot is relaxed and having coffee as his autopilot is switched onto "Red Route 20," the standard course set for all airliners out of Anchorage to avoid coming within 25 miles of Russian territories north of Japan. At 3:18 a.m., Japan time, the pilot radios that his position is 115 miles south of Hokkaido Island in northern Japan. Ground radar, however, locates the plane 115 miles *north* of Hokkaido and well into Soviet airspace. At 3:27 a.m., a garbled distress call goes out from the plane — the last message to be sent from KAL 007. Glance at our illustration of the path of the plane on the UVG 120 Sphere and imagine this scenario. KAL 007 crosses planetary grid point 6, approximately 1800 miles east/southeast of Anchorage, Alaska about 1:00 a.m. Thursday, September 1, 1983. The positions of the sun and moon begin bringing enormous energy into the vector line which stretches from the tip of the Aleutian chain to the Mongolian/Soviet mainland west of Sakhalin Island. (See illustration #19). Silently, without alerting Captain Chun the pilot, the geo-compass in the autopilot's guidance system is slowly pulled 22.24^{0} off its corrected north bearing, altering the course of the plane by that amount while simultaneously beginning to energize and speed up the magnetic odometer in the plane's computer navigational system. A fractional addition of a mile is added to each actual mile travelled at an accelerating rate. As the crew and passengers talk about the festivities ahead in Seoul, other smaller aircraft appear behind the 757 airliner. No communication takes place because the pilots of the smaller aircraft are never given international radio frequencies for fear they will defect. Then an explosion, and another, thunder into the ears of the crew. Captain Chun begins his radio distress call, but in four short minutes the lives of all 269 aboard are gone.

Compare the above to the flight of KAL 902 out of Paris, bound for Anchorage. The date is April 20, 1978. In the predawn sky over grid point 11, in northern Scotland, the 707's guidance system compass begins to read to an energized line running up from the Bermuda Triangle. Captain Kim Chang Kyu, a veteran KAL pilot, doesn't notice the bearing of his plane changing slowly to 82.25^{0} off his near polar great circle route. The plane moves onto an infill grid line over Greenland. By the time the plane moves into the next basic grid triangle, a passenger notices that the Arctic sun which had been on his right is now on his left. Before he can alert Captain Kyu, a Russian missile slams into the fuselage, killing two passengers and forcing the plane to land on a frozen lake south of Murmansk. As Russion troop vehicles appear on the shore, Captain Kyu apologizes to his passengers saying that he had felt something had gone wrong with his compass before the Russian planes had appeared.

Illustration #19

An activation of the grid system appears responsible for the demise of two modern jetliners dependent upon computerized navigational systems. On September 1, 1983, KAL 007 left Anchorage (A) on an intended flight to Seoul, South Korea (K). It was diverted down a minor grid line to a crash sight near Sakhalin Island (S). KAL 902 left Paris (P) bound for Anchorage (A) on April 20, 1978 but was diverted down a minor grid line and shot down near Murmansk (M) in the Soviet Union.

Both incidents, KAL 007 and KAL 902, were based on predawn crossings of major grid points (6 and 11) by sophisticated aircraft which then, unbeknownst to their crews drifted off their programmed course and followed minor grid lines until shot down by uncommunicative Russian pilots.

We predict that there will be other incidents such as these occuring in the future, and not just off the Russian coastline. We feel that incidents such as these help pinpoint the evidence about which Ivan Sanderson theorized in 1972 — that there is a predictable physical pattern of energy events working through the system Chris Bird called the planetary grid.

The "predictable physical pattern" was discovered in quite a different context from earth energy research. While discussing the physical structures which support his theories of geometry (in *Synergetics I*), R. Buckminster Fuller presented evidence that the micro-photography of balloon skin layers has, under near ideal conditions, produced visible patterns identical to our UVG 120 Sphere surface structure. As interior gas molecules ricochet off the inner surface of the balloon, they manifest their kinetic energy in "great circle" patterns of "shortest distance" frequency. If the ambient temperature of the balloon's exterior can be delicately balanced and equalized — the pattern of the UVG 120 sphere can become visible.

Given that the earth's original formation was based upon the clustered gravitational packing of quadrillions of vibrating cosmic dust particles and gases, in the early eons of our solar system — we feel the analogy of the balloon skin is strongly comparable to the lines of vectorial energy we hypothesize are transitting the earth's surface. Our Basic UVG Triangle reveals

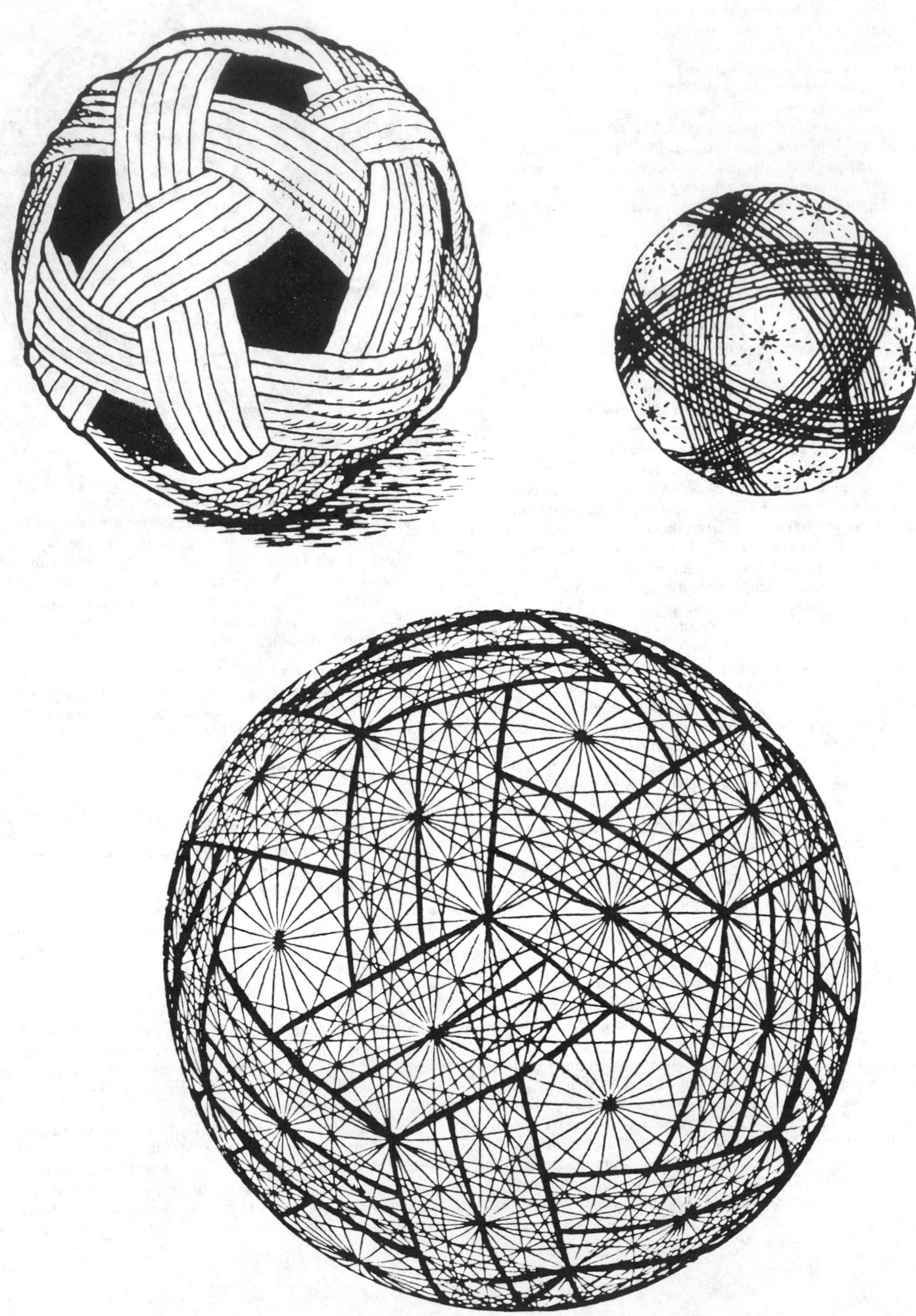

Illustration #20
R. Buckminster Fuller's configuration of electromagnetic band widths (small sphere) is a hidden master pattern in the UVG 120 Sphere. The similarity to hand-held decorative reed spheres from Southeast Asia is further evidence that such "planning models" have been in common use throughout human history. "If you could only see the reams of tracing paper which spill out of the drawers in my office," writes A.M. Davie. "I have been doing the same exercise with electromagnetic band widths for years. To forecast an event in the Catastrophe Theory, this principle must be used. Whether on a Planetary scale or down to full Earth surface scale of fractions of inches, it is basically the same theory...I have done experiments (with band widths of frequency tunability) in the lab and found the same experiences as reported in the Bermuda Triangle and UFO incidents. This experiment is too dangerous to repeat, and Edinburgh University has agreed to a ban on all attempts to re-enact the experiments. It is potentially lethal. The theory of this phenomenon was known to Artistotle...It is definitely TIME-SPACE-COLOUR-HARMONY syndrome in content, and therefore obeys a numerical law of nature to allow forecasting the event."

a 120th section of these energy lines — and we think that it is totally predictable to find detailed physical manifestations of these lines, particularly on continental land masses.

A possible piece of supporting evidence comes from the Vail/Cyr canopy theory — which proposes a more equalized world climate during the Megalithic period (see footnote 7). If the global climatic ambience were more regularized than it is today, it is possible that grid energy manifestations were also more visible and potentially more available for applied use. Extending the speculation back further in time, the deluge myth found in the myths of virtually all cultures can perhaps be traced to some (Atlantean?) technological endeavor that caused a partial and devastating collapse of the canopy. Before this collapse, the poles may well have been free of ice (hence the existence of maps such as Piri Reis and Buache). Polar ice caps may have formed relatively rapidly in the period of climatic disequilibrium. In this light, Cyr's Megalithic canopy theory is correspondent with our own findings in analyzing Megalithic sites. We have documented in the illustrations of Ireland, Britain, and Europe which follow; a patterned interface of man-made constructions, dating to the Megalithic period, which correspond to our proposed "infrastructure" for the icosa/dodecahedral planetary grid. New evidence that we are just beginning to analyze[13], and which includes patterns of mounds within the central United States and the curious "lines" of the Nazca area of Peru, exhibits the same close correspondence. This proves to us that past cultures have been aware of, and attuned to, the energies of the UVG 120 Sphere.

A second analogy to earth's processes we feel comfortable with is the Russian crystal earth concept, whereby coalesced volcanic matter which formed the earth settled initially into a crystal for (UVG 120 Polyhedron). The Russians theorize that with rotation and centrifugal redistribution of molten surface material, the earth soon took on its spherical form but retains the deep crystal structure and its predictable manifestations. One of these is based on the principle that crystal edges and vertexes carry most of the thermal, structural, and electromagnetic energy events developing from within and imposed upon the surface material. Satellite cameras and infrared/radar intruments have already documented thermal/structural energy developments along the globe's UVG 120 Polyhedral edges. It remains for traditional science to develop instruments as sensitive as an experienced dowser's "earth sense" before the full spectrum of the earth's electromagnetism can be tuned like a "crystal set" radio to a wide range of frequency band widths. (See illustration #20)

It is clear to us that Megalithic peoples knew all that we now know about the planetary grid and then some. The stones which they so carefully placed upon ley lines were used to communicate with anyone else linked via common telluric energy flows. (See illustration #21) These energy flows are being mapped today

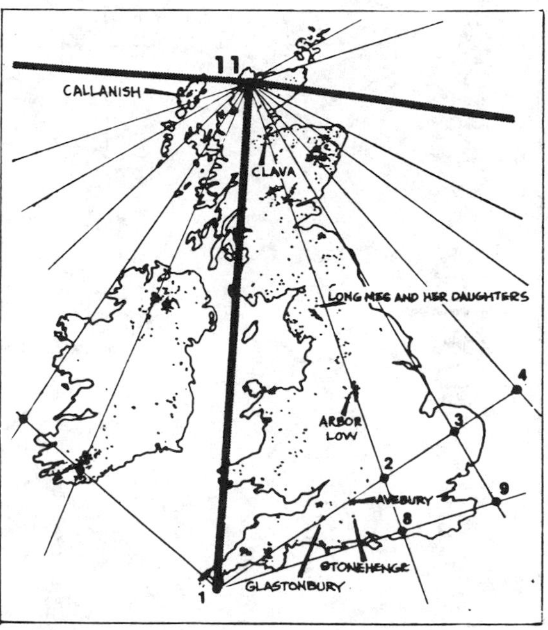

Illustration #21
Unobstructed minor grid energy lines focus into a Basic Triangle corner in the British Isles, which have probably the largest clustering of megaliths in northern Europe. Stone circles are indicated by dots.

Illustration #22
Both ley line hunters and dowsers have wondered at the persistent site line-ups of ancient megaliths and more recent sacred constructions (cathedrals, capital cities, shrines, etc.). The diamond-pattern line superimposed on our map shows a transcontinental system of energy ley lines published by Golin Bloy an experienced dowser in Europe. Most of the line has been confirmed by dowsing. The correspondence with the UVG 120 Sphere is apparent. In Triangle 11-20-2, we find Oxford (2); North Sea oil deposits (4-5-6); Rotterdam (9); Hameln, village of the Pied Piper (17); Berlin (13); Chartres (17); Alta Mira (24); Frankfort (19); Barcelona (35); Cordoba (32); Hamburg (12); and Lourdes (line 24-36). In Triangle 20-2-1, we find Athens (10); Delphi (19); and Assisi, home of St. Francis (43).

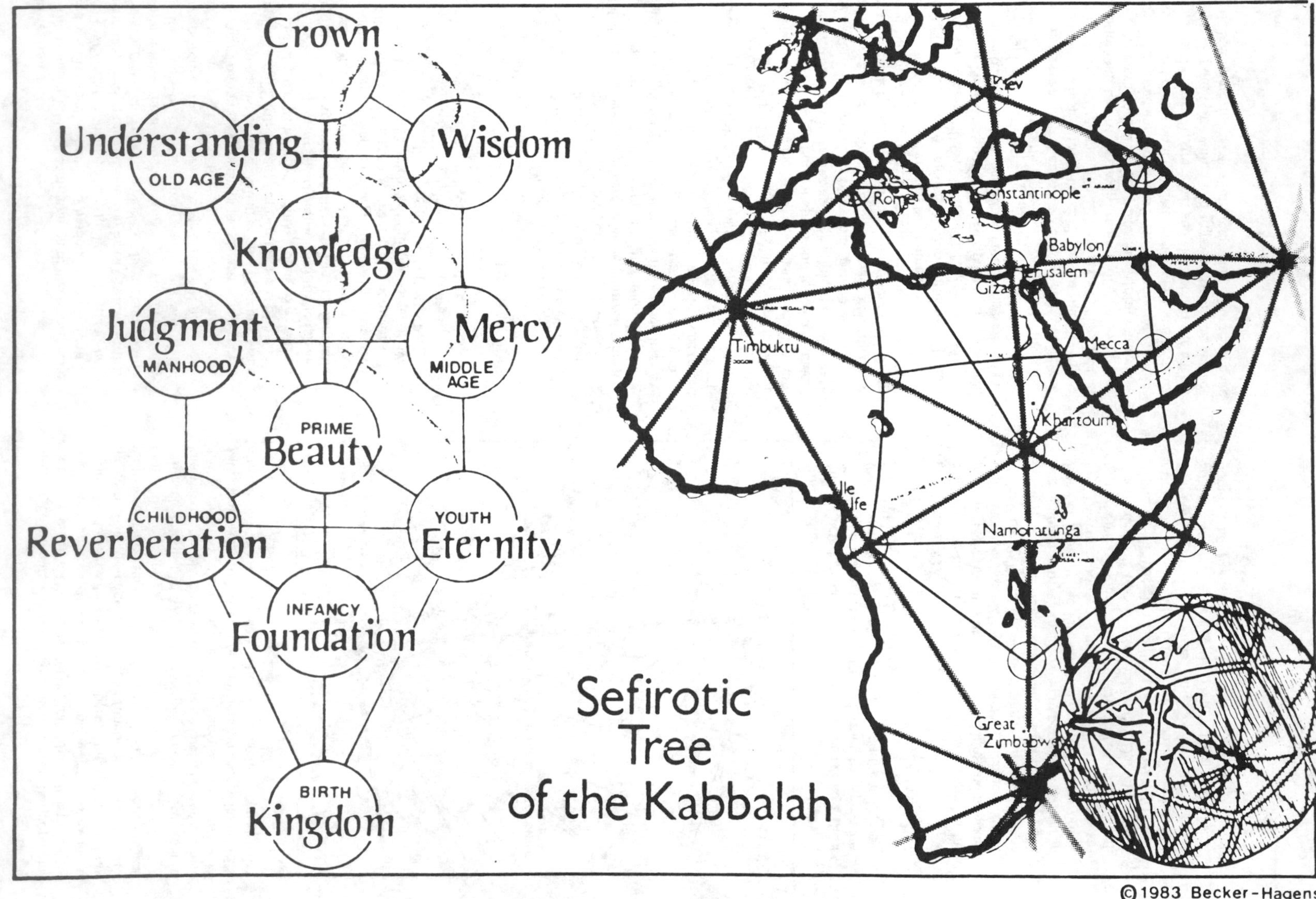
Crown
Understanding
OLD AGE
Wisdom
Knowledge
Judgment
MANHOOD
Mercy
MIDDLE AGE
PRIME
Beauty
CHILDHOOD
Reverberation
YOUTH
Eternity
INFANCY
Foundation
BIRTH
Kingdom
Sefirotic
Tree
of the Kabbalah
Rome
Constantinople
Babylon
Jerusalem
Giza
Timbuktu
Mecca
Khartoum
Ile Ife
Namoratunga
Great Zimbabwe
©1983 Becker-Hagens

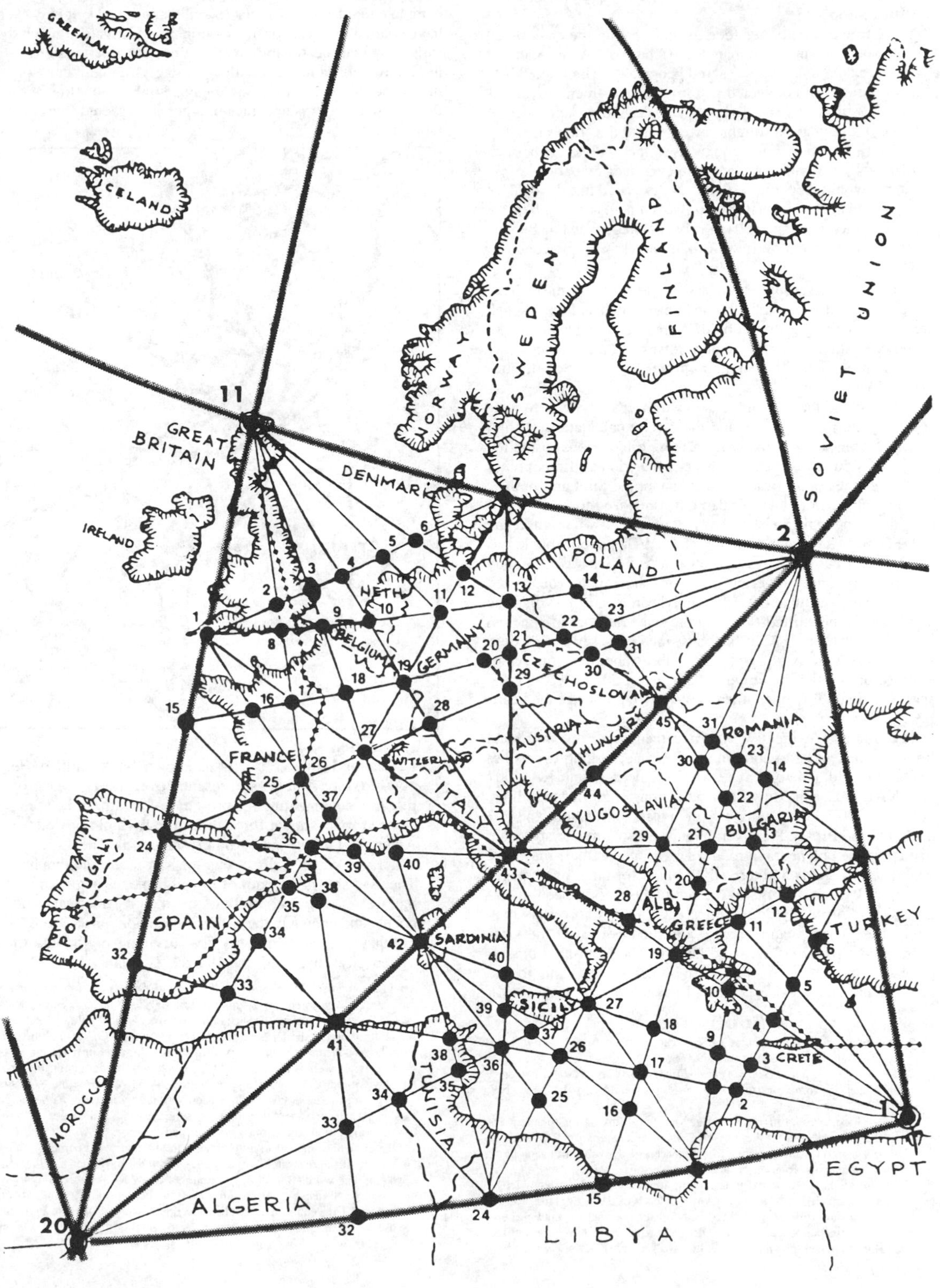
GREENLAND
ICELAND
NORWAY
SWEDEN
FINLAND
SOVIET UNION
GREAT BRITAIN
IRELAND
DENMARK
POLAND
NETH
BELGIUM
GERMANY
CZECHOSLOVAKIA
AUSTRIA
HUNGARY
ROMANIA
FRANCE
SWITZERLAND
ITALY
YUGOSLAVIA
BULGARIA
PORTUGAL
SPAIN
SARDINIA
ALB.
GREECE
TURKEY
SICILY
CRETE
MOROCCO
TUNISIA
ALGERIA
LIBYA
EGYPT

Illustration #23
"The tree can be understood as representing the chakras in the body of universal man, the Anthropos...Adam Kadmon. Sacred anatomy = sacred geography. There would be a number of connected patterns of 'trees/men' covering the surface of the globe which, depending upon the scale or application, might correspond to the 'root races' or 'sub-root races' or perhaps even the twelves 'tribes' of Israel (mankind). As there are ever finer gradations of 'trees' within the Sefirotic Tree, the 'extended trees' would create chains and great circles woven across the sphere like the electromagnetic band widths of frequency tunability." Communication from Robert Gulick in Englewood, Colorado.

both by dowsing groups interested in this rarest form of "harmony of the spheres" and ley line hunters (such as John Michell and others in the great tradition of Alfred Hawkins) who wonder at the coincident siting of modern towns and significant structures upon ancient stone remains from the past. (See illustration #22)

We also hold that a major reason why Megalithic groups were so interested in astronomy and the precise calculation of solar and lunar phases was that within these calculations rested the predicted "pulses" of energy through the grid at different times of the year. Captain Bruce Cathie, an airline pilot and prolific grid researcher from New Zealand, has theorized for years regarding the grid's pulsing harmonic pattern and how it might relate to UFO and "sky light" phenomena. UVG is applicable to this research in a curious way. R. Buckminster Fuller was constantly experimenting with spherical packing — how many equal sized spheres can you fit into a given polyhedron, and how can the arrangement be shifted (keeping the same number of spheres) into a different one. As it happens, the UVG 120 Polyhedron shifts back and forth with the cubeoctahedron (or vector equilibrium model, as Fuller calls it) that Cathie uses and that seems to map UFO phenomena. We can hypothesize the heartbeat of Gaia.

The ancients evidently patterned their universal and local holidays and feasts to conjoin with the interlocking events between the grid and solar system energy fields. Both KAL 007 and KAL 902 tragedies occurred during significant holiday periods — 007 during a major Hindu feast for Vishnu, and 902 during Good Friday/Passover. We have also come to speculate that the stone polyhedra introduced early in this article may have been used as charts and terrestrial guides for large pilgrimages which took place over major regions of the globe. (See illustration #23) Spiritually and intellectually hungry travellers may well have visited major energy collection points on the grid, each having its own flavor and delight. The hand-held model, or map, attuned as it was to the solar system and to the monuments and towns one would pass along the way, was a complete tool for the voyager. (See illustration #24) It may even have charted the cycle of transcontinental festivals in much the same way that the Australian aborigines are able to coordinate huge religious gatherings with (seemingly) no deliberate planning. The "bureaucracy" is maintained only in the flow of time through lines of kinship, lines of sight, and sacred lines of the tchuringa.

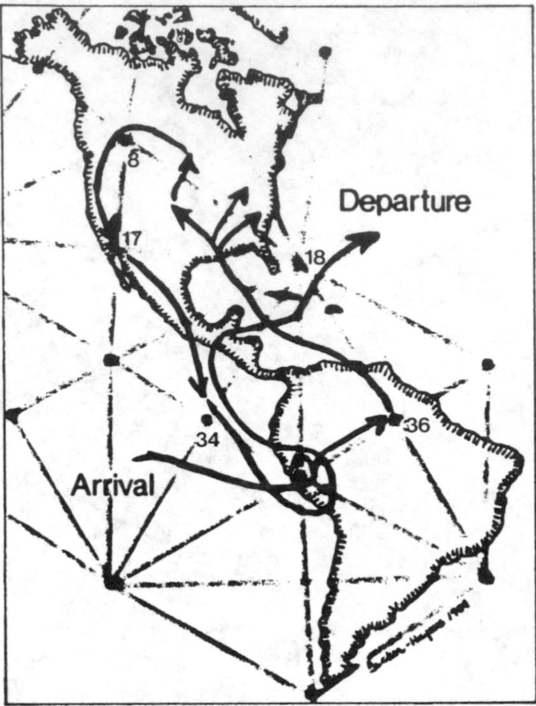

Illustration #24
L. Taylor Hansen, in a little known book entitled *He Walked the Americas*, presents over thirty years of research documenting the presence of a white-robed fair-skinned man known throughout the mythologies of the Americas (among many other names) as The Lord-of-Wind-and-Water, Tah-co-mah, or Kate-Zahl, the Prophet. The map shows the path of his pilgrimage, beginning in the western ocean, circling the major American grid points, and ending in the eastern ocean horizon. It is possible that "Jesus Christ" is our surviving mythology of sacred pilgrimages on the "Gizeh Crystal."

Footnotes

1. Let us pray that another plague (AIDS, cancer, heart disease...) will not be necessary in completing this scenario.
2. Taken from "*Gathered Notes Among Friends on: The Crystal's Dance*," a publication from Chrystal Hill Farm, 9411 Sandrock Rd., Eden, NY 14057.
3. Jeffrey Goodman is a highly controversial, free-thinking independent archaeologist and author (*We Are the Earthquake Generation: The Genesis Mystery*) who was among the earliest pioneers of "psychic archaeology." His current work focuses on health and crystals.
4. We want to thank Robert Cowley of the Research into Lost Knowledge Organization (RILKO, 8 The Drive, London N11 2DY England) for introducing our work to A.M. Davie of Alloa, Scotland. In our long, enjoyable correspondence with Mr. Davie, we have found him to be a gifted scholar of ancient languages and cultures, a keen observer of coincidence, and (as evidenced by reports of his work with SRI in California) inventor of a predictive system for events as seemingly unrelated as earthquakes, spontaneous combustion, cardiac infarction, mechanical failure, and crime.
5. We call this figure the Unified Vector Geometry (UVG) 120 Polyhedron, and hope that the new planetary grid terminology we introduce will be both clear as well as reflective of the ancient and modern contributors to its development. In one of his first letters, A.M. Davie wrote: "I came on one word yesterday which has been adopted by modern mathematics, and causes me considerable problems. Where two lines intersect, the word to describe this intersection is now termed 'Vector.' "An Bheachd-Or" is the ancient name for 'The Golden Circle,' and is a geometric figure of definite lineal measurements associated with the movements of the Solar System. The word 'Bheachd,' pronounced as 'Vect,' is according to my dictionary: Notice, Attention, Observation, Perception, Feeling, Ambition, Ideas, Conception, Distinct Recollection/Memory, Opinion, Behavior, Sense/Wisdom, Judgment, Conceit, Aim, Intention, Carriage, Vision, Eyesight, Surity, Covenant, Multitude, CIRCLE and RING."

6. Curiously, "armilla," the root in armillary spheres, has the meaning of, "iron ring" and "golden coronation bracelet."
7. Donald Cyr, editor of *Stonehenge Viewpoint*, and his friend Lawrence W. Smith have championed and greatly expanded the ideas of Isaac N. Vail since their high school days in the 1930s. As an archaeoastronomer, Cyr's notion is that much can be gained in understanding past civilizations if we do not make the uniformitarian assumption that things (such as climate) have always been roughly as they are now. The Vail/Cyr "Canopy Theory" supposes that during the Megalithic period, a layer of ice crystals formed over the earth at a height of about fifty miles. This could have produced something like the greenhouse effect — a mild, relatively windless climate with the atmosphere at the dew point — over much of the earth, with spectacular halos around the sun and moon. The light of the sun shining through the ice crystals would have been so brilliant that it would have been impossible to gaze at it directly. Because of the optics of light refraction through the ice crystals, however, each halo edge would fall 22 + degrees from the center of the sun — with a less common, but equally regular secondary halo occuring 46 + degrees from the center. This glorious sky phenomenon could have given man the world over a predictable common unit of measure. A related effect of the canopy may also help explain the seemingly phenomenal knowledge of astronomy among the ancients. Joe Jochmans (writing as Jalandris) received an honorary doctorate for his interpretation of Genesis based upon canopy and other earth energy effects. He claims that the canopy may have magnified the light from the stars and planets and made them appear closer and much easier to view with the unaided eye than is possible today. His other fascinating theory is that the Megalithic canopy was preceded by an even larger more magnificent canopy that ultimately collapsed — producing the great deluge and rain of forty days and forty nights that is recorded in the sacred tradition of virtually every culture on earth.
8. Sir J. Norman Lockyer, writing in the early part of this century, was perhaps the first contemporary archaeoastronomer — having discovered significant alignments between megaliths and celestial bodies. His work was largely rejected, as were his very humanitarian politics that echo his British predecessor Alfred Russel Wallace, though it forms the base for later work reinitiated by Alexander Thom.
9. Dick Benson's work, formally presented in June of this year to the U.S. Psychotronics Association meeting in Atlanta, holds the promise of a unified field of letters and numbers. His "World's Oldest Jesus ø Map" is reprinted to give not only a glimpse of the complex geometry employed by the ancient planners at Cairo but to hint at the sophistication and refinement of Benson's work. One of his most exciting archaeological discoveries is a virtually identical "site plan" based on the pyramids at Teotihuacan in Mexico.
10. "Morphogenetic fields" were introduced by British biologist Rupert Sheldrake in another controversial book, *A New Science of Life: The Hypothesis of Formative Causation*, suggested for burning by *Nature* magazine in Britain. The theory is complex, implying that once something comes into existence (an idea, a gene code, a chemical structure...) it exclusively fills a specific cosmic niche; sends a kind of formative energy throughout Gaia; and makes its appearance quickly and with increasing ease throughout the world. Currently the Tarrytown Group in New York is offering a prize of $10,000 for the best experimental design to test Sheldrake's theory.
11. Over the past year and a half, students in anthopology and environmental planning at Governors State University have undertaken the tedious, not-yet-computer assisted task of checking the fantastic claims of the Russian visionaries. (Several students, among them Penny Frick, Tim Donovan, Jay Rick, Denis Chapman, John Lerch, and Mary BoyaJean, have put in far beyond the required time and effort and have been brave enough to criticize and question almost everything!) In general, the students' work has involved the translation of data from various atlases and sourcebooks from their Mercator, conical and spherical projections to the hexakis icosahedron and rhombic triacontahedron that we use for standardizing data. For the most part, the Russian claims hold up but are substantially over-generalized — particularly with respect to electromagnetic aberration.
12. EarthStar is printed in full color on heavy cardstock, 17½" x 22½", and is suitable for framing — but has been pre-punched and scored for folding into an 8"-diameter rhombic triacontahedron globe with stand. A plastic UVG 4/30 Diamond overlay infilled with UVG 120 Sphere lines is included. It is available for $7.50, tax and postage included, from Conservative Technology, 105 Wolpers Rd., Park Forest, IL 60466. Dealer and bulk order discounts are available.
13. There are many people whose contributions, insights, and encouragement have been essential in keeping us so absorbed in this research — especially Tim Wilhelm, Robert Warth, Robert Gulick, Edwin Wright, John Michell, R. Gary Smith, Robert Lawlor, Jose A. Arguelles, the Rev. Dorothy Leon and L. Taylor Hansen.

CHART: Becker-Hagens Planetary Grid System Coordinates

1	31.72°N	31.20°E	On the Egyptian continental shelf, in the Mediterranean Sea, at approximately the midpoint between the two outlets of the Nile at Masabb Rashid and Masabb Dumyat
2	52.62°N	31.20°E	On the Sozh River east of Gomel, at the boundary junction of three Soviet republics — Ukraine, Bellorussia, and Russia
3	58.28°N	67.20°E	In marshy lowlands just west of Tobolsk
4	52.62°N	103.20°E	In the lowlands north of the southern tip of Lake Baykal, at the edge of highlands
5	58.28°N	139.20°E	In the highlands along the coast of the Sea of Okhotsk
6	52.62°N	175.20°E	Slightly east of Attu at the western tip of the Aleutian Islands
7	58.28°N	148.80°W	Edge of continental shelf in the Gulf of Alaska
8	52.62°N	112.80°W	Buffalo Lake, Alberta, at the edge of highlands in lowlands
9	58.28°N	76.80°W	Just east of Port Harrison on Hudson's Bay
10	52.62°N	40.80°W	Gibbs Fracture Zone
11	58.28°N	4.80°W	Loch More on the west coast of Scotland
12	26.57°N	67.20°E	On the edge of the Kirthar Range bordering the Indus River Valley, directly north of Karachi
13	31.72°N	103.20°E	At the east edge of the Himalayas in Szechuan Province, just west of the Jiuding Shan summit
14	26.57°N	139.20°E	At the intersection of Kydshu Palau Ridge, the West Mariana Ridge, and the Iwo Jima Ridge
15	31.72°N	175.20°E	At the intersection of Hess Plateau, the Hawaiian Ridge, and the Emperor Seamounts
16	26.57°N	148.80°W	Northeast of Hawaii, midway between the Murray Fracture Zone and the Molokai Fracture Zone
17	31.72°N	112.80°W	Cerro Cubabi, a highpoint just south of the US/Mexico border near Sonoita and lava fields

18	26.57°N	76.80°W	Edge of continental shelf near Great Abaco Island in the Bahamas
19	31.72°N	40.80°W	Atlantis Fracture Zone
20	26.57°N	4.80°W	In El Eglab, a highland peninsula at the edge of the Sahara Desert sand dunes
21	10.81°N	31.20°E	Sudan Highlands, at the edge of White Nile marshfields
22	0°	49.20°E	Somali Abyssal Plain
23	10.81°S	67.20°E	Vema Trench (in the Indian Ocean) at the intersection of the Mascarene Ridge, the Carlsberg Ridge, and Maldive Ridge into the Mid-Indian Ridge
24	0°	85.20°E	Ceylon Abyssal Plain
25	10.81°N	103.20°E	Kompong Som, a natural bay on the southern coast of Cambodia southwest of Phnom Penh
26	0°	121.20°E	At the midpoint of Teluk, Tomini, a bay in the northern area of Sulawesi
27	10.81°S	139.20°E	Midpoint of the mouth of the Gulf of Carpentaria
28	0°	157.20°E	Center of the Solomon Plateau
29	10.81°N	175.20°E	Midpoint of abyssal plain between Marshall Islands, Mid-Pacific Mountains, and the Magellan Plateau
30	0°	166.80°W	Nova Canton Trough
31	10.81°S	148.80°W	Society Islands
32	0°	130.80°W	Galapagos Fracture Zone
33	10.81°N	112.80°W	East end of the Clipperton Fracture Zone
34	0°	94.80°W	Junction of the Cocos Ridge and the Carnegie Ridge, just west of the Galapagos Islands.
35	10.81°S	76.80°W	Lake Punrrun in Peruvian coastal highlands
36	0°	58.80°W	State of Amazonas, at tip of minor watershed highlands
37	10.81°N	40.80°W	Vema Fracture Zone
38	0°	22.80°W	Romanche Fracture Zone
39	10.81°S	4.80°W	Edge of Mid-Atlantic Ridge in Angola Basin, just southeast of Ascension Fracture Zone
40	0°	13.20°W	Gabon highlands, at the intersection of three borders
41	26.57°S	31.20°E	L'uyengo on the Usutu River in Swaziland
42	31.72°S	67.20°E	Intersection of the Mid-Indian Ridge with the Southwest Indian Ridge
43	26.57°S	103.20°E	Tip of the Wallabi Plateau
44	31.72°S	139.20°E	In a lowland area just east of St. Mary Peak (highest point in the area) and north east of Spencer Gulf
45	26.57°S	175.20°E	At the edge of the Hebrides Trench, just southwest of the Fiji Islands
46	36.72°S	148.80°W	Undifferentiated South Pacific Ocean(!)
47	26.57°S	112.80°W	Easter Island Fracture Zone
48	31.72°S	76.80°W	Nazca Plate
49	26.57°S	40.80°W	In deep ocean, at edge of continental shelf, southeast of Rio de Janeiro
50	31.72°S	4.80°W	Walvis Ridge
51	58.28°S	31.20°E	Enderby Abyssal Plain
52	52.62°S	67.20°E	Kerguelen Plateau
53	58.28°S	103.20°E	Ocean floor, midway between Kerguelen Abyssal Plain and Wilkes Abyssal Plain
54	52.62°S	139.20°E	Kangaroo Fracture Zone
55	58.28°S	175.20°E	Edge of Scott Fracture Zone
56	52.62°S	148.80°W	Udintsev Fracture Zone
57	58.28°S	112.80°W	Eltanin Fracture Zone
58	52.62°S	76.80°W	South American tip, at the edge of the Haeckel Deep
59	58.28°S	40.80°W	South Sandwich Fracture Zone
60	52.62°S	4.80°W	Boivet Fracture Zone
61	North Pole		
62	South Pole		

DIAMAGNETIC GRAVITY

VORTEXES

by

Richard Lefors Clark, PhD.

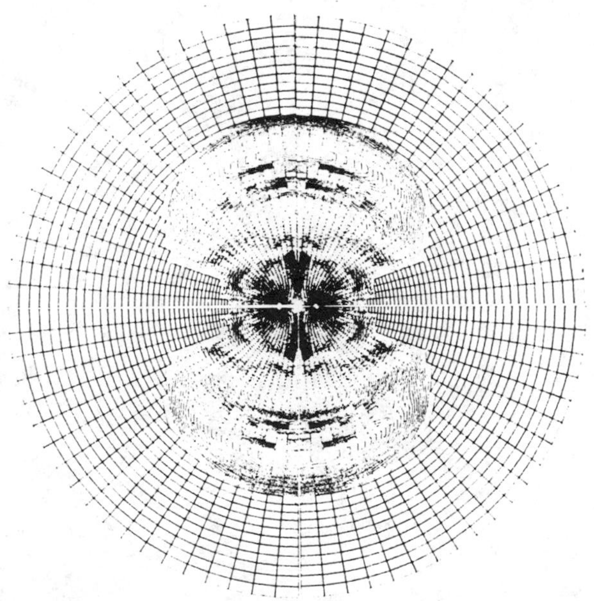

Waves of gravity pour from an extraordinary (and imaginary) cosmic accident —a head-on collision of two black holes approaching from left and right. Kenneth Eppley and Larry Smarr used a computer to calculate and draw contours of the variable curvature of space that constitutes the radiation. Such a collision would convert about a thousandth part of the rest-energy of the black holes into gravity waves. *(Photo: L. Smarr and K. Eppley)*

THE EARTH GRID, HUMAN LEVITATION AND GRAVITY ANOMALIES

Knowledge of the Earth Grid or "crystalline Earth" is very ancient and has been utilized by a number of civilizations. The pyramids and ley lines are on the power transfer lines of the natural Earth gravity Grid *all* over the world. The Earth Grid is comprised of the geometrical flow lines of gravity energy in the structure of the Earth itself.

While the subject of the Earth Grid has by now been covered in a considerable number of publications, one point in the Grid, marked by a long and strange history, at the eastern tip of Lake Ontario, is worth special mention. Most interesting here are two individuals, living one hundred years apart, who were both directly affected by this same Earth Grid point. These men were Daniel Home, the 19th century psychic, and Wilbert Smith, the 20th century scientist.

Daniel Home is the world famous levitator of the 19th century who lived in this Lake Ontario Grid point area. The period from 1820 to 1850 was apparently very active for this Grid point as many of the crowned heads of Europe and many noted scientists and world dignitaries visited Home and verified his feats of levitation. It is speculated that the Lake Ontario region may have acted as a biolectric triggering device conducive to Home's psychic development.

Meanwhile in the 20th century, because of numerous aircraft crashes in the Lake Ontario Earth Grid area (known as the

About the author

Richard Lefors Clark, Ph.D lives in San Diego and is one of the world's best known alternative energy, anti-gravity and World Grid researchers. His articles have appeared in a large number of journals and newsletters over the years.

Correspondence and requests for his free newsletter may be directed to:

Richard LeFors Clark
4015 Crown Point Drive, P-3
San Diego, CA 92109

Marysburgh Vortex, and regarded as "the Other Bermuda Triangle" and "the gateway to oblivion on the eastern end of Lake Ontario"), the Canadian National Research Council and U.S. Navy began *Project Magnet* in 1950 to investigate the area's magnetic anomalies and possible magnetic utility. This has been the *only known official governmental* research program into the Earth Grid system. A considerable number of planes and ships had mysteriously vanished from this region, while many UFO sightings were reported, and other bizarre and unearthly phenomena were noted. (For more information, refer to Hugh Cochrane's *Gateway to Oblivion*, Avon Books, NY)

Wilbert Smith, a Canadian communications engineer in the Department of Transportation, was director of the team of scientists involved in this project. Project Magnet was later officially terminated when the results became too sensitive for the two governments, as the research seemed to touch upon top secret UFO data. Afterwards Wilbert Smith designed several inexpensive gravity devices, such as the Anti-Gravity Proximity Detector, the Magnetic Deflection Detector, and the EMF Collapse Collector.

Smith's speculations are most intriguing. He noted large and sometimes mobile gravity anomalies all over the Lake Ontario area. He noted areas of "reduced binding" in the atmosphere above the Lake; the areas were described as "pillar-like columns" a thousand feet across and extending for several thousand feet up into the atmosphere. Moreover, they were invisible and only detectable with sensitive equipment. Peculiarities in gravity and magnetism were noted inside these columns, possibly related to a reduction (or weakening) in the nuclear binding forces holding matter together; the nuclear binding forces seemed stronger in the north and weaker in the south. Some of these mysterious columns appeared to be mobile changing location over time.

Smith theorized that when the weakened nuclear binding forces encountered matter under stress (such as an airplane in flight) the forces holding matter together ceased to exist, exactly along the lines of maximum stress, and the material disintegrated resulting in aircraft disasters. Later theorists suggested that ionization of the air within these columns could generate luminous anomalies, and that increasing energies could make rocks and other dielectrics in the immediate area *appear* to rise from the ground into the air.

It was also proposed that deep Earth-caused gravity stresses produced the strange atmospheric columns. In a gravity-structured Earth which is part of a gravity universe, that is the mildest form of truthful statement possible. On a planet so determined by gravity, this would be only one of *many* such gravity-magnetic anomalies present on the Earth Grid. And underlying many of the magnetic peculiarities observed around the Earth is the special principle of *diamagnetism,* the root of anti-gravity. First we'll see this principle at work in the local context of human-induced levitation.

HUMAN DIAMAGNETISM GRAVITY ANTENNA LEVITATION

The principle of diamagnetism which underlies human-induced levitation and anti-gravity vortexes on the planet can be demonstrated simply in what I call the human gravity antenna. *Diamagnetism* (explained below) is essentially a magnetic-neutral zone existing between a north and south magnetic field, which can be exploited for purposes of levitation. As I will indicate below, there are many such "magnetic flow reversal points" on the Earth marked by Grid points.

An arrangement of five human beings can be used as a quadruple gravity antenna to perform levitation of the central person. The weight of the central person, the levitatee, does not matter nor is the lack of strength or size of the four levitators important. What is important is the *form* of the quadropolar positions around the central levitatee (See Diagram 1). Here are a few pointers to keep in mind.

First, the levitators should be positioned 45 degrees off the magnetic compass direction of north, south, east, and west for maximum effectiveness. Second, alternation of male and female sex of the levitators adds to the gravity antenna`s power. Third, the hand stack on the head of the central levitatee by the levitators should not have like-gendered (male/male, female/female) hands touching. Fourth, there's no need to think of *anything*---just hold the hands stacked on the levitatee`s head for a count of ten. On the tenth count remove the stacked hands quickly and place one finger each on the four corners of the chair. The person in charge of counting says "lift" and up goes the levitatee. Now let's examine this phenomenon I like to call "Party Levitation" in more specific and practical detail.

To do Party Levitation you will need five people, one to be levitated---henceforth to be called the levitatee--- and four to do the levitating---henceforth to be called the

Diagram 1

Party Levitation in action

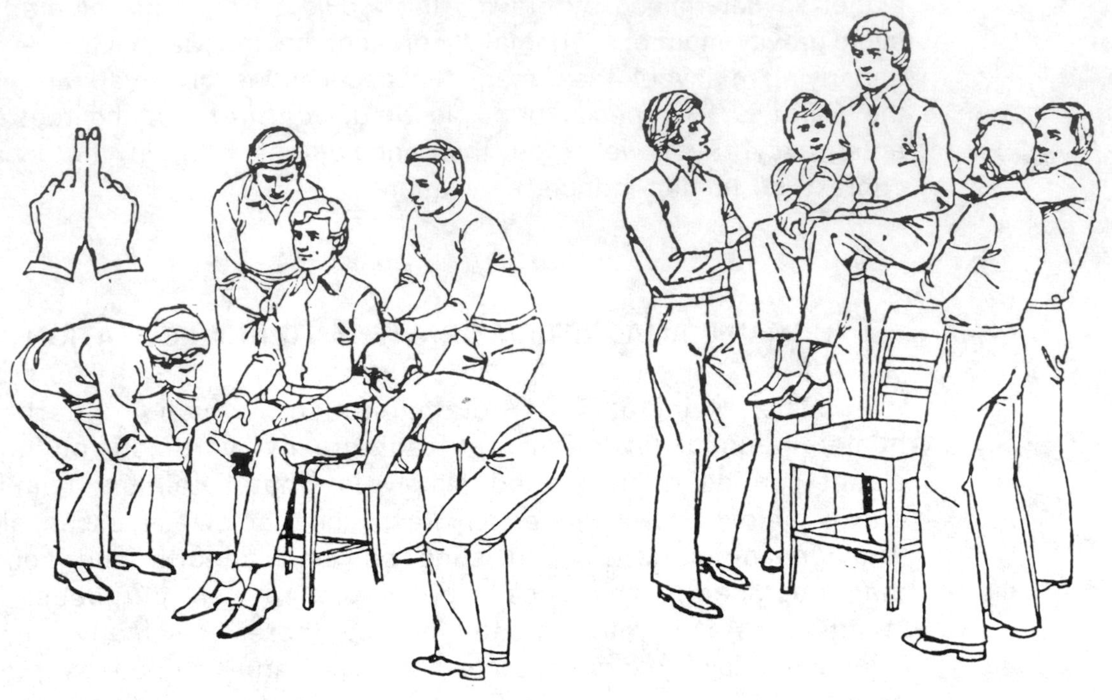

Diagram 2

Human Quadropolar Gravity Antenna

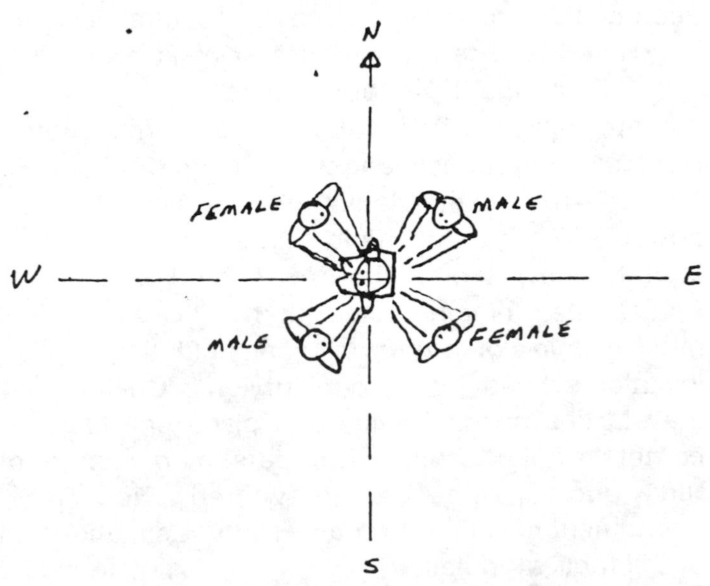

levitators.

The levitatee sits in a chair and the four levitators stand around him so that they form a square. One levitator should stand to the levitatee's left, and just behind his shoulder. Another levitator should stand in front of him and to his left, close to his left knee. The other two should stand on the right side of the levitatee's body and in similar positions.

Now the object of Party Levitation is to make the levitatee's body so light in weight that the four levitators can lift him several feet into the air using a single finger each. If the experiment is performed properly none of the levitators will feel the slightest resistance to their efforts. It will be as if the levitatee's body has lost its weight entirely.

While the levitatee is sitting, the four levitators surround him in the manner indicated and place their hands, one atop the other, on his head, as if they were healing him by the laying on of hands.

The person who is going to float must sit relaxed in a straightbacked chair with his legs together, his feet on the floor, and his hands in his lap. The other four participants now stand two on each side of the seated party, one at each shoulder and one at the knee. Instruct all four to extend their arms and place their closed fists together, closed except for the forefingers which should be extended and touching each other along their lengths as shown. The person nearest the seated man's left shoulder is now asked to place his two extended fingers, palms downwards, beneath his left armpit. Likewise, his opposite number inserts his forefingers beneath the right armpit, and again the other two respectively beneath the seated man's knees.

Now invite the four assistants to lift the man in this position, using only these extended fingers. However hard they try, it is impossible. As soon as you have registered their inability to do so, ask them to stack their hands alternately, one on top of the other on the man's head, in such a way that no person has his own two hands together, and then to exert a steady pressure downwards. As they keep this up you count to ten. On the count "nine", they must withdraw their hands quickly from his head and resume their earlier positions with their extended forefingers. On the count of "ten" they must try again to lift the man with those fingers alone. This time he will go soaring into the air with no difficulty whatsoever.

Diamagnetism And Levitation Accomplished at Earth Grid Points

Now, kind reader, reconsider Party Levitation and perhaps do the experiment again *but* this time have *no* central person (levitatee). Instead use the heaviest chair you can find. Just stack the hands, touching on the top of the massive chair back and *lift* (levitate) the heavy chair. Next, place hundreds of pounds of "dead" weight (heavy books) on the chair seat and still levitate it *easily* with four weak children lifting. What is happening here?

You have created a small, short-duration diamagnetic levitation vortex which is identical in function to the Earth`s big, permanent diamagnetic levitation vortexes at such places as Coral Castle, Florida, or Alice Springs, Australia.

Now, reconsider the diagram of the four persons levitating the massive chair. As humans they are the "mighty four" of the four cardinal compass points. Each one of the four is an *energy lobe* around the central object to be levitated. If I call any one of them north, you can call the others, turning counterclockwise, west, south, and east (See Diagram 2). Try doing the levitation with only three people, positioned off-center to the appropriate 90 degree spacing. We know that both the *exact* number and pattern of the human levitator element, but not their exact size or physical strength, are critical to the levitation. Also we know that inanimate weight levitates as easily as animate through using a human diamagnetic vortex. We might try a piano or even a Volkswagen in place of the chair.

The remarkable thing about Party Levitation is that it works *anywhere* on the Earth`s surface, whereas the equivalent big, permanent Earth Grid diamagnetic levitation vortexes all have fixed geographic locations (e.g., southern Florida or central Australia).

Whether it's on the surface of the Earth, or within the human sphere of the four levitators, the mechanism for levitation or anti-gravity is identical. In either case there are four energy lobes or directions. The north-south axis elements are usually called *magnetic* and the east-west axis elements are called *diamagnetic.*

Levitation is produced by diamagnetism existing on the surface of the Earth. (or near it). Diamagnetism operates at 90 degrees from magnetic, but in *three* directions, and not flat and two-dimensional on a sheet of paper as usually drawn. If magnetism flows in the plane of the Earth's surface, then diamagnetism flows straight *up*. And straight up is the direction that we call levitation or anti-gravity.

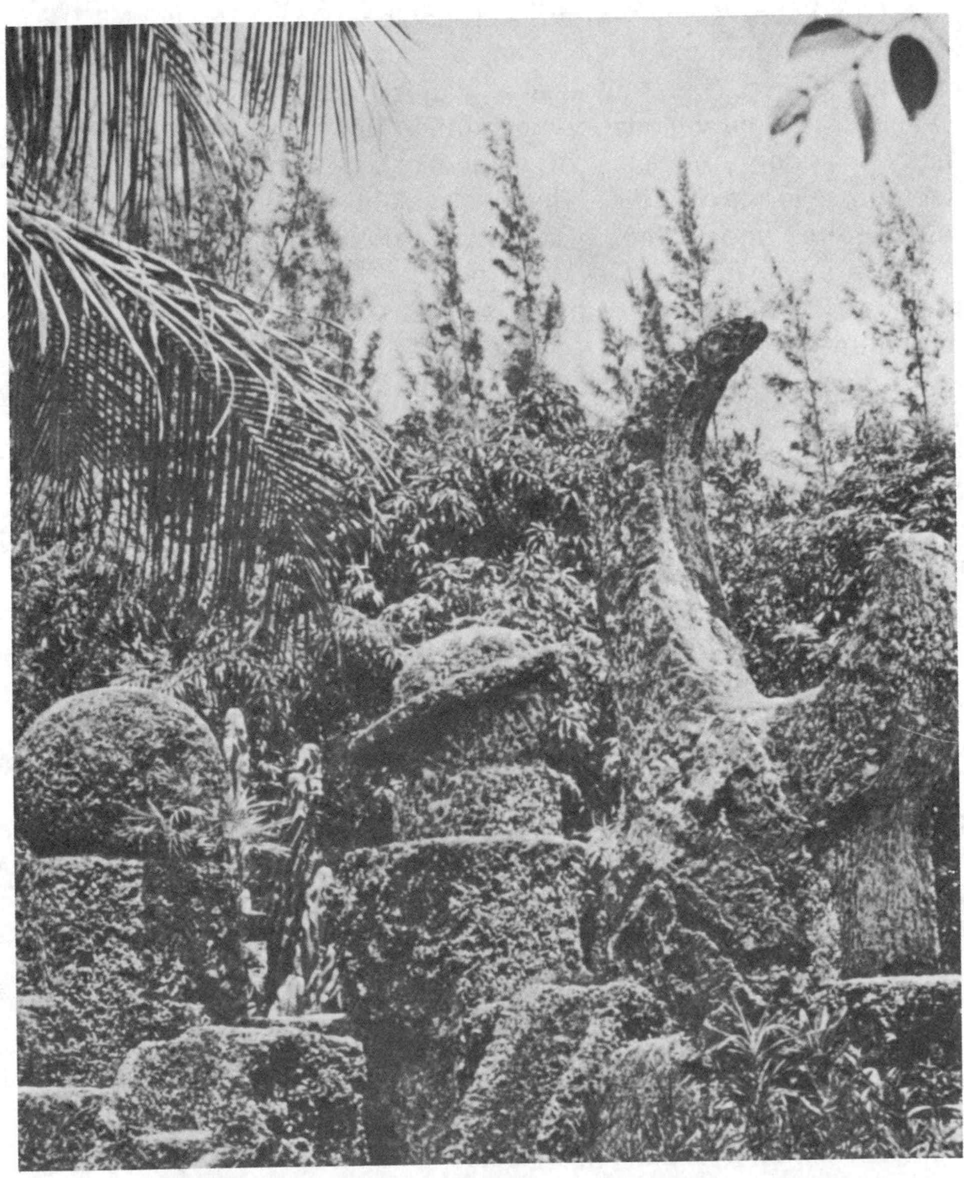

Sculpture symbolic of the moon and planets, constructed by Edward Leedskalnin at Coral Castle, Florida. With elementary tools and equipment this Latvian immigrant created artifacts whose construction defies "logical" explanation.

In the accompanying diagram (See Diagram 3) Coral Castle`s location is shown as Earth grid point #18. The west lobe is what pulled Florida down and opened the Keys area up. The east lobe is the Bermuda Triangle. Coral Castle will be referred to throughout this chapter, so a few words here of introduction to this impressive project are necessary. Coral Castle is a marvellous demonstration in stone and coral of many hidden principles of magnetics, designed and built in southern Florida by the "amateur" scientist Ed Leedskalnin in the 1930s and 1940s. This coral-based temple/residence includes stone furniture, a Moon pond, a North star telescope, a precise Sundial, and other features of exact astronomical alignment.

Look at the larger map of the Earth grid (See Diagram 4) and see the diamagnetic (east-west) lobes of Earth grid point #18 in southern Florida. The tip of the Yucatan and the Mexico/Texas coastline clearly show the west diamagnetic lobe shape of Earth grid point #18. The famous Bermuda Triangle is the east diamagnetic energy lobe of Earth grid point #18 (in season).

One thing we will immediately note is that the east-west diamagnetic lobes of #18 look like a horizontal "bow tie". This happens to be another descriptive name for what is now called in the magnetic sciences a **Bloch Wall.** The Bloch Wall is central to our understanding of diamagnetism, gravity vortexes, and levitation.

A Bloch Wall is a neutral center region at the junction of two magnetic poles (north/south). (See Diagrams 5, 6, 7) It is thereby a "magnetic flow reversal point" and is also known as a "diamagnetic vortex point". The Bloch Wall is the point of division of the circling vortex, or spin, of the electronic magnetic energies of the north and south poles. The negative energy pole and north pole magnetism spins to the *left;* the positive energy pole and south pole magnetism spins to the *right* . The point of zero magnetism and no-spin, and also the point of magnetic reversal where the two spin fields join, is the Bloch Wall.

We have two antithetical elements (polarities) meeting and generating a third element, the Bloch Wall, which is a weak pressure (gravity) generator. The south pole is the *source* and the north pole is the *sink* . The individual pole energy rotations are three component vectors and the conjunction (Bloch Wall) is a tensor. The resulting "Broken 8" figure is a two dimensional concept of a quadropole pattern. We can visualize it as the spin 2, circularly polarized, gravity wave force field source.

Diagram 3

Coral Castle, southern Florida, Earth Grid Point #18

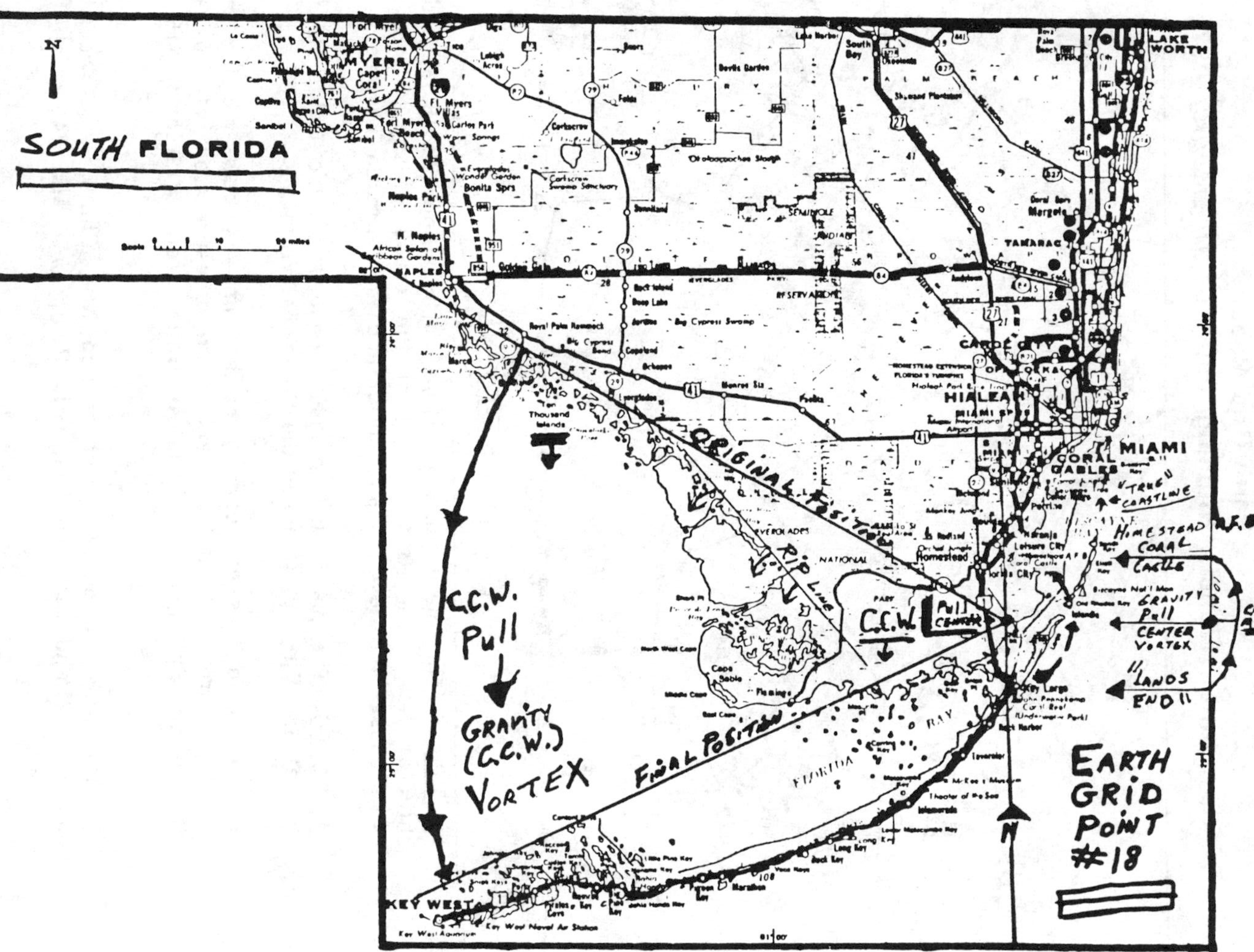

Diagram 4

Earth Grid Model
(after Francis Hitching data, *Earth Magic*, 1978)

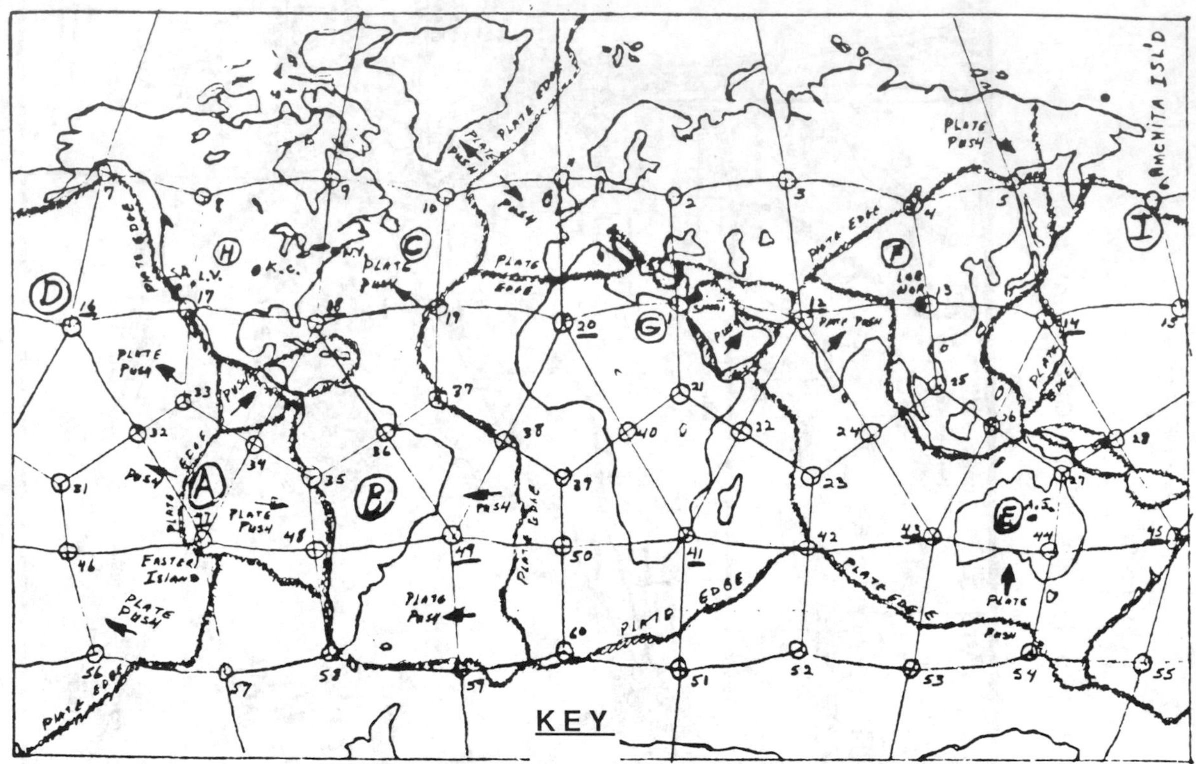

KEY

A, B, C: The plate push pressure north along #58,48,35, and 18 hits at New York (Brookhaven) at the cross pressure from #19. This causes the New England Vortex and the Bermuda Triangle.

A,B,C,+D: The plate push pressure centers on the California fault line at San Diego and causes the Southwest Vortex.

E: The plate pressure coming north from #54 bows up the cross pressures from #43 and #45 and down pressure from #14 to cause the Alice Springs/Pine Gap, Australia area; #12 and #16 are pressure top sides.

F: The pressure center point at Lop Nor, China, is between the points #12 and #14 and #43; Grid Points #41 and #45 push from below.

G: The minor pressure center point at Sinai is between points #20 and #12, with up pressure from #41; the plate breakup and slide pressure just below it has made Sinai useless now.

H: Las Vegas, Nevada, and Phoenix, Arizona, (Superstition Mountain) as center of #16, #17, and #18; the push comes from A below.

I: Amchita Island on #6, centered between #14 and #16, plate bucking pressure #5 and #33).

Diagram 5

Bloch Wall as Neutral Zone in Earth's Dipolar Magnetic Field

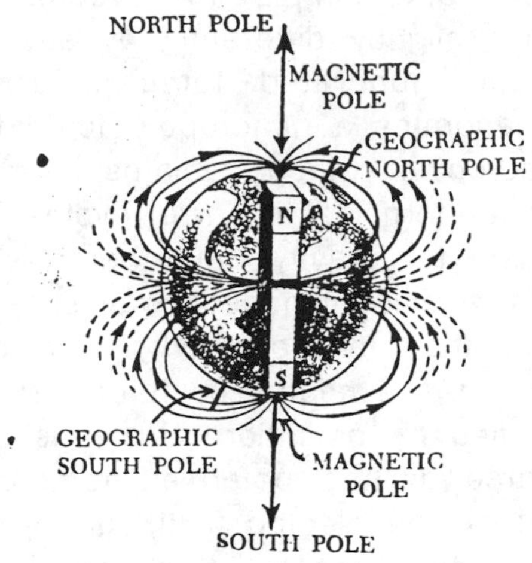

Diagram 6

Bloch Wall Illustrated in a Magnet

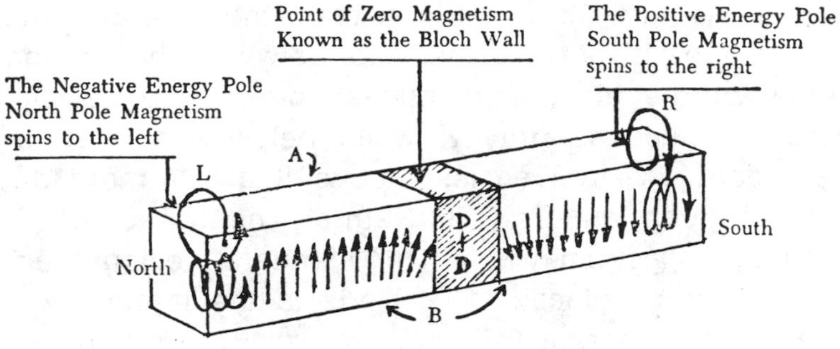

Diagram 7

The "Broken 8" Wave Zone in the Bloch Wall

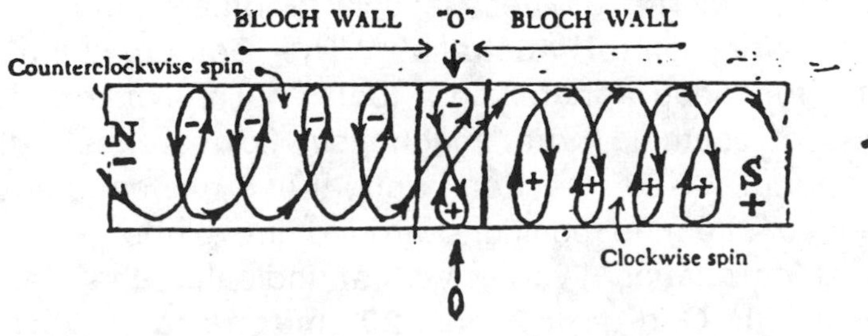

Two antithetical force fields, the magnetic and the electric (two vector force fields) meet and generate gravity, a neutral center force field and simple two vector system (tensor). We can state this slightly differently by saying the conjunction of two dipolar generated force field vectors (magnetic and electric) generates a quadropole force field, or gravity. Gravity, as a quadropole source, radiates in a circular 360 degrees polarization pattern, taking two cycles; thus a "spin 2" characteristic exists for gravity, and therefore gravity waves have twice the spin of electromagnetic waves.

The lack of polarization in the gravity field explains why it cannot be neutralized. As a neutral center force element, gravity cannot have polarities by definition. But it is still just as basic a generated force as the polarized forces of the magnet or the electric fields. The electric field, as well as the magnetic field, has a *neutral* center effect that is also a gravity wave field source. The two polarized main antithetical force fields (magnetic and electric) are triadic in themselves, as polarization by definition requires, and thus they are both gravity field sources.

In all electromagnets the Bloch Wall is actually external to the unit (See Diagram 8). The Bloch Wall, the neutral center gravity wave source, is now in the gap between the magnet faces. In terms of the electromagnetic spectrum, the point of 10^{12} Hertz is marked as gravity, while below this is radar, radio, and standard EM frequencies; above it are infrared and optical energy frequencies. This is Nature's neutral center in the radiant energy spectrum where Her standard design triadic system demanded it be placed. 10^{12} Hertz is the frequency of radiated gravity (See Diagram 9).

In terms of the Earth Grid, where the Bloch Wall of gravity wave field source exists, certain physically anomalous events can take place---such as spontaneous levitation.

The Earth`s diamagnetic flow field hits a reversal *Bloch Wall* area (south to north) at these special anomaly points like southern Florida or central Australia. The Equator Line is merely a myth for geographers and fools. The *magnetic reversal* areas of south to north magnetism flow are near the Tropics of Capricorn and Cancer; and these "spaced out" anomalies seem to alternate positions around the globe.

The best calculation I've arrived at indicates that there are within the Earth Grid a total of **20 magnetic reversal points,** with 10 nearly on the Tropic of Capricorn and 10 magnetic reversal points nearly on the Tropic of Cancer. The two sets of ten points are offset almost equally from each

Diagram 8

Bloch Wall as Independent of the Magnetic Fields

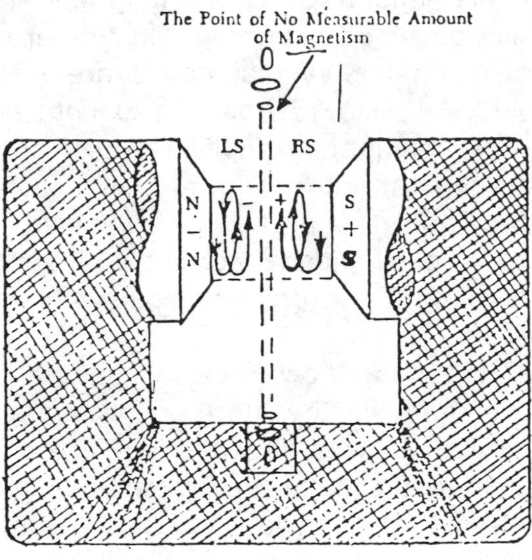

Diagram 9

Bloch Wall/Gravity Wave Field Source as a Function of the Electromagnetic Spectrum

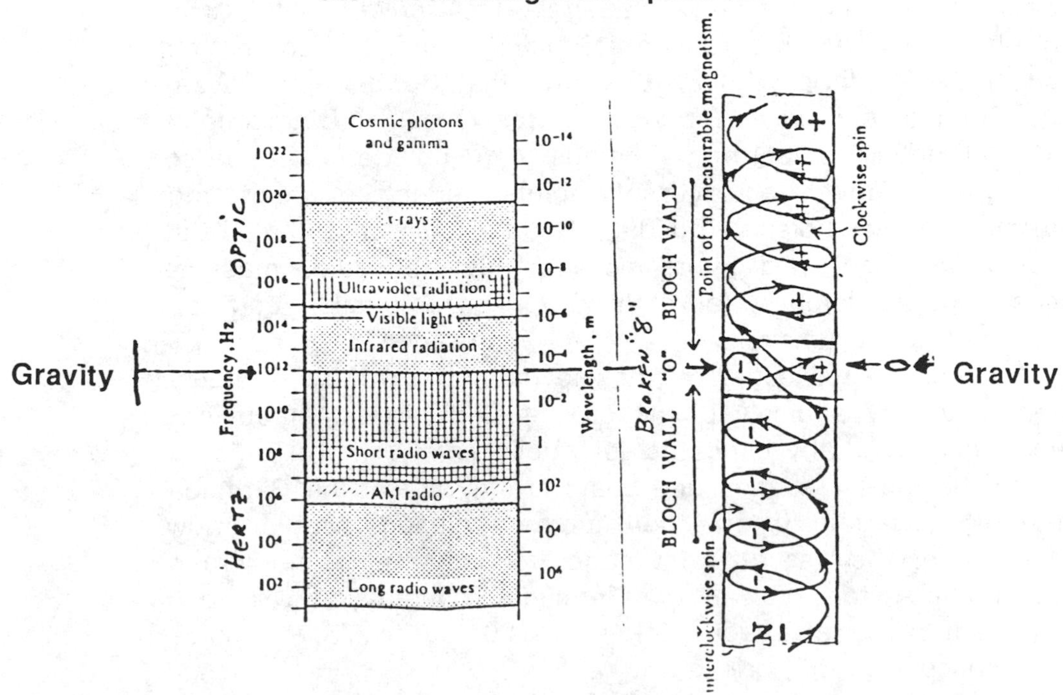

other going around the globe; the northern set is roughly midway between the southern set (See Diagram10).

The planetary distribution of these magnetic reversal points is indicated on the accompanying map. On the large Earth Grid map the northern magnetic reversal points are *near* #16, 17, 18, 19, 20, 1, 12, 13, 14, and 15 from left to right near the Tropic of Capricorn. The southern magnetic reversal points are near the Tropic of Cancer near Earth grid #46, 47, 48, 49, 50, 41, 42, 43, 44, and 45. The grid map has to be shifted leftward in the South to space it more nearly correct. The North is closer to true. The resulting Earth grid map puts #44 between #13 and #14, for example.

This is the *real* magnetic flow reversal pattern on the Earth such that above #44 is the northern magnetic flow reversal point (*Bloch Wall*). This has a beautiful bow tie of diamagnetic energy flows that can be clearly seen as the east and west coastlines of Australia. The plate push from below forced the diamagnetic bow tie up some but it is still very usable.

Why haven't we known about the existence of these 20 magnetic-gravity anomaly points on the Earth Grid before? A compass points North-South anywhere, and so, *hiding* facts and using the myth of the Equator`s magnetic polarity was expedient for our cunning "masters"---the "power elite" who control this planet. The reason for hiding it is obvious: If you knew this truth then you would *know* that Coral Castle, Giza, Alice Springs, etc., were *Bloch Wall* (bow ties) or Diamagnetic Vortex Points. Extraordinary things can be done at these diamagnetic bow tie reversal points, such as levitating extremely heavy objects (building Coral Castle and the Great Pyramid of Giza) and launching (secretly) the real, massive space ships and probes (as at Alice Springs, Australia, and Lop Nor, China, for example).

Official knowledge of the considerable *utility* of many magnetic-gravity anomaly points on the Grid has taken obvious precedence over any concerns for public safety. If the officials warned the fools in planes and boats to stay out of the Bermuda Triangle at certain times, then ordinary citizens would know too much of their secret knowledge. If you are in the wrong place on the wrong day in the Bermuda Triangle you will be a permanent piece of space junk some 20,000 to 75,000 miles out in space.

The Bermuda Triangle off the Florida coast, when active, is a powerful diamagnetic levitator. Usually the Earth contains the energy flow, but with extra stress from the Sun, Moon, and

Diagram 10

Earth's 20 Magnetic Reversal Areas

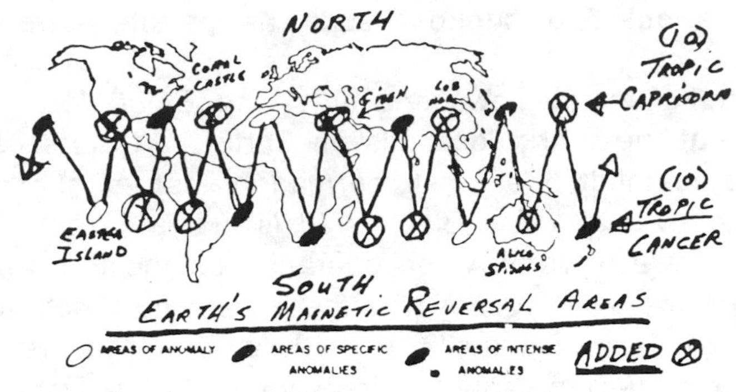

Diagram 11

United States Gravity Flow Vortex Map

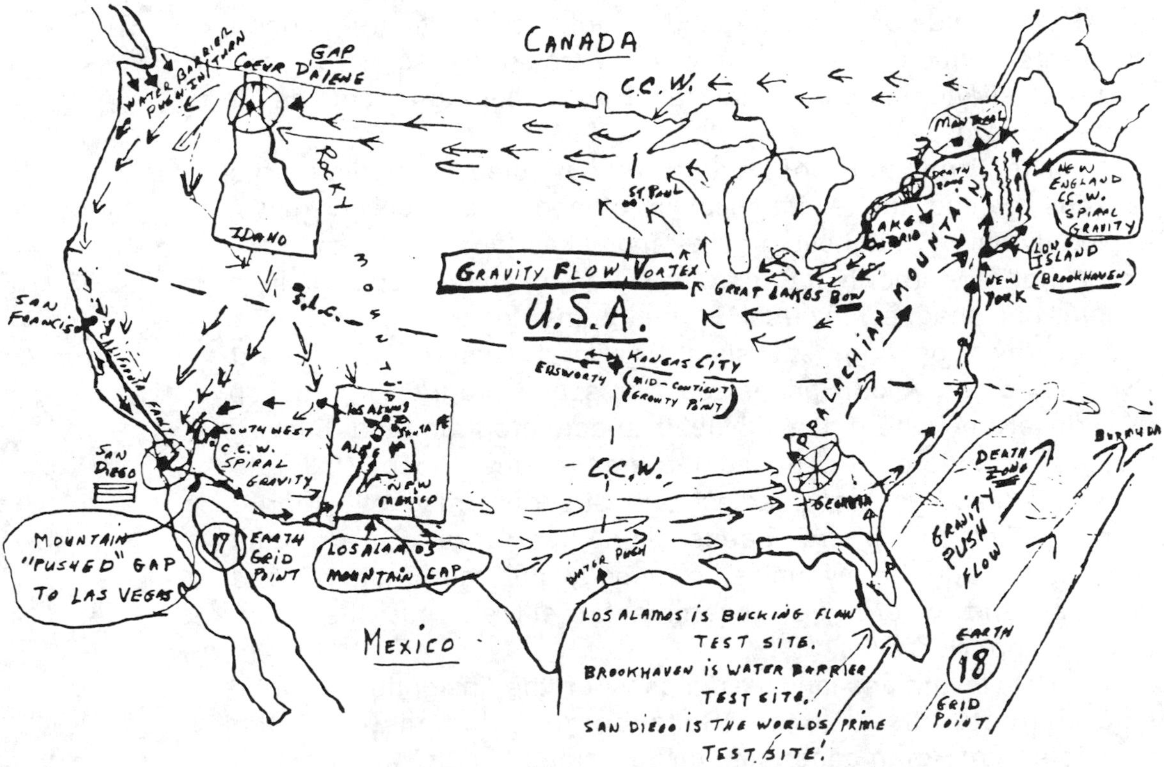

temperature factors, it ruptures upward and levitates anything over the "blow" points. Smaller ruptures will levitate anything under about 500 pounds---such as people---but not the ships they are on.

The magnetic energy flows encounter the *Bloch Wall*, or bow tie reversal, at these grid locations on Earth. Nature uses the *exact* same method in a small permanent bar magnet for magnetic polarity reversal. The Bloch Wall is just a great deal larger and much more powerful when operating on the Earth.

Didn't anyone ever wonder why there were no Bloch Wall effects on the mythical Equator? If all the Bloch walls for South to North magnetic polarity reversal were at the Equator, no one would have ever crossed it. That is why Nature designed the criss-cross mesh reversal system for polarity reversal. And that is why there are Earth Grid points where the unusual diamagnetic systems exist. These points work extremely well, facilitating the construction of places like Coral Castle or the Great Pyramid or aiding the functions of secret space programs---which are all only large-scale versions of our Party Levitations, using natural Earth diamagnetism as a levitator force.

The principles of diamagnetism clearly explain the reasons behind the exact location of secret or publicly-known exploitations of magnetic-gravity anomalies on the Earth Grid. The "knot" top (north) on the "bow tie" magnetic reversal in a simple bar magnet reversal is the prime location to stage a major gravity-defying feat such as Coral Castle, the Great Pyramid, or an Alice Springs/Lop Nor space program (The Lop Nor desert is where the Chinese space program and nuclear testing is centered). The center area of the Bloch Wall (the bow tie`s knot) is the steadiest and strongest magnetic (north) point, which is where Leedskalnin put Coral Castle, the Egyptians put the pyramids, somebody put the Easter Island statues, and where the governmental elites put the Alice Springs/Lop Nor sites.

The inventions and researches of the insightful Austrian scientist/naturalist Viktor Schauberger demonstrate the principles of diamagnetism on a small scale of polarity reversals operating in a simple bar magnet. His levitations are *diamagnetic* systems using water flows. Diamagnetism is the product (or effect) of a flow polarity reversal, like the Bloch Wall of the magnetic flow. Some waterfalls and streams have natural flows of diamagnetism or flow reversal effects. Schauberger simply built artificial water flows with internal powerful reversals in flow energy. These are simply a tubed version of a Bloch Wall system.

The Schauberger water levitators are all continuous type devices for anti-gravity effects. The trout fish, after which Schauberger named his water turbine, senses the coldest area in a waterfall for levitating up it. The waterfall's central spiralling cold flow is an anti-gravity effect area where the energy is driven out (reversed) to directionalized momentum as a natural anti-gravity system. A waterfall's center registers as a zero (or under) on a stressed gravity detector due to the reversed anti-gravity momentum. Schauberger copied this natural design of spiralling cold water flow for levitating system, in his logging flumes and turbines.

Schauberger's implosion turbines interrupted the water suction flow by a special shutoff valve, thus creating a reactive back-pressure force in the same direction as the implosion turbine. This reactive back-pressure force is the lifting (discharge cycle) or levitating action (directional momentum) of these types of devices. The Schauberger water turbines were used as the levitators in his versions of the German World War II Project V-7 Fighter aircraft.

Thus both Victor Schauberger and Edward Leedskalnin, the builder of Coral Castle in Homestead, Florida, wrote about and demonstrated magnetism and the mechanism of levitation applying natural Earth Grid principles of diamagnetism. (*Editor's Note* : Refer to *Living Water--Viktor Schauberger and the Secrets of Natural Energy*, by Olof Alexandersson, Turnstone Press Ltd., Wellingborough, England, 1982. Also: *Magnetic Current* , Edward Leedskalnin, Homestead, FL, 1946)

Leedskalnin had two secrets. First, he knew where, in terms of the Earth Grid, to build Coral Castle. Second, he knew how to do Party Levitation all alone. Try to figure that one out!

Leedskalnin could levitate huge pieces of coral by using the center of mass for the needed slight uplift launching pressure. In Party Levitation, the four outside levitators are lifting the center of mass from the outside edges. If three of the four levitators were to step back at the end of the count of ten hand-stack (charge cycle) and the one remaining levitator would then quickly bend down and reach under the chair to the center of mass and use only two fingers to push upward, then the center man in the chair will levitate. Leedskalnin used a stick or board to push upward at the exact center of mass of his coral slabs to levitate them.

Two of the humans (180 degrees apart) in the Party Levitation scenario are “seen” by Nature as diamagnetism sources. The four people are a small, temporary Earth grid point as far as Nature is concerned. Thus the Bloch Wall reversal effect, or diamagnetism, is created and thus levitation of the central area object results. Schauberger put the mechanism in water tubes and Leedskalnin played alone with his massive stones, but in either case, it is exactly the same process of diamagnetic levitation.

We must remember Leedskalnin was working on a Diamagnetic Earth Grid Point, so all mass objects in that area are always "charged" and easily lifted at their center of mass by a slight upward pushing pressure. Incidentally, due to the shifts in the north and south magnetic poles, Grid Point #18 is now inside Homestead Air Force Base; thus Coral Castle could no longer be built where it is now located.

Here are some additional comments on the subject of anti-gravity, or levitation. The reason for the weight of a mass in a gravitational field is the counterpush of the two masses` gravity radiations. As humans we push more powerfully on the Earth via our stress body than the Earth pushes on us. The total of the two pushes of gravity is so-called weight. If we lose gravity (stress push) by radiating it, as in the Party Levitation central element (levitatee), we push less. As our push (gravity) decreases, the Earth`s push-effectiveness on us increases. This is "weight loss" or levitation, which is really just letting the Earth push us away. It is not the total quantity of the masses that counts but the effective local gravity field`s relative strength.

For example, in the fire hose there is a decrease in the gravity (push) of the water. Thus the Earth *pushes* the water away, or in other words, the "weight loss" carries further. The circular (quadropolar) pattern of the whirling fire hose nozzle radiates (relieves) some of the water`s gravity (stress). It's important to note that Schauberger`s designs are based on this kind of water stress (gravity) control.

Levitation (weight loss) control is generally stress lowering via radiation, using gravity's natural characteristics. It works on either organic or inorganic mass, as gravity is the same for both. Think of it as the resultant pushes of two radiating sources, taken locally (These are "near field" design problems). Humans are locally a more powerful source of gravity than the Earth because we *push down* on it. But as we lose gravity (stress push) power, the Earth pushes us away.

Here are two final observations in this regard. The forms of self-levitation or single operator induced human levitation appear to be hypnotic trance-state "shut downs" of the human body`s gravity (stress) generation. Inorganic object levitation, if it is possible, is the "shut down" of the gravity (stress) generation of the object itself. Theoretically this object levitation is possible (as suggested by Coral Castle, pyramids, etc.).

A general theory of levitation systems must cover all of the various methods known to exist. This means there is a common factor among the diverse approaches of Earth Grid, Party Levitation, Dean Drives, Hooper/Over-Unity Electrical Generators, and Schauberger's devices. The common factor is the **Zero-Spin Energy Transfer**, or the flowing of the nonspin energy. This nonspin energy is a neutral center type of energy flow related to the Bloch Wall phenomena and is the cause of the various types of levitation.

In the Earth Grid Magnetic Reversal Points the straight-up, diamagnetic energy flow is a nonspin energy flow. This energy flow is exactly halfway between counterclockwise (north) and clockwise (south) flow and therefore it has no spin. Thus the Bow-Tie Knot levitation energy is a nonspin energy flow.

In Party Levitation the four levitators drain or temporarily stop the spin energy flow around the levitatee or the inanimate objects. Thus they create a very temporary nonspin energy center which easily levitates.

The Dean Drive type devices cross-cut or dump energy during the Critical Action Time that is, in fact, a nonspin energy. Mechanical as it is, the Dean Drive can generate directionalized momentum (nonspin energy flow) and therefore can be used as a levitator system.

The electromagnetic collapsing field reversals of Hooper or Over-Unity Generators, generate a nonspin energy flow for short periods during each cycle of operation. Any energetic flow reversal generates some nonspin energy flow. Therefore, electrical coils reversals generate some nonspin energy flow and can be used as levitator devices.

Schauberger energetic water flow systems are reversed by valving, identical to the electrical coil systems. Therefore the Schauberger turbines generate some nonspin energy flow and can be used as levitators.

In a universe of basically spinning energy and particle systems, this nonspin energy has very powerful effects. The nonspin energy is the neutral center force field, belonging to neither side of a generally polarized universe. As such, it is reacted with and repelled very strongly by all energy and particle systems. By the generation of nonspin energy flows and the directional vectoring of these flows, we can design most powerful levitating devices.

If Nature follows rules, which *She* does, then all we need do is understand *Her* methods then apply them. Since diamagnetism is a reaction vector at the reversal point of an energetic flow system, all levitation methods must be similar in Nature.

Vortex-Gravity Research Areas Strategically Sited on Earth Grid Points

A most interesting pattern of vortex-gravity research exists in the United States and Canada. The pattern is a counterclockwise vortex with four turning points or main centers/corners. The four main centers of vortex research are the extreme southern California area (San Diego and vicinity) , northern Idaho (Coeur D'Alene area), northern New York State (Hudson River/Montreal area), and northern Georgia (See Diagram 11).

This box-shaped pattern *bows* both inward and outward as it widens in the North-South axis, which is made of the two-bowed continental coastlines and the major interior mountain ranges on each coast, with a center at Kansas City (Ellsworth). On the western vortex flow the bowing widens and follows the Pacific Ocean coastlines on one side and the Rocky Mountains on the other side going *southward*. On the eastern vortex flow the bowing widens and follows the Atlantic Ocean coastline on one side and the Catskill/Appalachian Mountains on the other side going *northward*. The east-west vortex flows are relatively straight and narrow between the coastal vortex flows, to complete the general description of the box shape. (Consult the Earth Grid maps below to see these patterns clearly)

Another interesting aspect of the Eastern vortex flow is that "pressure" flexing out of the southern Caribbean Ocean coming north *against* the flow produces the anomalous Bermuda Triangle and Lake Ontario phenomena. Once this Earth Grid energy vortex flow gets pushed over or across or into water, *massive spontaneous* levitation phenomena will occur. The vanished planes, ships, and people often reported are actually thousands of miles *out in space* from the vortex-gravity toss. NASA knows this fact.

Schauberger's water vortex-gravity levitators are based on the same effect (though on a small scale) as the Bermuda

Diagram 12

Worldwide Gravity Vortex Research Areas Plotted on the World Grid

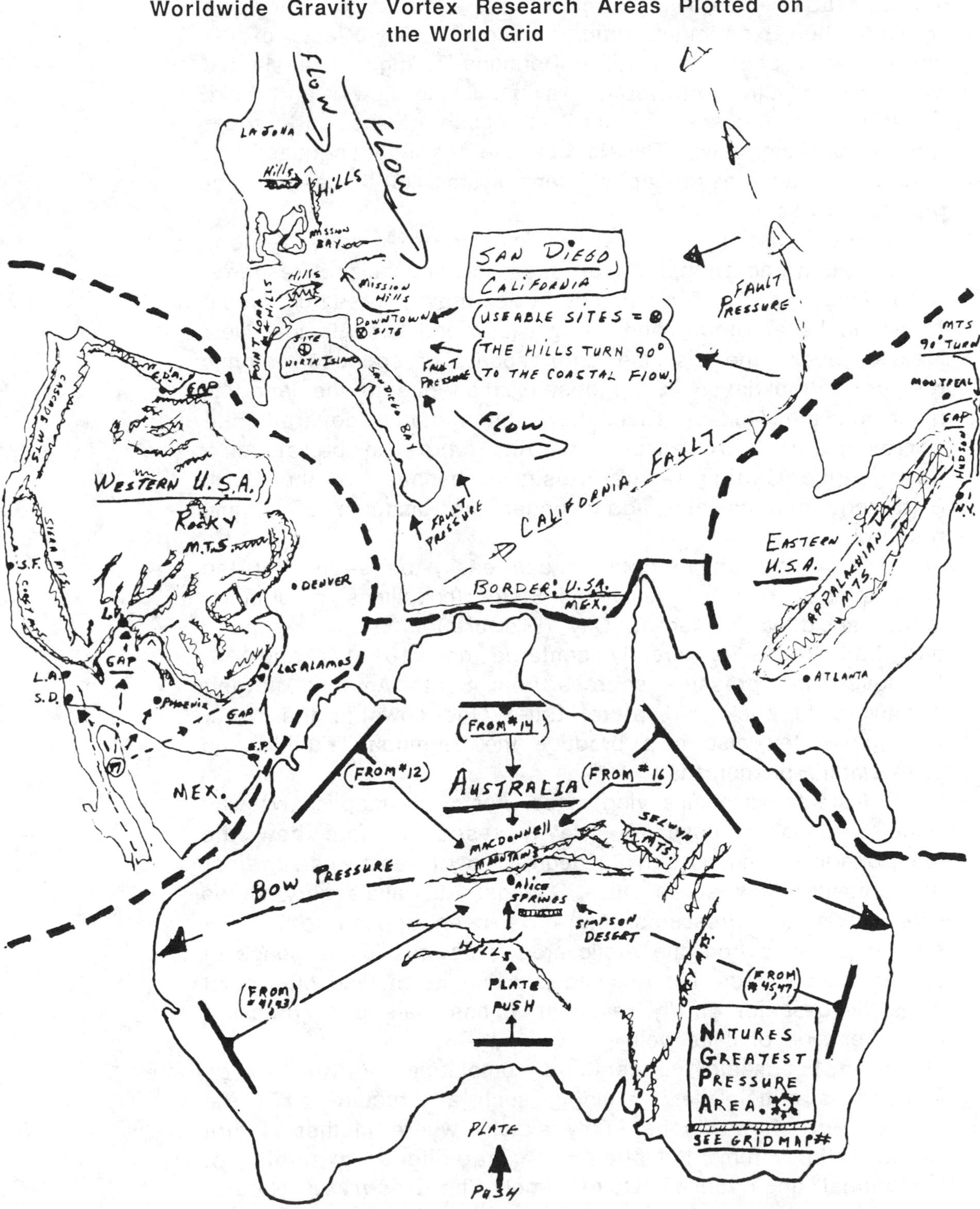

Triangle/Lake Ontario phenomena. The old Eldridge (Philadelphia Experiment) data recounts side-effects of the vortex-gravity phenomenon. The Bermuda Triangle is a slanted *out* push of the north-south gravity-bucking flows, and Lake Ontario is a focussed slanted *in* push of the north-south gravity- bucking flows. This is because the Atlantic coastline's land shape acts as an optical lens system to these bucking-gravity flows.

The location of these special vortex-gravity regions makes them most appropriate sites for specialized research (See Diagram 12). Government vortex-gravity research would *have* to be at Brookhaven, Long Island and Los Alamos, New Mexico, under the disguise and security of supposed atomic research. Brookhaven is the best location due to the land fall pinch on the Hudson River flow. International governmental vortex-gravity research would *have* to be at Alice Springs/Pine Gap in Central Australia, because of the Earth Grid requirements and again under the disguise of atomic research.

From the above data, it can easily be seen that the geographical shape of the United States (coastlines, mountains) is not accidental. Kansas City (Ellsworth) is a midway point and Las Vegas is directly centered as #16, 17, and 18. Moreover, the pressure sources from South America flowing northward to buck the natural Earth Grid flows in the North America vortex also help produce the Bermuda Triangle and Lake Ontario phenomena.

Note the accompanying maps. Australia's map shows why Alice Springs is used for gravity research---note how the MacDonnell Mountains turn 90 degrees to run east-west *against* the pressure flow above Alice Springs. Australia's very shape gives away the pressures that have been applied to it. The bowing pressure from the Arctic area is obvious in the shape of the Aleutian Islands, but Amchita Island right on Grid Map point #6 is the *best* for gravity research. It has plate push pressure on either side of it as well.

Ed Leedskalnin understood completely that the *exact* location is critical for building such a structure as Coral Castle. But how did he know exactly where Mother Nature would allow him to site this marvellous example of levitational engineering? Quite simply, he *observed* Nature, which is all it takes to have true knowledge of the natural forces of Earth.

Nature's Gravity Vortex Center pulled Florida counterclockwise around some 90 degrees to its vortex center

Diagram 13

Earth Grid Wars

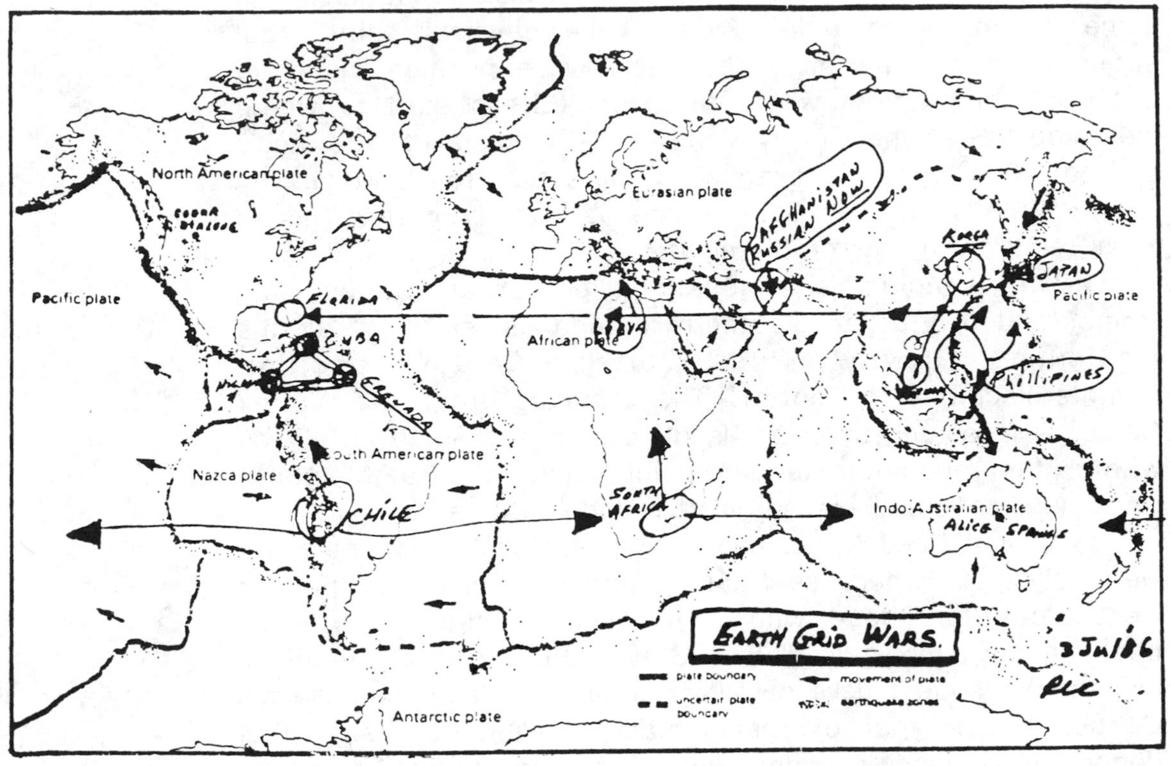

like a gate-leg table. The Gravity Pull Center Vortex energy also pulled counterclockwise on the southern end of Florida itself. On the map of southern Florida I have drawn the opening arc and the exact Gravity Pull Center, which is at maximum some 10 miles on either side of the physical center, but strongest in the maximum counterclockwise position of North. Draw a triangle from where the Florida Keys start to where they stop to see the Gravity Vortex Pull Center point. The land's end, at Key Largo, is exactly as far south from the Gravity Vortex Pull Center as Coral Castle is directly north. This is what Leedskalnin saw on his maps.

The specific site location for Coral Castle and Homestead A.F.B. in southern Florida is situated at the maximum Gravity Pull Vortex Center position (counterclockwise or north). The distance from the Vortex Center is measured by using "land's end" at the South to tell you where the maximum equal point location straight North (maximum counterclockwise) of the Vortex Center is.

All that Leedskalnin had to do was "see" what the maps were telling him, because Nature draws vivid, exact pictures of Her forces for those who have eyes to see them. Then Leedskalnin simply used this Gravity Pull Vortex Center to levitate the huge blocks of native coral into place to make his Castle. A five year old could stack up automobiles in that general area. Once the operation of the Mother Earth's gravity system is known, then engineering artificial systems is simple.

The patriarchal scientists of the cunning and stupid varieties who study gravity at these locations will fail because they all *hate* Nature, the female, and reality. Whereas "simple" men who like Nature and only *observe* Her thereby accomplish great things---witness Schauberger and Leedskalnin. The control attitude of patriarchal religions or secular humanism cannot *force* Nature with their writings, equations, and bulldozers to do anything. If you really want to engineer Nature's systems and forces, you must *adore* Nature, the female, and reality, an attitude which is the total inverse of the present patriarchal/scientific system.

Our newfound awareness of the geopoltical importance of certain diamagnetic Earth Grid Points introduces the subject of Earth Grid Wars.

The "Three Floridas" (Florida, Korea, and Vietnam) are still critical Earth Grid points after two bloody wars(See Diagram 13). The "boost shock-point" to this triangle is Libya. The Caribbean Plate has more recently seen a triangulation attempt that ended in military invasion. The Caribbean Plate triangle shock-wave system was to have been Grenada-Cuba-Nicaragua. The next try in this general area is absolute control of the Chilean Earth Grid point. The Union of South Africa's Grid point is critically necessary for control of both Europe and Australia. The Phillipines position on the major fault/plate system is pivotal to control of both Australia and Japan in the Pacific Basin. The Soviets already have secured and activated the site in Afghanistan.

Now, read again about the targeted countries in the daily newspapers and figure out who is currently winning the Earth Grid Wars. However, a truly expert knowledge of the Earth Grid system with a true understanding of Mother Nature's ways could still reverse this bleak picture of geopolitical control through command of Earth Grid locations.

A discussion of the Grid would be incomplete without some commentary on the Earth Grid Shifts. The Earth's magnetic poles do not completely shift (reverse or flip). Only the Earth's Bloch Wall Magnetic Reversal Anomalies move positions in both the northern and southern hemispheres to balance the Earth. The Bloch Wall anomalies were much further north some 10-15,000 years ago, at the time of their last estimated major movement. This Bloch Wall Magnetic Reversal area movement is caused by the Earth's expansions and possible contractions, land mass weight shifts, and changes in the Sun.

The so-called deluge and glacier phenomena are really caused by the massive ocean/sea tides and levitation effects at these times of balancing by the Earth Bloch Wall Anomaly position movements. There were no deity-caused floods or Ice Age glaciers; there were only the Earth Grid Magnetic Reversal Anomaly movements. These movements would have been Earth-shakingly impressive to observe; later they were recalled in myth and religious lore worldwide. Moreover, our knowledge of the Earth Grid mapping systemenables us now to plot major geopolitical, meteorological, and geological anomalies and disturbances with reference to possible magnetic-gravity coordinates (See Diagram 14).

Did we really think that a dynamically changing fly-wheel/gyro-like Earth sphere, at about 1000 miles per hour spin rate, didn't need or didn't have a correctional balance system? If it were not for the 20 movable locking points, or what we now call *Earth Grid Magnetic Reversal Anomalies* , this Earth would tear itself apart (See Diagram 15). Meanwhile all we humans can do with this perfectly elegant design of Mother Nature is to use it as the grounds for yet another stupid war of

Diagram 14

Geopolitical, Meteorological, and Geologic Anomalies Plotted on the Earth Grid

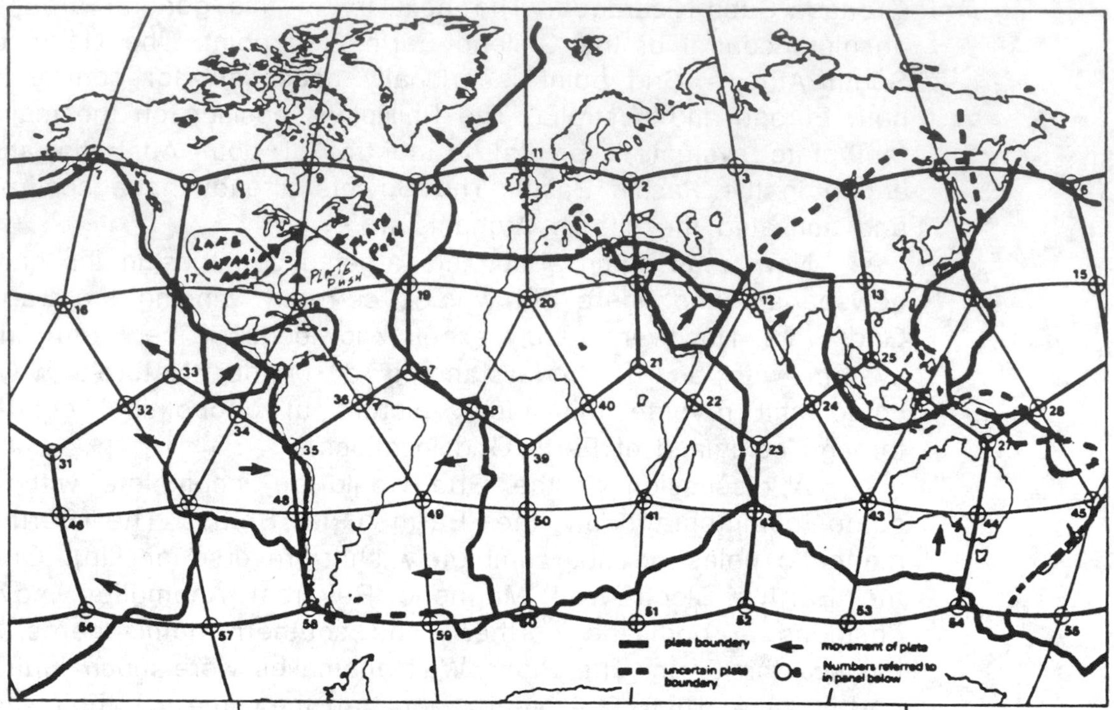

'Vile Vortices' – ten areas of violent magnetic and climatic disturbance spread symmetrically round the globe, according to the investigator Ivan T. Sanderson. They include the Bermuda Triangle (page 219), and are said to be places where phenomena are concentrated: 16, 18, 20, 12, 14, 47, 49, 41, 43, 45.

Volcanoes – the geometrical lines are said to follow the edges of the lithospheric plates, where volcanic activity takes place.

Magnetic anomalies – said to 'overlap with the vertices of the polygons'.

Meteorology – centres of cyclones and anti-cyclones lie at the nodes of the grid, giving birth to hurricanes, whose path then follows the ribs of the grid; so do many prevailing winds and water currents.

Earth faults – the mid-Atlantic underwater ridge lies between 10 and 37.

Solar radiation – maximum amounts of solar radiation (map page 45) are received at 1, 17, 41.

Atomic explosion – 1700 million years ago, a spontaneous atomic reaction based on U-235 occurred at 40.

Mineral ores – mineral deposits are concentrated along lines of grid that coincide with edges of continental plates; oil deposits are found at intersections (e.g. huge Tyumen oil find at 3).

Space photographs – photographic data collected by US and Russian satellites have recently made the map of the world more accurate, and confirm some of the oddities suggested by the grid: a 'fault-line' from Morocco to Pakistan is marked by the line from 20 to 12; Gemini spacecraft have shown circular geological structures 200–350 kilometres in diameter located at 17, 18 and 20.

Soil content – lack of certain elements in soil at 2 and 4 has led to freak evolution of plant life; at 4 (Lake Baikal) three-quarters of plants and animals are unique.

Bird migration – birds overwinter (page 86) at 12, 20, 41.

Ancient civilizations – people unconsciously sited their early centres at key intersections: Egyptians (1), Indus Valley (12), megalith builders (11), Peru (45), Easter Island (47), northern Mongolia (4).

Diagram 15

Earth Gravity Focus Points

Note: The numbers on the map are Earth Grid Point reference coordinates; see Diagram 4). U.S. has access or control of the four prime sites (Alice Springs, Easter Island, San Diego, Brookhaven, New York).

VIKTOR SCHAUBERGER

conquest and control. The asteroid belt could easily be the result of some other planetary group like our own that held a disastrous Earth Grid war. If we rip the "buttons" off this Lady's blouse, we'll find out instantly why raping the Earth is such a fatally bad idea.

THE IMPLOSION THEORY BY VIKTOR SCHAUBERGER:

The secret of life is dipolarity

Without opposite poles in nature
there is no attraction and repulsion.

Without attraction and repulsion
there is no movement,
without movement there is no life.

THERE ARE TWO NATURAL MODES OF
OPPOSITE HYPERBOLIC SPIRAL MOTIONS:

Excentric spiralling:
(centrifugence)

Concentric spiralling:
(centripetence)

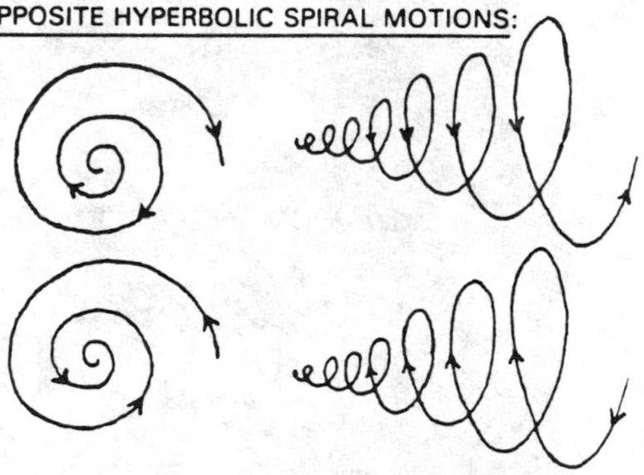

MATHEMATICS OF THE WORLD GRID

By

Bruce L. Cathie

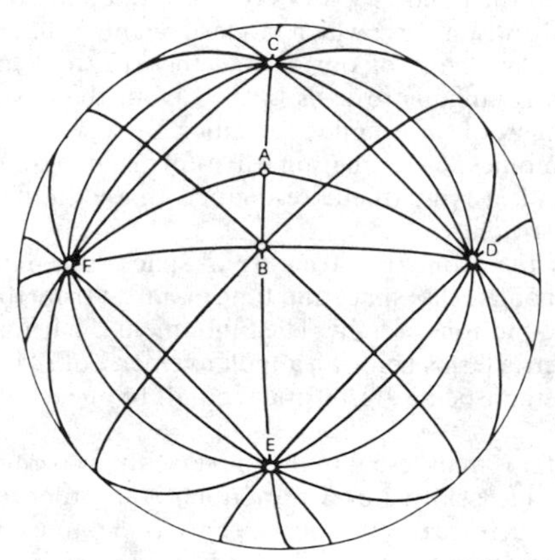

DEFINITIONS OF TERMS

Harmony and harmonic etc. as defined by the Britannica World Standard Dictionary:

1. HARMONY: A state of order, agreement, or completeness in the relations of things, or of parts of a whole to each other.

2. HARMONIC: Producing, characterised by, or pertaining to, harmony.
(a). Music: Pertaining to a tone whose rate of vibration is an exact multiple of a given primary tone.
(b). Mathematical: Derived from, or originally suggested by, the numerical relations between the vibrations of the musical harmonies, or overtones, of the same fundamental tone: Harmonic functions.
(c). Physics: Any component of a periodic quantity, which is an integral multiple of the fundamental frequency.

In this book I discuss the fundamental harmonies of the vibrational frequencies which form the building-blocks of our immediate universe; and those of the theoretical anti-universe which modern scientists have postulated as existing in mirror-like image of our own. I theorise that the whole of physical reality which is tangible to us is formed from the basic geometric harmonies, or harmonics, of the angular velocities, or wave-forms, of light. From these basic harmonies, or resonating wave-forms, myriad other waves are created which blend in sympathetic resonance, one with the other, thus forming the physical structures.

Einstein stated that the geometric structure of space-time determines the physical processes. I theorise that space and time manifest from the geometric harmonies of the wave-motions of light. The fundamental harmonic of light, in free space, in geometric terms being an angular velocity of 144,000 minutes of arc per grid second, there being 97,200 grid seconds to one revolution of the earth.

When physical matter is manifested in the universe the wave-forms of light from which it is formed are slowed down fractionally in order to release the energy required for the formation process. This is demonstrated by the unified harmonic equations in Chapter One. It was found that to calculate the values of harmonic wave-forms that have sympathetic resonance it was possible to disregard zeros to the right, or left, of whole numbers and extract the values direct from the mathematical tables.

My interest in the increasing UFO activity in the New Zealand area led me to the discovery that the surface of the world was crisscrossed with an intricate network of energy grid lines. I began my research in 1965. The information in this chapter regarding the structure and mathematical values built into the system will consist of material condensed from my first three books plus the findings derived from my recent research up to early 1982.

In a general way I was convinced that UFOs were actively engaged in a survey of the earth for some definite reason. I felt that their visits were not haphazard; they were not just on casual sightseeing tours. Quite a number of investigators around the world had come to the conclusion that the sightings were beginning to form a pattern. At this period, however, this pattern was so complex as to defy any definition, or solution. By the correlation of sightings small sections of track had been identified, and some saucers had been seen moving along these set paths. Some of these had hovered over certain spots at set intervals. But these bits and pieces of tracklines were so scattered around the surface of our planet that it was quite impossible to fit them together into any semblance or order.

I was certain that if an overall pattern could be found and plotted, it might be possible to establish the reason behind UFO activity. I considered that the pattern would be geometric if these things were intelligently controlled, and that if somehow I could find the key to one section then I might solve the rest by duplication and inference.

I had sighted a number of unidentified objects in the sky over a period of several years, and by correlating two of these with other data I was eventually able to construct a grid system which covered the whole world.

One of the sightings was in 1956. I was a DC3 co-pilot crewing a flight from Auckland to Paraparaumu. It was about 6pm, conditions were calm, and there was unlimited visibility. We were just south of Waverley at 7000 feet when I saw this object at an extremely high altitude in the east. I drew the captain's attention to it and together we watched it travel in a curved trajectory from east to west across our track until it disappeared in a flash of light at about 10,000 feet in the area of D'Urville Island. It appeared to travel across New Zealand in the vicinity, or slightly to the north, of Cook Strait, and it was so large that two streaks, similar to vapour trails, were seen to extend from either side of its pale green disc.

When about halfway across the Strait a small object detached itself from the parent body and dropped vertically until it disappeared. It looked almost as if the main disc was at such a high temperature that a globule had dripped from it. I thought about this later and decided that if that were so, the small object would also have a curved trajectory in the direction of the parent body. But this was not so; it detached and dropped *vertically* down at great speed. There could be only one answer for this action: the small body must have been controlled.

Calculations at a later date proved this UFO to have been between 1500—2000 feet in diameter. A report in a Nelson newspaper on the following day described an explosion at a high altitude to the north of the city. The shock-wave broke windows in some local glasshouses.

The other sighting occurred on 12 March 1965. This was the best and most interesting of them all, and from then my investigations were pressed on with all speed until they culminated in my present findings.

I had always expected to see UFOs in the sky, and that was where my attention was usually focussed. When I was flying I was alert and ready to analyse any object sighted from the aircraft. I never expected to find a saucer landing at my feet and so far this has never happened. This sighting however, was different from all the others because I observed it lying under thirty feet of water.

I was scheduled to carry out a positioning flight from Whenuapai, Auckland's main airport at the time, to Kaitaia. Departure was at 11am and as no passengers were involved and the weather was perfect, I decided to fly visually to Kaitaia along the west coast. An officer from the operations department was on board and this was a good opportunity to show him some of the rugged country to the north. (I must stress that air-traffic regulations were strictly observed during the flight).

On leaving Whenuapai I climbed to clear the area and when approaching the southern end of the Kaipara Harbour, just north of Helensville, I dropped to a lower altitude to have a better look at anything in the flight path. The tide in the harbour was well out, and the water over the mudflats and estuaries was quite shallow.

I suppose we were about a third of the way across the harbour when I spotted what I took to be a stranded grey-white whale. I veered slightly to port, to fly more directly over the object and to obtain a better look.

I suppose a pilot develops the habit of keeping his emotions to himself. As far as I can remember I gave no indication of surprise, and I said nothing as I looked down. My "whale" was definitely a metal fish. I could see it very clearly, and I quote from the notes I made later.

A. The object was perfectly streamlined and symmetrical in shape.
B. It had no external control surfaces or protrusions.
C. It appeared metallic, and there was a suggestion of a hatch on top, streamlined in shape. It was not quite halfway along the body as measured from the nose.
D. It was resting on the bottom of the estuary and headed towards the south, as suggested from the streamlined shape.
E. The shape was not that of a normal submarine and there was no superstructure.
F. I estimated the length as 100 feet, with a diameter of 15 feet at the widest part.
G. The object rested in no more than 30 feet of clear water. The bottom of the harbour was visible and the craft was sharply defined.

Inquiries made from the navy confirmed that it would not have been possible for a normal submarine to be in this particular position, due to the configuration of the harbour and coastline.

An American scientist checked this spot on the harbour with a depth-sounder in September 1969. He informed me afterwards that a hole had been detected in the harbour bed approximately one eighth of a mile wide and over 100 feet deep, which I consider would indicate some activity had been carried out in this position some five years previously. I published the scientist's report in my second book.

I had a further key to the puzzle in April 1965. My wife saw an advertisement in the local paper seeking members for a UFO organisation called New Zealand Scientific and Space Research. I contacted this organisation and found that a vast amount of information had been very efficiently compiled. Material had been collected from twenty-five different countries over a period of twelve years. I was invited to study the information at leisure.

Amongst this mass of data I discovered the reports of a UFO that had been seen from several different localities in both islands of New Zealand on March 26 1965. People in Napier, New Plymouth, Palmerston North, Wanganui, Feilding and Otaki Forks in the North Island; Nelson Coast Road, Blenheim and Westport (Cape Foulwind) in the South Island, had all reported sightings.

It was decided that I try to plot the track of this UFO. From the considerable amount of information available I found that the maximum variation in the times of sightings from all areas was 15 minutes. Most reports gave the time as 9.45pm. This proved that the object must have been very large and at a high altitude during the greater part of its trajectory.

There was nothing of any great significance or originality in these accounts, and they followed the pattern of many other sightings. However from the mass of detail supplied by so many different people over so wide an area, it was possible to plot the track of the object with reasonable accuracy. I started work on a Mercator's plotting chart, and after several hours of checking one report against the other, and calculating possible elevations and trajectories, I felt I had refined the plot sufficiently to draw in the final track of the object, or objects. The result is shown on map 1.

The track began about seventy nautical miles north of New Plymouth, passed just over to the west of Mt Egmont, and finished at D'Urville Island. When first seen the altitude would have been about 30,000 feet curving down on a flight path to somewhere around 10,000 feet when it disappeared.

Some time after those sightings on 26 March 1965 I had another look at the plot I have made. I could find no flaws in my thinking, but I needed more information. As I was to discover many times later, the clues were quite obvious, but I was not then sufficiently expert in realising their significance. In point of fact this first trackline was to be the starting point of a whole string of discoveries of which I have yet to find an end.

I pored over that plot for a long time before it suddenly occurred to me that the track appeared to be in line with the position where I had sighted the unidentified submarine object, or USO, on 12 March 1965. On extending the line back I found it was in line with the sightings of 26 March. I was positive there had to be a connection — but to prove it was a different matter.

I checked my report files again and found that on 2 March some fishermen just north of the coast of New Plymouth had seen a large object plunge into the sea and disappear. They thought it was an aircraft and reported the incident to the appropriate authorities, but no aircraft or personnel were missing. I checked this position on the map and found that it also fitted the established trackline. Was this connected with the USO of 12 March, and could the two sightings be of the same object, sighted twice in ten days? Could it be working slowly up this track carrying out some project on the sea bed? I tucked this thought away for future reference and carried on with the search.

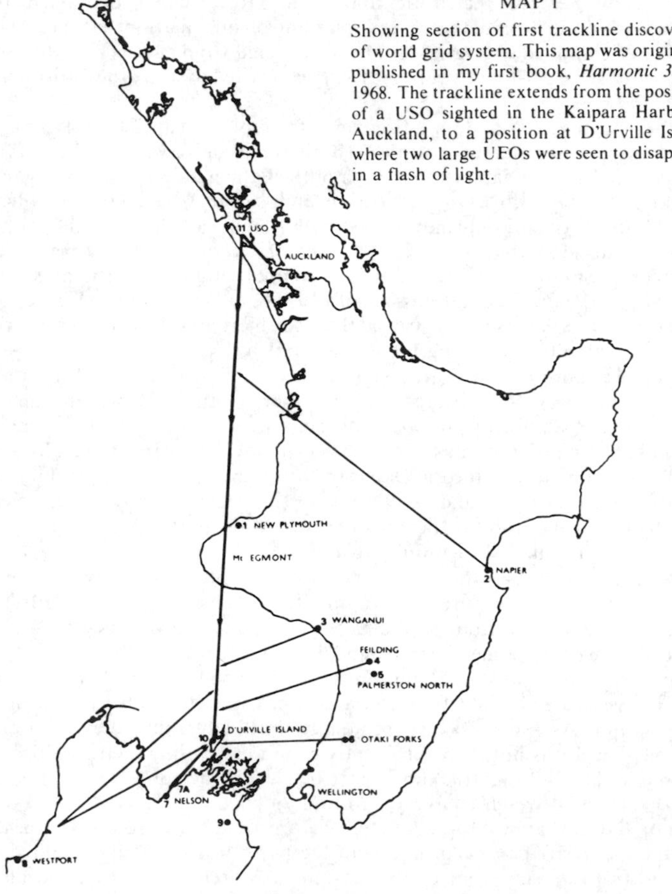

MAP 1

Showing section of first trackline discovered of world grid system. This map was originally published in my first book, *Harmonic 33*, in 1968. The trackline extends from the position of a USO sighted in the Kaipara Harbour, Auckland, to a position at D'Urville Island where two large UFOs were seen to disappear in a flash of light.

It was some days later that I remembered the UFO I had seen in 1956. This object was similar and, most significant of all, both objects had apparently travelled at 90° to each other, and finished in the same grand all-illuminating flash in the area of D'Urville Island.

If these objects were *not* controlled, how could anyone explain such coincidences? No two meteors or other natural phenomena could coincidentally carry out similar manoeuvres, travel at 90° to each other, and both decide to end their existence at the same point in space, within nine years of each other. Also, in both cases, objects had been seen to emerge from the parent bodies. Was this irrefutable evidence that they were intelligently controlled vehicles?

I plotted the track of the 1956 UFO on the map at 90° to the north-south line. I realised that I had no definite proof that they were at exactly 90° to each other or that the 1956 track was not a few miles north or south of this position — still, I had to start from somewhere, and I would assume this to be correct unless and until other evidence proved me wrong.

Two track lines at 90° meant little on their own. If I found several at 90°, I might have something — a grid perhaps? These two lines hinted at this, and I believed that if I could solve the system of measurement, then I had two ready made baselines to work from.

Once again I went to the UFO files and found that a Frenchman by the name of Aime Michel had been studying UFOs for a number of years and had found small sections of tracklines in various areas of Europe. Saucers had been seen hovering at various points along these tracklines, and Mr Michel had observed that the average distance between these points was 54.43 kilometres. By itself this was only a small grain of information but, like a starting gun, it set me off again.

Using the Kaipara Harbour as a starting point, I marked off the 54.43 kilometre intervals along the trackline I had found. I was disappointed when I was unsuccessful in obtaining an even distribution of positions to the D'Urville Island disappearing point. I checked and re-checked, but nothing worked out. I slept on the problem, and at some time during the night inspiration turned up the wick; once more the light grew bright.

I remembered that a great number of sightings had occurred around the Blenheim area. Even before the advent of ordinary aircraft in New Zealand, this area had been visited by UFOs. I had read about them in old copies of the local papers, and many recent sightings suggested again that this area had something special about it.

So I dragged out my map and extended the trackline until it cut a 90° coordinate from the town of Blenheim. The distance from this point to the Kaipara position I found to be exactly 300 nautical miles, and one nautical mile is equal to one minute of arc on the earth's surface. Could it be that the rough interval of 54.43 kilometres discovered by Michel was, in fact, an interval of 30 nautical miles when corrected? If so then this interval could be evenly spaced along my trackline ten times. Was this the system of measurement used by the UFO's? There was no proof, of course, but it seemed a reasonable assumption. A minute of arc is a measurement which could be applied to the whole universe.

University personnel and others in the academic field attacked me repeatedly over this issue. They maintained that degrees and minutes of arc were arbitrary values set up by the ancient mathematicians and that therefore my calculations were meaningless. I finally found proof of my argument in the works of Pythagoras. As my research progressed I discovered that the harmonic of the speed of light in free space had a value of 144. If this was divided by 2, to find the harmonic of one half cycle, or half-wave, the answer was 72. If this value was then applied to the Pythagoras right-angled 3, 4, 5 triangle and each side was extended in this ratio then the figure had sides of 216, 288 and 360 units. The harmonic proportions thus derived were equal to:

216 = 21600 = the number of minutes of arc in a circle.
360 = 360 = the number of degrees in a circle.
288 = (144 x 2) = 2C, where C = the speed of light harmonic.

It appeared from this that the harmonic of light had a very definite relationship with the geometry of a circle, and that the early mathematicians were fully aware of the fact. This will become clearer as you read through this book.

The fifth interval of 30 nautical miles from the Kaipara position coincided with the position off the coast of New Plymouth where the mysterious object had plunged into the sea. The plotted points of disappearance of the two large UFOs at D'Urville Island did not quite match up with the ninth interval, but this did not worry me unduly as I expected that a small percentage of error must be expected in my original plot. I readjusted this position to the ninth interval, and carried on the search to see how many other sightings I could fit into this pattern.

The results exceeded my expectations. I found that by using units of 30 minutes of arc latitude north-south, and 30 minutes of arc longitude east-west, on my Mercator's map, a grid pattern was formed into which a great number of UFO reports could be fitted. I eventually had a map with sixteen stationary and seventeen moving UFOs plotted on grid intersections and tracklines.

Having satisfied myself that my reasoning and plotting were not false, I considered that I had good proof that New Zealand, possibly other countries, and probably the whole world, were being systematically covered by some type of grid system.

In my first book I demonstrated that the main grid pattern consisted of grid lines spaced at intervals of 30 minutes of arc (latitude and longitude). In my second book I probably confused the issue a bit as I stated that the east-west grid lines were spaced at 24 minutes of arc. This was due to the spacing being measured in nautical miles, or values in minutes of latitude. The actual length of a minute of longitude varies mathematically from one nautical mile at the equator, to zero at the north and south poles.

The value of 30 minutes of arc in terms of longtitude in the New Zealand area happened to be an average of 24 nautical miles, which can be confusing those readers who are not familiar with map scales.

Reference to the grid structure will therefore be stated from now on in minute of arc values only, for latitude and longitude, to minimise confusion.

I subsequently discovered that the grid lattice could be further divided. It is now evident that the grid lines in the main system are spaced at intervals of 7.5 minutes of arc north-south, and east-west. The importance of this will prove itself when compared with the rest of the calculations in this book. There are 21,600 minutes of arc in a circle, and when this is divided by 7.5 we get a value of 2880. The grid lattice therefore is tuned harmonically to twice the speed of light (288), as will be shown in other sections.

It appeared that I had found a section of geometric grid pattern in the New Zealand area. I now had to form some theory of construction for the whole world. I could then possibly fit the New Zealand section into it.

By drawing a series of patterns on a small plastic ball I finally found a system which could be used as a starting point for a global investigation. (The basic pattern is shown in diagram 1).

I was sure I was on the right track, but now I had to super-impose this pattern on the world globe. It was essential that I find a point position somewhere on the earth upon which to orientate the geometrical pattern. I finally came up with an item of news that gave me a very important clue on how to proceed.

On 29 August 1964 the American survey ship *Eltanin* was carrying out a sweep of the sea-bed off the coast of South America. A series of submarine photographs was being taken of the area by means of a camera attached to a long cable. A surprise was in store when these photographs were developed. On one of the points, in marvellous detail, was an aerial-type object sticking up from an otherwise featureless sea-bed.

This object appeared to be metallic and perfectly symmetrical in construction. The array consisted of six main crossbars with small knob-like ends and a small crossbar at the top. Each cross looked to be set at angles of 15° to the others, and the whole system stood about 2 feet in height. The position where this object was found was given as latitude 59°08′ south, longitude 105° west.

As this bit of ironmongery was situated at a depth of 13,500 feet below the surface, I was certain that no human engineers had placed it there.

Scientists may be able to descend to those depths in specially constructed bathyspheres, but I don't think they could work as deeply as that on a precision engineering problem. In view of my earlier sightings in the Kaipara Harbour, I was willing to accept that the aerial-type object had been placed there by an un-identified submarine object, or USO.

Since this photo was taken there has been a determined attempt by the scientific world to label this object as nothing more than a plant of some sort. A journalist friend and I managed to visit the *Eltanin* during one of its few visits to New Zealand and when we discussed this object with some of the scientists on board, the comment was that it was classed as an artefact. This was before the great hush-up but, regardless of that, I believe that the mathematical proofs will show without doubt that the object is artifical, and most probably an aerial of some sort.

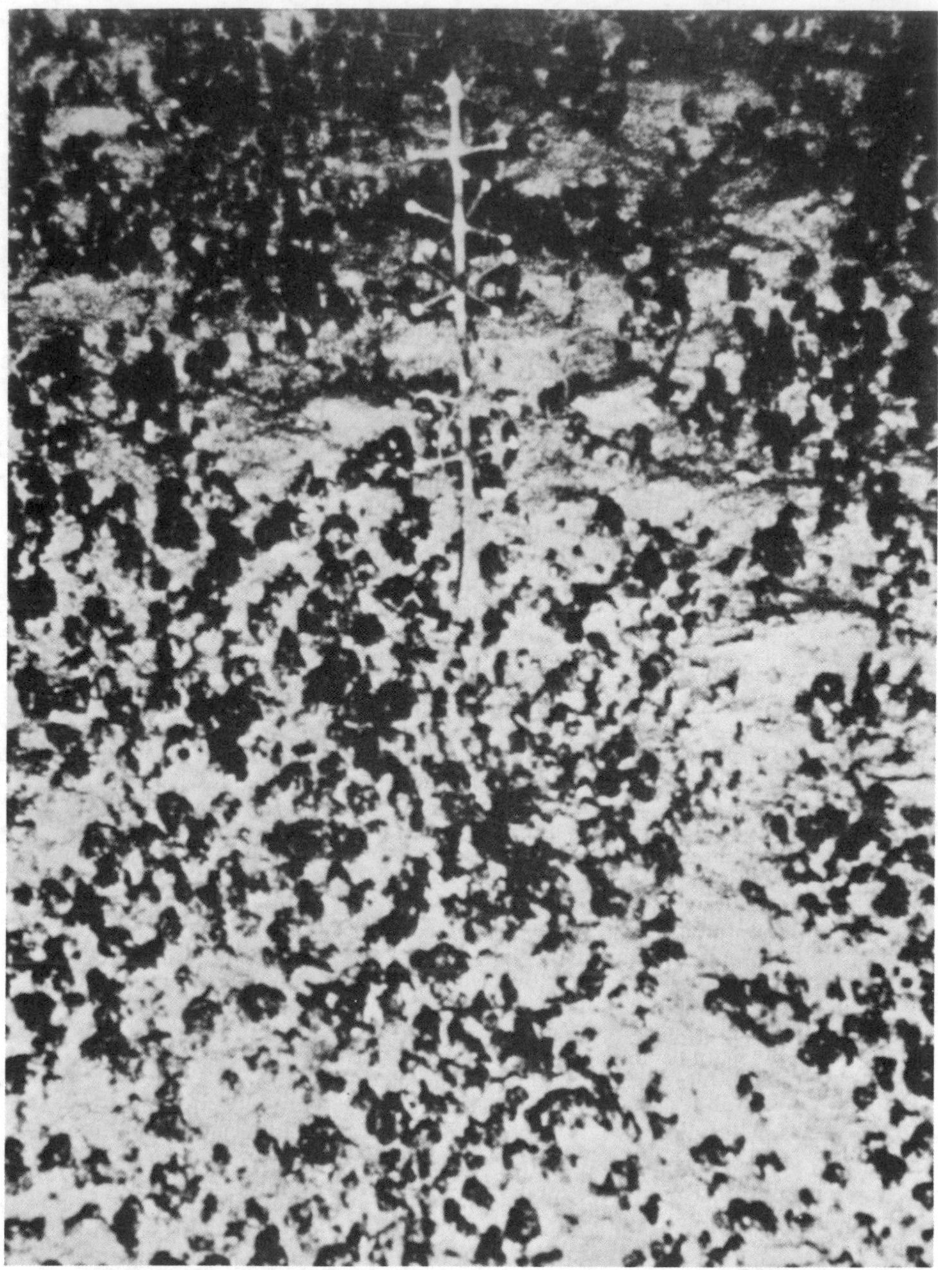

An "OOPART". Photographed on the sea-bed at a depth of 2,500 fathoms, 1,000 miles west of Cape Horn, by US survey ship *Eltanin*, whose officers are close-lipped about it. "It's a marine organism," maintained an *Eltanin* officer in Auckland in 1968. Pressed further, he admitted: "But it still looks like an artifact to me!"

DIAGRAM 1

Showing relationship of grid structure to the geographic poles. Each of the two grids has a similar pattern, the interaction of which sets up a third resultant grid. The poles of the three grids are positioned at three different latitudes and longitudes.

C, D, E, F = Corner aerial positions of grid polar square. Similar to aerial discovered by the survey ship *Eltanin*.

J — K = Polar axis.

A = Geographic pole
B = Grid pole

Distance C — G — D = 3600 minutes of arc.
Distance C — H — D = 3418.6069 minutes of arc.
Distance C — I — D = 3643.2 minutes of arc

(3600 — 3418.6069) = 181.39308

(181.39308 x 4) = 725.57233

$\sqrt{725.57233}$ = 26.93645 = 2693645 harmonic.

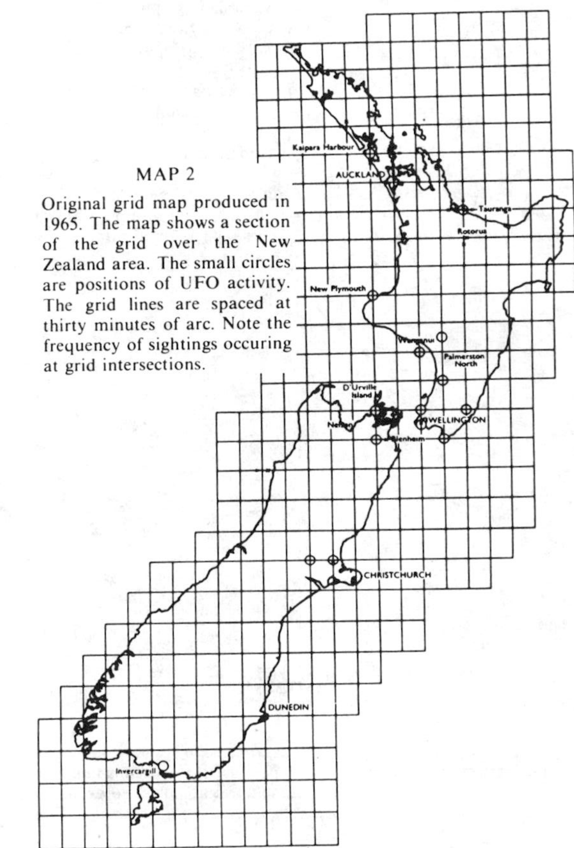

MAP 2

Original grid map produced in 1965. The map shows a section of the grid over the New Zealand area. The small circles are positions of UFO activity. The grid lines are spaced at thirty minutes of arc. Note the frequency of sightings occuring at grid intersections.

DIAGRAM 2

Showing the relationship of a grid polar square to the geographic pole. Each grid has a similar pattern.
The pole of each grid is set at a different latitude and longitude.

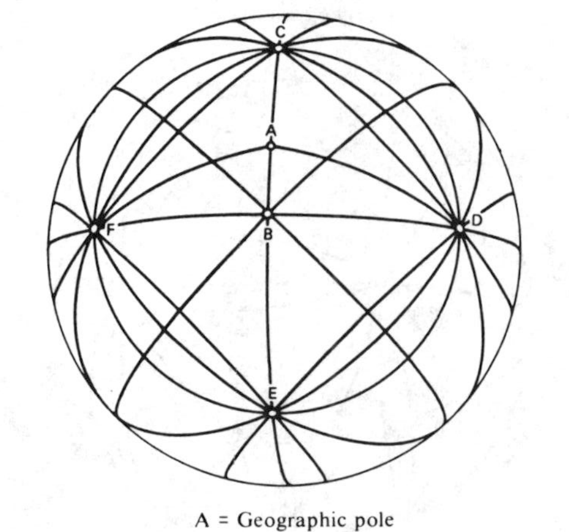

A = Geographic pole
B = Grid pole

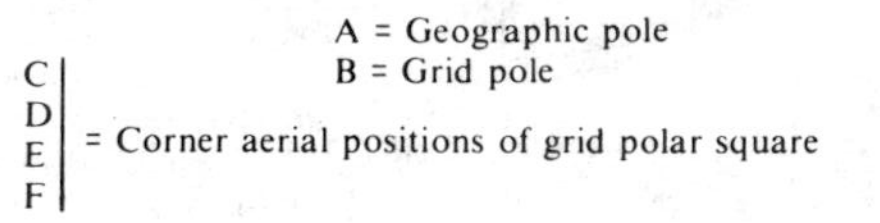

C, D, E, F = Corner aerial positions of grid polar square

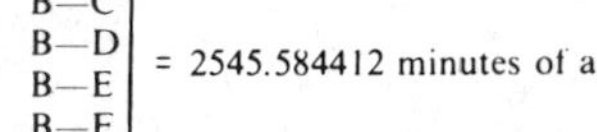

B—C, B—D, B—E, B—F = 2545.584412 minutes of arc

A—B Grid "A" = 1054.4 minutes of arc
A—B Grid "B" = 694.4 minutes of arc
A—B Grid "C" = 864 minutes of arc (resultant grid)

DIAGRAM 3

Showing the relationship of grid polar squares A, B, and C. The polar squares are orientated in reciprocal positions around both the north and south geographic poles.

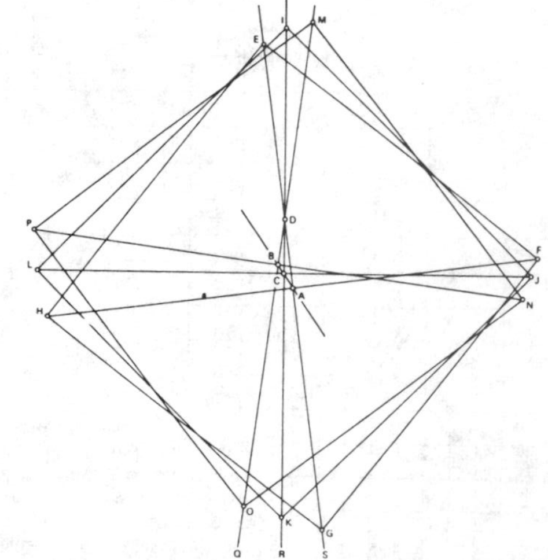

A: Grid pole "A": 1054.4 minutes of arc from geographic pole
B: Grid pole "B": 694.4 minutes of arc from geographic pole
C: Grid pole "C": 864 minutes of arc from geographic pole

D: North geographic pole
E, F, G, H: Polar square "A"
I, J, K, L: Polar square "C"
M, N, O, P: Polar square "B"

Q: Longitude 105 degrees west
R: Longitude 97.5 degrees west
S: Longitude 90 degrees west

The form of this aerial-like structure also fitted in with the general pattern of the grid as I had envisaged it on the plastic ball. The six main crossbars denoted the radiating points of six or twelve great circles which form the main structure of the grid.

I centred the grid on the position of the object found by the *Eltanin*, and the 180° reciprocal of this in Russian Siberia, lining the whole thing up with the section I had found in New Zealand. I found the system to be lined up very closely with the magnetic field of the earth. The equator of the grid followed very closely the line of zero dip around the world. (That is, the positions on the earth's surface where a magnetic compass needle has only a horizontal and no vertical component).

In my first two books I discussed the methods I used to line up the system and calculate the first estimates of the grid pole positions, and the maior focal points of the grid similar to the *Eltanin* "aerial" placement.

The reciprocal position of the *Eltanin* "aerial" is at latitude 59° 08′ north, longitude 75° east, in Siberia. I calculated the length of the diagonal of what I call, for simplicity, the "polar grid square" and found it to be 5091.168825 minutes of arc long. I plotted a track from the Siberian position through the north geographic pole and measured off this distance to locate another corner "aerial" of the polar square. (Square is not technically the right word to use as the four sides are formed by sections of small circles which are in different planes to each other. When the "polar square" areas are transferred from the surface of the earth sphere on to a flat plane such as a map, then a perfect square is formed with sides 3600 minutes long and diagnals of 5091.168825 minutes of arc).

In my first two books I stated, in error, that the sides of the "polar squares" were formed by sections of GREAT circles 3600 minutes of arc long, instead of SMALL circles. The great circle distance between these points is in fact 3418.606915 minutes of arc, which is very confusing to any investigator attempting to reconstruct the grid. I apologise to my readers for this error, which was caused by my lack of access to calculators during my earlier research. In the grid pattern there are actually two small-circle segments, and one great circle segment connecting each of these points which form the polar squares. Each of the segments has a different path over the earth and some tricky calculating is necessary to ascertain the true length. Although I used the wrong term in my earlier publications, the actual calculations derived from the grid system are not altered in any way, and still stand the test of time. Over the last few years I have slightly refined the values I demonstrated previously, derived from a mixture of practical and theoretical studies. I have now set up what I see as a completely theoretical system, discovered by working entirely by calculator. Time will prove how close my calculations are. I have no doubt that I, and others, will continue further to perfect the system as more facts come to light.

Once I had established this first base line I found it quite easy to construct the main skeleton of the grid over the whole surface of the earth.

As my work progressed I found that there were in fact two similar grids, interlocked with each other. The poles of the grids were spaced at different distances from the north geometric pole, and this arrangement set up a series of geometric harmonics which were directly related to the speed of light, mass, and gravity. The interaction of the two grids created a harmonic resonance which, in turn, formed a third resultant grid.

After ten years of work and correlating information I have now calculated theoretical positions for the three grid poles in the northern hemisphere which are very close to my original estimate. Reciprocal positions will give similar values for the southern hemisphere.

Grid pole (A) = Latitude 72.4266°/longitude 90° west 1054.4 minutes of arc from the north pole.

Grid pole "B" = Latitude 78.4266°/longitude 105° west 694.4 minutes of arc from the North Pole.

Resultant grid pole "C" = Latitude 75.6°/longitude 97.5° west 864 minutes of arc from the North Pole.

The diagonal of the "polar square" of 5091.168825 units can be broken down into a series of values:

$$5091.168824 \div 2 = 2545.584412$$
$$2545.584412 \div 7.5 = 3.39411255$$
$$3.39411255^2 = 11.52$$
$$11.52 \div 8 = 1.44 \text{ (speed of light harmonic)}$$
$$2545.584412^2 = 6480000$$
$$\text{Reciprocal of } 2545.584412 = .03928371$$

The harmonic value of 3928371 is of extreme importance as it has a direct relationship with the earth's magnetic field. The harmonic 648 was also shown, in my earlier books, to have many interesting associations. In particular the harmonic table for temperature.

The many other harmonic factors, centred around the "polar square" corner "aerial" positions, form a series of complex mathematical associations, and this can be left for those who wish to carry out their own research. If I can show how to construct the main "bones" of the grid my part of the job will be complete. I have found it impossible, so far, to plot the fine grid structure of lines 7.5 minutes apart, over the whole world, because of the complexity of such an exercise. (A full computer programme would be necessary and I do not have the finance required for such an undertaking).

So far I have confined myself to the New Zealand area, with the small section of finely-spaced grid lines that I originally discovered. Over the years I have been able to plot into this map a great many interesting facts which indicate activity by various scientific groups. This has helped me to gradually build up my own knowledge of the system.

My nosiness has not gone unnoticed — as evidenced by the constant probing of interested parties endeavouring to find out the extent of my discoveries. I hope that in the near future the international combines involved in this advanced research will make known to the public the vast amount of scientific knowledge they have aquired. Possibly this will only happen if and when a world government has been set up to control the scientific wonders which are now within our reach. Enough is known already to make most of our energy and transport systems obsolete — which may explain why the facts are being suppressed?

I have been able to check activity in other parts of the world by applying harmonic calculation to certain positions of latitude and longitude. It is not necessary to use the grid structure, and such, for some types of calculation once the harmonic process is understood. Eventually, when the whole grid has been plotted, the work will be much easier.

In my second book I stated that the first glimmerings of how true space travel might be achieved came to me when I uncovered the clues that led me to the UFO grid which laces about our globe.

I was aware that my calculations were not precisely accurate — in the strict mathematical sense — but I could see that the system was based on space-time geometrics, and at least there was the best possible support for this: none less than the theories of Einstein.

Somewhere, I knew, the system contained a clue to the truth of the unified field which, he had postulated, permeates all of existence. I didn't know at the time that this clue had already been found by scientists who were well ahead of me. I know now that they must have understood something of the grid system years ago. They knew that Einstein's ideas about the unified field were correct. What's more, for many years they had been carrying out full-scale research into the practical applications of the mathematical concepts contained in that theory.

We were told that Einstein died without completing his equations relating to the unified theory. But in more recent times it has been said that he did in fact complete his work but that the concepts were so advanced that the full truth was not released.

The only way to traverse the vast distances of space is to possess the means of manipulating, or altering, the very structure of space itself; altering the space-time geometric matrix, which to us provides the illusion of form and distance. The method of achieving this lies in the alteration of frequencies controlling the matter-antimatter cycles which govern our awareness, or perception, of position in the space-time structure. Time itself is a geometric, just as Einstein postulated; if time can be altered, then the whole universe is waiting for us to come and explore its nook and crannies.

In the blink of an eye we could cross colossal distances: for distance is an illusion. The only thing that keeps places apart in space is time. If it were possible to move from one position to another in space, in an infinitely small amount of time, or "zero time", then both the positions would coexist, according to our awareness. By speeding up the geometric of time we will be able to bring distant places within close proximity. This is the secret of the UFOs — they travel by means of altering the spatial dimensions around them and repositioning in space-time.

I decided to concentrate specifically on three harmonic values which appeared to have a close relationship with each other. Previously I had shown this connection and had truthfully pointed out that I did not know why the relationship was there at all.

The harmonic values which occupied my full attention:

1703 — This was the four-figure harmonic of 170,300,000,000, which is the expression in cubic minutes of arc of the mass, or volume, of the planet earth, and its surrounding atmosphere.

1439 — A four-figure harmonic of 143,900 minutes of arc per grid second, representing the speed of light in grid values.

2640 — This figure expressed in minute of arc values is built into the polar portion of the grid structure, as a geometric coordinate.

I found that when I matched these values harmonically the results were as follows. Zeros to the right-hand side can be ignored in this form of harmonic calculation:

1703
-264
1439

In other words the difference between the harmonic of mass and the harmonic of light was the harmonic of 264 (or 2640).

It was apparent that if my calculations were more accurately worked out it should be possible to find out just what the 2640 figure referred to.

After more calculation the following terms were found:

17025 Earth mass harmonic
-2636 Unknown harmonic
14389 Speed of light harmonic

Checking through some five-figure mathematical tables, I found to my surprise that 2.6363 is the square root of 6.95 (from the 1-10 square root tables). In harmonic calculation decimal points as well as zeros to the right or left of a figure can be ignored; so it could be said that the square root of 695 was 2636. I could perceive from this the first steps necessary to solve the elusive equation. I had established that 695 was the harmonic reciprocal of the speed of light, or 1 / 1439 subject to the accuracy of my calculations at the time. It was now possible to substitute algebraic values — although obviously a computer would be necessary to solve the true values to extreme accuracy.

17025 (earth mass)
-2636 square root of speed of light reciprocal
14389 (speed of light)

If C = The speed of light, and
M = Mass

Then $M = C + \sqrt{\frac{1}{C}}$

I had the first part of a unified field equation in harmonic values. To take the next step I first had to go back to Einsteinian theory, particularly the famous equation $E = MC^2$, where E is energy, M is mass and C the speed of light.

Einstein declared that physical matter was nothing more than a concentrated field of force. What we term a physical substance is in reality an intangible concentration of wave-forms. Different combinations of structural patterns of waves unite to form the myriad chemicals and elements which in turn react with one another to form physical substances. Different wave-forms of matter appear to us to be solid because we are constituted of similar wave-forms which resonate within a clearly defined range of frequencies — and which control the physical processes of our limited world.

Einstein believed that M, the value for mass in the equation, could eventually be removed and a value substituted that would express the physical in the form of pure energy. In other words, by substituting for M a unified field equation should result which would express in mathematical terms the whole of existence — including this universe and everything within it.

Einstein maintained that the M in his equation could be replaced by a term denoting wave-form. I had found a substitute for M in terms of wave-forms of light. So the obvious step, to me, was to replace Einstein's M with the values of C found from the grid system . The results are as follows:

Einstein $E = MC^2$

Cathie grid $M = C + \sqrt{1/C}$

Therefore $E = (C + \sqrt{1/C})\, C^2$ (Harmonic equation 1)

I now had a harmonic unified field equation expressed in terms of light — or pure electromagnetic wave form — the key to the universe, the whole of existence: to the seen and the unseen, to forms, solids, liquids and gases, the stars and the blackness of space itself, all consisting of visible and invisible waves of light. All of creation is light.

It was now necessary to refine my calculations and attempt to discover a way to practically apply this initial equation.

The equation is that from which an atomic bomb is developed. by setting up derivatives of the equation in geometric form, the relative motions of the wave-forms inherent in matter are zeroed, and convert from material substance back into pure energy.

This explained the workings of a nuclear explosive device, but it still did not yield the secret of space-time propulsion. The grid system which I discovered by the study of the movement of unidentified flying objects was harmonically tuned to this basic equation, yet a UFO does not disintegrate when it moves within the resonating fields of the network.

There had to be an extension of the equation which so far I had missed that would produce the necessary harmonics for movement in space-time.

In the polar areas of the grid the geometric values of some of the coordinates appeared to be doubled up. The coordinate of 2545584412 was doubled in the diagonals of the polar squares, with all of its associated harmonics and other factors appeared to be doubled when the pattern was projected onto a flat plain.

I reasoned that a way to check this idea was to increase the values of C in the equation, and observe the changing harmonic of E to see what relative values might emerge. I thought at the time that a direct antigravitational harmonic might become evident, but my recent research has proved this line of thought to be incorrect. In terms of mathematical values I found what I was hunting for in the form of two more equations. In the case of one of the equations I erroneously believed that the derived harmonic value related to the reciprocal of gravity. I know now that what I had hold of was an equation related to the magnetic field of the earth.

The earth being simply a huge magnet, a dynamo, wound with magnetic lines of force as it coils, tenescopically counted to be 1257 TO THE SQUARE CENTIMETRE IN ONE DIRECTION AND 1850 TO THE SQUARE CENTIMETRE IN THE OTHER DIRECTION (EDDY CURRENTS), indicates that natural law has placed these lines as close together as the hairs on one's head.

The spectroscope shows that there is an enormous magnetic field around the sun, and it is the present conclusion of the best minds that magnetic lines of force from the sun envelop this earth and extend to the moon, and THAT EVERYTHING, NO MATTER WHAT ITS FORM ON THIS PLANET, EXISTS BY REASON OF MAGNETIC LINES OF FORCE.

This I agree with, according to my own research. We are taught in our schools and universities that the magnetic field passes through one magnetic pole, then through the body, and out the other magnetic pole. I disagree with this explanation. I believe that the magnetic lines of force enter the body at the poles, then carry out a looped path through the body before passing out the opposite poles.

The flow is not in one pole and out the other, but in both poles, and out both poles, although the field intensity both ways is unbalanced.

If we can visualise one line of force so that we can trace out its path we can form an analogy by imagining it to be similar to a piece of string. First of all we make a loop in the piece of string. Now imagine it being fed through a fixed position with the loop remaining stationary relative to a fixed point. With the length of string as the axis we can now make the loop revolve in a path which is at 90° to the movement of the string. The loop in fact would trace out a spherical-shaped form in space.

The lines of force of the magnetic field would form a lattice, or grid pattern, due to the spin of the planetary body. A good analogy would be an ordinary machine-wound ball of string. The length of string has taken on the form of a ball, and at the same time has formed a crisscross pattern. If we again visualise this as a physical body being formed in space then we can now imagine a small vortex being created at all the trillions of points where the lines of force cross each other in the lattice pattern. Each vortex would manifest as an atomic structure and create within itself what we term a gravitational field. The gravitational field in other words is nothing more than the effect of relative motion in space. Matter is drawn towards a gravitational field, just as a piece of wood floating on water is drawn towards a whirlpool. The gravitational fields created by the vortexual action of every atom would combine to form the field of the completed planetary body.

The world grid that I speak of is the natural grid that is formed by the lattice pattern of the interlocking lines of force.

The unbalanced field of 1257 lines of force per square centimentre in one direction and 1850 in other does not tell us very much in itself. But if we use the information to calculate the field strength over an area which has a harmonic relationship with the unified fields of space, and if the basic information is correct, we should find some mathematical values of great importance.

At the time of writing my last book I was not aware of the extreme importance of the values at that stage of accuracy. I was close enough to see how they fitted into the equations, but a further fine tuning was necessary to reveal the knowledge locked within these two simple numbers.

The basic unit for harmonic calculation is the geodetic inch, or one seventy-two thousandth of a minute of arc; one minute of arc being 6000 geodetic feet. If we take the values 1257 and 1850 lines of force per square centimetre and calculate the field strengths for one square geodetic inch, the field density is 8326.71764 and 12255.08864 lines of force respectively. The fields being in oppostion to each other. The combined field density is equal to 20581.80628.

Allowing for very slight variations in the conversion factors the difference in field strengths (12255.08864 minus 8326.71764) is equal to 3928.371. We could say that the resultant field density one way is equivalent to field 'A' minus field 'B', or 3928.371 lines of force. This value I found to be the harmonic reciprocal of the grid coordinate 2545.584412.

The combined field strength of 20581.80628 lines of force can be harmonically associated with several other interesting facts, to be demonstrated in other sections of this book.

We can now formulate another equation in order to demonstrate the association of the earth's magnetic field with the speed of light.

Harmonic equation 2

$$\text{Field (A} - \text{B)} = (2C + \sqrt{1/2C})\,(2C)^2 = 3928.371 \text{ harmonic}$$

$$\text{Where } C = 144000 - 90.9345139 = 143909.0655$$

The reduction in light speed of 90.9345139 minutes of arc per grid/sec. creates a very interesting factor, because:

$$90.9345139 = \frac{3928371}{432}$$

The reduction in light speed is therefore equal, in harmonic terms, to the resultant field strength divided by the radius of spherical mass. In this case the radius being the distance, in minutes of arc, from the earth's centre to the average height of the atmosphere. (432 being a harmonic of 4320 minutes of arc).

In my last book, "The Pulse of the Universe", I had shown this reduction to be equal to three times the gravity acceleration harmonic as the values matched very closely within the accuracy of my work at that time. The relationship with gravity is still there but not so directly obvious.

We can now formulate a third equation by inserting the value for the speed of light at the earth's surface. By mathematical conversion this was found to be 143795.77 minutes of arc per grid second, where one grid second was 1/97200 part of the time taken for one revolution of the earth.

Harmonic Equation 3

$$2693645 = \sqrt{(2C + \sqrt{1/2C})\,(2C)^2}$$

Where C

$$= 144000 - 204.23$$
$$= 143795.77$$

In my third book I had again used the gravity factor as the basis for the reduction, making the value equal to 6G. I feel that this new approach based on extended knowledge is the more correct one, although, as above, the gravity factor is not so obvious. I believe that there is yet another factor in the light reduction process to be found but this will require further research.

The research will be extended until all the answers are in but the results appear to back up my belief that as the harmonic of light is fractionally decreased, the energy which is released is converted to form physical matter.

From this we can get a glimmering of how an unidentified flying object is able to create a series of resonating frequencies which alter the physical properties within and around it, thus causing a change in the space time frames of reference in relation to the earth or other planetary body.

As I have stated in my previous publications, natural law is not erratic. The universe does not rely on chance to manifest within itself the physical substances which we perceive and call reality. A very strict ordered system of mathematical progressions is necessary to create the smallest speck of matter from the primeval matrix of space.

During my years of research into the complexities of the earth grid system I have gradually built up a picture in my mind of the possible geometric combinations necessary to form matter from resonating, interlocking waveforms.

Matter and anti-matter are formed by the same wave motions in space. The waves travel through space in a spiralling motion, and alternately pass through positive and negative stages. Matter is formed through the positive stage, or pulse, and anti-matter through the negative pulse.

Each spiral of 360° forms a single pulse. The circular motion of an electron about the nucleus of an atom is therefore an illusion. The relative motion of the nucleus and electrons through space gives the illusion of circular motion. The period during the formation of anti-matter is completely undetectable, since obviously all physical matter is manifesting at the same pulse rate, including any instruments or detectors used to probe atomic structures.

The period or frequency rate between each pulse of physical matter creates the measurement which we call time, as well as the speed of light, at the particular position in space of which we are aware, at any given moment.

If the frequency rate of positive and negative pulses is either increased or decreased, then time and the speed of light vary in direct proportion.

This concept would explain time as a geometric, as Einstein theorised it to be.

A rough analogy of physical existence can be made by reference to a strip of motion picture film. Each frame or static picture on the film strip may be likened to a single pulse of physical existence. The division between one frame and the next represents a pulse of anti-matter. When viewed as a complete strip, each frame would be seen as a static picture — say one at either end of the strip — then the past and the future can be viewed simultaneously. However, when the film is fed through a projector, we obtain the illusion of motion and the passage of time. The divisions between the static pictures are not detected by our senses because of the frequency, or speed, of each projection on the movie screen. But by speeding up or slowing down the projector, we can alter the apparent time rate of the actions shown by the film.

To continue this analogy: our consciousness is the projector. The conscious 'I am' part of our individuality passes from one pulse of physical matter to the next within the framework of the physical structure which we term our body, thus giving the illusion of constant reality, and the passing of time.

It is logical to assume that we have a twin stream of consciousness on the anti-matter side of the cycle, which in fact creates a mirror-image of our own individual personality. (This postulate has already been put forward by scientists). The frequency of manifestation of both streams of consciousness, that is, the plus and the minus 'I am', would position our awareness of the illusion of reality at a particular point in space and time. In other words, if the frequency of pulse manifestation is altered, even fractionally, our awareness of reality, in the physical sense, will shift from one spatial point to another. In fact, we would travel from one point in space to another without being aware that we had traversed distance in the physical sense. This would be space travel in the truest sense.

Lets's look at another analogy: we can consider a simple spiral spring as representing the wave motion of an electron through space. Every second 360° spiral of the spring represents the path of the electron in physical matter, while the opposite applies to anti-matter.

The theory outlined above explains why light has been described as being caused by both a wave motion and a pulse. Both explanations are correct.

A pulse of light is manifested when the energy level of the atomic structure is altered by outside influences (theory of Max Planck). In the physical plane, the electron of the atomic structure appears to jump from its orbit. According to my belief, the electron *does not jump orbit*. But this is the illusion we obtain, since we are not equipped to perceive the path of the electron during the anti-matter cycle. What actually happens is that the radius of the spiralling motion is increased or decreased in order to absorb or release the energy imparted to, or removed from, the atomic structure. If the energy is imparted, then the electron must extend orbit in order to maintain balance in the system; and vice versa. Light, or any other radiant energy above or below light frequency, is therefore manifested by undetectable changes in the radius of the spiral motion of the electron during the anti-matter cycle.

If this hypothesis is correct, movement from one point in space to another point, regardless of apparent distance — in other words, true space travel — is completely feasible. By manipulating the frequency rate of the matter-anti-matter cycle, the time and speed of light can be varied in direct proportion to any desired value.

All the mathematical evidence amassed so far indicates that the maximum number of individual elements to be found in the universe will be 144. Each of these elements will have, in theory, six isotopes, which will make up a completed table of separate substances numbering 1008. An isotope is an atom of the same element which has a different nuclear mass and atomic weight.

Mathematically, the progression would create 144 octaves of separate substances giving a theoretical value of 1152. The difference between the total number of substances (1008) and the harmonic value in octaves (1152) would be 144, the light harmonic.

Once the precipitation of physical matter has occured, the buildup of substances takes place according to a very well ordered mathematical sequence. Light-waves, guided seemingly by superior intelligence, form intricate interlocking grid patterns which graduate from the simple to the more complex, as the elements from hydrogen at the lower end of the scale, to element 144, come into being.

When we think of reality we must think of mass in relation to any physical manifestation, and the smallest particle of physical matter that we are aware of is the electron. Therefore electron mass must be the starting point in our quest for a feasible theory to explain the structure of matter.

The average radius of action of the electron around the atomic nucleus must also have a constant harmonic value in order to set up a system of expanding spheres which encompass the structure of each element. As the number of protons in the nucleus increases with the buildup of each element, the spherical space which houses the electron shell must expand to accommodate an equal number of electrons. Although the protons and electrons are nothing more than extremely concentrated wave-forms, we consider them as physical particles in order to build up a picture of our model. As each electron cloud, or shell, expands outward from the nucleus, we find that it can accommodate only eight electrons. The shell is then filled up and another expansion must take place in order to form a new shell or harmonic zone, which again builds up to a maximum of eight electrons. As the magnitude of the harmonic resonance intensifies, heavier and heavier elements are produced until we reach a maximum of 144 elements. The light harmonic is then equal and the cycle has been completed. The whole series is a repetition of octaves of wave-forms forming more and more complex structures.

In my earlier work I had assumed that the harmonic radius of the atom was equal to the mass ratio of the proton and electron. I now realize that although I was on the right track, the theoretical model demonstrated was partly in error. This necessitated another search into the physics books and I now feel that the following calculations based on the experimental values are getting close to the truth.

It would be logical to base the harmonic interaction on the geometric structure of the hydrogen atom. If harmonic equivalents can be derived from the basic values established by experimetal physics, and remain within the laid down tolerances, then almost certainly a new theory should be evident. Especially if the harmonic values closely match those found in the unified equations previously demonstrated.

The distance given between the electron and the proton in the hydrogen atom is approximately 5.3×10^{-11} metre. (Physics Part 2, Halliday & Resnick)
I have discovered that a value of:
5.297493×10^{-11} metre fits in very neatly with the previously established harmonic terms. If we convert this value into its geometric equivalent, then:
5.297493×10^{-11} metre
$= 17.15150523 \times 10^{-11}$ geodetic feet
$= 205.8180628 \times 10^{-11}$ geodetic inches

The radius of the hydrogen atom is therefore very obviously tuned to the harmonic value of 20581.80628, which is the number of magnetic lines of force per square geodetic inch. The diameter of the hydrogen atom would be, 411.6361256.

If we calculate the circumference of the atom in terms of harmonic geodetic feet then:
$17.15150523 \times 10^{-11}$ geodetic feet radius
$= 34.30301$ harmonic diameter
$= 107.7660$ harmonic circumference.

Now if we allow spacing on this circumference for eight electron positions we have:
107.7660 divided by 8
= 13.47 units

But an electron has only half a spin value; the other half taking place during the anti-matter cycle, so:
13.47×2 to allow for the double cycle,
= 26.94

Allowing for the accuracy of the conversion factors etc. would make the harmonic geometrics of the hydrogen atom comply fairly closely with the geometric energy value derived from the unified equation (2693645). A comupter program set up for curved geometry should, in theory, show a perfect match.

We can now use the hydrogen atom as a base line to form a theory regarding the formation of the complete atomic table of elements. I believe that the harmonic radius of 205.8180628 units would remain constant throughout the whole range of elements. The orbits of electrons in all substances taking up harmonically spaced positions to the power of ten. In other words by shifting the decimal point to the right or left of this basic harmonic, the orbital radius of all electrons can be calculated. (See diagram 5).

This would apply to the whole range of 144 elements and their isotopes. Physical reality, as we perceive it, being manifested by the concentrated interlocking of harmonic wave-forms, which are built up progressively from a foundation of fundamental wave-packets.

The square of the diameter of the hydrogen atom (4116361257) is equal to the harmonic of mass at the centre of a light field, 1694443. This value also shows up in the cycle of element formation due to the introduction of neutrons into the atomic nucleus. It is stated in the physics books that the maximum number of neutrons that can be contained in the atomic nucleus is 1.6 times the number of protons. The theory of harmonic formation agrees with this. If the ratio of protons and neutrons in the basic element is taken as 1:1 then as each isotope is built up due to the introduction of neutrons we have the mathematical progression of 1:1, 1:1.1, 1:1.2, 1:1.3, 1:1.4, 1:1.5, 1:1.6, for the element and the six isotopes; then as the harmonic increases to 1:1.694443, and above, towards 1:1.7, we get the formation of the next higher element. The cycle would then repeat itself.

The rest mass of the proton is given as 1.67252×10^{-27} Kg, and a mass ratio of 1836 is laid down for the proton and electron. I believe that the harmonic values approach those found in the unifed equations when the atomic structure is accelerated towards the speed of light. According to Einstein the mass increases, and I believe the mass of the proton increases towards the 1694443 harmonic. If the energy level is built up above this point a condition would be reached where a change in physical state would occur. That is, the harmonic would be approaching 1.7 to 1.7018, the surface mass harmonic for an atomic structure, and a change would be triggered.

A gravitational connection with mass becomes evident when the normal gravitational acceleration is converted into grid equivalents. The physics books state that gravity acceleration varies according to latitude on the earth's surface, and also with altitude, or distance from the centre of the earth. The variation at sea level from 0° to 90° latitude is equal to 32.087829 feet/sec^2 to 32.257711 feet/sec^2.

I decided to calculate the grid gravity acceleration at latitude 52.8756° which is 37.1244° from the geometric pole. The reciprocal harmonic of this position (371244) is equal to 2693645. The interpolated standard gravity acceleration at this latitude is 32.194417 feet/sec^2.

The grid time factor I discovered has stood up to scrutiny over the years and is based on 27 periods for one revolution of the earth. Normally we use 24 periods of one hour each. The 27 periods, I call 27 grid hours. A grid hour is slightly shorter than a normal hour, and is divided into sixty grid minutes, each of which is equal to sixty grid seconds.

Therefore for one revolution of the earth we have a standard time of 86,400 seconds as against a grid time of 97,200 grid seconds. The ratio is 8:9.

So: $32.194417 \times \frac{6000}{6080} \times \frac{8}{9} = 28.24071667$

If this acceleration factor is multiplied by 6 then:
$28.24071667 \times 6 = 169.4443$
1694443 harmonic = $(C + \sqrt{1/C})$ Where C = 143000 minutes of arc per grid/sec.
So harmonically, gravity acceleration is equal to:

$\frac{(C + \sqrt{1/C})}{6}$ At the centre of a light field, forming spherical mass.

As my own research has shown me that physical reality is manifested by the harmonic nature of light, it appears logical that a vehicle constructed to the principles of harmonics will be required to set up the space-time fields necessary. If this is so, then the first criterion will be that the vehicle must resonate in perfect harmony with the complete table of elements in our physical universe. If it does not, then it would be more than probable that any element or particle of matter not in harmonic resonance within the vehicle structure, or payload, would be left behind when the space-time field was activated. The results would be embarrassing, to say the least!

It would be impractical to construct a vehicle made from an alloy of the whole range of 144 elements in the theoretical atomic table. Apart from this, such an alloy is no doubt a physical impossibility.

The clue which suggests a method of overcoming this problem is the way matter is built up in octaves of wave-forms. If an octave of elements could be combined, which would set up a resonating field tuned to all the elements in the table, and the unified fields of space then, maybe, we would have a method of crashing the time barrier.

I put forward the following proposal for consideration. If an octave of elements is the answer let us make a selection from the theoretical table of elements of 144. If we divide 144 by 8 we get divisions of 18 units, therefore we will select each of the elements we require, 18 units part, as follows:

Atomic number 18: argon
Atomic number 36: crypton
Atomic number 54: xenon
Atomic number 72: hafnium
Atomic number 90: thorium
Atomic number 108: X
Atomic number 126: Y UNDISCOVERED ELEMENTS
Atomic number 144: Z
Total number 648

It can be seen that the total harmonic value of the atomic numbers of the combined elements is 648. The square root of this number is 25.45584412, the harmonic of which is found in the polar sections of the world grid. Three new elements just recently discovered have atomic numbers of 116,124 and 126. Do the scientists know something, and are they now looking for numbers 108 and 144.

DIAGRAM 4

Showing the harmonic wave formation of a basic element and the six associated isotopes.

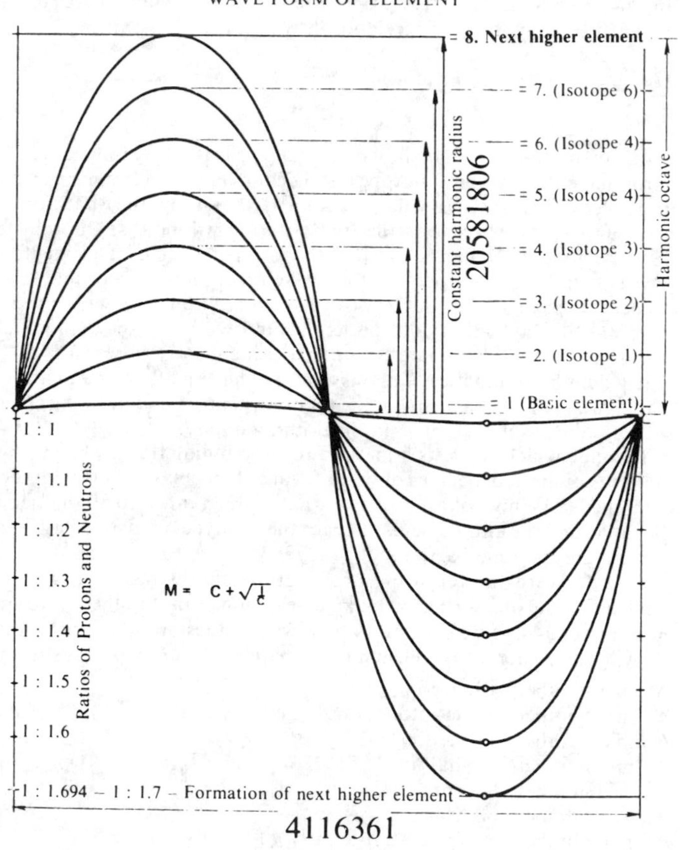

DIAGRAM 5

Showing the harmonic wave-form which creates an atom of matter and antimatter, in alternate pulses.

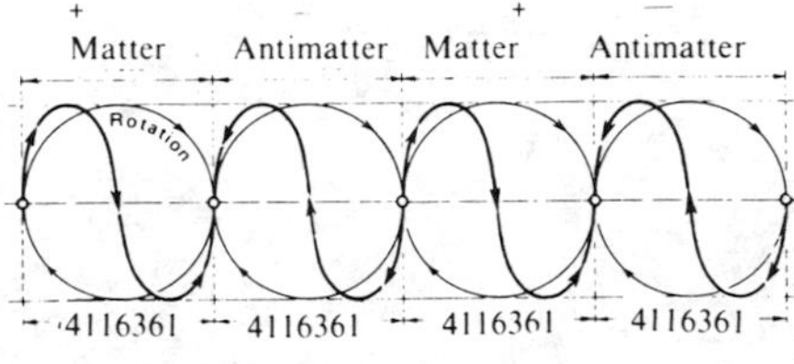

A point on the surface of the spherical mass would be rotated through the equivalent of 371.2766511 degrees for each of the matter and anti-matter cycles. (742.5533022 degrees for the double cycle). Spiral Pi in this case would be equal to 3.24.

Electron Orbits

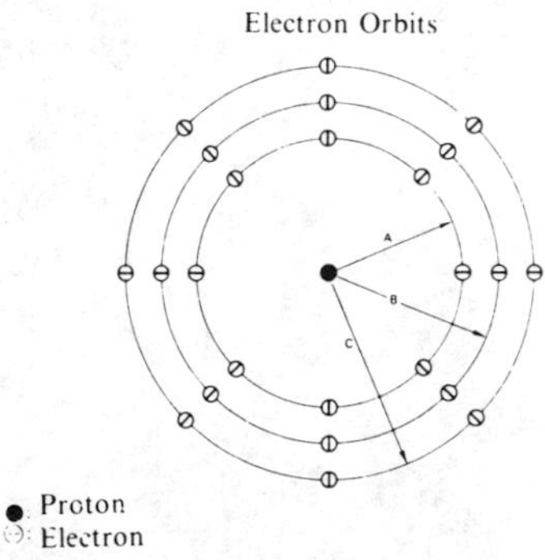

● Proton
⊖ Electron

A: Harmonic radius 205.818062
B: Harmonic radius 2058.18062 (In terms of harmonic geodetic inches)
C: Harmonic radius 20581.8062

A: Harmonic radius 17.1515052
B: Harmonic radius 171.515052 (In terms of harmonic geodetic feet)
C: Harmonic radius 1715.15052

The circumference remains a constant harmonic of 107766085 giving an electron spacing harmonic of 1347076. By doubling this harmonic to allow for the matter and anti-matter cycle we have a value of 2694 which closely complies with unified field equation (3) 2693645. A full computer program should make these values match exactly.

Harmonic values based on the Hydrogen Atom.

THE PHILADELPHIA EXPERIMENT

by

HARRY OSOFF

Albert Einstein conferring with naval officers in his study at Princeton, New Jersey, July 24, 1943. (*National Archives*)

Regional Philadelphia Newspaper Article

October 1943

Strange Circumstances
Surround Tavern Brawl

Several city police officers responding to a call to aid members of the Navy Shore Patrol in breaking up a tavern brawl near the U.S. Navy docks here last night got something of a surprise when they arrived on the scene to find the place empty of customers. According to a pair of very nervous waitresses, the Shore Patrol had arrived first and cleared the place out - but not before two of the sailors involved allegedly did a disappearing act. ***"They just sort of vanished into thin air. . . right there,"*** *reported one of the frightened hostesses, "and I ain't been drinking either!" At that point, according to her account, the Shore Patrol proceeded to hustle everyone out of the place in short order.*

A subsequent chat with the local police precinct left no doubts as to the fact that some sort of general brawl had indeed occurred in the vicinity of the dockyards at about eleven o'clock last night, but neither confirmation nor denial of the stranger aspects of the story could be immediately obtained. One reported witness succinctly summed up the affair by dismissing it as nothing more than "A lot of hooey from them daffy dames down there." Who, he went on to say, were just looking for some free publicity.

Damage to the tavern was estimated to be in the vicinity of six hundred dollars.

The **"Philadelphia Experiment"** is the name that has commonly been given to an *alleged* Top-Secret experiment conducted by the United States Navy in 1943 in which the Destroyer Escort U.S.S. Eldridge, outfitted with several tons of specialized electronics equipment capable of creating a tremendous pulsating magnetic field around itself, was first made ***invisible*** and then ***transported***, in a matter of moments, from the Philadelphia Navy Yard, to the Norfolk Docks and back again, a total distance of over 400 miles (640 kilometers).

The United States government for the last 43 years has officially denied that this experiment ever took place. Challenging this statement, however, are several unanswered questions: What caused the death of some of the crew members aboard ship in a safe and secure harbor? Why was the remainder of the crew discharged as medically unfit? If one concludes that the Philadelphia Experiment did really occur, then was the untimely death of an independent researcher investigating the alleged experiment really suicide? How could the Navy possibly accomplish such a fantastic experiment? In any case, the story begins with Morris Ketchum Jessup, an astronomy and mathematics Professor at the University of Michigan.

Morris Ketchum Jessup was born in Rockville, Indiana, March 20, 1900 and named after his uncle, a railroad and financial baron (who also had a Cape in the northernmost tip of Greenland named after him). In the late 1920s while a Doctorate student at the University of Michigan, the young Jessup's research was responsible for the discovery of many physical double stars now catalogued by the Royal Astronomical Society of London.

While the country was in the firm grip of the Depression and jobs were hard to find, Jessup, like so many other highly technical people, took work wherever he could. He was first assigned by the U.S. Department of Agriculture to go to the Amazon to study sources of crude rubber. From there he became a photographer on an archaeological expedition to the Mayan ruins in Central America. Then Jessup went to Peru to study pre-Incan culture. It was in Peru that Jessup, after studying these massive ruins with their incredible exactness and implicit construction skills, speculated that they could have been built only with the aid of levitating devices from sky ships of some sort. This theory places Jessup among the first of modern scientists to believe in the "Ancient Astronauts" theory. This view, naturally, did not put him in high regard among his employers and colleagues, and he was soon on his own.

Jessup continued his research at his own expense. He found some very interesting craters in Mexico that were similar in structure and type to the mysterious craters on the Moon. Further research disclosed that the United States Air Force had highly classified photos of the Mexican craters. Running out of money, Jessup returned to the U.S. in 1954 to raise funds for further research. When the flying-saucer craze ran rampant in the late 1940s and early 1950s, Jessup became interested, first casually, and then quite seriously. His major focus was the possible propulsion power for these sky ships.

From what he had learned in Central America, Mexico, and Peru, Jessup was convinced that UFOs were a real possibility, and he had enough foundation to prove it. Jessup moved to Washington, D.C. and devoted the next year to extensive research. On January 13, 1955, he gave his publisher the completed manuscript of his book, *The Case for the UFO.*

The book sold well enough such that in the fall of 1955 Bantam issued a paperback edition. Shortly after this book was published, Jessup received a most unusual letter. It was written in several different colors of ink and the spelling and punctuation were most odd. The subject of the letter, however, was even stranger than its grammatical oddities. The correspondent, a Mr. Allende (who signed his letters "Carl Allen") was markedly interested in Jessups' ideas about levitation and went to great lengths to agree with Jessups' theory---that many of our megaliths were built using the technique of levitation. In fact, he assured Jessup that levitation was not only scientifically possible but was commonplace on Earth in our recent past. Jessup was so fascinated by the style of the letter and the agreement with his own theory that he wrote back to Allende asking for more details.

These events concurred with several other pressing matters. At this time Jessup was doing the publicity and lecture circuit and was also preparing his second book, *The UFO and the Bible.* He soon forgot about the mysterious letter.

During the next year Jessup pushed for research into the unified field theory, something Einstein had worked on during the last twenty years of his life. It was this consuming interest that brought the "Philadelphia Experiment" back into the limelight. On January 13, 1956, exactly one year after his

Carlos Allende (alias Carl Allen) is the single most important individual in the story of the Philadelphia experiment. He it was who claimed to have seen the *Eldridge* – DE 173 – disappear at sea in 1943. He also claimed to have read that it had been made to vanish from its docks in Philadelphia, materialise in the Norfolk area of Virginia and then return to Philadelphia – a total distance of over 400 miles (640 kilometres). Many years later Allende recalled the experiment at sea: 'I watched the air all around the ship . . . turn slightly, ever so slightly, darker than all the other air. . . . I saw, after a few minutes, a foggy green mist arise like a thin cloud. . . . I watched as thereafter the DE 173 became rapidly invisible to human eyes'

the Philadelphia naval docks, Pennsylvania, USA, where, said Allende, the *Eldridge* was the subject of a strange scientific experiment, being teleported to Virginia and back again

first book was published, Morris Ketchum Jessup received the following letter. (*Editor's Note* : It is reprinted here exactly as Jessup received it. This letter contains many typographical errors and odd capitalizations of certain words; these have not been corrected, as they contain a significant part of the key to the whole matter. However a few new paragraphs have been made in the long text to aid readability)

My Dear Dr. Jessup,

Your invocation to the Public that they move en Masse upon their Representatives and have thusly enough Pressure placed at the right & sufficient Number of Places where from a Law demanding Research into Dr. Albert Eienstiens Unified Field Theory May be enacted (1925-1927) *is Not* at all Necessary. It May Intrest you to know that The Good Doctor Was Not so Much influenced in his retraction of that Work, by Mathematics, as he most assuredly was by Humantics.

His Later computations, done strictly for his own edification & amusement, upon cycles of Human Civilization & Progress compared to the Growth of Mans General over-all Character Was enough to Horrify Him. Thus, we are *told* today that the Theory was "Incomplete."

Dr. B. Russell asserts privately that It is complete. He also says that Man is Not Ready for it & Shan't be until after W.W. III. Nevertheless, "Results" of My friend Dr. Franklin Reno, *were used*. These Were a complete Recheck of That Theory, With a View to any & Every Possible quick use of it, if feasible in a Very short time. There Were good Results, as far as a Group Math Re-Check AND as far as a good Physical "Result," to Boot. YET, THE NAVY FEARS TO USE THIS RESULT. The Result was & stands today as Proof that The Unified Field Theory to a certain extent is correct. Beyond that certain extent No Person in his right senses, or having any senses at all, Will evermore *dare* to go.

I am sorry that I Mislead You in My Previous Missive. True, enough, such a form of Levitation has been accomplished as described. It is also a Very commonly observed reaction of certain Metals to Certain Fields surrounding a current, This field being used for that purpose. Had Farraday concerned himself about the Mag. field surrounding an Electric Current, We today Would NOT exist *or if* We did exist, our present Geo-Political situation would have the very timebombish, ticking off towards Destruction, atmosphere that Now exists. Alright, Alright! The "result" was complete invisibility of a ship, Destroyer type, *and all* of its crew, While at Sea. (Oct. 1943)

The Field Was effective in an oblate spheroidal shape, extending one hundred yards (More or Less, due to Lunar position and Latitude) *out* from each beam of the ship. Any Person Within that sphere became vague in form BUT He too observed those Persons aboard *that* ship as though they too were of the same state, yet were walking upon nothing. Any person without that sphere could see Nothing save the clearly *Defined shape of the Ships Hull in the Water.* PROVIDING of course, that that person was just close enough to see yet, just barely outside of that field.

Why tell you Now? Very Simple; If you choose to go Mad,

then you would reveal this information. Half of the officiers and the crew of that Ship are at Present, Mad as Hatters. A few are even Yet confined to certain areas where they may receive trained Scientific aid when they, either, "Go Blank" or "Go Blank" & Get Stuck." Going-Bland IE an after effect of the Man having been within the field too Much, IS Not at all an unplesant expierence to Healthily Curious Sailors. However it is when also, they "Get Stuck" that they call it "HELL" INCORPORATED" The Man thusly stricken can Not Move of his own volition unless one or More of those who are within the field go & touch him, quickly, else he "Freezes".

If a Man Freezes, His position Must be Marked out carefully and then the Field is cut-off. Everyone but that "Frozen" Man is able to Move; to appreciate *apparent* Solidity again. Then, the Newest Member of the cres Must approach the Spot, where he will find the "Frozen" Mans face or Bare skin, that is Not covered by usual uniform Clothing. Sometimes, It takes only an hour or so Sometimes all Night & all Day Long & Worse *It once took 6 months,* to get the Man "Unfrozen". *This "Deep Freeze" was not psycological.* It is a Result of a Hyper-Field that is set up, *within* the field of the Body, While the "Scorch" Field is turned on & this at Length *or* upon a Old Hand.

A Highly complicated Piece of Equipment Had to be constructed in order to Unfreeze those who became "True Froze" (*Editor's Note* : This could be "Free Freeze") or "Deep Freeze" subjects. *Usually a "Deep Freeze" Man goes Mad, Stark Raving, Gibbering, Running MAD,* if His "freeze" is far More than a Day in our time.

I speak of TIME for DEEP "Frozen Men" are Not aware of Time as We know it. They are Like Semi-comatoese person, who Live, breathe, Look & feel but still are unaware of So Utterly Many things as to constitute a "Nether World" to them. A Man in an ordinary common Freeze *is* aware of Time, sometimes *acutely* so. Yet They are *Never* aware of Time precisely as you and I are aware of it. The First "Deep Freeze" As I said took 6 months to Rectify. It also took over 5 Million Dollars worth of Electronic equipment & a Special Ship Berth. If around or Near the Philadelphia Navy Yard you see a group of Sailors in the act of Putting their Hands *upon* a fellow *or* upon "thin air", observe the Digits & appendages of the Stricken Man. If they seem to Waver, as tho within a Heat-Mirage, **go quickly** & Put YOUR Hands upon Him, *For that Man is **The Very Most Desperate** of Men in The World. Not one of those Men ever want at all to become again invisible.* I do Not think that Much More Need be said as to Why Man is Not Ready for Force-Field Work. Eh?

You Will Hear phrases from these Men such as "Caught in the Flow (or the Push) or "Stuck in the Green" or "Stuck in Molasses" or " I was "going" FAST", These Refer to Some of the Decade-Later after effects of Force-Field Work. "Caught in the Flow" Describes exactly the "Stuck in Molasses" sensation of a Man going into a "Deep Freeze" or Plain Freeze" either of the two. "Caught in the Push" can either refer to That Which a Man feels Briefly WHEN he is either about to inadvertantly "Go-Blank" IE Become Invisible" or about to "Get Stuck" in a "Deep Freeze" or "Plain Freeze."

There are only a few of the original Expierimental D-E's

Crew Left by Now, Sir. Most went insane, one just walked "throo" His quarters Wall in sight of His Wife & Child & 2 other crew Members (WAS NEVER SEEN AGAIN), two " Went into "The Flame," I.E. They "Froze" & Caught fire, while carrying common Small-Boat Compasses, one Man carried the compass & Caught fire, the other came for the "Laying on of Hands" as he was the nearest but he too, took fire. THEY BURNED FOR 18 DAYS. The faith in "Hand Laying" Died When this Happened & Mens Minds Went by the scores. *The experiment Was a Complete Success . The Men were Complete Failures.*

Check Philadelphia Papers for a tiny one Paragraph (upper Half of sheet, inside the paper Near the rear 3rd of Paper, 1944-46 in Spring or Fall or Winter, NOT Summer.) of an item describing the Sailors Actions after their initial Voyage. They Raided a Local to the Navy Yard "Gin Mill" or "Beer Joint" & caused such shock & Paralysis of the Waitresses that Little comprehensible could be gotten from them, save that Paragraph & the Writer of it, Does Not Believe it, & Says "I only wrote what I heard & them Dames is Daffy. So, all I get is a "Hide-it" Bedtime Story."

Check observer ships crew, Matson Lines Liberty ship out of Norfolk, (Company MAY Have Ships Log for that Voyage or Coast Guard have it) The S.S. Andrew Furnseth, Chief Mate Mowsely, (Will secure Captains Name Later) (Ships Log Has Crew List on it.) one crew member Richard Price or "Splicey" Price May Remember other Names of Deck Crew Men, (Coast Guard has record of Sailors issued "Papers") Mr. Price Was 18 or 19 then, Oct. 1943, and Lives or Lived at that time in His old Family Home in Roanoke, VA. a small town with a Small Phone book. These Men Were Witnesses, The Men of this crew, "Connally of New England, (Boston?), May have Witnessed but I doubt it. (Spelling May be incorrect) DID witness this. I ask you to Do this bit of Research simply that you May Choke on your own Tongue when you Remember what you have "appealed to be Made Law"

Very Disrespectfully Yours,
Carl M. Allen

Days Later

Notes in addition to and pertaining to Missive.

(Contact Rear Admiral Ransom Bennett for verification of info Herin. Navy Cheif of research. He may offer you a job, ultimately)

Coldly & analytically speaking, without the Howling that is in the Letter to you accompanying this, I will say the following in all Fairness to you & to Science. (1) The Navy did Not know that the men could become invisible WHILE NOT UPON THE SHIP & UNDER THE FIELDS INFLUENCE. (2) The Navy Did Not know that *there would be* Men Die from the odd effects of HYPER "Field" within *or* upon "Field." (3) Further, They even yet do Not know Why this happened & are not even sure that the "F" within "F" is the reason, for sure at all. *In Short* The Atomic bomb didn't kill the expierimentors thus the expieriments went on-but

Left: the SS *Andrew Furuseth*, which Carlos Allende (using the name Carl Allen) joined in August 1943. In the photograph of the ship's officers and crew (above), the man standing immediately to the left of the right-hand ventilator is thought by some reseachers to be Allende, who served on the ship until January 1944 eventually one or two were accidentally killed But *the cause* was known as to *Why* they died.

Myself, I "feel" that something pertaining to the Small-boat compass "triggered" off "The Flames." I have no proof, but Neither Does the Navy. (4) WORSE & Not Mentioned When one or two of their Men, Visible-within-the-field-to- all-the-others, *Just Walked into Nothingness,* AND Nothing Could be felt, of them, either when the "field" Was turned on OR off, THEY WERE JUST GONE! Then, More Fears Were Amassed. (5) Worse, Yet, When an apparently Visible & New-Man Just walks semingly "throo" the Wall of his House, the surrounding area Searched by all Men & thoroughly scrutinzed by & with & under an Installed Portable Field developer AND NOTHING EVER found of him. *So Many Many Fears were by then in effect that the Sum total of them all could Not ever again be faced by ANY of those Men or by the Men Working at & upon the Experiments.*

I wish to Mention that Somehow, also, The Experimental Ship Disappeared from its Philadelphia Dock and only a Very few Minutes Later appeared at its other Dock in the Norfolk, Newport News, Portsmouth area. This was distinctly AND clearly Identified as being that place BUT the ship then, *again,* Dissappeared And Went *Back* to its Philadelphia Dock in only a Very few Minutes or Less. This was also noted in the newspapers But I forget what paper I read it in *or* When It happened. Probably Late in the experiments, May have been in 1956 *after* Experiments were discontinued, I can Not Say for Sure

To the Navy this Whole thing was So Impractical due to its Morale Blasting effects Which were so much so that efficient operation of the Ship was Drastically hindered and then after this occurence It was shown that even the Mere operation of a ship could Not be counted upon at all. In short, Ignorance of this thing bred Such Terrors of it that, on the Level of attempted operations, with what knowledge was then available It was deemed as impossible, Impracticable and Too Horrible.

I believe that Had YOU *then* been Working upon & With the team that was Working upon this project With yourself knowing what You *NOW* know, that "The Flames" Would Not have been *so unexpected,* or Such a Terrifying Mystery. Also, More than Likely, I must say in All fairness, None of these other occurances could have happened without some knowledge of their possibility of occuring. In fact, They May have been prevented by a far More Cautious Program AND by a Much More Cautiously careful Selection of Personnell for Ships officers & Crew.

Such Was Not the case. The Navy used whatever *Human Material* was at hand, Without Much, *if any,* thought as to character & Personality of that Material. If care, Great Care is taken in selection of Ship, and officers and crew AND If Careful Indoctrination is taken *along* with Careful watch over articles of apparel Such as rings & Watches & Identification bracelets & belt buckles, *Plus* AND ESPECIALLY the effect of Hob-Nailed shoes or Cleated-shoes U.S. Navy issue shoes, I feel that some progress towards dissapating the fearfilled ignorance surrounding this profect Will be Most surely & certainly accomplished. The Records of the U.S. Maritime Service HOUSE Norfolk, Va. (for Graduated Seamen of their Schools) Will reveal who was assigned to S.S. Andrew Furuseth for Month of either Late Sept. or Oct. of

1943. I remember positively of one other observer who stood beside Me When tests were going on. He was from New England, Brown Blond Curly Hair, blue eyes, Don't remember name. I leave it up *to you* to Decide if further work shall be put into this or Not, and Write this in Hopes there Will be.

Very Sincerely,
Carl M. Allen

So here was a mysterious correspondence from a man who talked like he knew intimately about levitation, disappearing ships, and invisible men. He wrote in different color inks and with a style of writing that would not win any good grades anywhere. Jessup, meanwhile, was being pushed around by his agents in New York to run the publicity circuit and to get a new book out while the interest was still hot on his last one. But all he wanted was to make some cash and get back to those craters in Mexico. It would have been easy to just forget the whole Allende matter, but Jessup sent him a postcard asking for more details and five months later he received the following reply. (Once again, this is reprinted as it was received by Jessup)

Dear Mr. Jessup:

Having just recently gotten home from my long travels around the country I find that you had dropped me a card. You ask that I write you "at once" and So after taking everything into consideration, I have decided to do so. You ask me for what is tantamount to positive proof of something that only the duplication of those devices that produced "This Phenomenon" could ever give you. At least, were I of scientific bent, I presume that, were I of Such a Curiosity about something, the which has been produced from a theory that was discarded (1927) as incomplete, I am sure that I would be of such dubiousness towards that I would Have to be *shown* those devices that produced such a curious interaction of Forces & Fields, in operation & their product.

Mr. Jessup, I could NEVER possibly satisfy such an attitude. The reason being that I could not, Nor ever would the Navy Research Dept. (Then under the present Boss of the Navy, Burke) ever let it be known that any such thing was ever allowed to be done. For you see, It was because of Burkes Curiosity & Willingness & prompting that this experiment was enabled to be carried out. It proved a White-elephant *but* His attitude towards advanced & ultra-advanced types of research is just *"THE" THING* that put him where he is today. (Or at least, to be sure, it carries a great weight). Were the stench of such an Experiments results ever to come out, He would be crucified.

However, I have noticed, that throo the ages, those who have had this happen to them, once the vulgar passions that caused the reaction have cooled-off AND *further* research OPENLY carried

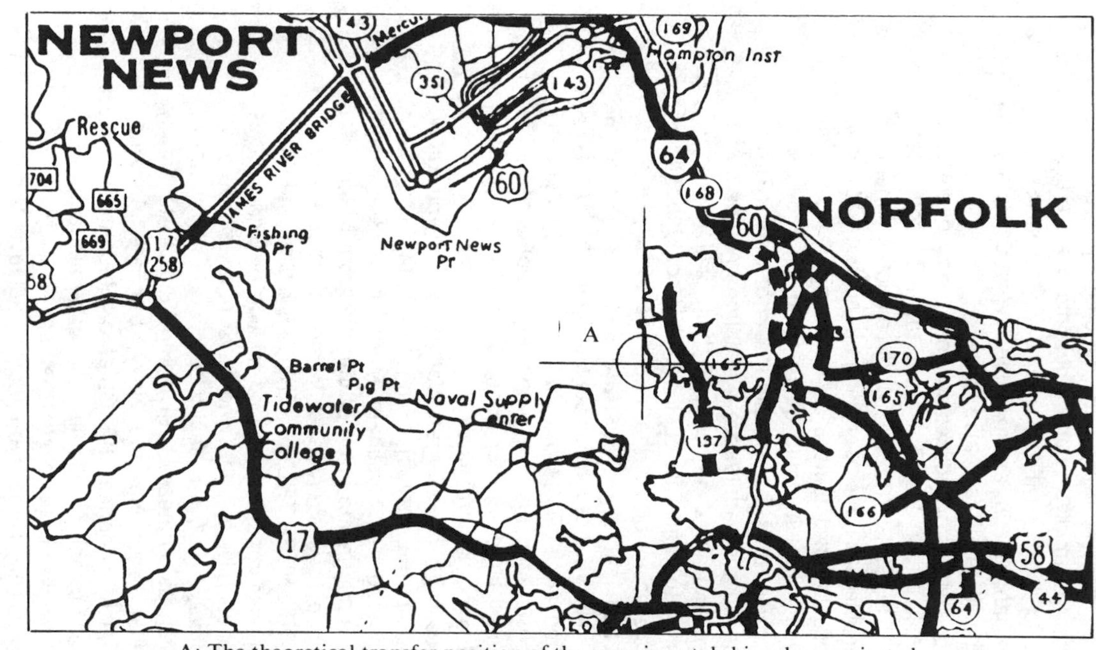

A: The theoretical transfer position of the experimental ship when projected from the Penn's Landing area.
The position would be further to the west if projected from the point adjacent to the Philadelphia College of Science.

on, *that* these crucified ones achieve something akin to Saint hood. You say that this, "is of the greatest importance". I disagree with you Mr. Jessup, not just whole Heartedly, *but vehemently.* However at the same time, your ideas & your own sort of curiosity is that of mine own sort and besides my disagreement is based upon philosophical Morality and not upon that curiosity which Drives Science so rapidly. I can be of some positive help to you in myself *but* to do so would require a Hypnotist, Sodium Pentathol, a tape recorder & an excellent typist-secretary in order to produce material of *Real* value to you.

As you know one who is hypnotized cannot Lie *and* one who is both hypnotized AND given "Truth Serum" as it is colloqually known, COULD NOT POSSIBLY LIE, *AT ALL.* To boot, *My Memory* would be THUS enabled to remember things in such *great detail,* things that my present consciousness cannot recall at all, or only barely and uncertainly that it would be of far greater benifit to use hypnosis. I could thus be enabled to *not only* Recall COMPLETE names, but also addresses & telephone numbers AND perhaps the *very* important Z numbers of those sailors whom I sailed with them or even came into contact with. I could too, being something of a Dialectician, be able to thusly talk exactly as these witnesses talked and imitate or *illustrate* their Mannerisms & *Habits of thought,* thus your psychologists can figure IN ADVANCE the Surefire method of dealing Most Sucessfully with these. I could NOT do this with someone with whom I had not observed at length & these men, I lived with for about 6 months, so you are bound to get good to excellent results.

The mind does NOT ever forget, Not really, As you know. Upon this I suggest this way of doing this with Myself but further, the Later usage of Myself in Mannerisms & Thought pattern illustration is suggested in order that the Goal of inducing these Men to *place themselves* at & under your disposal (HYPNOTICALLY OR UNDER TRUTH-SERUM) is a Goal, the Which could Have Far greater impact, due to co-relation of Expieriences remembered Hypnotically *by Men who have not seen or even written to each other, at all, for Nearly or over TEN years.* In this, with such Men as Witnesses, giving irrefuttable testimony It is my belief that were, Not the Navy, *but the Airforce,* confronted with such evidence, (IE Chief of Research) there would be either an uproar or a quiet and determined effort to achieve SAFELY "that which" the Navy failed at.

They did NOT fail to, I hope you realize, achieve Metalic & organic invisibility nor did they fail to, unbesoughtedly, acheive transportation of thousands of tons of Metal & Humans at an eyes blink speed. Even though this latter effect of prolonged experimentation was (to them) The thing that caused them to consider the experiment as a failure, I BELIEVE THAT *FURTHER EXPERIMENTS* WOULD NATURALLY HAVE PRODUCED ***CONTROLLED*** TRANSPORT OF GREAT TONNAGES AT ULTRAFAST SPEEDS TO A *DESIRED* POINT *THE INSTANT* IT IS DESIRED throo usage of an area covered by: (1) those cargoes and (2) that "Field" that could cause those goods, Ships or Ship parts (MEN WERE TRANSPORTED AS WELL) *to go* to another Point. Accidently & to the embarrassed perplexity of the Navy THIS HAS ALREADY HAPPENED TO A WHOLE SHIP, CREW & ALL. I read of this AND of THE OFF-BASE AWOL ACTIVITIES OF THE crew-Men who were at the time invisible in a *Philadelphia* NEWSPAPER. UNDER NARCO-HYPNO-HYPNOSIS I CAN BE ENABLED TO DIVULGE THE NAME, DATE & SECTION & PAGE NUMBER of *that* Paper & the other one.

Thus this papers "Morgue" will divulge EVEN MORE POSITIVE PROOF ALREADY PUBLISHED of this experiment. The Name of the Reporter who skeptically *covered & wrote* of these incidents (OF THE RESTAURANT-BARROOM RAID WHILE INVISIBLE & OF *THE SHIPS* SUDDEN AWOL) AND WHO INTERVIEWED the Waitresses CAN THIS BE FOUND, thus HIS and the Waitresses testimony can be added to the Records. Once on this track, I believe That you can uncover CONSIDERABLY MORE evidence to sustain this----(what would you call it---SCANDAL or DISCOVERY?) You would Need a Dale Carneigie *to Maneuever these folks* into doing just as you wish. It would be cheaper than paying everyone of all these witnesses & *Much more Ethical.* The Idea Is, to the Layman type of person, utterly ridiculous. However, can you remember, all by yourself, the Date of a Newspaper in which you saw an interesting item more than 5 years ago? Or recall names of Men, their phone #'s that you saw in 1943-44.

I do hope you will consider this plan. You will Progress as Not possible in any other way. Of course, I realize that you will need a Man Who can cause people to want to have fun, to play with Hypnotism, one that can thusly dupe those he-you need to: #1 come to His Demonstrations & thus call on them to be either both "Honored" as Helping with the show & doing Him a Great favor, &/ or being part of the act for the mite of a small fee He would HAVE to be a Man of such an androit ingenuity at Manufacturing a *plausable story* on the-instant-he-sizes-up-his-"*personality-to be dealt with* THAT had cost PLENTY. The ability to convince people of an outright Lie as being the absolute truth would be one of his prime prerequisites. (Ahem.) Yes, some such skulduggery would have to be thought well out & done. THE ULTIMATE END WILL BE A TRUTH TOO HUGE, TOO FANTASTIC, TO NOT BE TOLD. A WELL FOUNDED TRUTH, BACKED UP BY UNOBFUSCATIVE PROOF POSITIVE.

I would like to find where it is that these Sailors live NOW. *It is known* that some few people can somehow tell you a mans name & His Home address UNDER HYPNOSIS EVEN THOUGH *NEVER* HAVING MET OR SEEN THE PERSON. These folks have a very high or just a high PSI factor in their make-up that can be intensified under stress or strain OR that usually is intensified under extreme fright. It also can be RE-intensified by Hypnosis, thus is like reading from the Encyclopedia Brittanica. Even though that Barroom- Restaurant Raid was staged by invisible or partly invisible men, those men *CAN SEE EACH OTHER* THUS NAMES, in the excitement, were sure to have been Mentioned, whether last or first Names or Nicknames. A check of the Naval Yards Dispensories or Hospital or aid stations or prison RECORDS of that particular day that the Barroom-Restaurant occured May reveal the EXACT NAMES OF PRECISELY WHO WERE THE MEN, THEIR SERVICE SERIAL NUMBERS & THUS THE INFORMATION ON WHERE THEY ARE FROM BE SECURED & by adroit "maneuvuerings" of those still at Home, THE NAME OF *THE PLACE* where they are at present can be secured.

> HOW WOULD YOU LIKE TO ACTUALLY SPEAK TO (or some of THE MEN) A MAN WHO WAS ONCE *AN INVISIBLE HUMAN BEING?* (MAY BECOME SO IN FRONT OF YOUR VERY EYES IF HE TURNS OFF HIS HIP-SET). Well, all this fantastically Preposterous sort of rubbish *will be* necessary, Just to do that, the Hypnotist-psychologist & all that. Maybe I suggest something too thorough & too Methodical for your taste but then, I, as first subject, Don't care to be Hypnotised at all. But too, feel that certain pull of curiosity about this thing that, to me, is irresistable. I *want* to crack this thing wide open. My reasons are simply to enable *more work* to be done upon this "Field Theory."
>
> I am a star-gazer Mr. Jessup. I make no bones about this and the fact that I feel that *IF HANDLED PROPERLY, I.E. PRESENTED TO PEOPLE & SCIENCE IN THE PROPER PSCHOLOGICALLY EFFECTIVE MANNER,* I feel sure that Man will go where He now dreams of being---to the stars via the form of transport that the Navy accidentally stumbled upon (to their embarrassment) when their EXP. SHIP took off & popped-up a minute or so later on several Hundred sea travel-trip miles away at another of its berths in Cheasapeake Bay area. I read of this in another newspaper & only by Hypnosis could *any* Man remember *all* the details of which paper, date of occurance & etc., you see? Eh. Perhaps already, the Navy has used this accident of transport to build your UFO's. It is a logical advance from any standpoint. What do *you* think ??

One could conclude from the beginning of the letter that Jessup had asked for some specific hard cold facts. He could even have been looking for the actual equipment design. What he got back as an answer was: "I can't give you those things, but how about truth serum and hypnosis?" Allen's answer was too fantastic to believe and since he provided no new information, Jessup disregarded these letters as ramblings from a crazy person with a fondness for UFOs. There wasn't anything else to do. Jessup was too busy raising capital to return to Mexico and resume his grand passion---those mysterious craters---than to pursue some crackpot talking about invisible ships and men. However, there were events happening elsewhere that would soon bring this fantastic story back into Jessup's life.

In late July or early August a copy of **The Case for the UFO** arrived at the Office of Naval Research (O.N.R.). However, this was not an ordinary copy. It had been sent to Admiral N. Furth in a manila envelope and across the front of it had been scribbled "Happy Easter". The book itself was well worn and contained handwritten comments at the top, bottom and margins of the pages. The comments were written in three different colors of ink as if the book had been passed back and forth between three people. The comments suggested a knowledge of UFOs, their method of propulsion, and the origin and background of the beings operating them. The book at that time fell into the possession of Major Darrell L. Ritter (U.S.M.C. Aeronautical Project Officer at O.N.R.) who took a great interest in these comments. It was obvious that a great deal of time and effort had been put into this book.

Major Ritter was also aware of the government's momentary interest in anti-gravity research, and felt that the comments about undersea cities built by two groups of extra-terrestrials (called the LMs and SMs) were quite intriguing. There were explanations for mysterious ship and plane disappearances in the Bermuda Triangle. Also included was an extensive commentary on the origins of odd storms and clouds, of objects falling from the sky, of strange marks and footprints that Jessup had written about, and many odd words (such as: "mothership", "home ship", "dead ship", "great ark", "great bombardment", "great return", "great war", "little men", "force fields", "deep freeze", "measure markers", "scout ships", "magnetic fields", "gravity fields", "sheets of diamonds", "cosmic rays", "force cutters", "inlay work", "clear talk", "telepathing", "nodes", "vortices", and "magnetic net") that were used throughout the book and which might be of some value for later research. Afterwards, Major Ritter passed the book on to two other O.N.R. officers, Commander George W. Hoover (Special Projects Officer) and Captain Sidney Sherby. These men were intimately involved in the Navy's *Project Vanguard*, the code name for the U.S. effort to develop the first artificial earth satellite.

Commander Hoover and Captain Sherby, reviewing the book, and the mysterious comments within it, invited Jessup to come to O.N.R. and discuss his book. By this time it was the spring of 1957 and 18 months had passed since the book had first arrived at the O.N.R. As Jessup read the annotated book he reportedly became more and more distressed, because the comments referred to subjects he had heard about *but which had not been mentioned* in his writings. The person or persons who had written these comments had a good understanding of the current "myths" of UFOs, extraterrestrials, and other subjects mainly the concern of psychics, cultists and mystics. Jessup became confused as to why the United States governmentwas so interested in the scribblings from such an apparently cluttered mind. As he read further he came across a comment concerning a secret Navy experiment in 1943 and immediately he knew who had been responsible for the crazed and disjointed comments.

Jessup then shared his discovery with the Naval Officers and they in turn asked if the O.N.R. could have the letters. Next they informed Jessup that a special edition of his book was being produced by them and it would include all the additions. Jessup consented to the new edition and made three additional trips to the O.N.R. concerning this matter.

Shortly after these meetings Jessup was involved in a car accident. At the same time he began experiencing marital difficulties; close friends say he was never quite the same after that. He seemed quite disturbed by the Navy experience and after receiving the promised copies of his own book he spent considerable time adding his own comments. Hoover and Shelby would, in the days to come, make many attempts to find the elusive Allende (Carl Allen) but with no success. Jessup was still confused as to why the Navy was so interested in this matter, and spent considerable time researching the details of the operation known as the "Philadelphia Experiment".

In the meantime all his efforts to get back to Mexico had come up blank, and he now devoted himself to writing and publishing. He moved back to his native Indiana and started publishing a small astrological journal. During October of 1958, Jessup left Indiana for New York on publishing business and around the 31st paid a visit to a friend, Ivan T. Sanderson, founder of the Society for the Investigation of the Unexplained (S.I.T.U.). Over dinner Jessup gave Sanderson the copy of the book he had been making notes in; Jessup, being visibly disturbed, asked Sanderson in great sincerity to read it and then lock it up for safe keeping---"In case anything should happen to me."

Jessup was scheduled to return to Indiana within a few days. When he failed to return, his publisher became concerned and contacted one of Jessups' associates concerning his whereabouts. His associate related that he had no information. Six weeks after his New York departure Jessup, was located in Florida; apparently, he had gone there from New York and had been involved in another major car accident from which he was still recovering. Jessup, during those next months, was in terrible spirits. His publisher rejected his manuscripts as being "not up to par." His writings were drawing considerable criticism from all around the country. On April 20, 1959, two years after meeting with the O.N.R., Jessup was found dead in his car close to his Florida home: a victim of carbon-monoxide poisoning. A hose had been attached to his car exhaust and passed into the passenger side window.

Jessup had killed himself. Or had he? Jessup's death has

been the subject of substantial speculation. Some of his friends have said that Jessup was not the type to kill himself. Others have suggested he was murdered when he refused to abandon his UFO research. Rumors were then circulating about the "Men In Black", the name given to government agents who allegedly visited several UFO researchers and "persuaded" them to cease and desist their work. Other friends said that Jessup was depressed about personal problems and that he had sent a suicide note to a close friend. However, the handwriting was not checked to see if it matched with Jessup's.

The truth about Morris K. Jessup will probably never be known, placing him in that same file cabinet along with Karen Silkwood, John F. Kennedy, Martin Luther King, and other humans regarding whom certain factions in our society would have an easier time of things if they were invisible or dead.

So we might ask, Did the Navy really make a Destroyer-class ship disappear and transport itself over four hundred miles of ocean in a matter of moments, or is this just some fantastic story? And if this is not just a story, why did they do it? We know by the results why the Navy might have wanted to keep things quiet. Governmental cover-ups are not new; they seem to come with the institution. Maybe we can reach a conclusion more easily if we learn more about the last day of Jessup's life.

Dr. J. Manson Valentine, an oceanographer, archaeologist, and zoologist, had been a friend of Jessups' for the last fourteen years of his life while he resided in Florida. Jessup, as we know, was very upset during the last months of his life and was reaching out more than ever to talk with someone. Dr. Valentine was that someone. It was during these last months that Jessup shared his innermost feelings about the Philadelphia Experiment with him. It's very probable that Dr. Valentine was the last person to talk with Jessup. He had spoken to Jessup on April 20, 1959, and had invited Jessup to dinner; Jessup accepted his invitation, but never showed up.

When asked, "Why do you think Jessup killed himself?", Dr. Valentine's answer was: "If he committed suicide it was probably due to extreme depression. He had been approached by the Navy to continue working on the Philadelphia Experiment or similar projects, but had declined, as he was worried about its dangerous ramifications... Perhaps he could have been saved. He was still alive when he was found .... Perhaps he was allowed to die." Dr. Valentine went on to say that Jessup had researched the question of the Philadelphia Experiment, "pretty thoroughly. You must remember that he was not a crank writer, but a distinguished and famous scientist."

Dr. Valentine remembers Jessup relating some strange things he had learned concerning the Navy's experiment. Jessup said the invisibility effect had been accomplished by using magnetic field generators, called degaussers, which were "pulsed" at resonant frequencies to create a huge magnetic field around the Destroyer. In Dr. Valentine's opinion Jessup was well informed of the alleged experiment and had met with the Navy officers and scientists several times. He had said to Dr. Valentine: "The experiment is very interesting but awfully dangerous. It is too hard on the people involved. This use of magnetic resonance is tantamount to temporary obliteration in our dimension but it tends to get out of control. Actually, it is equivalent to a transference of matter into another level or dimension, and could represent a dimensional breakthrough if it were possible to control it."

According to Valentine, Jessup believed he was "on the verge of discovering the scientific basis for whatever was happening." Jessup explained: "An electric field created in a coil induces a magnetic field at right angles to the first, and each of these fields represents one plane of space. But since there are three planes of space, there must be a third field, perhaps a gravitational one. By hooking up electromagnetic generators so as to produce a magnetic pulse it might be possible to produce this third field through the principle of resonance." Jessup thought the Navy had discovered this by accident.

This brings up the interesting possibility of a fourth dimension. It is known, by abstract mathematics, that it is possible to have as many as fifteen dimensions. If they exist as a mathematical *concept*, they exist in *fact* (according to Pythagoras). It is a widely held belief among scientists that basic atomic structure is essentially electric in nature rather than material. A vast interplay of energies is involved. This concept gives us great flexibility in visualizing the universe such that if multiple phases of matter don't exist it would be quite surprising.

The transition from one phase (our world), to another world would be equivalent to the passage from one plane of existence to another in a sort of interdimensional metamorphosis. It is a case of worlds within worlds. Magnetism is thought to be the key factor in the control of these dimensional changes. Magnetism is the only phenomenon for which scientists have no mechanical explanation. We can visualize electrons travelling along a wire to create electric current, and we can envision waves of different frequencies to create heat, light and radio.

But a magnetic field defies mechanical interpretation. In addition, when UFOs do their materializations/dematerializations, intense magnetic disturbances are always present.

With these thoughts in mind let's see how the concept of a "World Grid" could be a key factor in the location and function of the alleged Philadelphia Experiment.

The Philadelphia Experiment is fantastic because it disturbs our sense of what we *think* exists in a particular time and space. And when we speak of space and time, we invariably think of Einstein. Jessup believed Einstein's theories held the key to UFO propulsion; after all, Carl Allen had confirmed that it not only was the key but full scale research and experimentation of Einstein's mysterious mathematical concepts was already a reality.

Researching Naval employment records we find that Albert Einstein was hired as a Scientist for the Office of Naval Research (O.N.R.) on May 31, 1943, a post he maintained until June 30, 1944. Also on July 24, 1943, Einstein met with Naval Officers in his Princeton study---just three months prior to the Philadelphia Experiment.

One way to cross the tremendous distances of space would be to alter the structure of space itself. This could be accomplished by modifying the space-time geometric matrix. It is this matrix that gives us the illusion of form and distance. One method of changing the matrix is through the modification of frequencies controlling the matter-antimatter cycles. These in turn control our perceptions of things existing in apparent space-time. Einstein's premise is that time is a geometric concept; therefore, if this could be altered, then all of the universe would become available to us at any single moment.

In one second we could travel great distances, for at that point distance would be revealed as an illusion. According to a prevalent view, Time is the factor that keeps objects apart in space. With the possibility of moving from place to place in what is called "Zero Time", then both places exist *in* the same place according to our perception. By speeding up the geometric of time we are able to bring distant objects closer together. This is the secret of extra-terrestrial spacecraft; they travel by altering the space dimension by bringing time to zero.

Einstein believed that physical matter was nothing more than a concentrated field of force. What we see visually as a physical substance is in actuality a combination (or four-dimensional matrix) of frequencies. Different frequencies combine in different ways thus creating different physical masses. These masses seem solid to us because we are also

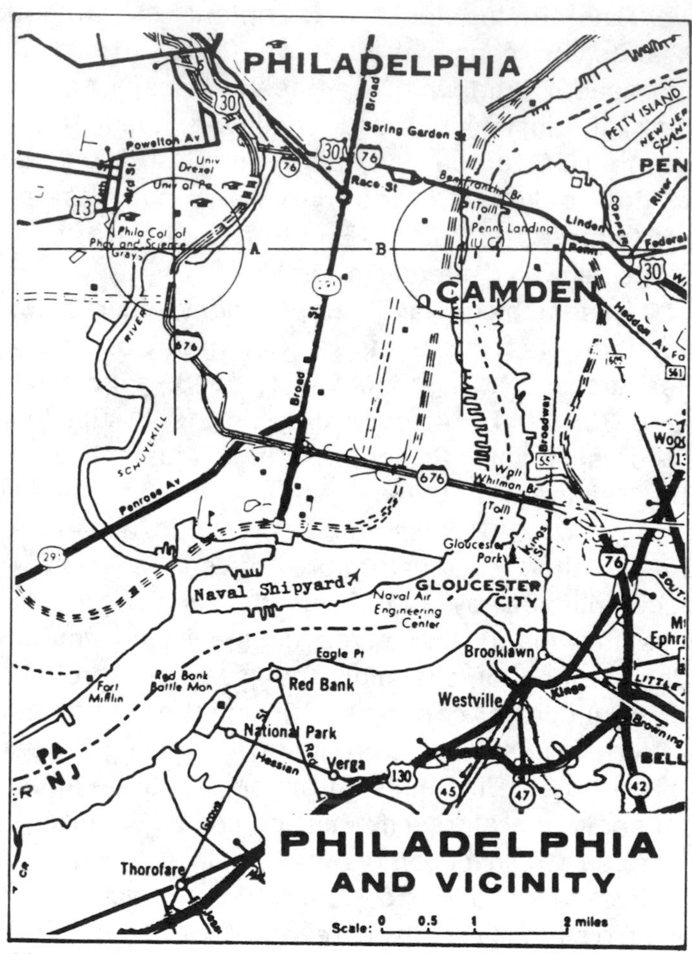

Position A: Theoretical experimental site in the vicinity of the Philadelphia College of Science.

Position B: Theoretical experimental site in the vicinity of Penn's Landing.

Latitude A — B = 143795.77 seconds of arc north. The speed of light harmonic at the earth's surface.

made up of similar wave-forms which vibrate within a defined band-width, and this band-width makes up the limited perspective of our visual, physical world.

In the famous equation **$E=MC^2$, M**, the value for mass, can be replaced by a value representing a specific waveform. According to Bruce Cathie's mathematics of the world grid, the substituted term is a function of the velocity of Light.

Einstein $E=MC^2$

Cathie grid $M=C+\sqrt{1/C}$

Therefore $E=(C+\sqrt{1/C})\ C^2$ **(Harmonic equation 1)**

Within this unified field equation, expressed in terms of pure electromagnetic energy, lies the key to the universe: the whole of existence, the seen and unseen, forms, solids, liquids and gases, the stars and the blackness of space itself. All is perceived to consist of visible and invisible waves of light. All of creation is Light.

The earth is simply a huge magnet wound with magnetic lines of force. The coils are 1,725 cm^2 in one direction and 1,850 cm^2 in the other. These lines of force form a grid pattern due to the spin of our planet. At any given point there are a trillion lines of force crossing and creating small vortices. Each vortex manifests as an atomic structure and creates within itself a gravitational field. The gravitational field is nothing more than the effect of relative motion in space. Matter is drawn towards a gravitational field, just as a piece of wood is drawn into a whirlpool. The gravitational fields created by the vortexual action of every atom combine to form the complete field of our planet Earth. The lattice matrix of the world grid is the natural grid formed by these interlocking lines of force.

(*Editor's Note* : Actually, the magnetic field density at the surface of the Earth, in gauss, is approximately 0.5 lines per cm^2.)

The basic unit for harmonic calculation in relation to this grid is the **geodetic inch**, or 0.172 minutes of arc, one minute of arc being 6,000 geodetic feet. By taking the values of 1,725 and 1,850 per cm^2 and calculating the field strengths for one square geodetic inch, the field density is found to be 8,326.71764 and 12,255.08864, respectively. When the fields are in opposition, the combined field density is 20,581.80628

The Pantagraph

Thursday, August 21, 1986

Bloomington-Normal, Illinois

Navy has lots of tricks to make carriers disappear

WASHINGTON, D.C. (AP) — U.S. Navy aircraft carriers, despite their incredible size, are becoming adept at a form of magic.

Utilizing weather, speed, advanced logistical planning and high-tech tomfoolery, several carriers in recent months have managed to vanish from antagonists' eyes into the vastness of the oceans, reappearing only at the moment of attack.

Last April, dogged by airplanes rented by American television networks and by Soviet intelligence vessels, the carriers Coral Sea and America dropped from sight off the coast of Sicily. Less than 24 hours later, their planes bombed targets in Libya.

And just over a month ago, a much lengthier case of a "missing" carrier occurred during an exercise named RIMPAC 86. The USS Ranger, although the target of an intense search that included satellite reconnaissance, escaped detection for two weeks while sailing across the Pacific.

The performance was considered all the more remarkable by an Australian admiral who monitored the exercise because the carrier's planes were flying sorties throughout the period, staging mock attacks against surface ships, submarines and land targets.

Rear Adm. I.W. Knox of the Royal Australian Navy disclosed recently the "Orange" forces in RIMPAC could not locate the Ranger "from the time it departed Southern Californian exercise areas until it steamed into Pearl Harbor some 14 days later."

Reports of such exploits delight Navy brass, who must answer critics who think carriers are sitting ducks in an age of nuclear-powered submarines and cruise missiles.

Modern-day carriers have yet to be tested in combat against Soviet weaponry. But they are practicing hard at what the Navy calls "maneuver strategy" — if the enemy can't find you, you have surprise. And with surprise, you can win.

Navy spokesmen decline to discuss the war-fighting tactics, citing military secrecy. But several officers interviewed recently, who asked not to be identified, say the idea of a "stealthy carrier" is not so far-fetched.

Consider:

- The Coral Sea and America accomplished their feats through a variety of tricks, but the most important were "masking" and "EMCON." The details of masking are classified, but essentially it involves making another ship — a destroyer, for example — look and sound like a carrier and a carrier look like something else.

Please see CARRIERS, page A5

CARRIERS

From A1

The process normally begins when a carrier is under radar surveillance, but beyond visual sight. The decoy ship maintains the carrier's previous course, while the carrier speeds away.

"We can make the Soviets believe another ship is the carrier," says one official. "The radar image, broadcasting pilot talk and the radio sounds of flight operations, the lighting at night: It looks like a duck and sounds like a duck so it must be a duck. So they follow the duck and make a mistake."

The carrier, meantime, can employ lighting at night that makes it look like a tanker.

• Also employed by the Coral Sea and America, and the key to the Ranger's disappearing act, was EMCON. This is the equivalent of a submarine "rigging for silence" or a convoy traveling under blackout conditions.

EMCON is a Navy acronym for emission control. Emission, in this case, refers to the electronic signals that are radiated by such equipment as radars, sonar and radio. When a carrier goes to EMCON, it literally shuts down much of its electronic gear to avoid detection.

Navy officials say a carrier can operate for long periods in EMCON because "we go mute, but not deaf or blind."

The procedure works by utilizing E2-C Hawkeye radar planes, flying at some distance from the carrier. Everything the Hawkeye sees is relayed electronically to the carrier and its escorts, providing a picture of aerial activity as well as surface forces.

While transmitting, the Hawkeye is far from the carrier, which gets the plane's signals passively without any transmission of its own. The Hawkeye also takes on the role of air-traffic controller for the carrier's planes.

Replenishment oilers, meantime, are told well in advance to make their own way to a specific position in the ocean. Again, radio silence is maintained.

• Aviation tactics. Even if radar can't pick up a carrier sailing beyond the horizon, the ship's location can be betrayed by jet aircraft scrambling into the air. The Navy's answer is called "offset vector."

"To be simplistic, the planes don't climb," says one officer. "They catapult off and literally hit the deck. If planes are suddenly popping up 100 miles from the ship, you have no idea where they came from."

— Speed. Publicly, the Navy says its carriers are capable of speeds "in excess of 30 knots." Privately, officers acknowledge the floating cities can approach 40 knots.

"We can literally outrun the Soviet tattletales (intelligence ships)," says one. "And in (heavy) weather of any kind, there's no contest. The carrier can outrun its own escorts."

— Weather and Satellites. Anyone who's been caught in the rain after the weatherman forecast sunny skies has his own thoughts on meteorology. But there have been solid gains made within that science in recent years.

"Although really heavy weather can hurt flight operations, these guys know how to follow weather patterns and use rain storms and above all, cloud cover," says one official. "The carriers can receive weather data via satellite, passively, without portraying their position."

"And we know the orbital parameters of Soviet reconnaissance satellites as well as our own," adds another. "If there's a recon bird coming by and you can duck into some weather, you duck into the weather. Or if you know there's a blind spot in coverage, you sail there."

"Once you succeed in slipping away," summarizes one officer, "the odds shift in your favor. Most people don't have any conception of how big the oceans are. You can be lonely if you want."

for one square geodetic inch. The difference in field strengths is calculated to be 12,255.08864 minus 83,26.71764 which equals 3,928.371. From this we can say that the resultant field density one way is field *A* minus field *B* or 3,928.371 lines of force per cm^2. This value is the reciprocal of 1/2 the distance of the polar grid square size.

We can now formulate another equation in order to demonstrate the association of the Earth's magnetic field with the speed of light.

Please note that 144,000 is a speed of light harmonic value in free space. The figure of 143,900 minutes of arc grid per second will be explained below.

Harmonic Equation 2

Field (A - B)=(2C + √1/2C) (2C)2= 3,928.371

Where C= 144,000 - 90.9345139
= 143,909.0655

The value of 90.9345139 is of interest because

$$90.9345139 = \frac{3{,}928.371}{432}$$

The reduction in the speed of light is equal in harmonic terms to the resultant field strength divided by the radius of the spherical mass. In this case the radius is equivalent to the distance in minutes of arc, from the Earth's center to the average height of the atmosphere (432 being a harmonic of 4,320 minutes of arc).

We can now generate another equation by inserting the value for the speed of light at the Earth's surface. By mathematical conversion this was found to be 143,795.77 minutes of arc per grid second, where one grid second was 1/972,000 part of the time taken for one revolution of the Earth.

Harmonic Equation 3

2,693,645 =√(2C +√1/2C) (2C)2
Where C = (144,000 - 204.23) = 143,795.7
(Harmonic of the speed of light at the surface of the Earth.)

Theoretical geometric pattern for the Philadelphia Experiment.

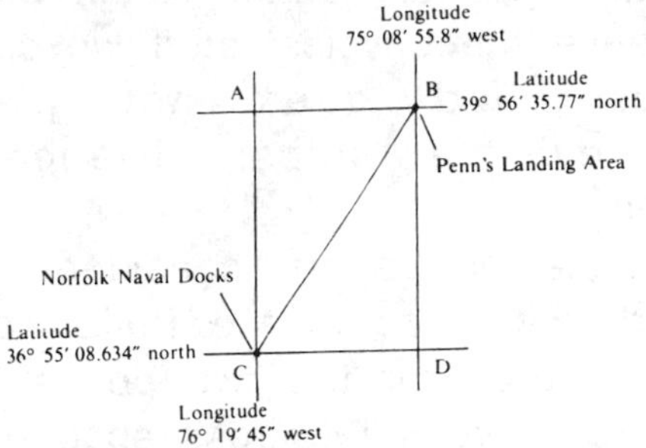

Latitude 39° 56′ 35.77″ = 143795.77 minutes of arc north, which is equal to the harmonic of the speed of light at the earth's surface.

Dislplacement of Norfolk position from North Pole	= 53.080935 degrees
Displacement of Norfolk position from Equator	= 36.919065 degrees
Difference	= 16.16187 degrees
Divided by 60	= 0.2693645 harmonic

Distance B — C = 189.7366596 minutes of arc = 3.16227766 degrees. This number group has its own mirror image reciprocal. The circular area swept out by a wave-front of this radius would be harmonically equal to Pi, or 3.141592654.

Latitude displacement A — C = 181.452266 minutes of arc. The square root of this number equals 13.47042 which is a harmonic of electron spacing in the atomic nucleus.

Longitude displacement C — D = 1.1803288 degrees. The reciprocal of this value equals 0.8472215. Double this value equals 1.694443 harmonic.

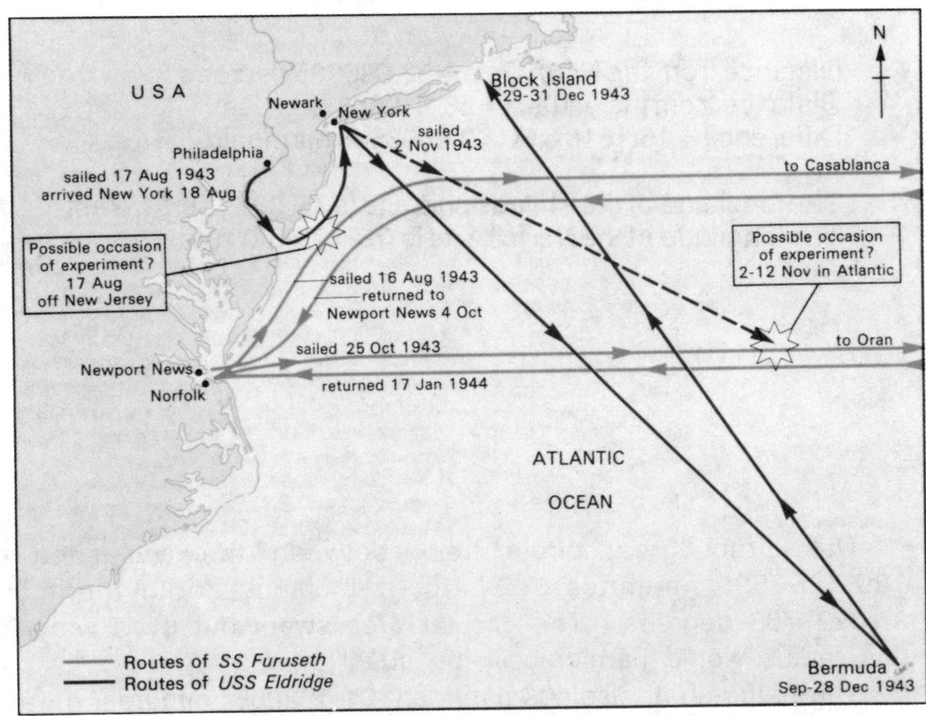

Now, let's surmise that as the harmonic of light decreases, the energy which is being released converts its form into physical matter. You wouldn't think that the universe would leave to chance the physical stuff we call reality. As Einstein once said, "God does not play dice with the universe!"---invisible ships, disappearing men, reality, notwithstanding. . . .

Bruce Cathie has spent considerable time studying the latitudes and longitudes of the Philadelphia and Norfolk Navy Yards in a search for the two points that were harmonically correct for the movement across space-time.

The latitude of the Philadelphia Naval Base, namely, 39° 56' 35.77" North, set up a prime harmonic of the speed of light, which was 143,795.77 seconds of arc. It is an interesting coincidence that the College of Science was established at this latitude. This latitude is equivalent to 143,795.77 seconds of arc North. The latitude in the Norfolk area is 36° 55' 08" North.

Distance from the North Pole = 53.080935 degrees
Distance from the equator= 36.919065 degrees
Difference = 16.1618 ÷ 60 = 0.2693645 harmonic

The longitude of the Philadelphia site is 75° 08' 55.8" West
The longitude of the Norfolk site is 76° 19' 45.0" West

The direct great circle track between the two sites is 189.7366596 minutes of arc, which is equivalent to 3.16227766 degrees. The circular area swept out by a wave of this radius would harmonically be equal to π.

The latitudinal displacement is 181.452266 minutes of arc. The square root of this number equals 13.47042, which is a harmonic of the electron spacing in the atomic nucleus.

The longitudinal spacing would equal 1.1803288 degrees. The reciprocal of this number is 0.8472215; when doubled this number yields the 1.694443 harmonic.

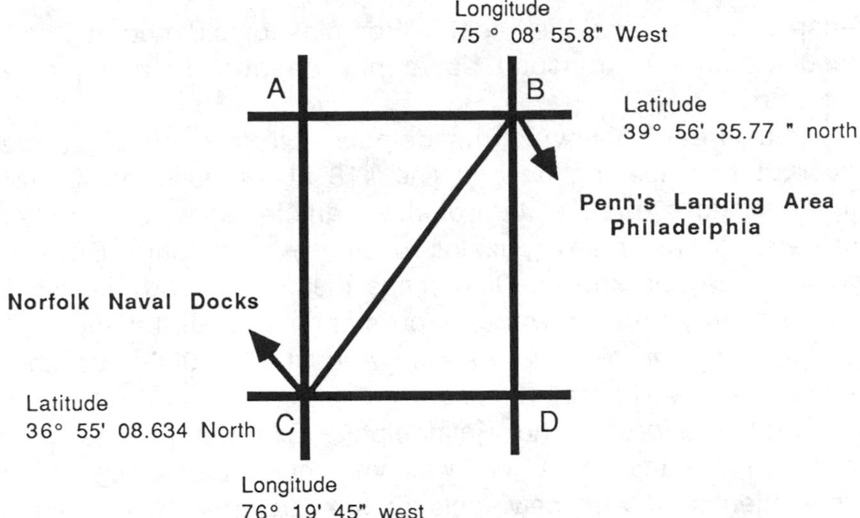

Another interesting coincidence exists here. Line B-C in the diagram is very close to and parallel with grid line #18 on the Becker-Hagens world grid system (See their chapter "The Planetary Grid: A New Synthesis," above). This line connects the Philadelphia docks and the Norfolk docks with the Bermuda Triangle. Could it be that the vessel in its dematerialized state was actually on this grid line? Could it be that the energy that makes all this possible is a magnetic field transmitted at the correct frequency by the powerful field generators aboard the ship?

Maybe it is true that the Navy scientists didn't expect what resulted from their unique experiment; maybe, in fact, the results were terribly counter to the desired effects. If indeed the goal had been just to make the ships invisible to radar (similar to modern day Stealth systems), or to magnetically repel torpedos, perhaps instead the Navy found something of much greater import than anyone had ever imagined.

It seems to me that the experiment was just that---an experiment. We will never know what the true purpose of this experiment was. The purpose of the last experiment in the series was most likely the actual transport of the ship, a possibility the Navy might have learned of through earlier tests. But originally they were looking for radar invisibility or a magnetic torpedo/mine shield. The War was going to be won on the sea and thus the opportunistic Navy exploited Einstein's misgivings about the rise of Nazi Germany to persuade him to assist the U.S. government in developing a passive protection device. In the process they found incredible mysteries regarding pulsating magnetic fields, and through the course of their experimentations, literally led themselves into matter transport. Perhaps the most incredible coincidence is that the presumed matter transport apparently happened along a world grid line.

I can hear it now: "Philadelphia---Norfolk physical matter transport now leaving on grid line #18 at 1400 Greenwich Mean Time. Visitors please board the vehicle at this time." The answers to the many puzzles of the Philadelphia Experiment will some day be known. Or perhaps they are already known by a few. Anyway the mystique persists. The following article appeared in *The Pantagraph* on August 21, 1986, published in Bloomington - Normal, Illinois.

(*Editor's Note* : The Philadelphia Experiment has been a mystery for many years. We welcome the reader's comments on this subject and any new facts or speculations they might have so that this continuing enigma can finally be solved.)

Ley Lines and the Meaning of Adam

by

Richard Leviton

"As Above, So Below" ---Hermes Trismegistos

Hermes' Geomancy

Looming behind all concepts of the planetary Grid stands the ancient magus, Hermes Trismegistos, Thrice-Greatest Master Geomancer of Earth, with his Smagdarine Emerald Tablets, the keys to Gaia's (Earth's) energy body. That same master Grid engineer, the Gods' messenger for Earth, later passed the flame of his mastery, for our time, to the Archangel Michael with his solar initiatory sword. Michael, say the Hebrews, is the Keeper of the Secrets of the Relations between Heaven and Earth---the nurturing bond of geomancy. The message of both Hermes and Michael to us today as neophyte Grid engineers is this: The Grid is the paramount spiritual phenomenon of Earth.

Our Ariadne's thread out of this bewildering maze of physical life on Earth is the ley line. The rediscovery of ley lines in this century is only a fragment, however, of the eventual unveiling of the secrets of Nature. Ley lines are the luminous strands that many are pulling at today, hardly suspecting what riches lie at the end of these subtle light lines. All ley lines lead to the planetary Grid, the primary light and energy matrix, creating, enveloping, and maintaining planet Earth, our Gaia.

The Grid has been variously described by poets and clairvoyants in recent times. Ley lines are "the radial threads on a spider's web."[1] Ley lines form the "focal points in a vast multilayered cobweb somewhat reminiscent of a micrograph of nerve cells and their ganglia" as "the circulation and nervous system of the body of earth." [2] The Grid is "a geometrically precise web" punctuated with "Grids of Light, focal points," a "receptor web complex with nexi of entrance." [3] The British novelist Doris Lessing writes intimately of the Grid as "the enclosing web of subtle light (that) touched the earth globe...All over the globe ran these pulses or lines" which make "a colored spinning membrane" and "a great web of patterning oscillations and quiverings." [4] A personal acquaintance of mine in England summed it up lucidly: "I saw the Earth as a fishnet web of light lines. My body was the same, and there were lines of light radiating from the intersections of the planet's surface to link with the web network surrounding other planets."

The Hermetic Keys to the planetary Grid are inscribed on the

Messenger's mythical Emerald Tablets, which summarise the 7 Hermetic Principles underlying all manifestation. These are the keys to Hermes' Geomancy: The Principle of Mentalism (The Universe is Mental, the All is Infinite Mind, which is the fundamental reality and the womb of all universes). The Principle of Correspondence (Whatever is Below is like unto that which is Above, and whatever is Above is like that which is Below, to accomplish the miracles of The One). The Principle of Vibration (Nothing rests; everything moves and vibrates). The Principle of Polarity (Everything is dual, has poles, and pairs of opposites). The Principle of Rhythm (Everything has its tides, its rise and fall, its equal pendulum swings to the right and left, its peaks and troughs). The Principle of Causation (Every effect has its Cause, every Cause has its Effect, all proceeding by Law, never by chance). The Principle of Gender (Everything has its "masculine" and "feminine" aspects). [5]

Experiential knowledge of Hermes' principles through meditative interfacing with the Earth Grid leads us into the secrets of geomancy. The Grid is not something *out there* , away from us, safely, abstractly separate from our daily lives. Our molecular bodies and human consciousness as we walk on Earth live within the Grid. The Grid is like a unified tuning fork vibrating with our Light/Life/Electromagnetic spectrum for Earth as we receive it daily from our specific Star Evolution paradigm, the Sun, the astrophysical center of our local solar system Grid. Our King Sun is an evolving star, and our lives as humans on Earth are breathed within the Grid-mediated parameters of "His" body, our familiar solar system.

The Grid is the forgotten nexus between humankind, as embodied, Earth-walking consciousness, and the starry heavens. The Grid is the spiritual link for the blending of cosmic and terrestrial energies in the consciousness experiment known as Humanity; it is the pervasive means for the harmonious fusion of the energies of the solar system in human consciousness. The Grid actually predates physical Earth and is more like Mother Gaia's exterior skeletal energy structure, her prototypal design and predetermined matrix of energy and light from which her physical body was manifested. Our relations as embodied humans with the Star Evolution we call the Sun is mediated through the Grid enveloping Earth.

The key word here is **homologous**. The human body is conical, rectangular, while the Earth's body is spherical; yet Hermes speaks truthfully when he says, As Above, So Below. What exists in Heaven is embodied on Earth and in the Human but in specific manners appropriate to the morphology. This is the meaning of "equal Logos" (homo-logous),i.e., the same Word. Just as the human has an intricate subway system of acupuncture meridians, carrying *ch'i*, the life force, so has the Earth a myriad weblike matrix of ley lines and focal points,

Geomancy and somamancy are two more pivotal Grid-explicating words. **Geomancy** initially means "divination of the Earth's secrets" (From the Greek, Gaia-mantos), but after a meditative experience with the planetary Grid, the word emerges for us into its larger meaning as "*divinization* of the Earth," because positive, loving human consciousness interfacing with the Heaven-bestowed Grid completes its intended divinization process. **Somamancy** (Greek: body-mantos) is the equivalent word operating in the human dimension. As we breathe meditatively with Love from Above, which is the fundamental energy behind light and matter, at focal points on the Grid, not only do we bring the Earth's light lines into clarity, we manifest our own inherent divinity, perceive our own bodily ley lines, and come to embody, knowingly, somamantically, this inseverable nexus between the Earth, cosmos, and human. Another name for this nexus is the Grid. Thus geomancy and somamancy are two sides of the same coin. When we harmonise and enlighten *geo*, we do reciprocally the same for *soma*.

Eastern esoteric yoga informs us that the human has not only the apparent physical body, but a series of overlapping, multidimensional bodies which form a kind of Jacob's Ladder away from the familiar body of bones and flesh into the Body of Light. These bodies are variously described according to different traditions, but essentially they include the etheric/electromagnetic body (seat of the meridians and chakras), the emotional body (or astral body, the basic formative dimension for emotions as polarised expressions), the mental body (the sphere of abstract knowledge and concrete thinking, the realm of Forms), and the causal body (seat of the Soul, the timeless, spiritualized agent behind sequential human incarnations).

These 5 Bodies form an interpenetrating consciousness grid, like a series of Chinese boxes,or like the layers of an onion, with always another inside. The Earth, similarly, has this multidimensional overlay of grid bodies. This convenient, linear abstraction of what is indivisible, whole, simultaneous, and synchronous, is nonetheless useful as a model in explaining the different functional aspects of the planetary Grid. Thus we begin with an examination of Gaia's 5 Grid Bodies.

Diagram 1

Human Acupuncture Chart Showing Meridians and Points

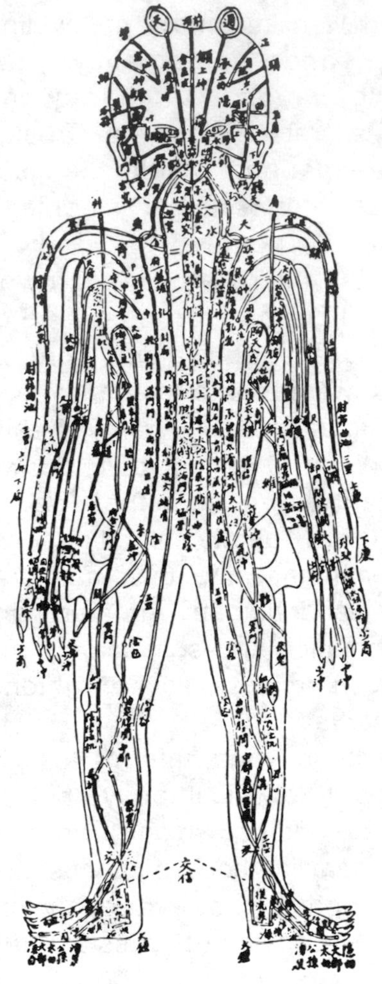

(From: *Acupuncture,* Marc Duke, Pyramid House, New York, 1972, p. 127)

The Electromagnetic 1746 Grid

This grid, the first dimensional expression away from the physical Earth, is the foundation of the material Earth and what *Ecclesiastes* called "the Golden Bowl." It is an etheric energy duplicate, though more subtle, of the physical, whether human or planetary, and it is here that most contemporary geomancers, dowsers, and ley hunters are conducting their investigations. This body vitalises and energises the physical. It is the clearinghouse for all in-coming energy fields and transmits them intelligently to the organic body matrices (organs or power points). It is the channel for physically-focussed consciousness to register the subtle worlds of energy and influence.

Through the electromagnetic body course the acupuncture meridians, the yin (negative, feminine) and yang (positive, masculine) polarised channels for the "two breaths of *ch'i*," the pervasive life energy, as catalogued by the ancient Chinese. These meridians traverse the physical Earth and human body in an intricate though rationally precise matrix, visually resembling something like the New York City subway system at its most obtuse (Diagram 1). Acupuncturists speak of 10 organ-related (and 2 affiliate) channels, 15 *Luo* that connect these major meridians, the 8 Strange Flow channels, the 12 muscle meridians---such that as many as 59 "rivers of *ch'i* " are documented in advanced Chinese medical texts, with a minimum of 365 treatment points (or subway stops) but with up to 1000 points potentially available and sometimes used.

Correspondingly the venerable Chinese geomancers, practicing *feng shui*, the elusive landscape science of "wind and water", delineated the terrestrial *lung mei* ("dragon paths" or ley lines) which flowed either as a white yang tiger in the high mountains or as a yin blue dragon in the low hills and valleys. Where the two *lung mei* (the "two breaths of *ch'i*") met and became one, this was a power point node, full of *ch'i* and suitable for a royal grave or temple. The masters of *feng shui* then intelligently placed their acupuncture "needles of stone" at these key power fusion points to clarify, harmonise, energise, and distribute the terrestrial *ch'i* in the Grid in accordance with daily, weekly, monthly, seasonal, and yearly calendars---which is precisely what the acupuncturist does with her assortment of tiny needles and treatment maps of the human body.

This is our conceptual background for entering the Electromagnetic 1746 Grid. The first key aspect of this grid is the treatment nodes, or power points, in the meridian system. These have been variously described by "Earth Mysteries" writers as energy cells, coordination points, exit points, energy vortices, time portals, subtle digestive systems. A more accurate name is **domes** because this clearly, though controversially, reflects the origin and purpose of these landscape energy centers.

There is on the Earth, state proponents of the Dome theory, a system of **dome centers,** or etheric energy canopies, occupying the space over sacred enclosures (creating them, in fact), from which extend numerous short-distance straight-running and spiralling **dome lines** of light radiating out over the landscape. The dome lines link the dome centers with each other in a subtle communications grid. The subtle landscape is characterized as an intricate pattern of spirals, straight lines, and pulsing circles of light, like a couple thousand blinking thimbles of multihued Light dotting the Earth in a geometric web of ribbony filaments flowing outwards in all directions. The Domes made the etheric structure of Earth what it is by imposing a conscious matrix upon the planet to make Earth a place for possible human conscious evolution.

According to Dome theory, when the Domes appeared on Earth they activated lines of light and energy already present in the etheric skeletal web of the planet. The Domes were Ships brought here as a response from what is called the Architect of Cosmic Destiny and in line with past proposals and future events for Earth. Technically, it's not accurate to say the Domes *came* and *went* because they exist spatially in between spirit and matter. However, they were present on Earth three times in planetary history. It is also not accurate to construe the Domes as mechanical material vehicles according to our customary understanding; they are more like transdimensional magnetic/energy facilitators overlaid on the physical landscape. In the first Dome Presence, there were no humans on Earth; in the second Dome Presence there was primitive human life; and during the third Dome Presence there were some humans who could clearly see the Domes and understand their function. What these early humans saw is recounted in various ancient mythologies (notably the Irish and Sumerian) as the Houses of the Sky Gods.

When the Domes were present, which by our reckoning, was for a very long time, they imparted immediate energy/ consciousness imprints (1/4 to 1 mile in diameter) on the Earth's surface. These were permanent resonance patterns shaped like domes (or like lampshades set over hills and mountains). This is an oscillating pattern which will persist until the Earth ceases to exist or until they are reaffirmed or altered by another Dome visit. Although clairvoyants today describe these etheric energy canopies resident over many hundreds of sacred mountains and past megalithic religious enclosures (e.g., Stonehenge, Machu Picchu, Palenque, Mt. Shasta, among many examples), these are actually etheric energy memories of the once quasi-materially present Domes. Though the Domes have "left", their powerful electromagnetic energy impressions remain in place, like the persistent retinal image of a light bulb held in front of our eyes in a dark room. The simultaneous presence and nonpresence of these Domes is a paradox of energy as created by the inadequacies of our language.

Morphologically, however, the Domes were of varying sizes, capacities, and functions, arranged around the planet in a predetermined, numerically-fixed matrix according to star formations above. Their precise distribution patterning on Earth was a microcosmic reflection of esoteric macrocosmic star geometries. The "Captain" Domes, for example, distributed Love, Light, and Energy to the smaller Domes. The overriding intention of the Domes was to bring Earth to biological, sentient life. Even today, millions of years later, etheric traces of their silvery energy pipework (different from ley or dome lines)are still clairvoyantly visible on the landscape in such geomantically heightened places as Glastonbury, England. Visually, we can imagine nearly 2000 huge spherical, kinetic lampshades simultaneously descending like twinkling party hats over mountains, hills, and plateaus around the world, fitting down snugly and brightly, electrifying the Earth with their incredibly brilliant light and distributing this light through a spinning pin wheel matrix of Dome centers.

The Domes were the originating homes of ley lines, or more accurately, within this conceptual model, the **dome lines**. These exist in two forms. Straight-running dome lines (averaging in length 5-30 miles) are lines of energy connecting one dome with another making an angular light matrix around the planet. An example of this pattern is found in California with Mt. Diablo (Contra Costa County) and Mt. Tamalpais (Marin County); both of these sacred mountains (as the native Indians originally perceived them), are just outside San Francisco, domed, about 25 miles apart, and are connected by a straight dome line. The dome lines, incidentally, are pulsating energy channels with marked variations in seasonal intensity.

Each Dome had the capacity to initiate up to 48 affiliate

Diagram 2

Engineering Model for Domes and Dome Lines

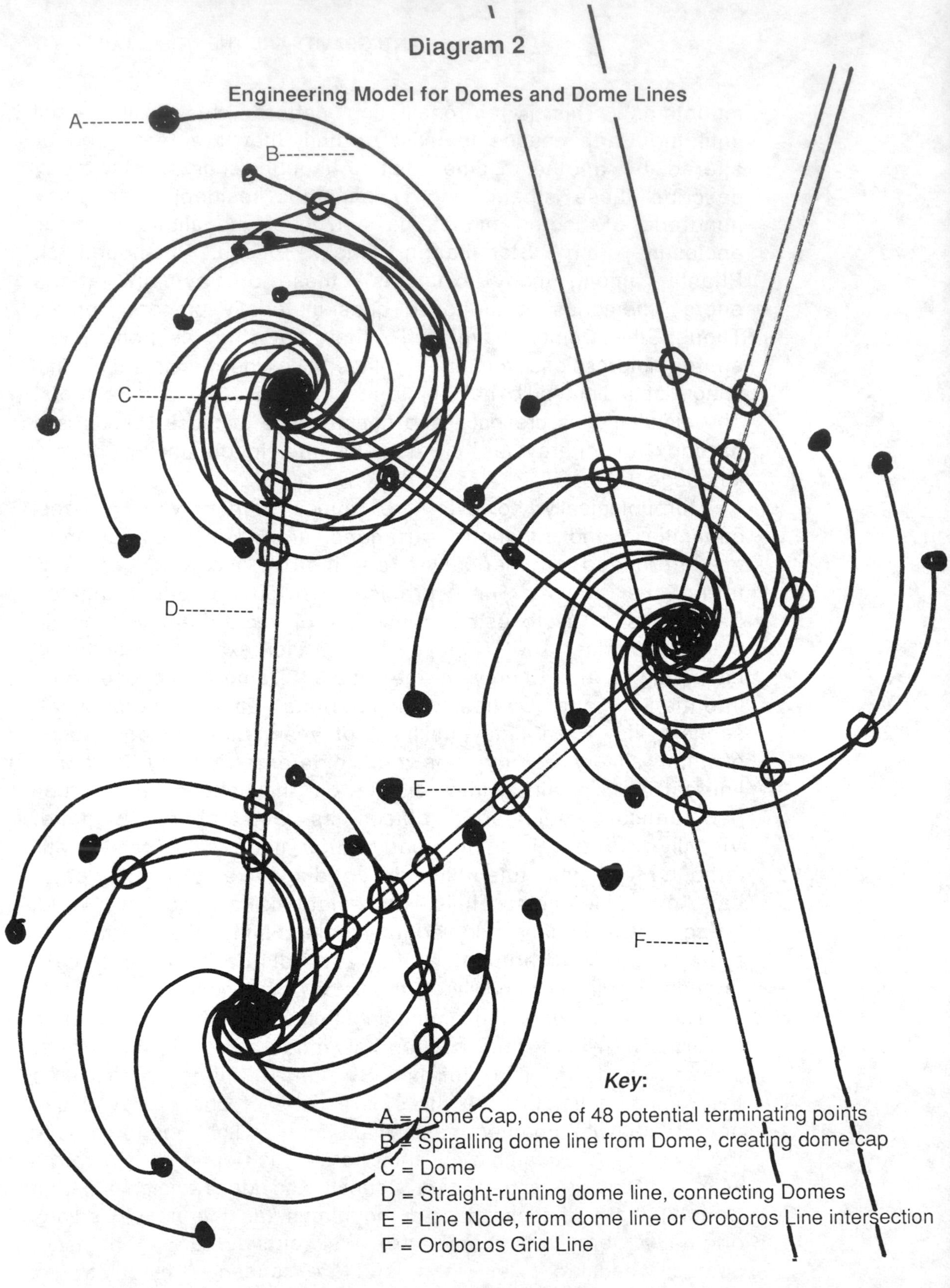

A---------

B------------

C---------------

D-----------

E--------------

F---------

***Key*:**

A = Dome Cap, one of 48 potential terminating points
B = Spiralling dome line from Dome, creating dome cap
C = Dome
D = Straight-running dome line, connecting Domes
E = Line Node, from dome line or Oroboros Line intersection
F = Oroboros Grid Line

energy centers, or smaller domes, through a series of spiralling dome lines with a smaller **dome cap** at the end. These became affiliate, spiritualized power points in the landscape,but directly related, like child to parent, with the initiating Dome. Potentially there are 83,808 such dome caps on Earth, a figure that amply explains the near planetary ubiquity of ancient religious sites. The specific radiating pattern for the spiralling dome lines was heliocentric, according to the phi ratio (or Golden Mean, Golden Proportion, Golden Section of sacred geometry, expressed as 1.618034, which is an asymmetrical spiral exemplified in the patterning whorls of the sunflower and the leaf distribution pattern for many plants and described as the Fibonacci Series). For example, Mt. Tamalpais sends out at least two dome caps into urban San Francisco, spiritually energizing the areas of the Palace of Fine Arts and Lincoln Park. The Dome at Mt. Diablo similarly sends dome caps into what are now urban Oakland and Berkeley.

Moreover, whenever any spiral or straight dome lines intersect, they form minor power points called **line nodes** (Diagram 2). These are copious, far more so than the considerably abundant dome caps, and are characterized as variously solar/positive, lunar/negative, some centrifugal, some centripedal, in effect. Domes, dome caps, and line nodes were sequentially marked by ancient geomancers with stone circles, major temples, barrows and stone chambers, and single standing stones, then afterwards in the Christian ecclesiastical ascendancy, by churches. The entire geomantic panoply was once positioned carefully as a set of Grid engineering instruments of spiritual science within this precise web of Domes, dome caps, and line nodes, energy remains of which are today being detected, increasingly, by Earth Mysteries researchers (e.g., the British Dragon Project, directed by Paul Devereaux, editor of *The Ley Hunter*). Remembered vaguely in myth, folklore, and local custom, these landscape temples, animated by Domes, linked by dome lines, may be forgotten, but they haven't been closed down.[6]

Furthermore, according to Dome theory, on a planetary basis all the Domes are linked by way of interwoven gold and silver lines which emanate like cords from their crowns, and these are joined together at one specific planetary node which is the Grid's umbilicus and Master Dome. The gold and silver cords represent the *balanced energy inputs* of positive/negative, or male/female entering each Dome. In popular mythology, this umbilical point is called King Arthur's Round Table of Camelot. The Domes were brought to Earth to create a Paradise for humankind. Each carried a light form, or seed crystal, of what was to be, both locally and globally, through the Grid. Of these Paradise crystals, some have been activated, but otherwise humankind has either not been aware of this divine potential or not bothered to make use of them to create the intended Earth Paradise. The option, however, still remains.

Because of their heightened electromagnetic fields, the Dome enclosures were like immaculate, high consciousness meditation halls where human awareness could be healed, uplifted, even interdimensionally transported through the domed exit points in the Houses of the Gods, facilitated by megalithic engineering. The Irish *Brugh na Boinne* (the House by the River Boyne) known today as the Newgrange tumulus, was the home of the Tuatha de Danann, the Irish deities, and often visited by intrepid humans seeking an audience with their Gods.

The domed coordination points in some cases contain psychic maps to the local esoteric geography. "These maps are used to provide points of resonance, release, and deflection "[7] and include details of the local layout of Domes, dome caps, line nodes, and dome lines and their energy/consciousness ratings. The Domes facilitate meditatively-acquired insight into the planetary thought matrix (what Teilhard de Chardin calls the "noosphere") which is present like a hologrammic library in the energy field of each Dome. This is why the Biblical Moses received the *Pentateuch,* or *Torah Or,* on Mt. Sinai, which was a pre-eminent sacred *domed* mountain. Furthermore, true to Hermes' Principle of Correspondence, and in a process of reciprocal inevitability, when the Domes arrived, their terrific heat brought up a dome of water from underground, with its multidirectional web of water veins, both to cool the searing Earth and to mirror the Light Dome above. Thus, even today, there are yang/centrifugal light lines and domes above ground, and yin/centripedal water lines and domes underground, etheric above, physical below. This is behind the phenomenon, constantly reported by dowsers of anomalous, copious water networks coincident with sacred enclosures.

Thus the Domes, metaphysically speaking, distributed the vibrations of Love and Light from Above through this imposed Grid system,thereby spiritually irradiating the landscape and, by extension, human consciousness, with these positive, evolutionary energies. This is the key: Before Adam, the Elohim. The meaning of this gnomic statement will emerge as we move through the Grid. However, the doorway for this key is expressed in a single number, i.e., the number of planetary

Diagram 3

The Human Chakra System

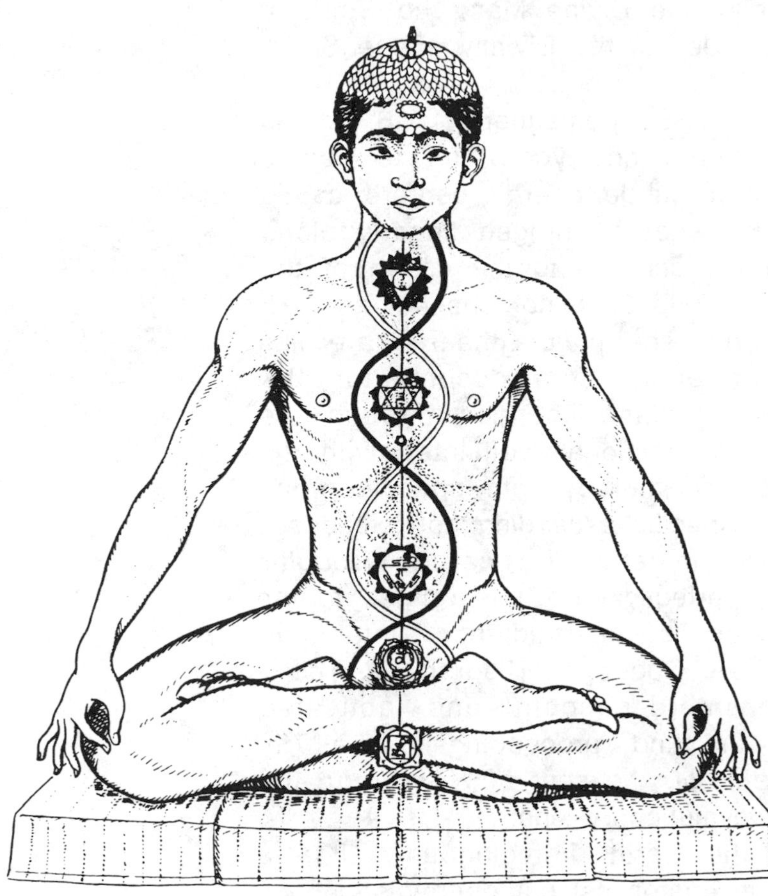

Chakras

7. Crown, *Sahasrara*

6. Brow, *Ajna*

5. Throat, *Visuddha*

4. Heart, outer, *Anahata*
inner, *Ananda-kanda*

3. Solar Plexus, *Manipura*

2. Sacral, *Svadhisthana*

1. Root, *Muladhara*

Channels

1. White spiral: *pingala nadi*, solar

2. Dark spiral: *ida nadi*, lunar

3. Central line: *sushumna nadi*, neutral

(From: *The Inner Reaches of Outer Space*, Joseph Campbell, Alfred van der Marck Editions, New York, 1986, p. 65)

Domes: **1746.** In the mystical science of Qabala and its mathematical language of gematria, this is a number of profound significance, for it is the fusion of the primary solar (666) and lunar (1080) the bipolar energies behind manifestation. In Qabala symbolism 1746 is the "grain of mustard seed" which the Christ likened to the Kingdom of Heaven; it is also, symbolically, the Divine Man, the Spirit of God on Earth, the Mysteries of Jesus, the Divinity of the Spirit, and others of similar import.

The second key aspect of the Electromagnetic 1746 Grid is **chakras.** According to esoteric Hindu yoga, in the human etheric body there are 7 major subtle energy centers called chakras (Sanskrit for "spinning wheels") ranged linearly along the vertical spinal axis from the scrotum to the crown of the head. There are anywhere from 7 to 22 minor chakras as well, distributed throughout the body. The major chakras are like electrical junction boxes, or energy transducers, for the physical body, mediating higher plane energies through the material form. The chakras are functionally affiliated with the 7 principal endocrine glands and thereby with specific organ regions of the body and with specific ascending consciousness states as well. For example, the throat chakra, called *Visuddha* (meaning "cleansed, clarified, perfectly pure.") is related to the thyroid gland and the mastery of clairaudience (intangible hearing, as in the "voices" of the Gods; see Diagram 3). The 7 chakras are energetically interdependent and activated sequentially, beginning with the 2nd, proceeding to the 7th, then returning to the 1st, the Root, the seat of *Kundalini*, the fundamental creative cosmic evolutionary energy.

Similarly in this model, the Earth, homologously, has a chakra system, arranged not in anatomical but energy sequence at 7 key Dome centers (Diagram 4). An **Earth chakra**, such as at the Great Pyramid of Giza, Egypt, or at Glastonbury Tor, England, is a huge energy vortex, several miles in immediate diameter (and extending much further in area of influence), like a two-way swinging Grid door. It is a subtle electromagnetic interface between higher, nonphysical stellar energies and the material embodiment of them in the Earth or human body. An Earth chakra may be pictured like this: Picture tiny flowers all over the Earth. Some form larger flowers and some of these form even larger flowers. Chakras are energy in one form flowing into another, like flowers opening as parts of another flower, each independent yet interdependent, similar yet dissimilar. Alternately, we can visualise a mighty wheel with many spokes. At each spoke there is a point of light. The wheel

Diagram 4

Planetary Chakras as Mapped on the Human

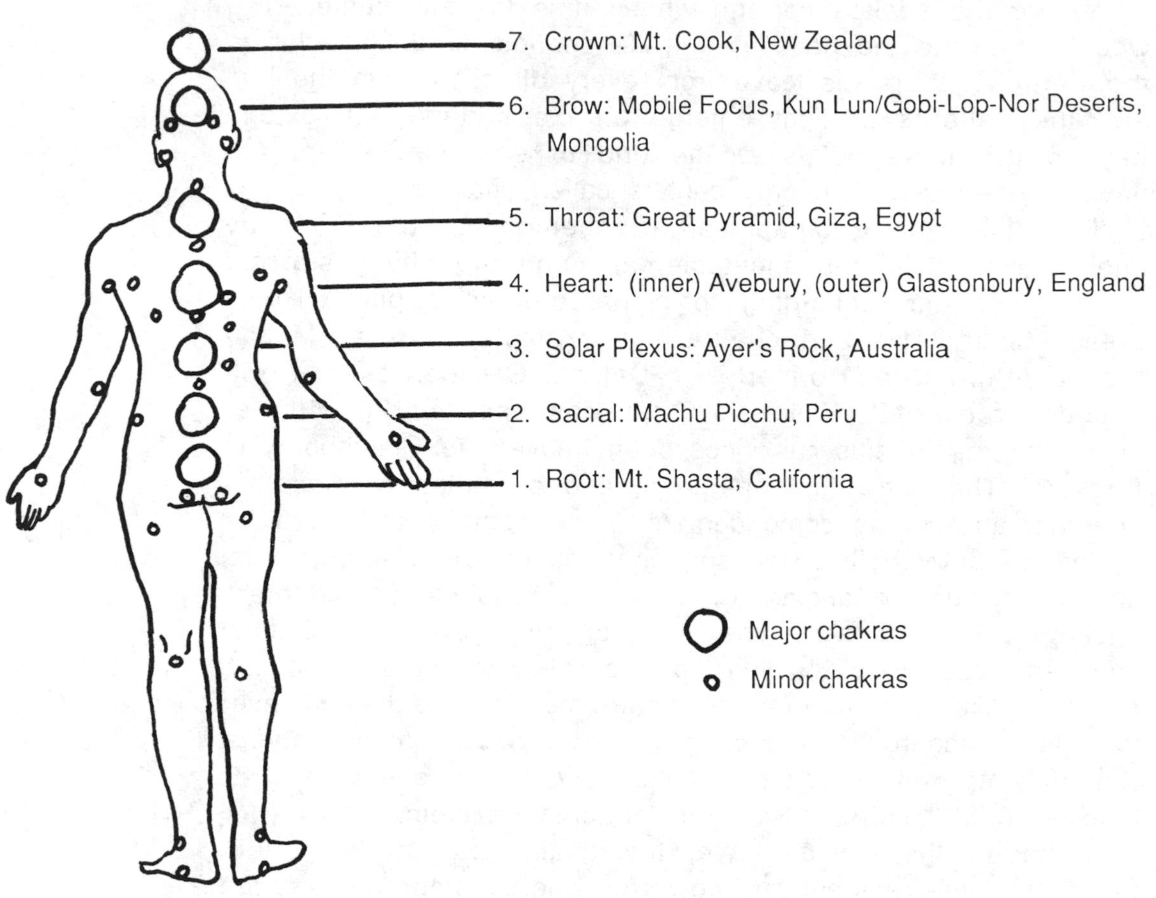

has a hub and each spoke has two ends. Each spoke is connected to the hub and to the wheel. The center of the hub is connected to neither the spokes nor the wheel; it is the still center. The wheel turns into the head of a white opened dandelion---this is the Earth. The spokes leave from every direction from the hub and the patterns of light emerge on the surface and extend beyond it. These points at the end of each spoke are the flowers, or nodes, or energy centers called chakras.

Curiously, the geographical arrangement of the planetary chakra system is not immutable, although the changes occur very slowly and according to a predetermined plan, like a preset timer. The 2nd chakra, for example, now at Machu Picchu, Peru, was formerly at Delphi, Greece, site of the famous oracle; Mt. Kailas in Tibet was once Earth's 4th, or heart chakra, but this has since been "moved" to Glastonbury in England. The activation, operation, and cessation of planetary chakras, as well as dome centers, was originally calibrated for a definite time/evolutionary sequence based on a fundamental clairvoyant understanding of the vast reaches of planetary destiny. The 6th chakra, (the Brow, or *Ajna,* discussed below) changes focus every 200 years and is called the Mobile Focus; it operates like a consciousness beam moving purposefully over the planet according to a pre-arranged schedule of activations. Presently it is focussed on Glastonbury, but at one time in its long eventful history, it was resident in Jerusalem.

Although the Domes have, technically, paradoxically, left, they are still resident as powerful energy imprints, as the Mothers of all sacred Earth enclosures. The Electromagnetic 1746 Grid, furthermore, is still operational,though at a somewhat reduced Light intensity compared to what it would be like if the Domes were materially present again. Gaia's etheric energy body remains sentiently active, just as Her living physical form breathes through its biosphere. This level of the Grid can be likened to a radio carrying the whole range of frequency transmission capabilities. The various parts of the radio band are assigned to the Dome receptor matrix, which are like individual antenna or radio towers. This is a system of Grid sonics, of tone modulations. The various Dome centers are energised as sonic receptor sites according to a graduated dial of master transmissions`. In many cases stone devices, electromagnetically-adjusted, were positioned at the Dome antenna sites to facilitate sonic reception. Not only were the Dome sites, according to this theory, calibrated planetarily in terms of radio beam receptivity, they were also calibrated in terms of a master electromagnetic spectrum geared to the consciousness and life support needs of humans and biosphere. Each Dome was like a specially-set tuning fork; when struck by the incoming beam it then resonated this tone through its local web system as a uniform vibration.

In recent years, many believe, the Grid has been undergoing a gradual, site-specific reactivation by the same agencies, the Elohim, that originally engineered and installed the system in accordance with Hermes' Principles. The Earth was made as a Home in Man's image. The Electromagnetic 1746 Grid anchors and differentiates the next dimensional Grid matrix called the Oroboric 15 Line Grid,which forms and maintains the biosphere and makes these higher energies available for human consciousness and technology interactions and for mutually-supportive human and Earth evolution.

The Earth is enveloped in a lace doily of electromagnetic fields and pulsing points of light which move the incoming intelligent cosmic/stellar energy streams through the matrix, always tending towards balance. The role of the geomancer, intelligently manipulating and cooperating with the Electromagnetic 1746 Grid, has been to harmonise these incoming streams against the chaotic entropic energy fields created by negative thought forms of resident humans, and to maintain the health of both human and Gaia. The geomancer has always been the Earth doctor and human metaphysician.

The Oroboric 15 Line Grid

The ancient Chinese geomancers had a comprehensive understanding of the manifold harmonious relations between Heaven, Earth, and the Human. They stated there was first the *Wu Chi*, the one primal vibration or Cosmic Sound (called OM in Sanskrit, the Logos in original Christianity) that differentiates into the *Tai Ch'i,* or Two Tones (yin/yang polarity), which then manifests as the 12 Tones, the *Lu.* The 12 *Lu* are the 12 fundamental pitches within the octave, related to each other by specific ratios. In the West this twelvefold differentiation of the octave is known as the Zodiac; this is another topology of the basic cosmic modulations of celestial harmonics. Moreover, the Chinese stated that the vibratory modulations influence Earth in a regular oscillation according to hourly, semi-daily, daily, weekly, biweekly, monthly, seasonal, yearly, and meta-annual cycles, all catalogued in astronomical/astrological tables. The geomantic year was apportioned into 12 Notes, 6 yin, 6 yang, each assigned to one of the 5 Elements (wood, fire, metal, water, soil).

Meanwhile the acupuncturists had charted the 12 primary energy meridians in the human body, assigning to each a yin/yang polarity (e.g., Absolute Yin, Lesser Yang), an organ (e.g., spleen, heart, liver, lungs), an element (e.g., Heart/fire, Liver/Wood, Kidneys/water), and a yearly-daily time of heightened activity, propitious for treatment (e.g., Heart/Summer/Noon-2 p.m.). And they tied the system conceptually together with a set of *4 Laws of Ch'i,* which basically operate in alignment with Hermes' Principle of Rhythm, including Mother-Son, Husband-Wife, Noon-Midnight, and the 5 Elements. These govern and describe the oscillating energy movements in both the human and Earth meridians (Diagram 5).

In the West the twelvefold permutations of the One energy were catalogued in terms of our familiar Zodiacal attributions (e.g., Sagittarius/fire, Taurus/earth, Gemini/air), each "ruled" by a planet (e.g., Venus rules Taurus, Mercury rules Gemini), and associated with particular body regions (e.g., Taurus with the throat, Gemini with the ears, arms, hands, chest, lungs, and Sagittarius with hips and thighs). In mythology this circuit of 12 has found expression in the image of King Arthur's Round Table of Grail Knights, each Knight representing one station of this spinning Zodiac House.

The Chinese acupuncturists further discovered that in addition to the 10 organ-related meridians and their two affiliate channels (Heart Governor/yin and Three Heater/yang),there were two additional regulatory channels, namely, the Governing Vessel (yang/solar/front of the body/directing) and the Conception Vessel (yin/lunar/back of the body/responding). Meanwhile the Indian yogis had described the three (related) subtle *nadis*, or channels of Kundalini through the chakras. These are the *pingala nadi* (solar/right side), *ida nadi* (lunar/left side), and *sushumna nadi* (neutral/central fusion pathway; see Diagram 3). The *pingala* carries the Fire of Matter; the *ida* channels the Fire of Manas; and through the *sushumna* courses the Fire of Spirit---from the Root to the Crown chakra, according to the evolutionary sequence of chakra awakenings. For the purposes of this model, we will consider the *pingala nadi* and Governing Vessel meridian to be homologous and the *ida pingala* and Conception Vessel to be similarly related.

This is all necessary conceptual foundation for appreciating the Oroboric 15 Line Grid. This is Gaia's emotional body, Her interactive sphere of formation for the biosphere which is the matrix for all life on Earth. This Grid makes differentiated

Diagram 5

A Human-Earth Oroboros Line

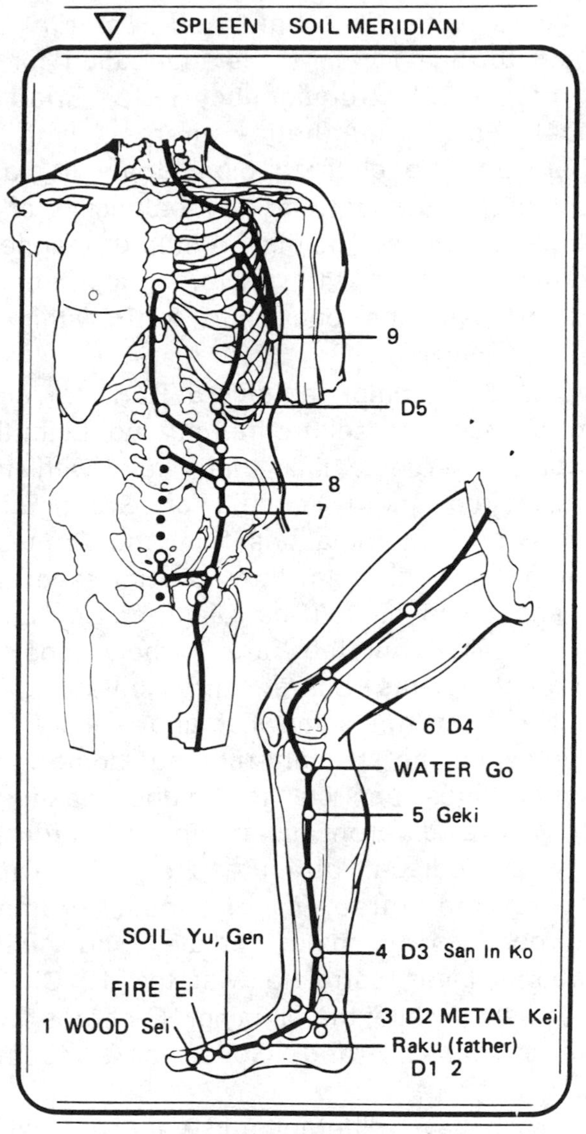

(From: *Acupuncture*, Michio Kushi, East West Foundation, Boston, MA, 1973, p. 11)

sensation possible (expressed as emotions, ruled, as described in astrology, by the planets and stars "in their courses"), and is the bridge between Mind and physical matter.

The Oroboric Grid, with its balanced *Tai Ch'i* of, alternatingly, 6 yin and 6 yang lines, is the foundation for the magnetic polarities of the Electromagnetic 1746 Grid and thereby for physical Earth. Magnetic energy, with its north/south poles operating in a charged biofield about matter, is concerned with establishing polarity or the balancing of the energy flow between two defined points. "Without magnetics there would be nothing to hold the universe together for it...contains the flow of vibrations back and forth within the theoretical limits of this universe." [8]

Thus the Oroboric Grid is comprised of 15 Earth-traversing Dragon Lines, broad avenues of solar-differentiated Light,that, like the mythic Oroboros serpent, link their tails with their mouths, making a complete energy circuit, or Great Circle, about the planet. These are not radiations from the Domes or dome caps, like dome lines, though they do intersect and interact with Domes and dome caps (See Diagram 2). Nor do these Oroboros Lines oscillate but they are, rather, consistent lines of energy surrounding the planet and containing the organic film of Earth life. They run somewhat above the Earth's surface, often parallel with the straight-running dome lines. Twelve major Oroboros Lines encircle the globe making 12 Great Circles; each has a different solar energy, ordinarily denominated by the 12 Zodiacal attributes (e.g., a Taurus Oroboros Line). There are three minor lines, ordinarily denominated by the qualities of male, female, and neutral. Basically the 12 Oroboros Lines correlate with the 12 Chinese *Lu* and 12 organ meridians, while the 3 minor Oroboros Lines correspond with the 3 *nadis* (and Governing/Conception Vessels).

The Great Circles each have different and varying levels of vibration, or color, but they do not involve all the colors of the spectrum. Gold is a principal color while lilac is found on occasion. The Oroboros Lines are primary energy tracks. After the birth of a biological being, such as Gaia, the primary energy lines determine the nature of its growth and environment, i.e., the biosphere. We can visualise a sphere with 15 golden, white, and lilac lines encircling it at geometric intervals, making a total of 62 points of intersection and 120 equal-sized triangles. Within each of these intersections is a positive and negative line running across the surface. These two are represented by pale blue lines which form the recessed side of the 120 triangles. The forward lines of these triangles are golden or white, and the positive/negative lines are not fixed but oscillate in a rhythmic pattern. This overall Oroboric figure incorporates the dodecahedron and icosahedron, two of the Platonic Solids (described below) forming the biosphere; in fact, the form for Earth is a combination of all 5 Platonic Solids (abstract forms of the 5 elements, which form the next dimensional Grid). This is the energy lattice covering the Earth; it is what produced Earth's environmental structure.

A well-known example of an Oroboros Line is the St. Michael Dragon Ley in England. Dowsers trace its course for 380 miles, extending from southwest Cornwall at Michael's Mount (at 62 degrees East of North, aligned with the May 1, or Beltane, sunrise,one of the Celtic quarterly calendar days) to northeast Suffolk at Bury St. Edmunds. Along the way it is dotted with numerous eponymous Christian Church and earlier megalithic dedications. The St. Michael Oroboros Line, however, is much longer than 380 miles; nor is it the exclusive property of Michaelic Britain. It extends entirely around the planet, joining itself again after a circumferential journey of some 24,000 miles. Its width varies at different points, being at some areas as narrow as 4 feet, while at others measuring several hundred yards in width. There are actually many Grid lines above the Earth, with the final one being two miles above the ground. Oroboros meridians particularly vary in width and intensity at nodal points (Domes, dome caps, line nodes, and Oroboric intersections) and may have thousands of major and minor treatment points arrayed along their length.

There is a specific site on Earth where the Michael/solar and Oroboros/Lunar Lines actually touch down, beginning and ending their planetary circuit and consequently activating the other 12 Zodiacal Ororobos Lines. This is also the site of the Master Dome, the original Round Table of Camelot, the Zodiacal Court of the Sun. This place is **Avebury Circle,** in central Wiltshire, England. Avebury, according to this model, is the planetary umbilicus. Avebury is Earth's primary cosmic/electrical socket. It's where the Earth plugs into the cosmos. Avebury is Grid Central, the planetary geomantic switchboard (See Diagram 6).

Each of the Earth's 1746 Domes has two vertical light cords---one gold, one silver---rising out of its top like an insulated lampshade cord. All these dual-weaved cords are joined together into one master interwoven cable at the Avebury Master Dome.

Moreover, Avebury is, to borrow another term from esoteric

Diagram 6

Avebury Circle as Planetary Grid Umbilicus

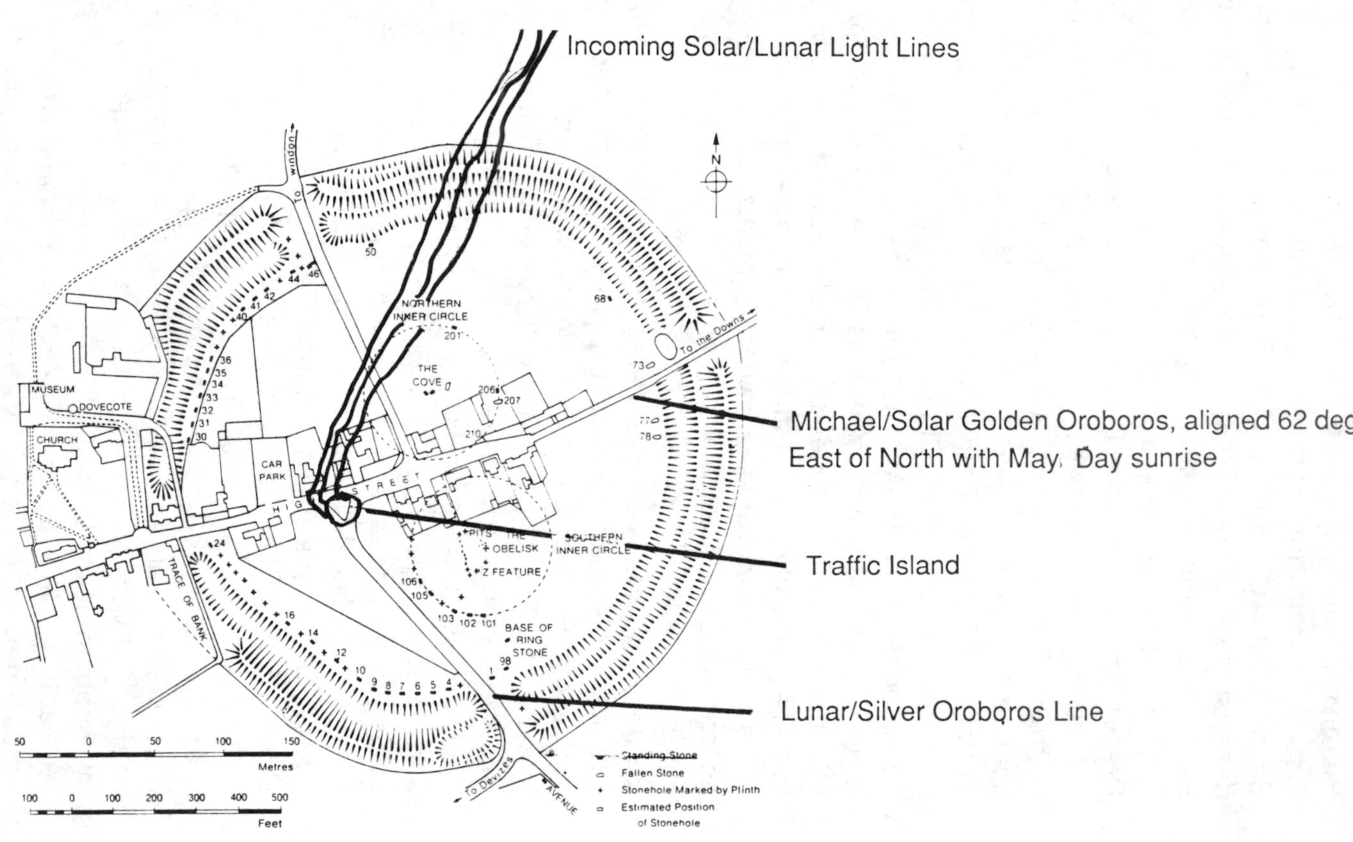

(From: *The Avebury Monuments*, Faith de M. Vatcher, Lance Vatcher, Wiltshire Department of the Environment, Her Majesty's Stationery Office, London, 1976)

yoga, the planetary *sutratma* . The sutratma is the channel through which the direct stream of life from the Spirit flows through the lower spiritual bodies and Soul to the personality and physical body; it is anchored in the etheric heart chakra. The life stream controls the circulation of the human blood and the planetary *ch'i*. For the Earth Avebury is the inner etheric heart, called *Ananda-kanda,* and operates in tandem with Glastonbury, the outer etheric heart, called *Anahata* (See Diagram 4). The sutratma at Avebury as the planetary tie-down for the basic solar/*pingala* and lunar/*ida* Oroboros Lines is also what is known in *Ecclesiastes* as "the Silver Cord, the thread that binds all the selves in the human being with the divine."

Thus the primary *Tai Ch'i*, or energy/consciousness polarity, enters the Earth Grid through her inner heart chakra at Avebury where it is then distributed throughout the Oroboric Grid as Gaia's emotional life blood. Each Grid line, vertical and horizontal, connects with the whole pattern covering the globe. Each of the two lines entering Avebury is connected at other points with each of the other 13 Oroboros Lines. The solar Oroboros comes in as a burst of pure Spirit, fiery, almost deadly, carrying absolute, eternal consciousness; it is assigned the gematria 666 by Qabala. The lunar Oroboros is cool, moist, refreshing, like a revivifying draught, carrying incarnate consciousness, subject to temporal cycles of birth and death, time and space; it is assigned the gematria 1080.

The two energies are fused at Avebury (just as they are within the dual human heart chakra), their currents sent coursing through the Grid. The number of their fusion is 1746, which is the sum of 1080 and 666. The dynamics of their interactive fusion, as a ratio of 666/1080 is the phi spiral of unfolding Light, namely, 1.618034. This is a fact fundamental to the nature of Light (described below) and at the heart of the Grid and the Human. While the solar and lunar lines are tied down at the planetary inner heart at Avebury, the Neutral Oroboros Line (equivalent to the *sushumna nadi*,carrying the Fire of Spirit) is anchored at Earth's crown chakra, Mt. Cook in western New Zealand,through which the dual Avebury-originating lines pass in their Great Circles.

What is at play here is that the primary yin/yang polarity of the Oroboros 15 Line Grid produces the balanced phi-described fusion of the 1746 Electromagnetic Grid, which is to say, Light finding balanced manifestation in the Earth Body. As Doris Lessing writes, "The outer web of musical light created the inner earthy one and held it there in its dance of tension." It is "a connecting feeding mesh (like an electric grid of humanity)". The Oroboric 15 Line Grid is Gaia's emotional body, her personality, expressed twelvefold as the Zodiacal archetypes of the 12 *Lu*---and thus ours, too, as human residents upon Gaia. This dimension of the Grid is our home on Earth such that, as Lessing says, "In the great singing dance, everything linked and moved together. My mind was the facet of a mind, like cells in a honeycomb."

Each of the Oroboros Lines was originally at some point anchored down to Earth by agency of special physical **Vibrating Stones** which came with the Domes. They were apparently material stones, as we know stones, about the size of a spherical suitcase. They were brought here by Plan of the Cosmic Chaplains and Elohim geomancers appearing here in the Domes; the stones were activated by the Domes, then positioned at key sites around the Earth to form what is called a Global Hermetic Megalithic Calendar, for the benefit of all living forms. Each Vibrating Stone had its time of significance, in accordance with all the synchronously overlapping Zodiac schedules of activity, from the 12-hour cycle to the Great Year of 25,920 years. All 12 stones resonated in harmony and in resonance with each other.

One such Vibrating Stone was placed, according to several geomancers, at Beckery Island, a small hill just outside the center of Glastonbury, Somerset, and tied down the Taurus Oroboros Line as it was intersected by the Michael/Solar Oroboros passing through the town. This particular site was also known in ancient Welsh myth as one of Britain's Three Perpetual Choirs (the Choir of Afallach, or Avalon). These were continual geomantic resonators, established on the landscape as reflections of a heavenly model related to three different aspects of consciousness translated to Earth. Activated long ago from a divine source, the Choirs were originally far more active than at present,and were related to healing. The Vibrating Stone from Beckery was subsequently removed but remains conspicuously visible though totally anomalously, elsewhere in Glastonbury. Thus in geomantic terms, the Taurus Stone was the primary receptor for the Taurean tone/vibration for the Oroboros Grid. It was the main reservoir, amplifier, disperser, and transducer/transmuter of this 1/12th differentiation of cosmic energy entering our biosphere. The 12 stones acting in concert formed the foundation of the Global Hermetic Calendar.

The central coordination point for this Global Stone Calendar of Zodiac energies is Avebury, the condensed planetary

Round Table of the Sun. The Round Table is a model for understanding the interdependent activities of the 12 Tones of the one Sound. The planetary Round Table is in effect the central receptor complex for the composite energies and consciousness of our solar system, for our particular Star Evolution paradigm of Light/Life/Consciousness whose King is our Sun.

Our solar system, ideally, is comprised of 12 revolving, rotating, inter-relating bodies (This figure includes the Sun and its reflector, the Moon, and the energy shell of the supposedly destroyed planet called Maldek or Marduk, now present as an asteroid belt between Mars and Jupiter). This was the original *ideal* solar octave of 12 planetary notes. Just as our Gaia is a living sentient being, so is our solar system a larger unified consciousness entity whose point of awareness is called by esotericists the **Solar Logos.** Each planet is directly related, in terms of "ruling" influence, to one of the 12 Zodiac Houses thereby producing a triangular pattern of influence of stars, planets, and Earth coordinates, mediated to this planet through the Oroboros Grid and Avebury Round Table of the Sun.

The planetary Round Table is the means by which Gaia can experience the differentiated energies of the Solar Logos, of which She is an integral part. The Oroboros Grid represents the 12 Knights of Gaia's Round Table, the means by which these 12 oscillating influences are distributed to Her body and eventually to the consciousness of Her human, Zodiacally-attuned residents. Gaia's Grid body is the personality of the Sun expressed twelvefold. As Above, So Below, said Hermes. We have, then, the Oroboros Grid interfacing the energy dynamics of the solar system and its organising consciousness, the Solar Logos, for embodied humanity. By meditative mastery of the Round Table we penetrate to the essence of our Star Evolution paradigm, of which we are biophysical miniatures, chemical holograms, and thus we stand on the threshold of transcendence, of attaining in consciousness that fourth dimensional quality called anti-gravity.

There are, of course, inherent limitations to our Grid conceptualizations through Zodiacal archetypes. Much of this descriptive symbolism is manmade and homocentric, and thus not necessarily truly accurate with respect to the realities of the Grid as the Elohim would describe them. From their vantage point, things are more cyclical and interdependent. It is not so much constellations and stones, but matter vibrating in synchronicity. Things are synchronously resonating in reciprocal maintenance with each other and thus feed the Earth. The Earth reciprocally maintains this relationship of interdependence.

Each of the 12 Stones resonates at a particular frequency that is in sympathetic harmony with certain astrological constellations. The most relevant point, however, is the *relationship*. The Earth is an active force as well as a receptive matrix. Each celestial, terrestrial and lunar body is in sympathetic resonance, one with the other, travelling at tremendous speeds through infinite space. As we chart the Oroboros Grid, and particularly the Polyhedronic Crystal Grid (described next) we steadily approach the barrier between third and fourth dimensions, with all the inherent inadequacies and difficulties of Earth-based language and linear conceptualization.

Thus the Earth Grid at this level, through the Avebury umbilicus, is the Round Table as a planetary hologram of the energy/consciousness body of the Solar Logos. It is the receiving/transmitting device expressed at the borderline between third and fourth dimensions. In the context of the Earth we have expressed the energy realities of the Sun's Royal Court, which itself is but a component of the far larger vibrational body of the Galactic Logos. Now, the Grid contains a practical, localised feature that makes the conscious human experience with the Sun's Zodiacal Court possible.

The **landscape Zodiac** (discussed below) is the local, accessible hologram of the Master Round Table of Avebury and the Solar Logos,and represents an experiential workshop for aligning human with planetary, solar, galactic, and universal energy streams. We could liken the function of the landscape Zodiac (i.e., in which the energy skeletons of constellations around the ecliptic are overlaid on a 30 mile circumferential band on the Earth, as in Somerset, England, with the Glastonbury Zodiac) to that of a geomantic concert hall wherein we hear the Music of the Spheres as played by the local affiliate orchestra.

There is some classical precedent for this musical interpretation of the Grid. Pythagoras and Plato both presented Grid models couched in musical terms. Pythagoras described a Cosmic Ship of Music comprised of our planets and neighboring stars, which sailed through the Heavens emitting *rhoizamata,* or "rushing sounds", which we could hear when we tuned the seven-stringed lyre of ourselves (the unified chakra system) to resonate with the celestial music (accomplished or played by the Grid). Plato spoke of the Spindle of Necessity which he envisioned as the solar system rotating about the axis of the universe. On each whorl of this Spindle sits a Siren who sings a single note. In either case the total resonance pattern, the total Sound, the complete concert, is the celestial music of our King Sun, what Doris Lessing calls "the controlling governor of them all... the majestic core of our web... the deep low organ note that underlies all being... God's singing center."

The Polyhedronic Crystal Grid

The Grid now operates in the fourth dimension as a function of crystal geometry, comprising the 5 Platonic Solids. This is Gaia's mental body, the sphere of abstract thinking and concrete knowledge, what Plato recognised as the world of Forms. Here the 15 Oroboros Grid Lines,which in the preceding Grid dimension beribbon the Earth sphere in a kinetic band of light, here are fused together into one unified polyhedron of 120 equal-sized triangles (or 10 hexagons, or 30 diamonds) with 62 intersection points. Grid mappers Bethe Hagens and William Becker call this geometrical Grid dimension the "Earth Star."

Whereas in the Oroboric Grid the 15 Great Circles collectively form and maintain the living biosphere, here in the Polyhedronic Crystal Grid the 5 elements (which are differentiated out in the Oroboros Lines, e.g., Taurus/earth, Gemini/air, Sagittarius/fire), exist in their abstract, more static, crystalline form, as Platonic Solids (e.g., fire/tetrahedron, earth/cube, air/octahedron, water/icosahedron, ether/dodecahedron). The Earth Crystal is the formative agent for the kinetic Oroboros Lines, which represent, in a sense, the elements in motion, manifesting the biosphere. We can visualise the Polyhedron as a multifaceted etheric crystal superimposed over the Earth, like an overcoat, or like a geometric padded hatbox for a most delicate and flowery headpiece. Here the 5 Platonic Solids (as the abstract form of the elements) form a unified etheric crystal, with all the predictable geometrical/consciousness/formative properties of the crystal---such as the containment and patterning of Light.

We can better appreciate how the Earth Polyhedron functions by reviewing the properties of crystals. Crystals are rightly called "windows of Light," as patterning and dimensional-transmitting doorways from the kinetic world of Light radiation down through the more apparently static material world of form---and the reverse. Crystals can amplify and project thought forms; facilitate interdimensional communication; operate as tuning forks at specific frequencies to key individuals and their environments to desired light harmonics; receive and transmit high energy inputs; maintain unified electromagnetic fields to provide balance and harmony; serve as cosmic batteries, storing and releasing energy on schedule; function as archetypal libraries, holding messages, codes, histories, schedules; work as light modulators; or act as psychic binoculars and telescopes seeing over great time/space distances.[9] These are documented applications of material plane crystals but their enumeration helps us understand the geometry of consciousness and Light at play in this more abstract Grid dimension.

Physical life on Earth is an oscillating dance of the 5 elements, as orchestrated to us through successively more material Grid interfaces, and as played for us by the symphonic interactions of the 11 planets (minus Earth), the 12 Zodiac Houses, and other influential star families (e.g., Sirius, Orion, Arcturus, among others). The Earth in its higher mental body manifestation is a crystal receptor floating in space, moving through the harmonic web of the stellar Grid, itself a vast unified crystal-polyhedron. We move with the Earth as a facet in the life and being of our King Sun, our Solar Logos,whose body is our solar system, source of our Light, Life, and Consciousness *parameters*.

We live, through these interpenetrating Grid dimensions, the stellar evolutionary life of our Sun in concert with his (once) 11 satellite planets, his Knights (now minus Maldek) and ecliptically-neighboring Zodiac. We are all on the same solar wave-length as mediated through the Polyhedronic Crystal Grid. "Every star evolution is on a valency of Light which determines its own evolutionary program," writes J. J. Hurtak.[10] This represents our Solar Fishnet, the specific conditions of Light, Life, and Consciousness that constitute our *home* in the solar system.

The fundamental Round Table of the Sun, of which planet Earth is a valiant Knight, is marked by the projected ecliptic our Earth makes through the 12 Houses of the Zodiac (or the apparent path the Sun takes) during a 12 month cycle; it is also described by the Sun's own ecliptic peregrination in 2160 year spurts (following the Precession of the Equinoxes) through these same constellations. Just as the Earth is visualised as this rotating, revolving crystalline receptor, wired for sound to the other planets and stars, dancing to the fivefold tune within the context of the evolutionary possibilities of this single Sun system and on the specific dance floor of planet Earth, so, too, is the local solar system a unified, evolving Being functioning within its own Light/Life/Consciousness paradigm within a larger controlling body.

The Sun and the totality of the solar system, when seen from a distance, free of time and space limitations, is a Light Crystal with interpenetrating Grids, surrounding each planet and linking them in a solar web. This is really a question of fundamental *limitations*. "Man is chained to his geomagnetic cycles," says Hurtak, living in "planetary bondage to its own Light field" or "solar magnetic field paradigm", operating under "the ancient astrophysical status of Light upon Earth." Humans exist on Earth, adds Doris Lessing, within their "terrible bondage, the chains of necessity that grasped them... This web was an iron, a frightful necessity, imposing its design." Our electromagnetic spectrum, dispensed by the Sun and mediated through the Polyhedronic Crystal Grid, is both our familiar *home* and our frightful *jail,* depending on our orientation. Gravity holds us rooted to the material Earth and the solar winds blow hard to keep us strapped to the Earth's surface and within Her electromagnetic field. However, at the doorway of the Polyhedron, the place where our evolutionary Light paradigm for Humanity on Earth is molded and transmitted, we have the possibility of lifting off in a rush of anti-gravity.

The Earth Grid represents the geometry of consciousness, the constraints on awareness and fourth dimensional transcendence, our biochemical/evolutionary parameters of expression. The crystalline Star Grid, of which our Earth is a component, is the form-dynamics of our local Star Evolution program, namely, the restrictions on consciousness, or that which upholds what Hurtak calls "the bioconsciousness of the old planetary cycles", or that which maintains "the electromagnetic ordering of the life code." Our interpenetrating Grid system is like a huge solar DNA hologram enveloping, infiltrating, and *living us* inescapably. It is a particular electromagnetic domain, or frequency/life spectrum, which is a partial expression (tailored for Earth, just as Venus and Mars have their own Grid realities) of the unified Star Evolution Grid, itself but a cosmic DNA hologram of a larger harmonic being. So here we live, as humans on Earth, breathing within and as sentient facets of this resonating matrix. It fits like a primary tuning fork over our noosphere and biosphere such that not one atom or electron or speeding quark escapes its dominant resonance.

Yet this same Crystal Grid represents the possible Grid

Doors out of this Sun-imposed paradigm. It holds the key to anti-gravity; here the stellar Grid restrictions can be transcended, here human consciousness can depart the solar system, soaring off the Earth in a burst of Light into the fourth and fifth dimensions. This is freedom from gravity, which is none other than the *weight* of the mind/body/emotions bounded by the linear time/space fishnet of the Grid. Anti-gravity, as we will see below, is fundamentally a consciousness technology, a transcending mastery of the Grid. Our stellar Grid, after all, is only one of billions of such star evolution crystal grids glittering in what Hurtak calls "the Sea of Crystal", which is our Milky Way seen through mystic eyes. Star systems now are seen as individual, interdependent, inter-resonating geometric harmonic Grids of Light.

Thus the Polyhedronic Grid is like a central distribution warehouse for a supermarket chain. Here all the groceries and produce are received and parcelled out, first for the regional distributors, then the individual units. The Platonic Solids, in this model, receive the abstract energy impulses, or bulk shipments, from the Zodiac Houses, other stars and planets, then parcel them out down through the succeeding 3 Grids to the physical Earth and our daily lives as Grid consumers---all in accordance with the inherent geometric/elemental design.

Here is an example of how this system works. Recently at the moment of the lunar eclipse and full Moon of Libra 1986, the Earth tetrahedron received a major solar activation. The 5 Platonic Solids form what is in truth an indivisible whole; but for the purpose of this illustration, let us envision the tetrahedron alone, as a 3-sided pyramid within a basketball, but with the corners protruding like big toes from old socks. From the apex of the pyramid/tetrahedron, rises a spiralling cone extending far into space, into the starfields. At the moment of activation, first the cone, then the pyramid, blushed an effulgent gold throughout. Momentarily the tetrahedron was radiant and vibrationally jubilant with powerful solar energy amidst the other Solids which formed a clear quartz crystal. Obviously, shortly afterwards the fire-energized pyramid began diffusing its new energies throughout the unified polyhedron. The planetary positioning point (apex up) for this now golden tetrahedron within the Polyhedronic Crystal Grid overlap on Earth is Richland-Balsam Mt. (or The Balsam; or Mt. Balsam Cone; current elevation 6500 feet, ancient elevation 6666 feet) in Western North Carolina, 20 miles south of Waynesville, just off the Blue Ridge Parkway (heading "north").

The Earth Crystal, then, is "wired for sound" with the other interior crystal organs of the Sun system by way of the Stellar Grid. The Stellar Grid is structured differently than the various Earth Grids. When we visualize a geodesic or other multi-faceted rhomboid solid, we see subtle lines of energy passing from one plane of experience or existence to a similar plane or facet in a rhomboid at another dimension. This is the Stellar/Earth Grid connection. It is linked with forces of an etheric nature. The Stellar Grid may be visualized from Earth as a lace curtain or pattern of interconnected snowflakes stretching across the entire night sky.

The Soul of Gaia

In the theory of Earth's higher bodies, this is Gaia's causal body, the inner Temple of Solomon, the Soul of our sentient planet. This is the prime consciousness Grid for Gaia, centered in a quasi-physical, quasi-etheric domain roughly coordinated topographically with the Kun Lun Mountains and Gobi/Lob Nor Deserts of Mongolia/Northern China. Like the brow chakra of the human, which is the seat of clairvoyance, the Soul of Gaia is an interdimensional realm, essentially hidden and mostly intangible. It can be physically entered, however, occasionally by human adepts or somewhat more easily in the visionary body, through various meditative/geomantic doorways around the Earth.

At this level we encounter the Planetary Logos called Sanat Kumara (The One Initiator) who presides over Earth's inner life as the Soul, mediating through the brow chakra the "Word of God" to the physical Being of Gaia (See Diagram 4). Through the activated brow chakra, one comes to know one's true divine identity and life purpose. This is echoed Biblically in St. John's *Revelation* where he describes the 144,000 Children of Israel on Mt. Zion, standing with the Lamb (Christ), each with the Name of God written on their foreheads (in their brow chakra). In our time,planetarily, the Soul of Gaia operates by means of the **Mobile Focus**. This consciousness beam contains the inner Soul awareness and evolutionary program for Gaia and all her residents and is usually mediated to the physical plane through the four succeeding Grids. However, in our special historical moment, the Mobile Focus is coming through the planet's outer heart chakra at Glastonbury.

The Mobile Focus is continually moving, travelling over the Earth's surface with no permanently fixed location. Theoretically it is fully resident in one locality for about 100 years but with an overspill of energy before and afterwards of 50 years each,making 200 years total presence in one locale.

The Mobile Focus,it is believed, was once resident at Jerusalem and Mt. Kailas, but in the course of Earth history, obviously it has been *many* places.

The Focus operates by means of a predetermined evolutionary activation mechanism. If we wind up a clock, it then proceeds through its mechanism to tell time. As the Domes supposedly came three times, they preprogrammed the matrix of energy lines over Earth to coincide with certain planetary and constellationary exactitudes existing in the far future. The action of the Mobile Focus is much like the effect a living Master, like the 14th Dalai Lama, for example, can have on a receptive human. We can experience a profound change in our consciousness just by sitting in the presence of such a Master, but only to the degree of our receptivity to his/her heightened pure vibrations. The Mobile Focus, as a geomantic Living Master for Gaia, has been moved, therefore, in accordance with a Master Plan, a vast far-seeing tablet of planetary destiny, over Earth's surface, to resonate equally at each culture, for each creed, for 200 year periods---facilitating the implementation of Gaia's Soul programs into the physical domain of human culture.

The Mobile Focus, in this model, is an initiatory energy beam designed by Adepts under guidance of the Elohim, for the transfiguration of consciousness from the human plane to one of angelic resonance. It is like a powerful spotlight of color/sound/vibration/energy shone steadily over a specific region (e.g., a Dome center). It has as its agenda the uplifting of human awareness into knowledge of the Master Plan and that particular bioregion's role in achieving this total Plan for Earth. Here we listen to Gaia's Soul telling Her (and us) the reason and purpose for our existence as an inhabited planet. Here we listen to the wise voice of Her Planetary Logos, Sanat Kumara, as He imparts spiritual qualities through the Grid matrix. Thus we begin to understand *why* things are precisely the way they are on the physical plane, according to Hermes' Principle of Causation. We begin to appreciate that Gaia's karma is largely the result of our ill-informed actions over the milennia. Indeed, when Gaia is appreciated as a sentient, coherent, living Being, then we will awake in horror at the scope of the injuries we've inflicted upon Her.

From the interpretive vantage of the mystical science of Qabala, Earth's 5 interpenetrating Grid Bodies may be seen as part of a basic abstract model for reality called the Tree of Life (Diagram 7). The Tree is composed of 12 spheres (called *Sephira* [plural; *Sephiroth*, singular] : 10 manifest, 2 subtle)

Diagram 7

Qabala Tree of Life

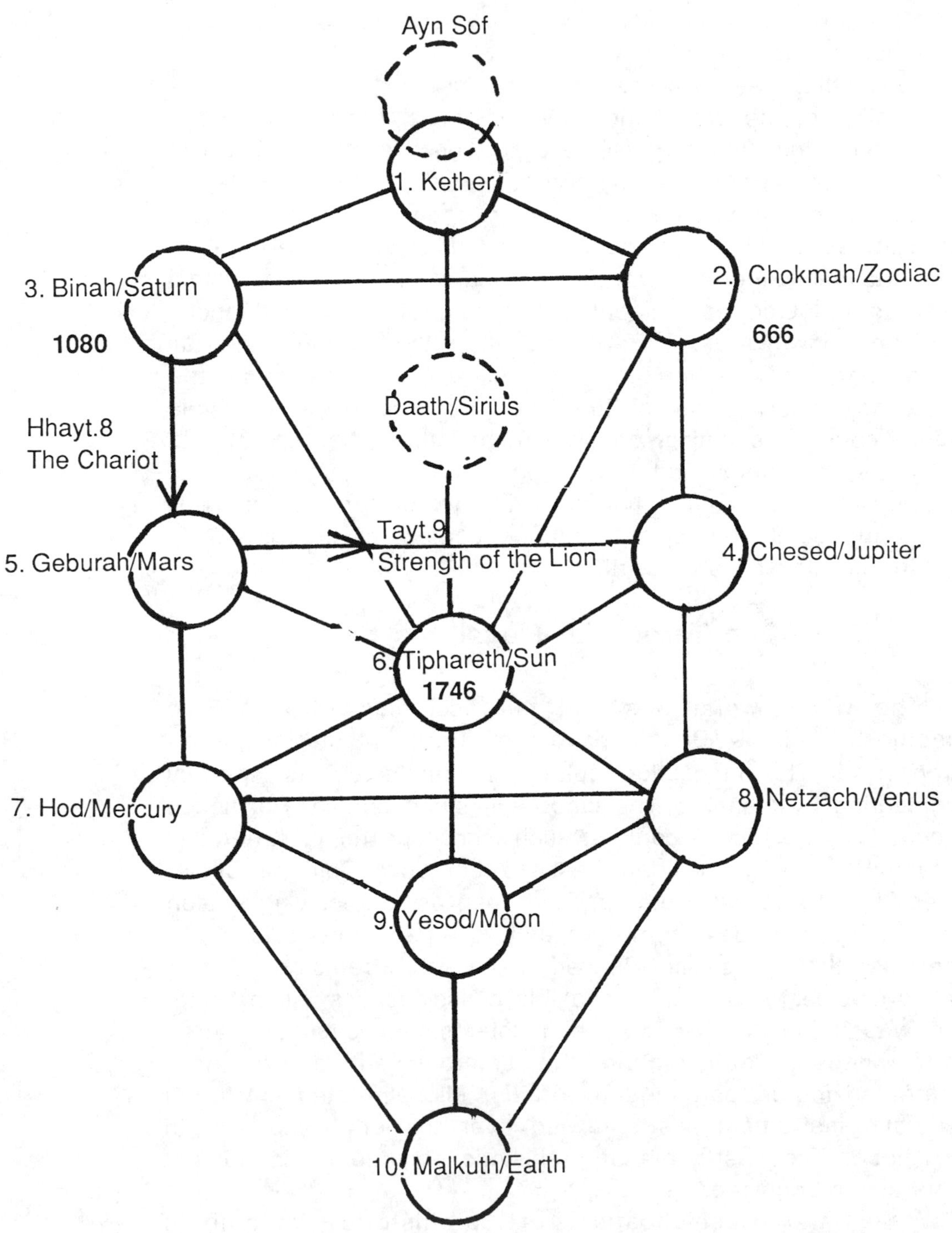

and 22 pathways linking these energy/consciousness domains. Earth, at the bottom sphere (*Malkuth*, 10th Sephiroth) is linked, through the pathways (The group name is *Autiot*, forming the 22 sacred letters, the later basis for the Hebrew language) to God, at Kether, at the top of the Tree.

Ideally the Tree resonates as one vibrational being with the Name of God, the unpronounceable, ineffable *Tetragrammaton*. The planets and Zodiac Houses are positioned on the Tree which as a totality operates synchronously in many levels of manifestation and understanding (e.g., human consciousness, the Earth Grid, the Solar Logos). One Grid system is always an interdependent tone in a broader Grid harmonic. The Tree model presents the Grid as a linear sequencing of higher influences mediating downwards to Earth; but in truth, it's more like an onion made of dozens of onion skins. The reality is the immediacy and integrity of the onion, or Grid---with all levels synchronously resonating, one within the other (Diagram 8).

The synchronous Grid resonance is finally brought down to the physical Earth---the ultimate Grid theater for this complex drama of cosmic energies within the context of ordinary daily human consciousness on Earth.

The Terrestrial Megalithic Grid

"The whole world was laid out according to a cosmic scheme," explains British doyen of Earth Mysteries, John Michell.[11] The megalithic culture accomplished its spiritual engineering by means of the landscape stone temple. Positioned geomantically at Dome centers, such landscape temples (e.g., in Britain, Stonehenge, Maiden Castle, Arbor Low, Rollright Circle, Maes Howe, and many others) functioned as "a receiving station for direct influences from heavenly constellations and earth energies" thereby uniting Heaven and Earth. Prehistoric Britain was an epicenter of such megalithic consciousness engineering, and was a land of "closely-linked, intercommunicating centers," adds Michell, "engaged in the same scientific program." Characterizing in part modern Britain, Michell noted, "A great scientific instrument lies sprawled over the entire surface of the globe. The vast scale of prehistoric engineering is not yet generally recognized."

While the sophistication of "prehistoric" megalithic engineering may remain as yet largely unrecognized, certainly its still copious and visible remains do not go unacknowledged. The extent and abundance of extant megalithic sites in Britain alone is staggering. Estimates state there are still 1000 stone

Diagram 8

The Grid as a Function of Interpenetrating Higher Dimensional Bodies for the Living Earth

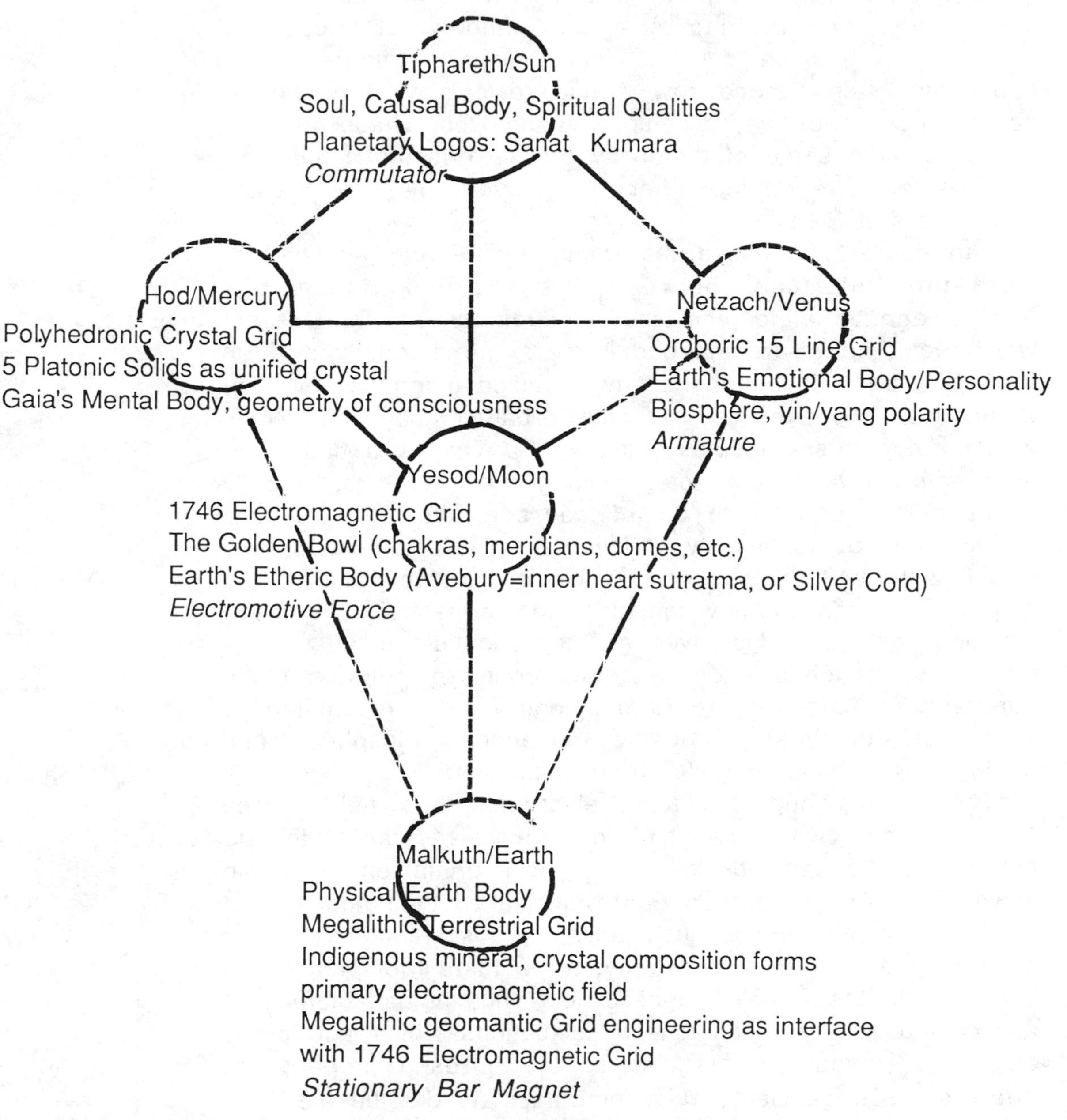

chambers, at least 30,000 barrows, 900 stone circles, 3000 hillforts, and countless thousands of single standing stones, all in varying states of decay and neglect. The names are multiple and various,too, for the scientific panoply of megalithic engineering: cromlech, dolmen, menhir, quoit, hill figure, fogou, souterrain, cairn, stone row, round tower, pyramid, brugh, gallery grave, causewayed camp, ring-and-ditch. These are best appreciated as some of the many precise geomantic tools for consciousness-technology once employed by the master geomancers of Gaia.

The context for these megalithic engineering applications was the interface between the Earth's indigenous electromagnetic field and the Electromagnetic 1746 Grid, which acted to re-arrange and harness the magnetized Earth field. The Earth is surrounded by a unified magnetic field and within this it behaves as if it were a ball of magnetized iron, with north and south poles (Diagram 9). This is a fluctuating field, with daily shifts in total geomagnetic force (from 0.0002 gauss at the Equator to 0.0005 gauss at the Poles, and a geomagnetic daily intensity variation of 20-50 gammas). Most scientists attribute these changes to the Sun; solar flares and magnetic storms thereby initiating geomagnetically traumatic situations on Earth. Moreover, geomagnetic field polarity, seen over time, switches often, and has done so perhaps many hundreds of times in the Earth's long history (estimated at every 230,000 years), causing tremendous biospheric and geologic alterations and life form extinctions.

The Earth's huge,oscillating electromagnetic field is the Mother to our own human biofields, themselves the Mother to our individual organ biofields. It acts as a primal energy womb in which all living forms on Earth have taken their nourishment and continuing energetic sustenance. In a system of magnetic ecology the human energy rhythms take their cue from variations in the Earth's magnetic field; thus human biorhythms are conditioned by geomagnetic fluctuations which act for us as timers, modulators, regulators, and, if used properly, as healers.[12] The ancient Druids of Britain, as did the old *feng shui* masters of China, comprehended these manifold energy bonds and knew how to work harmoniously, creatively, with the interdependent, multidirectional flow of electromagnetic pulses to maintain individual health, communal cooperation, and world peace. Their context was the Terrestrial Megalithic Grid and their means was consciousness technology.

The geomantic secret of the Druids was that they comprehended the Grid as a **supermagnetic armature.**

Diagram 9

Earth's Geomagnetic Field in 1965

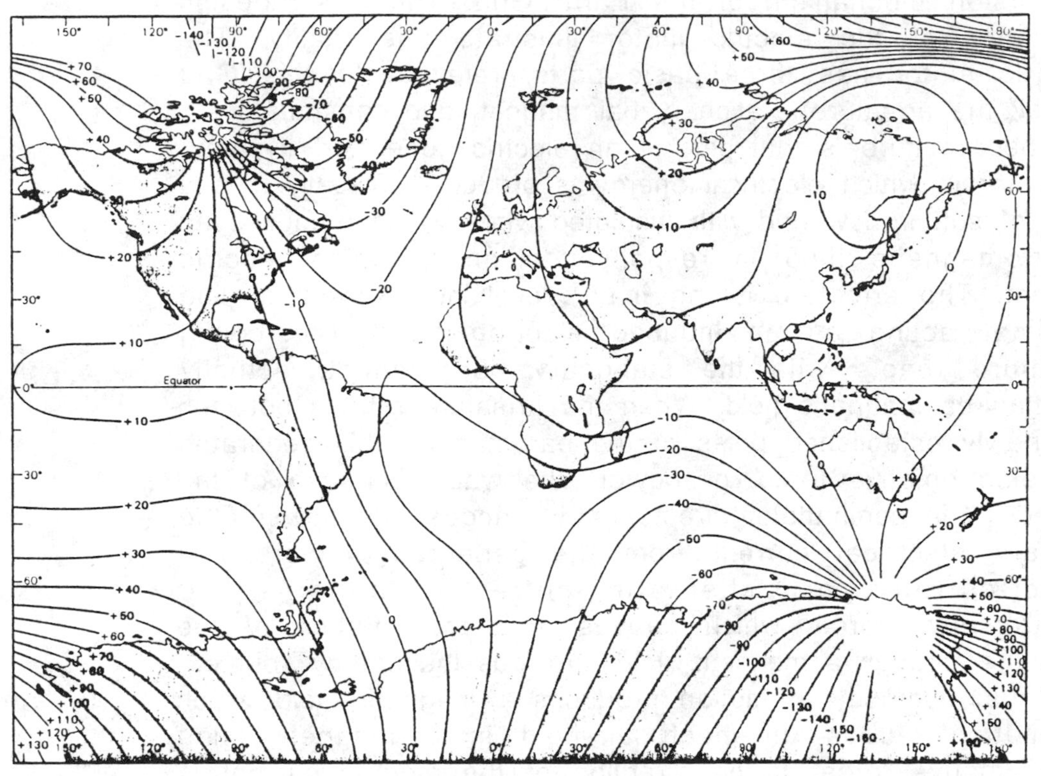

True to Hermes' Principle of Correspondence, the modern electric motor is a scaled-down version of the energy conversion mechanism of the Earth Grid. The basic design principles of the electric motor illustrate this reality. The electric motor has three basic parts, relevant to this Grid model: the armature, stationary bar magnet, and commutator.

The armature is that part of an electric generator, dynamo, or motor in which electrical energy is produced. Usually it is a core of soft iron wound with insulated wires which produces an electromagnetic field in response to an incoming electric current. The armature is the main, revolving, current-carrying winding, acting as an induced electromagnet. The coiled armature reacts with the stationary bar magnet, actually creating its magnetic field. When the armature rotates between the newly established poles of the bar magnet, this generates the electromotive force, or power---the whole purpose of the motor. The commutator directs (and changes) the flow of the primary electrical current from the generator, either in a direct-current or alternating-current manner. The electromotive force, which derives from the rotation of the armature through a magnetic field, provides the energy source.

Thus electricity in motion produces a magnetic field which in motion across an electrical field in a magnet yields electromotive force. If the direction of the electric current is changed through the commutator, the poles reverse direction when the armature accordingly changes its rotational direction. A direct-current of constant strength produces an unchanging magnetic field whereas an alternating -current makes the magnetic field reverse itself every time the current reverses.

Thus the Grid is a supermagnetic armature. The Oroboric 15 Line Grid is the coiled armature. The *sutratma* of interwoven gold/silver Oroboros Lines entering Avebury Circle represents the commutator, the channel for the variously positive/negative electrical current that produces the electromagnet in the Oroboros armature. The Oroboros armature produces the electromagnetic field in the stationary bar magnet of the Earth, in reaction with its indigenous mineral, crystal, and stone conductors. "The Earth's core, composed mostly of molten iron, conducts electric currents which amplify accompanying magnetic fields," explains Hurtak, "when energy wave bombardment pours in through the polar areas of the Earth." The electromotive force is drawn off through the Electromagnetic 1746 Grid centers interfacing with the natural electric/telluric flows of the Earth's magnetic field (See Diagram 9). This interface was the intelligent positioning of megalithic hardware (e.g., hollow, crystal-tipped, 100 foot-high pyramids) at key Grid junction boxes in a program of applied consciousness technology which re-arranged the indigenous magnetic field pattern into a workable energy Grid from which free and inexhaustible supplies could be drawn. This is the foundation of the Druidic sacred landscape science extolled by Michell.

The Electromagnetic 1746 Grid is the planetary Grid Engineer's energy matrix blueprint, his Con Edison route map. The advanced crystal technology of Atlantis, for example, represented the "home appliance" that plugged into this free energy system drawing off virtually endless reserves of energy to empower civilization (the technological aspect) while furthering the spiritual evolution of humankind (the consciousness aspect).[13] The electromotive force is not available, either functionally or conceptually, without this spiritual/scientific fusion expressed as consciousness technology and that comes from the proper understanding of the human/Grid interface. The Grid energy appliances were, and remain, a fusion as spiritual engineering. The Master Grid Engineers were, and remain, Knights of the Holy Grail. Thus the Grid is revealed as the context in which consciousness and technology are harmoniously integrated in a planetary *Tai Ch'i* for human and Earth enlightenment.

In accordance with this simple electric motor model of the Earth Grid, the much-prophesised Earth Changes, possible geomagnetic field and pole reversal, even the apocalyptic Second Coming of Christ, are all nested within the function of the Grid commutator.

Between geomagnetic field reversals, the Grid seems to function as a direct-current motor, with its steady stream of one-way electricity. But with the imminence of Earth Changes and field reversal, suddenly it seems that the Grid is actually an alternating-current motor, simply with long pauses between field reversals. A change in the polarity of the electric current flowing through the Grid commutator at Avebury fundamentally means the introduction of a new electromagnetic Light/Life/Consciousness spectrum for Earth, an upgrading of our physical life parameters by a literal electrification of matter---the biosphere, noosphere, and all our Grid bodies---into the fourth dimension, into the realm of anti-gravity. Everything will be vibrationally transfigured---As Above, So Below---from the Star Evolution Crystal to the Earth Polyhedron Crystal to the human molecules of DNA and ATP. It will happen unilaterally, instantaneously, synchronously.

This is because the primary message the reality of the Grid is telling us is this: We are all one crystalline vibrational body---galaxy, solar system, Earth, human.

The Human/Grid Interface

When the Earth is comprehended as a receiving/transmitting crystal harmonic and a resonant facet in the solar crystal harmonic, a note in the solar octave, then we need a unifying scheduling science with which to orient ourselves within this Grid totality.

The precise science of astrology is the Viewer's Guide for daily Grid programming. The Ephemeris is the *TV Guide* for the Grid. What programs shall we watch as the world turns? What maudlin soaps shall we participate in as our King Sun plugs us into His daily melodrama?

Astrology minutely calibrates the hourly, daily, weekly, monthly, yearly cycles of the planets---the movements of our orchestra. Through astrologically-attuned eyes, which is simply developing the interpretive aspect of astronomy, we can understand our lives, our world, our emotions, our movements, our reasons, habits, difficulties, and exaltations, according to this "web of iron necessity," this whirling elemental energy dance of our interwired human/solar psyche. The Polyhedronic Crystal Grid is like the master crystal chip that receives, through its 120 smooth triangular receptor plates, the myriad, though mathematically rational and orchestrated, energy/consciousness/Sound channellings from our biopsychic disc jockeys. Thus the Ephemeris, with its factual tables of numbers and degrees, when properly applied, represents the Grid Engineer's codebook for predicting, assessing, correcting, interpreting, and *transmuting* these steady, determining inputs from the solar radio station.

Transmuting is the key. We can change the channel if we choose,turn down the volume,fine tune the specific radio band. The Grid Engineer has the potential for transmuting (freeing the inherent energy by releasing it from its form bondage) the solar/celestial energies by intelligent interfacing with the Electromagnetic 1746 Grid through any of the 144 planetary Round Table holograms, or terrestrial Zodiacs resident on Earth. This Grid, we must remember, is the Golden Alchemical Bowl of electromagnetic differentiation, and the potential alembic of our transfiguration from gravitationally bonded humans to Humans of Light. Just because King Sun, our accustomed disc jockey, plays his favorite tunes on his radio station, doesn't mean we have to, ultimately, always dance to that rhythm.

The introduction of the reality of the local Zodiac workshops brings us to the crux of the possible interaction between the human and the Grid. This is where the Grid Engineer and Knight of the Holy Grail become one. This unification of seeking the Grail and serving the Grid is played out in the local geomythic theater of the landscape Zodiac. **Geomythic** means "the living myth in the landscape" and our direct involvement in this terrestrial symbology through a heightened consciousness interaction within a local Zodiac complex.

Our Zodiac conceptual model again operates as an interdependent series of homologous and attuned dimensional systems i.e., Zodiacs within Zodiacs. We begin with the Master Solar Round Table of the Earth/Sun ecliptic through the twelve Houses of the Zodiac---every year, every 2160 years, every 25, 920 years. Here we have both King Sun and planet Earth circuiting the heavenly twelve-gated Grail Castle as intrepid, dedicated Grail Knights. This vast cycling, and questing, is translated, homologously, down to Earth, first, through Avebury as Grid switchboard and concert maistro, the master point for the 12 Oroboros Zodiac Lines, and, second, through the expansive planetary distribution of these 12 Dragon Lines,thereby making a Round Table of both Avebury Circle (condensed) and the entire planet Earth (expanded). But how does an individual Grail Knight voluntarily, consciously experience this huge planetary Round Table? And how does the Grid Engineer make intelligent, compassionate, and timely adjustments in the geomantic web of this vast-revolving solar table on Earth? Through the local Zodiac hologram.

In this Zodiac model, an overlay of Qabala's Tree of Life with the mythic Round Table/Zodiac image is most illuminating. The Earth is one of the 12 resonating spheres, one of the 12 Round Table members, one of the 12 Notes in the solar octave, in the Solar Tree of Life. Thus we can picture these relations either in terms of the Tree or Round Table, which are essentially interchangeable for this illustration. Our Body of the Sun is expressed as a 12-sphered Tree of Life, with 12 Knights, or 12 Notes; Earth is Malkuth, the 10th Sephiroth, representing, appropriately, Earth (See Diagram 7; the 7th Sephiroth, *Hod*, for example, represents Mercury).

Next, and similarly, the Earth Body is expressed as a Tree of Life, and here Mt. Shasta is Malkuth and Root chakra. The Gaia Tree has 12 spheres which in terms of the Grid are 12 **Zodiac**

Vortices, major planetary Zodiac domains which correspond in legend to the camps of the 12 Tribes of Israel. These are primary geomantic sectors each organised into a major Zodiac complex of 12 sub-Zodiac temples. The unification of these 12 Zodiac Vortices is the planetary Round Table, or Tree, as the whole family of Jacob (who was Israel). Next, each of these 12 Zodiac Vortices has a subsystem of 12 **Zodiac Domes**, giving us a total of 144 Zodiac hologram temples on the planet (although all are not always available at one given time because of changing geologic/meteorologic conditions). Each of the 12 Zodiac Dome sub-systems comprises a Zodiac Vortex Round Table, of which there are 12 worldwide.

For example, what I call the Hyperborean Round Table occupies an approximate area ranging from the Orkney Islands of northern Scotland, through Ireland, Wales, and England, to Brittainy and southwestern France. This Domed Zodiac Round Table includes 12 interdependent local Zodiac systems. Each has a dominant myth-system Logos but all are primarily constellated around King Arthur and the Grail. One of these 12 local Zodiacs is the somewhat familiar Glastonbury/Somerset "Round Table of the Stars," as it's often called, or more poetically, *The Region of the Summer Stars* (which includes the famous mystical Avalon). Each local Zodiac (which may measure 10 miles in diameter, 20-30 miles in circumference) is topped and energized by a huge Zodiac Dome.

Each local Zodiac, such as The Region of the Summer Stars, is a hologram of the solar Round Table in the form of 144 quasi-etheric star center effigies dimensionally overlaid like a stellar template on the physical landscape. The landscape Zodiac is a double ecliptic, with one physical ecliptic including 96 star effigies (from the northern hemisphere skies) and one etheric ecliptic including 48 star effigies (from the southern hemisphere skies). The two ecliptics interlock forming a *vesica piscis* with Glastonbury in its cradle.

Within such a local Zodiac temple, a particular constellation, such as Canis Major (the Great Dog), will have an approximate material landscape reference point, a residence often reflected in place names, local legends, or actual landscape sculpturing, within or outside this defining ecliptic.

In central Somerset, for example, within The Region of the Summer Stars, Canis Major is called "The Girt Dog of Langport" and occupies a geographic region about 5 miles long and 1 mile broad, and includes 16 recognizable **star centers** in its geomythic body. Sirius, the brightest star in the night sky, touches down locally at Oath Hill which was once used by King

Diagram 10

Star Template of Canis Major Overlaid on Somerset Landscape with 16 Star Centers

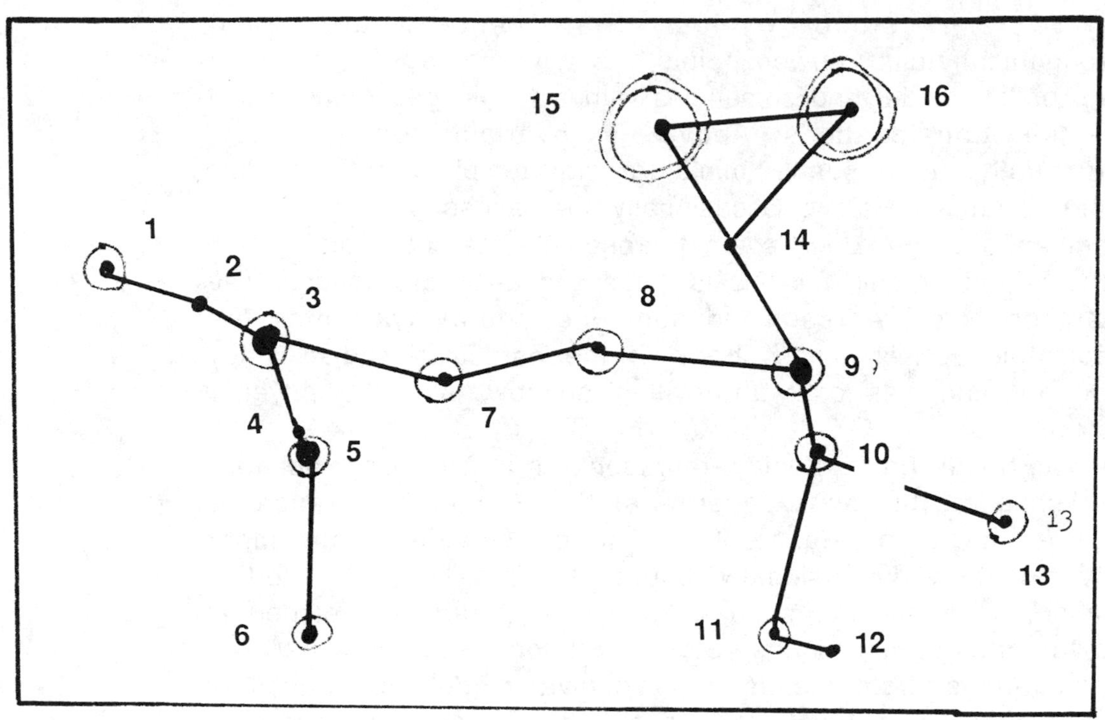

Key

1 Aludra: church
3 Wezea: church
5 Adhara: church
6 church
7 former church
8 church, formerly stone circle
9 Sirius: Oath Hill, former temple
12 stone monument
13 church, formerly barrow
15 church, formerly barrow
16 church, hollow hill (stone chamber)

Arthur to obtain oaths and fealty-committments from his Knights. About 6 star centers are occupied by 600-1000 year old Christian churches, many of which were preceded by barrows or stone circles. Star centers are local geomythically-cast power points, usually marked by a dome cap, or line node, and sometimes with a full-fledged dome. Each of the constellations Above is overlaid, energetically, structurally, as a subtle, miniature star template of landscape star formations Below. Occasionally the landscape, when seen from an airplane, does seem to resemble the morphology of a fish or goat or bull, but this is not essential by any means. The star centers represent dimensional doorways into the geomythic consciousness body of the particular Zodiac effigy whose being has cast an inviting shadow over the physical terrain.

The local Earth Zodiac represents a basic consciousness workshop for human experience of the Grid of solar energies that *is* the Solar Round Table, which comprises our inner psychic three-dimensionally bounded life. The local Zodiac embodies, in miniature, the astrophysical parameters etched in Earth and ether of the Star Evolution Grid and its 144 permutations, from the basic 12 octaval modulations. Each of the 144 Zodiacs has a different flavor, a different angle of vision, a different nuance and energy coloring. Why there are 144 is explained below.

Through hologrammic miniaturization, the local Zodiac makes the vast solar ecliptic Round Table accessible for human interaction and transmutation. The local Zodiac holds up before our meditative eyes a mirror made of geomancy for inner self-discovery. In circuiting the Zodiac temple we learn we are, psychically, made of the identical resonance pattern as the solar system, and we thank our Zodiac hologram for clearly mirroring this reality for us. The Zodiac is a means for individual attunement with the Music of the Spheres, for hearing the subtle cosmic crystal harmonics, orchestrated daily by the "rushing sounds" movement of planets and stars, the *Rhoizamata*, as Pythagoras would say, which are always resonating within our atomic/molecular/consciousness environment, but just below the range of common hearing. The local Zodiac radio turns up the volume on this unending solar resonance so we can hear our stellar heartbeat. So, transiting the Earth Zodiac under intelligent astrological guidance, is like having a personalized Sony Walkman strapped to our ears, tuned to the cosmic FM band of fine musical orchestration---Venusian rhapsodies, Martian reggae, Jupiterian symphonies---all courtesy of King Sun Broadcasting Network.

Each landscape effigy has its own internal templic structure modelled, again, on the Tree of Life. Our Girt Dog of Langport happens to be, geomythically, the canine psychopomp for the neophyte Grail Knight entering the starry Otherworld of the Zodiac temple, the spinning mystical Grail Castle. Mythologically, the Zodiac temple is the theater for the Grail Knight to seek, find, and fulfill the Grail Quest, which is none other than uncovering and opening the divine seed of Light and Spirit buried deep within human consciousness. The landscape Zodiac temple is energetically organised to facilitate this revelation. Our inner nature truly lies among the stars. And Merlin, legendary Enchanter and Bard of Britain and King Arthur's Star Worker, was the master geomancer who dispatched the Grail Knights out to the star centers for visionary/integrative experiences, each according to the coincidence of their individual natal charts, their own spiritual development status, and the larger astrological cycles---as mediated through the landscape Zodiac hologram.

This is the moment in which the Grail Knight and Grid Engineer shake hands and act as one out in the Grid. The field of our psychophysical organism, the electromagnetic and bioplasmic structure, is inherently linked into the Earth's electromagnetic and bioplasmic fields. When a human being inter-relates and unifies (through meditation) at the right point in time and space (according to the Ephemeris time tables) on the surface of the Earth (at the correctly chosen star center vortex), and in themselves (in attunement with their overall program of spiritual unfoldment, as calibrated by their Master), and there is coincidence, then we have individual and planetary resonance. Then we have direct, tangible, experiential knowledge of the human place in the solar system. When we walk through the Zodiac Grid Door into the realm of the Gods, we comprehend our true status in the solar paradigm. And that is to embody and transfigure it all in the Human Body of Light.

But how, exactly, does the meditating Grail Knight also function as Grid technician? Just as the Solar Logos is the Soul of the Being known as the solar system, and just as the Planetary Logos is the Soul of Gaia, so the Grail stands for the potential for humans *to know as* the Soul. The Grail is an electromagnetic consciousness doorway within the human mind/body complex which opens through individuation of the psyche (i.e., the harmonious integration of the twelvefold Zodiac archetypes of the Sun) into divinity. This is called by Qabalists the *Adam Kadmon*, the sacred template of human perfection, the Edenic Light Body.

The Grid, operating through its geomantically symbolic local star configurations, is a series of epiphanies, of harmonic unifications, octaval Notes of Trees within Trees, each sounding their note in a heavenly/terrestrial chorale. It proceeds step-by-step, beginning with the local Zodiac effigies. When Canis Major resonates within the Region of the Summer Stars Zodiac system, and when all 144 effigies within this Zodiac Dome are harmonised, then the system as a whole can resonate properly and fulfill its intended geometric place in the Zodiac octaval choir. When each of the 144 Zodiac Domes is harmonised, when the 12 Zodiac Vortices are resonating, then the global Round Table/Tree of Life through Avebury can sing within the choir of the solar system of which our Gaia is one sweetly singing voice. Thus is Gaia's position as Grail Knight at the King Sun's Round Table fulfilled and the solar harmonic completed.

When the human, myth-living one's true identity as a star-compounded Grail Knight walking through the local Zodiac temple, unifies consciousness at a star center through a variety of means (e.g., meditation, chanting, singing, dancing, crystal focussing, directed breathing, group rituals, channelling higher beings, performing color visualizations), this brings the local aspect of the Electromagnetic 1746 Grid into clarity, focus, and harmony. Human and planetary energies are balanced through aware human participation at Grid nodes.

When we comprehend the Grid as Gaia's immune and digestive system, and when we further consider the ubiquitous ecological disaster we have dumped in Her lap (not to mention the howling delusionary human astral plane we've created above the Earth like a permanent brown band of smog), then we can clearly see the urgency for purging, cleansing, and harmonising the Human/Gaia Being again. We are not separate: Gaia's ecology is our spirituality; Her imbalance is our psychosis. It's a question of **reciprocal maintenance.** As we maintain the Mother, so we maintain ourselves, Her children. As we purify Her body, so we cleanse our own. As we feed Her, so She feeds us. As the British geomancer Reshad Feild notes, "Although this grid system exists in the natural world, it,too, is made for man and woman, and so the necessary work of transformation has to go 'through' the vehicle of the human being." [14]

This is true planetary ecology, love for the "Earth Household", because it recognizes the indivisible bond between Earth and Human, House and Resident, Mother and Child, as mediated through our homologous Grid bodies. And we can count on the assistance of both the Elemental (the supposed "legendary "realm of gnomes, fairies, sylphs, etc.) and the Angelic Kingdoms, in concert with the Elohim, Adam's "parents" on Earth.

The Enlightening of Adam

The landscape temple made of stones and crystal, positioned at Dome centers, divinely empowered by the Elohim in concordance with the Elemental Kingdom, and ritually inhabited by consciously breathing humans, linked Heaven and Earth through Man. The terrestrial temple also functioned as a Grid Door by which human consciousness, initially bounded by the Earth's gravitational/consciousness field, could actually exit this plane and enter "the realm of the Gods." Through this Grid Door, the Gods could also channel their spiritual vibrations and messages.

The ancient ziggurat, for example, was a Grid Door or Heaven/Earth mediator. The Akkadian/Babylonian name was *zukiratu,* which connoted "tube of divine spirit;" while in the Sumerian tongue, ziggurats were called ESH, which meant "supreme" or "most high" or "heat source". Moreover the ziggurat at legendary Nippur (at the northern confluence of the Tigris and Euphrates Rivers) was considered the Gods' headquarters, called KI.UR (or DUR.AN.KI) which meant "place of Earth's root" and "the place where the bond between Heaven and Earth rose", the place where there was a "heavenward tall pillar reaching to the sky."[15] Clearly such a place was a major Dome center for Sumerian culture.

As the Irish myths attest, the *sidhe*, or raised stone-and-earth barrow, was the home of the Tuatha de Danann, the sanctified, potent residence of the ancient Gods. Domed Newgrange, the *Brugh na Boinne,* was their principal home in old Ireland. The Gods, through their residences, were the source of wisdom for early reverential humankind,and while the Gods may have occupied their etheric palaces at the Dome centers, humans meanwhile, and afterwards, constructed physical temples to mark the spots and serve as a two-way swinging door.

So the Domes which brought Love from Above for Gaia's meridians, also brought wisdom to Adam, the early man/woman inhabitant. The Domes were the source of wisdom, the **wise domes**. Megalithic culture was a sacred milieue best described as **magelithic**, meaning the time of the Magus Stones. But the agents of the Wise Domes, the Stone Magi (or Magicians), after a time judged it better to not leave their signature too prominently and removed the letter *e,* leaving us wisdom. But even in their omission did they leave their handwriting, for the *e* that was removed from the wise domes is the *e* of **Elohim.**

The Elohim also left the consciousness technology in place to facilitate the human retrieval of their angelic wisdom through the interdimensional structures positioned at the Dome sites. Stone Age indeed! The Elohim left a major calling card at Avebury, not the least tarnished after many milennia. Just as Avebury is central to the nature and operation of the Earth Grid, so it was, and remains, pivotal in the appearance (and eventual reawakening) of Adam, the first collective manifestation of physically individuated woman and man on Earth. When we understand Avebury a little better, we can begin to answer the fundamental questions underlying all this complexity of life: Why is there a Grid at all? Why is there an Earth? Why is there human life?

Avebury Circle originally had 94 stones, of which 72 were created by the Elohim, and 22 were later imported from elsewhere. Encircling the Avebury Circle is a massive ditch (about 30 feet deep) bordered on both sides by an embankment. The ditch is like a huge groove running around the Circle; it has an intensely feminine vibration, like a river of soft silent light flowing whitely through the earthen channel, like a susurrus between embankments. Walking slowly through the ditch one senses the primal Mother is whispering here to her Children of the Circle.

At Avebury Circle the earth has been taken out of a whole and removed. We can look at the circle as a giant record. The ditch is the groove on the record. If we play the record with the needle of our Spirit, then we hear some "hi fi" angelic music. The 94 stones are the amplifiers for the music. The Stone Circle is thus an outdoor cosmic sound system, the site of the original Rock concerts.

Here we have the concept of **geomantic harmonics** at work. The stone circle has a specific pre-encoded resonance harmonic, a specific musically-enscribed message, or Song. The composite shape of the circle represents a frozen cymatic sculpture, a permanent landscape stereo record from the Spirit. The stone circle embodies a Tone dropped into the ethers of the Earth then molded terrestrially into a playable record. The ditch is the primary record groove, and the first wave trough emanating from the place where the "stone" tone was originally dropped into the site (i.e.,the center of the circle). The Dome overhead is the bell that carries the tone when "struck" from

Above by the musician. The Dome site channels this Tone through its geomantically calibrated musical instrument, the stone circle, and the encircling stones are the "wrap-around sound" loudspeakers. The particular size and structural complexity of the megalithic stone record is directly related to the evolutionary importance of the Sound recorded. The truly biggest hit tunes get the largest diameter stone circles.

Avebury is thus one of Gaia's largest stone records, occupying an area in Wiltshire of 28 1/2 acres, with a ditch circumference of 4/5 mile. The 17th century British antiquarian John Aubrey, writing of Avebury, declared, "Avebury doth as much exceed Stonehenge in grandeur as a Cathedral doth an ordinary Parish Church." The 20th century British scholar Harold Bayley (writing in *The Lost Language of Symbolism,* 1913) corroborated Aubrey's enthusiasm, announcing "The English Temple of Abury (sic) typified not only Time but also the greater Absolute, the all-embracing and more *awe*-full Soul of time, the axis of Existence." Why is Avebury so important?

All the ley lines, it seems, lead to Avebury. All the energy in the Grid is focussed at Avebury Circle, our planetary Grid umbilicus. The purpose of Avebury is tuning human consciousness to its purpose on Earth. At Avebury resides the Earth-expression of the blazing Seed of divine Light. Within the human body, as the Grail Knight discovers, resides this same Light Seed, this fire of the Spirit, which we call the **Nimitta** or **Blazing Star**[16]. This Seed, whether within the human or at Avebury, is the same Blazing Star. It is the same blazing crystal Seed from which both Gaia and Adam were physically born, birthed by the Elohim, whom *Genesis,* in the standard confusing and exoteric translations, calls God. More properly, the Elohim are God's agents, the Sons of Light, and the agents of our local creation.

This fundamental aspect of the Grid and human life will make more sense when we examine a few key words. Avebury, Adam, and Elohim, are coded symbolic words created by the Elohim through the sacred language of Qabala (which matches letters with numbers, i.e., gematria).

ADAM (1.4.40, technically written as ADM) means "the Aleph (A.1.) buried in the Blood of Earth (DAM, 4.40)." Aleph here means the Blazing Star of the eternal Spirit, the universal flame of the Nimitta, implanted as an imperishable seed of Light within the human body of clay and blood (DAM). In other words, the Kingdom of Heaven blazes within us as this Star (Aleph). AVEBURY is the place (BRY, 2.200.10) where the Aleph was implanted (or buried) in Mother (AVE, 1.6.1) Earth. Avebury is the Mother's Village, the place of the Mother's berry, or seed. Avebury, as the inner heart of Gaia, was Adam's heart/womb door, the terrestrial place where Adam first came into Earth incarnation from the Garden of Eden Above. Adam arrived with the Blazing Star burning like a blinding furnace within his/her mind/body complex. Adam appeared on Earth through Avebury as a terrific flame of Heaven walking in the form of the human. Avebury remains the place we can go to on Earth to remember our fiery, spiritual arrival on the planet.

ELOHIM, an angelic hierarchy, were the Creator Gods for Adam and Gaia, the master mancers of geo and soma. Elohim implemented the translation of the Blazing Star from the spiritual realms into the sentient, organic, evolving life form of Adam, following the same homology whereby the Aleph was clothed in planet Earth, becoming our sentient, organic, evolving life form of Gaia. Elohim, in a sense, supervised and midwived the co-creation of Adam and Gaia as homologous beings.

Let's examine this still more closely. This will clarify our composite model of the Grid, Earth, Adam, and Elohim. Light, in Qabala, is AWR or 1.62 (Technically, it's 1.6.200, but final zeros are redundant). AVE the Mother is 1.61. The phi ratio of the light spiral is 1.61 (or, precisely, 1.618034, which can be rounded off to 1.62). Earth and Adam have a mathematically homologous relationship whereby ADAM is 144 and Earth, through its Grid (i.e., Electromagnetic 1746 Grid, the Golden Bowl, and Christ Body) is 1746. Both numbers are related through the phi ratio.

The Silver Cord, the primary dual-weaved umbilical electrical cable entering Avebury, is comprised of 666 (the solar Father of Light, the Seed, the Nimitta, Aleph, or Blazing Star,and golden line) and 1080 (the lunar Mother of Forms, and silver line). Their relation as polarised light (666/1080, positive/negative) is expressed as phi 1.61 while their summation is 1746, also a function of phi. We have, then, **Light** (AWR 1.62) moving through the umbilicus as **Electricity** (positive/negative charges, expressed as 666/1080) and manifesting as **Electromagnetism** (the polarised north/south nodes of the 1746 Electromagnetic Grid, as manifested through the yin/yang qualities of the 12 Oroboros Lines). This channelling of Light to Electricity to Electromagnetism births physical **Life**, expressed as Adam and Gaia, as the bioorganic theater for their interplay, as mediated through the Megalithic Grid.

Earth, incidentally, is written in Qabala as ARTZ (or ERTZ,

1.200.90, or 291, whose digits total 12, the prime number of the Oroboros Grid and Zodiac Temple), In terms of mythology, the Mother of Forms (1080) creates the Holy Grail to contain the Father's Seed of Light (666, Blazing Star), while the Elohim (angelic Grail Maidens) bring the Grail (now 1746, both Seed and Vessel) down to Earth (ARTZ, the 12-sided Grail Castle) for Adam (144), the Grail Knight and Grail Bearer.

But what creates the Light originally? What starts this whole generative procession culminating in Adam walking the Earth bearing the Grail? Undifferentiated, undivided, inexhaustible, unfathomable **Love from Above**.

Adam is the key to unlocking the secret of this **light harmonic**. The New Zealand Grid theorist Bruce Cathie speculates that "All the mathematical evidence so far indicates that the maximum number of individual elements to be found in the universe will be 144." Each element can have, theoretically, 6 isotopes, making 864 possible combinations. Cathie proposes "144 octaves of separate substances" in which an octave is comprised of an element family of 6 isotopes each. Each electron cloud, or shell, as it expands outwards from the atomic nucleus, can accomodate a maximum of 8 electrons. Thus each shell expansion is a function of 8 (the original basis of the octave) and forms a new electron shell. This Cathie calls the "harmonic zone" or "light harmonic" totalling 144. "The light harmonic is then equal and the cycle has been completed. The whole series is a repetition of octaves of wave forms" whereby physical reality is "manifested by the concentrated interlocking of harmonic wave-forms."[17]

This is clearly controversial yet keenly intriguing. To date 107 elements have been discovered; this leaves 37 undetected, or should we more accurately say, "as yet *unmanifested* ?" The number 144, we've seen, is pivotal in the Grid and Adam. A closer look at our key numbers will amplify Cathie's suggestions.

How can we arrive at 144 elements? Let's postulate 18 solar octaves, as representing the maximum expressive potential of the solar Father (666, whose digits total 18) acting on the material archetypal Forms of the Mother. From the Mother of Forms, say the Qabalists, issues the heavenly Chariot (The Mother's sphere, Binah, the third Sephiroth, manifests the *Hhayt*. 8, a downward manifesting pathway called in Tarot the Chariot [See Diagram 7]). The Chariot of Hhayt. 8 refers to the maximum number of electrons in an atomic shell thereby comprising an element as the fundamental form. Now, let's rearrange the Periodic Table of the Elements, momentarily, and postulate 8 families of elements, each occupying 3 solar octaves. By the mathematics of light (18 x 8) we have the full light harmonic, 144, expressed as Adam, on Earth. Thus Adam 144, as a sentient, organic life form comprises, the full expressive potential for the 144 elements in this universe. The 144 elements, themselves, represent the dramatic interplay (based on phi 1.61, as the unfolding physics of Light) of the Father 666 and Mother 1080. Their combined electrical impulse 1746 (i.e., the Grail with the Blazing Star inside) is the spark within the form of Life, for Adam and Earth. And in either case, the Elohim are the quantum midwives, heavenly benefactors, and, literally, God-parents of this grand astrophysical experiment.

This complex, terrestrial drama all reduces to the number **9,** called *Tayt* in Qabala. All the key numbers in this Light interplay of Earth, Adam, and the Grid, it seems, digitally total 9: 1746, 144, 1080, 666, 864, 83,808 (possible planetary dome caps), 20,736 (number of planetary Zodiacs multiplied by number of star effigies in each). Even affiliate numbers all point to 9: 86,400 (average human heartbeats/day), 25,920 (number of years in one Great Zodiac Year), 4,320,000 (years in the Mahayuga, the Hindu cosmic time cycle)---not to mention the 9 month gestation time for humans. What, then, is the 9 that pervades the inner structure of the Grid?

We must turn to the Qabala for illumination of the 9. Tayt.9 represents the archetype of the primeval "feminine" formative energy, which draws upon the *Hhayt.* 8 (the storage sphere, or Chariot), of all undifferentiated energy, which derives from Binah (the Sephiroth of the Mother of Forms) to build structures. *Tayt.* 9 is the elementary "Female", the prodigious proliferator of elementary form units, individual cells, expressive composites created from the Mother's electron clusters of *Hhayt* 8. In Qabala Tarot symbolism (Tarot is a pictorial system directly related to the Tree of Life as a visual/intuitive series of life/drama depictions affiliated, in part, with the 22 pathways) *Tayt.* 9 is the Path of "Strength of the Lion." Each pathway on the Tree is "ruled" by a Zodiac House; *Tayt.* 9 is ruled by Leo, which in turn is ruled by the Sun. *Tayt.* 9 is often depicted in Tarot symbology as the Scarlet Woman (alive with the fire of Life) and is pictured as an ecstatic, nearly drunken, lascivious, scarlet-clothed, and most powerful primal woman astride a Lion/Serpent, holding its jaws open in triumph. In world mythologies, 9 is the number of "the Goddess Mother of the World," the "Great Goddess of Many Names," She who is Matrix of the cosmic life process, and, in Greece, it was the number of the Nine Muses, Daughters of Mnemosyne (Memory, i.e., *Binah*).

But what is the Strength of the Lion that our archetypal generatrix is riding triumphantly? Qabala symbolism interprets the Lion variously. Regulus, the heart of the Lion, is the brightest star in that constellation and Leo was anciently regarded as the beginning of the Zodiac Round. The Lion also represents the first formation of the human individuality projected into the world of Form (Geburah, 5th Sephiroth) from the realm of the Spirit (Chesed, 4th Sephiroth). The Lion, says J.J. Hurtak, represents our Star Evolution, King Sun. Thus the entire solar reality, the **Drama of the Nine,** of our local Star Evolution system, is mathematically encoded into the light harmonic of Adam, Earth, Grid. The 9 is the Logos of our Sun, his metaphysical calling card, his secret telephone number. We have, then, the physics, geometry, and gematria of the specific light harmonic (the solar octaves) of our King Sun, encoded synchronously and thoroughly throughout all form manifestations in our world, within all dramatis personae (like an ineradicable blood type or permanent thumbprint) of his solar Crystal Theater. Through our human lives as the Mother's Children on Earth, our local Mother, we myth-live, as divinely made holograms, the Light valency, or Mind/Body/Spirit, of our solar system, *Tayt*. 9, the Strength of the Lion.

This is the Drama of the Nine in short form: **The** (Love from Above) **Light** (AWR, 1.61, the Logos of Light, phi) **Harmonic** (Electricity, phi differentiated as 666/1080, into positive/negative charges) **Expressed** (through the Elohim, the angelic verb, agents of the implantation of archetypal life into temporal form) **as Adam** (144, the human electromagnetic fulfillment of all elemental expressive potentiality, as 18 solar octaves x 8 element families) **on Earth** (ARTZ, 291=12, the 12-fold Zodiac/Round Table/Planetary Grid matrix). Thus do the Wise Domes of the Elohim teach us of the *Lion's Play* and purpose of Earth, Adam, and our loving bond, the Grid.

Adam's Geomancy

So Hermes throws the ball back to us. As humans we must all become geomancers for our Mother, Gaia, and for ourselves, Adam.

At the beginning of Time on Earth, the great geomancer Hermes arrived with the Elohim, the Sons of Light and Biblical "Giants in the Earth," and established the Global Hermetic Megalithic Calendar---the Grid. The Elohim further arranged for the human psyche to resonate in harmony with the Music of the Spheres as broadcast through our local twelvefold solar Round Table and as received through many radios of the templic stone grid. This was, supposedly, at the time of the second Dome Presence, just before Adam's Drama of the Nine was about to be staged. The Grid temple was designed to achieve the necessary biopsychic nexus between Heaven and Earth as embodied, as lived, as walked by Adam on Earth.

Thus Adam and Gaia were set in balance in an inextricable bond, as homologous manifestations and groundings of the same fundamental phi spiral of Light. The human psyche was wired into the Grid which itself was wired for sound as a sonic hologram of the Solar Logos. The planetary Grid and its local miniaturizations was the model/blueprint/directions for Home, Enlightenment, and Paradise. Through the Grid, Gaia and Adam were held in living harmony within the greater body of the solar system.

Thus we got off to a terrific start. After a while, the Elohim/Giants and their Domes departed. We were on our own.

Human geomancers, trained under Hermes, and in cooperation with the Elemental Kingdom, assumed responsibility for Grid maintenance (which is to say, really, for individual and communal enlightenment) although they could still rely on assistance from Above---first, from the Elohim, who had returned to angelic form and residence, and second, from the widespread extra-planetary network of benevolent Space Brothers. The presumed high civilization of Atlantis was the site of the Planetary College of Grid Magnetics graduating a succession of expert geomancers. The twelve-tiered Atlantean Temple of Oralin was geomancy headquarters, like a Pentagon for magnetic sciences. Here geomancers and magnetics technicians conducted continual analyses of Grid conditions, monitored terrestrial/solar energy fields, designed and installed various geomantic engineering instruments---all as part of an overall program of maintaining a harmonious and fruitful planetary Grid system for the benefit of all beings.[18]

We might construe these ultrascientific Atlantean Grid technicians as the archetypal computerized Druids, for even in later times, after the collapse of Atlantean high culture, the legendary Druids maintained the wisdom of the Grid and kept it in balance. The Druids fine-tuned the Earth Radio through all Her Dome receptor/dial sites and myriad transmission wires. The Druid geomancers kept Gaia's biosphere humming with a steady stream of life-supporting, life-enriching, life-evolving energy transmissions from Above.

The Druids and Atlanteans understood well the reciprocal agreement. Through Hermes, Adam learned the *divination* of the Earth, the secrets of geomancy. But through Adam, Hermes expected the reciprocal *divinization* of the Earth through intelligent, loving application of geomancy. Why? Because, fundamentally, this program of reciprocal maintenance would bring about the mutual enlightenment of Mother Earth and Child Adam, which is what the Elohim intended, as part of the Master Plan, for this particular astrophysical experiment on Earth. Gaia, through Her Grid, maintains our Blazing Star. We, through our geomancy, maintain Gaia's Blazing Star.

But why need we be concerned *today*, in our comfortable Western society of personal computers, credit cards and new Volvos? Why should we bother with all this ancient history and idealistic grandeur from a remote Druidic past? Because many interlocking universal, galactic, solar, planetary, and human evolutionary cycles are all synchronously coming to fruition and conclusion at this the end of the 20th century. Certain basic incarnational obligations all humans willingly agreed to, long ago, as a condition for inhabiting the Earth, have all come due. It's not a question of "the wrath of the Gods" or an "angry,displeased Jehovah". It's simply a matter of cosmic clockwork. A major cycle is nearly finished. New things are about to begin. All old business must be cleared up quickly. This kind of Grid teleology will assume sharper focus when we examine two further aspects of the Grid.

Planet Earth, within the theory of chakras, is the Muladhara Root Chakra in the Body of the Solar Logos. If we picture the solar system as a huge human-like figure, Earth sits very materially in the scrotum as the root energy center. The entire Earth Grid, in fact, is actually an organic multitiered model of the energy dynamics of a solar root chakra, functioning for the Sun just as Mt. Shasta functions for Gaia. What is the significance of the root chakra?

Sleeping within Gaia is the Goddess Kundalini, the tremendous creative, evolutionary spiritual energy that transfigures, when activated, the entire 7 chakra system---of the human, the Earth, the solar system. Kundalini, the Indian Tantric texts inform us, is "She who maintains all the beings of the world by means of inspiration and expiration and (who) shines in the cavity of the root Lotus like a chain of brilliant lights." Moreover, Goddess Kundalini "is the receptacle of that continuous stream of ambrosia which flows from the Eternal Bliss. By Her radiance it is that the whole of this universe and this Cauldron is illumined."[19] The sequence of chakra openings is reckoned as 2 through 7, then back to the root, from which the aroused Kundalini arises in a fiery burst like the soaring serpent and flames up the sushumna through the chakras illuminating everything with a divine light beyond brilliance. This is Gaia's potential and Her expected role in our local solar system.

Planet Earth is also the final Word in the Secret Name of God, called in Qabala, **Tetragrammaton**, the Word of Four Letters, i.e., **YHWH** (Yod-He-Wod-He, or Yahweh, or Jehovah, in translation). The Solar Logos, as we mentioned, can be modelled as a Tree of Life with Earth at Malkuth, the 10th Sephiroth. The *Tetragrammaton* in part pertains to that composite ineffable resonance, or harmonic, of all levels of expression of this Tree. This includes the Four Elements (fire, air, water, earth) in all their dimensions of subtle and physical expression. The Father of Light (Chokmah) is **Yod**; the Mother of Forms (Binah/Saturn) is **He** (pronounced *Hay* **);** the Soul of Adam (Tiphareth/Sun) is **Wod**; and Earth, the Body of Adam (Malkuth/Earth) is the final **He**.

The Earth is a Perpetual Choir in the solar system orchestra. Just as one stone circle on Earth is a cosmic Record, angelically recorded for Man, and just as individual stone circles are instrumental members of the planetary orchestra and all performing their parts of the overall solar symphony, so Gaia Herself is a planetary Record for those Above. Gaia is one Note singing proudly in the infinite space, finding its intended, necessary, and appropriate niche in the Music of the Spheres. When all the stone circle records are attuned, when the 12 Oroboric Lines resonate in equal measure through Avebury Circle, and when the necessary crystalline spirit needles are positioned throughout the Earth Record, then Gaia can sing **He** to the angels in Heaven.

This is the meaning of **reciprocal harmonics.** This is Adam's Geomancy. When Gaia sounds Her **He** in the Choir of the solar system, then the solar harmonic is completed. Then the solar octave is registered, every note, and altogether. Then everything begins to vibrate at a faster rate and the Solar Logos sounds His Note in the Galactic Choir---and so forth, into Infinity, as far as we're concerned.

This is why all the attention is focussed today on the Earth, on Her Grid. This is why the Space Brothers touch down so visibly into our third dimension, why so much interdimensional channelling (from Ascended Masters and angels, in particular) is happening today, why the Angelic Kingdom is returning to credible human awareness, why the Grid is coming into focus.

Everyone is waiting for us.

The Earth is one note in the solar choir. When Earth sounds Her **He** in the Choir, the light harmonic of this Star Evolution will be completed, in turn completing a more exalted light harmonic of which it is a part. The Earth and our King Sun are about to receive a major solar/spiritual initiation, one which will inaugurate a new Light valency, a new electromagnetic spectrum, which will be experienced by us as a quantum leap away from materialized consciousness into the free-floating fourth dimension.

This may sound remote, abstract, and unbelievable, too far away from ley lines, and therefore not worthy of our concern. Why should we be concerned, anyway?

Some time ago, it is believed, Hermes handed over his role as Gaia's Master Geomancer to his spiritual brother, the Archangel Michael. Michael, among other responsibilities, is called The Keeper of the Secrets of the Relations between Heaven and Earth; He is also the Tone Bearer for Earth and the Standard Bearer for the Christ, who is Adam's full potential, the source of the hologram of the Human. Michael approaches Gaia now with his Sword of Spirit poised for the initiatory stroke. Already He has touched Gaia at the apex of Her fire/tetrahedron at Mt. Balsam Cone, North Carolina. Gaia's inner heart at Avebury is scheduled for imminent reactivation. The Grid, under structural reassessment, is also about to be "switched back on", full power, but at a higher vibrational rate. Theoretically, the Domes and Elohim will return. The ancient British festival of Michael Mass (known traditionally as Michaelmas, September 29) will be radically enriched in planetary meaning.

Both Gaia and Adam will remember the Blazing Star set as an imperishable Seed of Knowing and Bliss within their planetary and human bodies. *We must again embody Adam* (as the Blazing Star buried in the Blood of Earth) *inhabiting Gaia* (as the Blazing Star buried in the Clay of the Mother).

What will happen then? Anti-gravity! There will be a new Light/Life spectrum for Adam and Gaia, resulting in a change in, even transcendence of, the ancient gravitational field holding us down with iron guy-wires to the physical plane of Earth awareness. Recently a new elementary substance was discovered; it was found to have possible anti-gravity properties and was named *levitonium.* The scientists speculated that *levitonium* might be capable of powering rockets out of the Earth's gravitational field.

With a small measure of British-earned cheekiness, I now

propose a term to describe the possibilities of anti-gravity within the terms of human experience: levitony. **Levitony** is a species of giddiness inspired by the angels---Elohim, if you like. It is an attitude, perhaps archetypal, of giggling detachment that lifts us right off the Earth in a free-floating feather of amusement and mirth, defying gravity, defeating the seriousness, the weightiness, the heaviness, of Earth life as we know it---those familiar "astrophysical consciousness parameters".

Levitony, I suggest with a cirrus-like grin,is native to our constitution, something we were naturally born with. With the bouyancy of levitony we will glide in Adam's transfigured Light Body high above dear Gaia and we will note She, too, is again looking pristine and sparkling in Her blazing light. She, too, once again, has become our Garden of Eden.

REFERENCES

[1] Hitching, Francis, *Earth Magic,* William Morrow & Company, New York, 1977.

[2] Graves, Tom, *Needles of Stone Revisited*, Gothic Image Publications, Glastonbury, England, 1978, 1986.

[3] Elkins, Don, Rueckert, Carla, McCarty, James Allen, *The Ra Material---An Ancient Astronaut Speaks,* The Donning Company, Norfolk, VA, 1984.

[4] Lessing, Doris, *Briefing for a Descent into Hell,* Alfred Knopf, New York, 1971.

[5] Three Initiates, *The Kybalion: A Study of the Hermetic Philosophy of Ancient Egypt and Greece,* Yogi Publication Society, Chicago, 1912.

[6] Leviton, Richard, "The Ley Hunters," *East West*, November 1986, pp. 70-75.

[7] Clow, Barbara Hand, *Eye of the Centaur: A Visionary Guide into Past Lives*, Llewellyn Publications, St. Paul, MN, 1986.

[8] Alper, Dr. Frank, *Exploring Atlantis,* Volume 1, Coleman Publishing, Farmingdale, NY, 1983.

[9] Baer, Randall N., Baer, Vicki V., *Windows of Light: Quartz Crystals and Self-Transformation*, Harper & Row, San Francisco, CA 1984.

[10] Hurtak, J.J., *The Book of Knowledge: The Keys of Enoch,* The Academy for Future Science, Los Gatos, CA, 1973, 1977.

[11] Leviton, Richard, "Message of the Stones," *East West*, June 1985, pp.

53-57.

[12] Leviton, Richard, "The Body Electric---Healing with Nature's Energy," *East West*, June 1986, pp. 54-61.

[13] Whitfield, Joseph, *The Treasure of El Dorado,* Treasure Publications, Roanoke, VA, 1986.

[14] Feild, Reshad, "Some Notes on the Subject of Ley Lines and Geomancy," published in Germany, 1986.

[15] Sitchin, Zecharia, *The 12th Planet,* Avon, New York, 1976.

[16] For more information on *Nimitta* and the *Blazing Star*, consult **Looking for Arthur, Volume 1: Joseph's Seed**, by Richard Leviton, 1987

[17] Cathie, Bruce, *The Bridge to Infinity: Harmonic 371244*, Quark Enterprises/Brookfield Press, Auckland, New Zealand, 1983.

[18] Alper, Dr. Frank, *op. cit.* , Volume 2.

[19] Avalon, Arthur, *The Serpent Power---The Secrets of Tantric and Shaktic Yoga,* Dover Publications, New York, 1974.

About the Author

Richard Leviton is the author of *Joseph's Seed*, the first volume of a trilogy about the relations between mythology, the megalithic landscape, and transformations in consciousness---under the general title of *Looking for Arthur*. He is also author of *Fraser's Angel,* a visionary tale about the adventures of a young boy travelling in the angelic realms. Both titles are published in 1987. Since early 1984 Leviton has lived in Somerset, England, where he has researched firsthand the subjects of geomancy and geomythics. He is also Contributing Editor for *East West* magazine in Boston, Massachusetts. For correspondence, please direct inquiries to: Richard Leviton, 8 Skinner Lane, South Hadley, MA 01075.

INTERNATIONAL HARMONY BASED UPON A MUSIC OF PLANETARY GRID SYSTEMS

by Barbara Hero

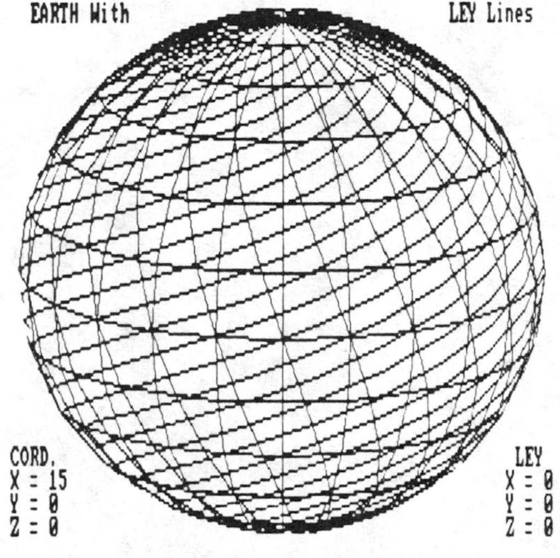

This paper will propose a method of correlating Earth Grid systems with specific musical notes, by a process of translating length to frequencies which can then be translated to musical notes.

A method of octave expansion and octave reduction was used to determine the specific frequency of a note.

When this theory is applied to the relationships of countries to sounds, a way of increasing harmony between countries can be suggested by knowing a key note of the distance between them.

A correspondence with Pythagorean Lambdoma of seven rays is suggested.

In September of 1983 I received a letter from Governors State University in Illinois requesting submission of information or research on a project called THE PLANETARY GRID SYSTEM. I wrote back a note saying that perhaps I could help by identifying the musical interval of the modular grid system if there is a module that has been determined in length. Then, a year later in December, 1984, Bethe Hagens and William Becker sent a copy of the magazine *Pursuit*[1] which featured their research. And in this article the distances in miles of the grid system they devised was given, so that I could get to work to determine certain musical relationships. I sent a letter detailing these relationships. After receiving my letter Bethe Hagens replied:

> Thank you so much for your letter. I wanted you to know that we had received it. I am kind of stunned by what you have found in the grid — and your political interpretations. It's one of the most fascinating responses we've ever received. I don't know that I told you, but I am a professional violinist when I am not being an anthropologist. Your work in harmonics begins to get at something I have felt intuitively must exist but had no way to express.
>
> . . . I have not had the time to sit with your letter and really absorb it. I will write again once I have something intelligent to say. Again, thanks so much for writing.

The Becker-Hagens report presented a theory of the growing structure of the earth, from the tetrahedron, octahedron, cube, icosahedron, and dodecahedron. These are the Platonic solids attributed to Pythagoras (500 B.C.). The dodecahedron and icosahedron together, Becker and Hagens found to be the grid system of our present age. When the line arrays of each of these solids is overlaid on a sphere, a grid emerges which they contend is a pattern the ancient peoples used for becoming one with the earth.[2]

Briefly, factors to consider when calculating the harmonic implications between countries, cities, or villages include the following:

- What is the great circle distance in miles between two points on the grid system?
- What are the major apex points?
- Is the assumption that Giza is the major point valid, or has the energy changed since the building of the Great Pyramid?
- Are significant places in history nodes of the grid system?
- Are fault lines energy lines?
- Are mountain ranges energy lines?
- What is the difference between the fault lines and the mountain range lines in terms of energy?
- Could certain distances portend problem areas in terms of harmonies?

The Becker-Hagens report mentioned the *Twelve Devils' Graveyards Around the World (Saga Magazine,* 1972) where magnetic and energy aberrations were located. These are found zig-zaging the equator at 30 degrees above and 30 degrees below the equator.

Using an "Atlas" software computer program, Robert Foulkrod found the distance in miles to be 4264 miles between adjacent "Graveyards." The corresponding musical frequency based on the speed of sound in air is 0.0000502 cps. By octave expansion to the middle "C" octave (multiplying by 2 to the "n" number of times), this translates to a musical note of "A". This particular distance or musical note might be an indication of disharmony between countries, if, indeed, distance is a factor.

The Becker-Hagens report sets the kite shaped grid dimensions as 1400 miles (short end of the kite), 2200 miles (the outside kite length), and 2600 miles (the brace down the middle of the kite). The musical notes are "E flat", "A flat", and "F", respectively. The latter note represents the distance between Gomel in the Soviet Union and

Sebha in Libya. Therefore the musical sound of "F" at 345 cps might be accentuated for harmony between these two countries.

The Becker-Hagens report mentioned the theory by Sinkiewitz who claimed that the present energy grid sytem is out of alignment with the ancient grid system, and that New Age Spiritual communities around the globe are rediscovering the new grid and building sacred sites to activate them.

The Aleutian Islands have been predicted to be the new North Pole. See Figures 1, 2, 3, 4, & 5. What is the distance involved when a diamond of a 70 degree apex is overlaid on the new North Pole, and the legs of the diamond terminate at the Equator? This is the shape which some have found intuitively very emotionally responsive as if from a long forgotten past.

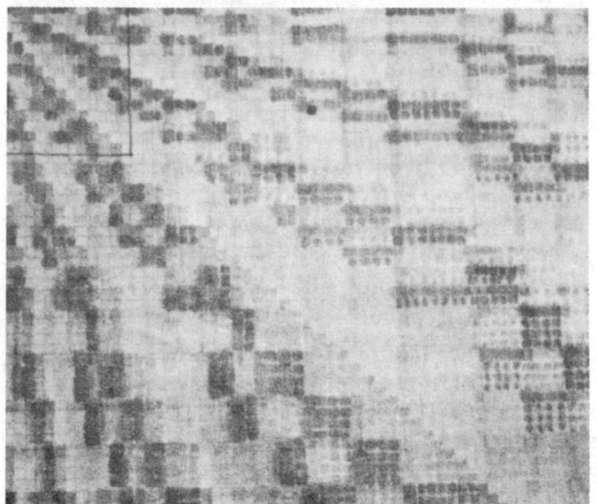

Figure 1. A Lambdoma Matrix (Color Coded).

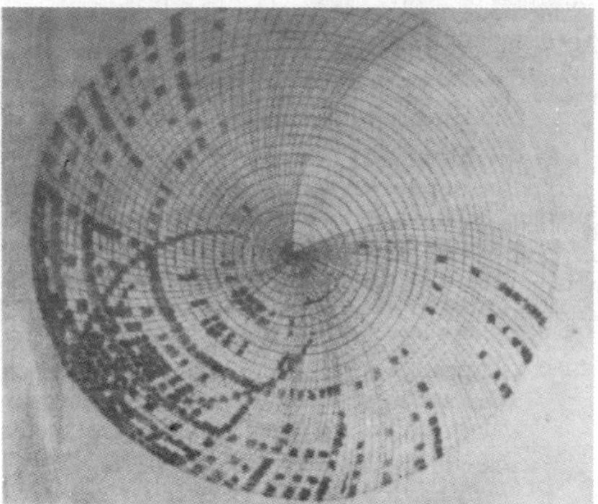

Figure 2. A Planetary Grid System based upon a Lambdoma Matrix originating at one of the poles.

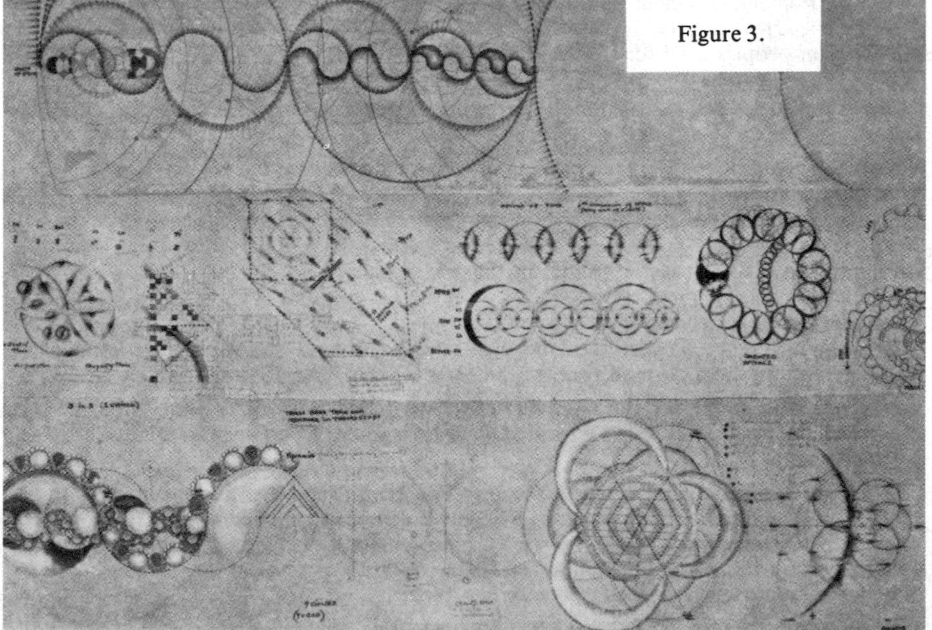

Figure 3.

Figures 3, 4, 5, & 6. Some Visual Ways of Interpreting musical intervals, as a prelude to applying to a planetary grid system.

Figure 4.

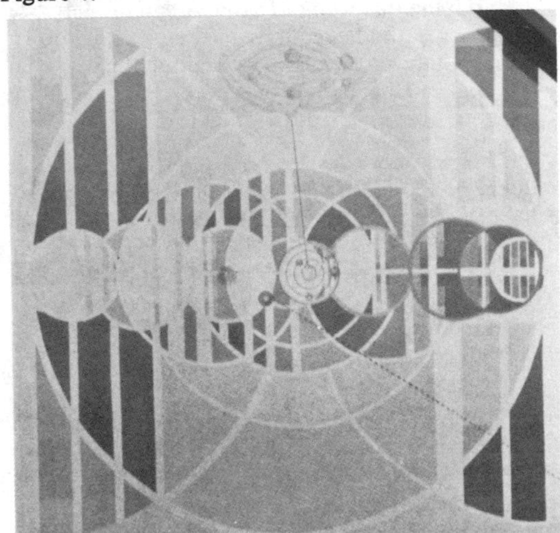

Figure 5.

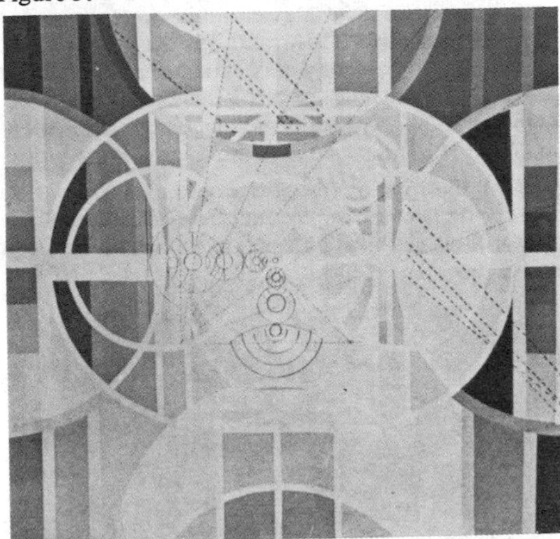

The method of determining the frequency of a distance is based on formula in physics which is stated in the letter to Becker-Hagens.

$$v = fw$$

where v = (1130) the velocity of sound in air at room temperature in ft/sec.

f = frequency in cycles/sec or Hertz

w = wavelength or distance in feet.

Because of the nature of the inverse properties of wavelength and frequency, the frequency and wavelength can be found if one knows the speed of sound for the material through which the sound travels.

Through the oceans the speed of sound would be faster and hence create a different musical note. The speed could have been taken to be the speed of sound through granite for mountainous ridges, and a different velocity in valleys, which would be of a less dense material. In valleys sound would travel slower than in the mountains, and slower still in air. One could assume that in earthquake faults the sound would travel even faster as the density of the entire earth would be a factor, it would seem, if in fact the earth is denser and not hollow. If the earth were hollow, as has been presented by some, sound would not travel in a vacuum, and would turn to light, since light and sound are on the same spectrum separated only by our measuring sound in frequency and light in wavelength. Light would travel faster in a vacuum, slower in air, slower still in water and become sound in a dense, non-transparent medium.

The note relating two cities or sites can readily be determined by the formula described earlier. When a third city or site is added one can readily determine whether the three are in harmonic accord by using a long forgotten method of determining geometrically and algebraically the arithmetic, geometric and harmonic means.

To illustrate, take the distance from a to b to be a given length in miles, then take a distance from one of these sites to another. Put the resulting lengths end to end, bisect them and draw a circle from the halfway mark. Draw a line orthogonal to the diameter of the circle at the point on the line of the first city or site. Where this line meets the circle determines the geometric mean. Then draw a line from this point on the circle to the center of the circle. This is the arithmetic mean, and the radius of the circle. Drawing a line orthogonal to this radius stretching to the first site defines the harmonic mean. These distances can be translated into sounds which would be harmonious with each one of the cities.

For example, let us take the distance between Gomel and Timbuktu of 1400 miles, and Timbuktu to Great Zimbebwe of 2200. Lets add these in one line making a total of 3600 miles, which bisected equals 1800 miles. The arithmetic mean would equal 1800 miles a "B" musically. The geometric mean would equal the square root of (2200 x 1400) or 1755 miles, a "C" musically and the harmonic mean 2 x (1400 x 2200) / (1400 2200), which equals 1711 miles, a "C#" musically. The length between the first two cities of 1400 is an "E flat", and the length between the second and third cities of 2200 is an "A flat". The cities exhibit an interval of a fourth between them or "A" to "E flat", which is a common harmonic used musically.

A "key note" of a country could be determined by means of a Lambdoma diagram (a Pythagorean model). See Figure 6, References 3 through 8. The apex of the Lambdoma diagram is divided equally as the diagonal down the center of the x and y axis. The diagonal has a ratio of 1:1, so that whatever the distance is along the diagonal of the grid would be its "key note". For example Gomel in the Becker-Hagens grid has seven rays radiating from the apex point, and the diagonal which represents the "key note" extends from Gomel to El Eglab, 2600 miles, an "F" musically. From Cairo to London is 2183 miles, a "G#".

Each of the rays of the grid would exhibit a unique energy, and much work has to be done to determine the quality of these differing energies. See Figures 7 & 8. In the case of the earth the circumference of the earth should be taken into account as a reference distance and frequency, the circumference is 24,860 miles. This is equivalent to a "D" musically (in air).

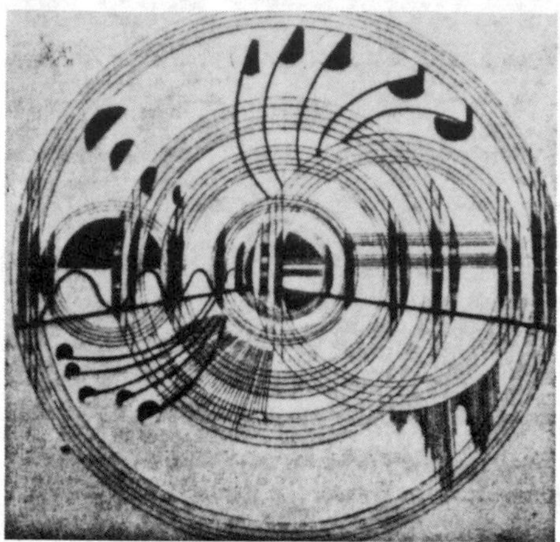

Figure 6.

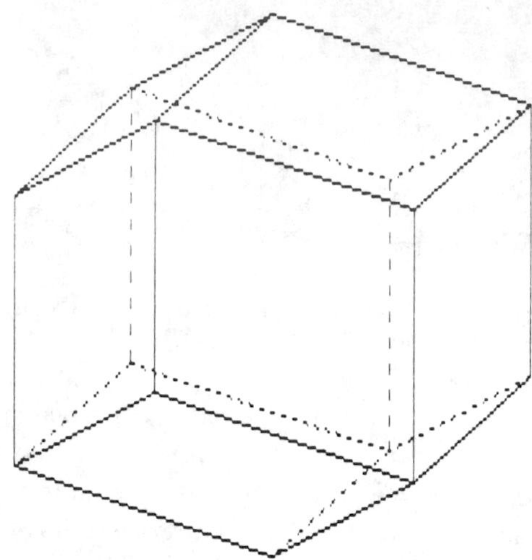

Figure 7. Recently rediscovered regular solid. It is in addition to the five solids known as the "Platonic Solids". All twelve faces are identical diamond shapes. The corner angles of each diamond are 70.52878 degrees and 109.47122. Solids of this shape will stack together without any empty spaces between them as is also true with cubes. We could call it a Rhombic Dodecahedron. Five views as a Grid. Computer Program by Robert Foulkrod.

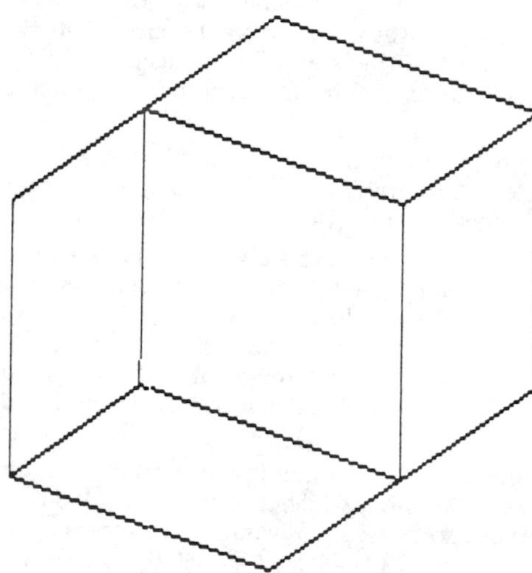

Figure 8. Front view of the Rhombic Dodecahedron showing the true shape of one of its diamond faces.

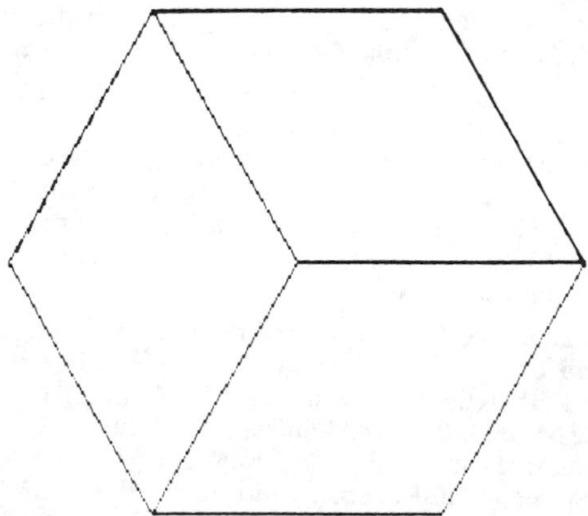

Figure 9. Top view of the Rhombic Dodecahedron.

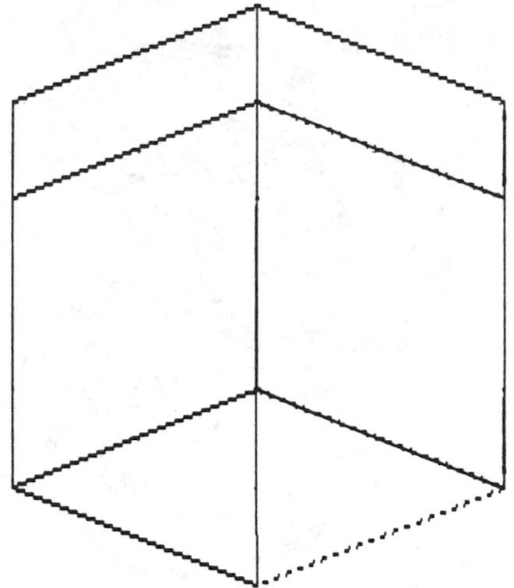

Figure 10. Right side view of the Rhombic Dodecahedron.

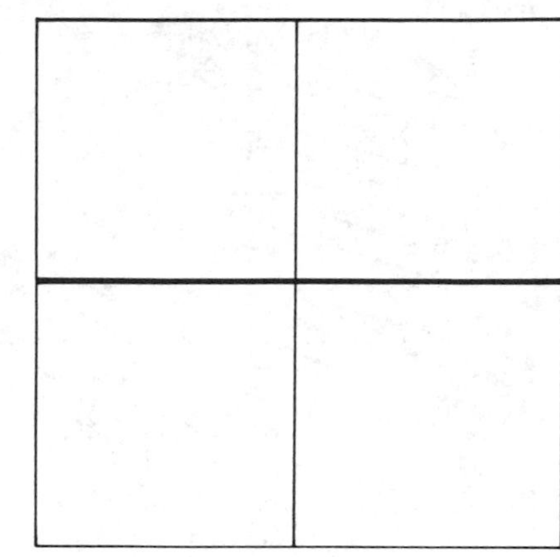

Figure 11. Oblique view of the Rhombic Dodecahedron.

Figure 12. Ratios of Frequencies — A Lambdoma Table

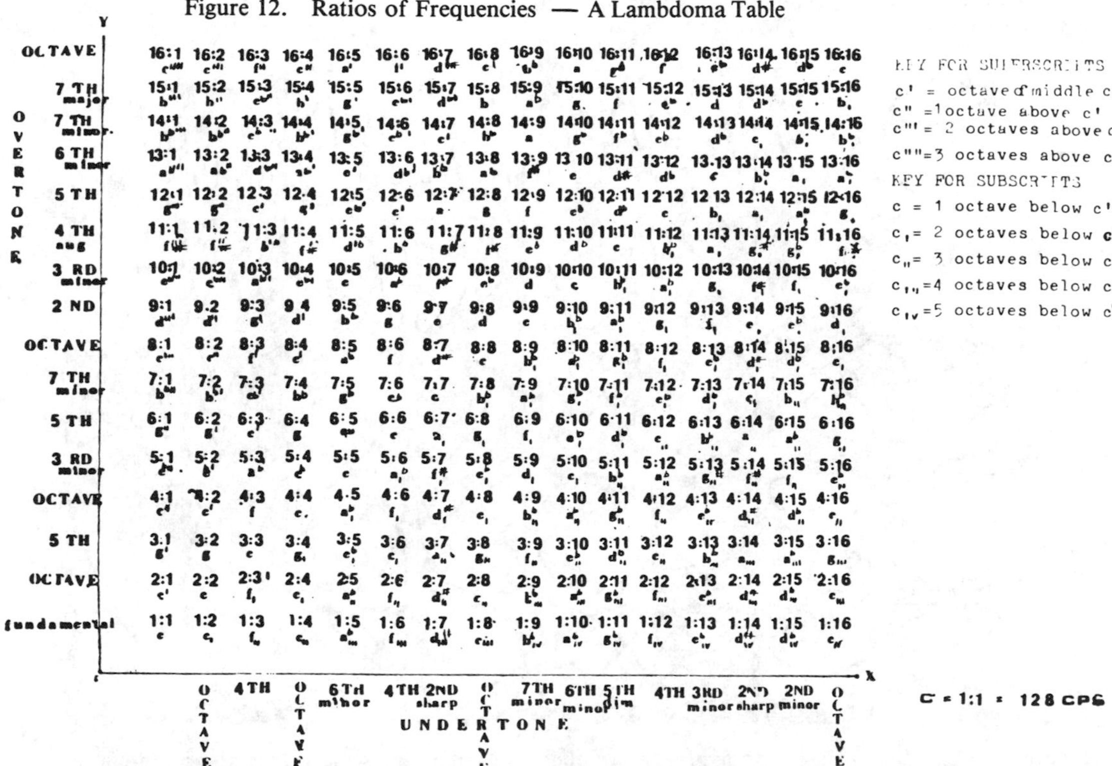

Y (OVERTONE)																
OCTAVE	16:1 c''''	16:2 c'''	16:3 f''	16:4 c''	16:5 a'	16:6 f'	16:7 d#'	16:8 c'	16:9 b♭	16:10 a	16:11 g♭	16:12 f	16:13 e♭	16:14 d#	16:15 d♭	16:16 c
7 TH major	15:1 b'''	15:2 b''	15:3 e♭''	15:4 b'	15:5 g'	15:6 e♭'	15:7 d♭'	15:8 b	15:9 a♭	15:10 g	15:11 f	15:12 e♭	15:13 d	15:14 d♭	15:15 c	15:16 b,
7 TH minor	14:1 b♭'''	14:2 b♭''	14:3 e♭''	14:4 b♭'	14:5 g♭'	14:6 e♭'	14:7 c'	14:8 b♭	14:9 a	14:10 g♭	14:11 f♭	14:12 e♭	14:13 d♭	14:14 c,	14:15 b,	14:16 b♭,
6 TH minor	13:1 a'''	13:2 a♭''	13:3 d♭''	13:4 a♭'	13:5 e'	13:6 d♭'	13:7 b♭	13:8 a♭	13:9 f#	13:10 e	13:11 d#	13:12 d♭	13:13 c	13:14 b♭,	13:15 a,	13:16 a♭,
5 TH	12:1 g''	12:2 g'	12:3 c'	12:4 g'	12:5 e♭'	12:6 c'	12:7 a	12:8 g	12:9 f	12:10 e♭	12:11 d♭	12:12 c	12:13 b,	12:14 a,	12:15 a♭,	12:16 g,
4 TH aug	11:1 f#''	11:2 f#''	11:3 b♭'	11:4 f#	11:5 d♭'	11:6 b♭	11:7 g#	11:8 f#	11:9 e♭	11:10 d♭	11:11 c	11:12 b♭,	11:13 a,	11:14 g#,	11:15 g♭,	11:16 f#,
3 RD minor	10:1 e'''	10:2 e'''	10:3 a♭''	10:4 e''	10:5 c	10:6 a♭	10:7 f#	10:8 e♭	10:9 d	10:10 c	10:11 b♭,	10:12 a♭,	10:13 g,	10:14 f#	10:15 f,	10:16 e♭,
2 ND	9:1 d'''	9:2 d''	9:3 g'	9:4 d'	9:5 b♭	9:6 g	9:7 e	9:8 d	9:9 c	9:10 b♭,	9:11 a♭,	9:12 g,	9:13 f,	9:14 e,	9:15 e♭,	9:16 d,
OCTAVE	8:1 c'''	8:2 c''	8:3 f'	8:4 c'	8:5 a♭	8:6 f	8:7 d#	8:8 c	8:9 b♭,	8:10 a♭,	8:11 g♭,	8:12 f,	8:13 e♭,	8:14 d#,	8:15 d♭,	8:16 c,
7 TH minor	7:1 b♭'''	7:2 b♭''	7:3 e♭'	7:4 b♭	7:5 g♭	7:6 e♭	7:7 c	7:8 b♭,	7:9 a♭,	7:10 g,	7:11 f♭,	7:12 e♭,	7:13 d♭,	7:14 c,	7:15 b,,	7:16 b♭,,
5 TH	6:1 g''	6:2 g'	6:3 c'	6:4 g	6:5 e♭	6:6 c	6:7 a,	6:8 g,	6:9 f,	6:10 e♭,	6:11 d♭,	6:12 c,,	6:13 b♭,,	6:14 a,,	6:15 a♭,,	6:16 g,,
3 RD minor	5:1 e''	5:2 e'	5:3 a♭	5:4 e	5:5 c	5:6 a♭,	5:7 f#,	5:8 e♭,	5:9 d,	5:10 c,	5:11 b♭,,	5:12 a♭,,	5:13 g#,,	5:14 f#,,	5:15 f,,	5:16 e♭,,
OCTAVE	4:1 c''	4:2 c'	4:3 f	4:4 c,	4:5 a♭,	4:6 f,	4:7 d#,	4:8 c,	4:9 b♭,,	4:10 a♭,,	4:11 g♭,,	4:12 f,,	4:13 e♭,,	4:14 d#,,	4:15 d♭,,	4:16 c,,
5 TH	3:1 g'	3:2 g	3:3 c	3:4 g,	3:5 e♭,	3:6 c,	3:7 a,,	3:8 g,,	3:9 f,,	3:10 e♭,,	3:11 d♭,,	3:12 c,,	3:13 b♭,,,	3:14 a,,,	3:15 a♭,,,	3:16 g,,,
OCTAVE	2:1 c'	2:2 c	2:3 f,	2:4 c,	2:5 a♭,,	2:6 f,,	2:7 d#,,	2:8 c,,	2:9 b♭,,,	2:10 a♭,,,	2:11 g♭,,,	2:12 f,,,	2:13 e♭,,,	2:14 d#,,,	2:15 d♭,,,	2:16 c,,,
fundamental	1:1 c	1:2 c,	1:3 f,,	1:4 c,,	1:5 a♭,,,	1:6 f,,,	1:7 d#,,,	1:8 c,,,	1:9 $b^{\flat}_{iv}$	1:10 $a^{\flat}_{iv}$	1:11 $g^{\flat}_{iv}$	1:12 f_{iv}	1:13 $e^{\flat}_{iv}$	1:14 $d^{\#}_{iv}$	1:15 $d^{\flat}_{iv}$	1:16 c_{iv}
UNDERTONE (X)		OCTAVE	4TH	OCTAVE	6TH minor	4TH	2ND sharp	OCTAVE	7TH minor	6TH minor	5TH dim	4TH	3RD minor	2ND sharp	2ND minor	OCTAVE

KEY FOR SUPERSCRIPTS

c' = octave of middle c
c'' = 1 octave above c'
c''' = 2 octaves above c'
c'''' = 3 octaves above c'

KEY FOR SUBSCRIPTS

c = 1 octave below c'
c, = 2 octaves below c'
c,, = 3 octaves below c'
c,,, = 4 octaves below c'
c,v = 5 octaves below c'

C = 1:1 = 128 CPS

This table shows the numerical (ratio) relationships of whole numbers to specific intervals in music. When reading across the rows from left to right an undertone series results. When reading up the columns beginning at the lower left an overtone series results. Superscripts indicate the octave above middle C, and subscripts indicate the octaves below middle C.

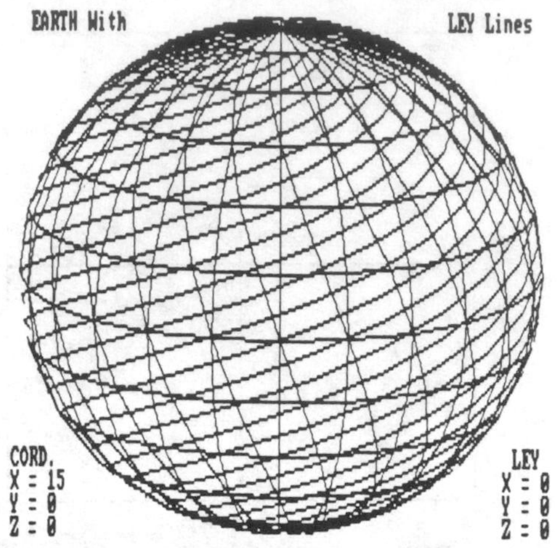

Figure 13. Computer plotted two-dimensional representation of three-dimensional earth with "Ley" (energy network) lines. The ley lines are separately rotatable in ley line location conceived by Prof. Donald Beaman. Computer programming by Robert Foulkrod.

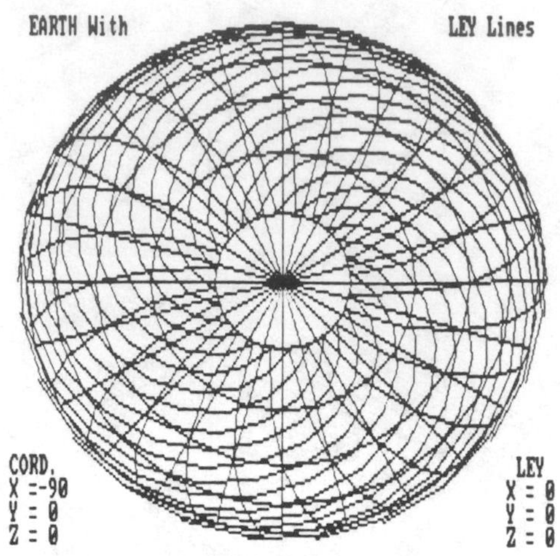

Figure 14. South Pole view of the Earth with ley lines, as conceived by Prof. Donald Beaman, computer program by Robert Foulkrod.

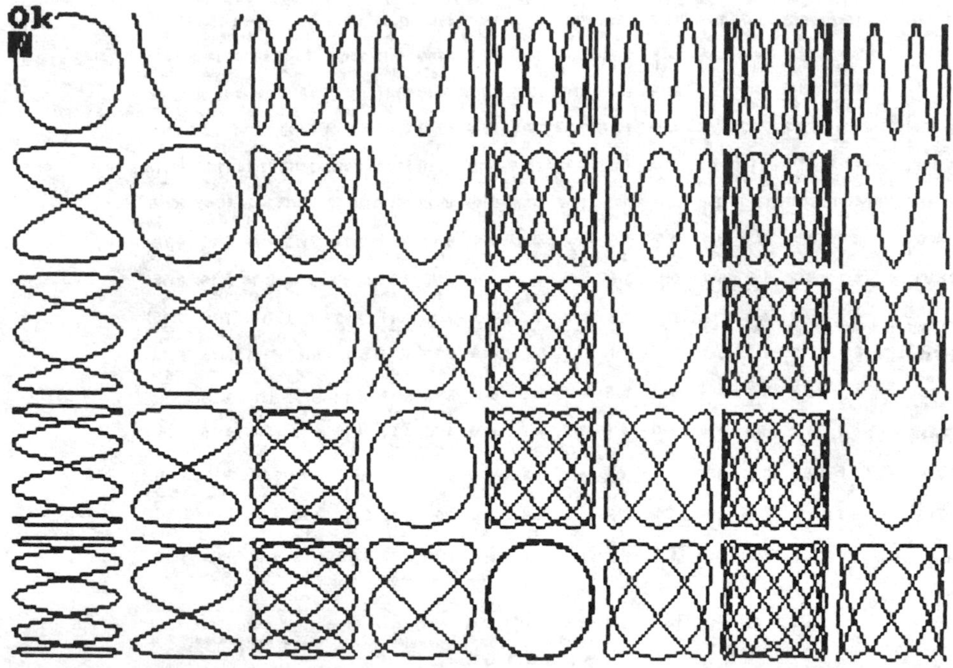

Figure 15. Lissajous Figures. Detail of a 5x8 Lambdoma Matrix representing an earth grid evolution as defined by Pythagorean intervals in sounds. The individual patterns shown are "Lissajous" patterns formed by whole-number ratios between a fundamental tone and its overtones and/or undertones. Computer program by Robert Foulkrod, programmed in "Basic" language on an IBM PC Jr.

Envision these Lissajous Figures arrayed on the Lambdoma Diagram matrix (Fig. 12) as a progressive series of grid lines encircling the globe of earth, each shape sounding its specific interval.

In conclusion, if the earth is in transition in terms of developing into a new phase of grid lines, this factor might indicate a shift of energy or frequency at different places on the earth. See Figure 9. The grid patterns would then take on different distances. See Figure 10. We might ask how can we as humans help the earth in this transitory phase?

First, recognizing that harmonies between cities or countries is based upon attunement to each other's energy patterns. Most of all let us attune ourselves to the earth's energies, recognizing the oneness of all things in our material universe, and learning the *importance of sound as a manifestation of different realities.*

Any grid system has to have distance as one of the factors, since wavelength is inherent in all sound vibrations, as the inversion of frequency. Even though we cannot hear the specific frequency of a grid line, the interval quality is present though inaudible. So lets make them audible.

REFERENCES

1) Becker-Hagens, "Pursuit Science: Pursuit of the Unexplained," *Journal of SITU,* The Society for the Investigation of the Unexplained, Vol. 17, Number 2, Whole Number 66, Second Quarer, 1984.
2) Jalandris, *Earthfire: Exploring the Energies of the Ancients,* Lincoln, Nebraska, 1981.
3) S. Levairie and E. Levy,*Tone: A Study in Musical Acoustics,* Kent State University Press, Kent, Ohio, 1968.
4) Kayser, Hans, *Akroasis: The Theory of World Harmonics,* translated by Robert Lilienfeld, Plowshare Press, Boston, 1964.
5) E. McClain, *The Pythagorean Plato: Prelude to the Song Itself,* Nicolas Hays, Ltd., New York, 1978.
6) B. Hero, "Paintings Based on Relative Pitch in Music," *Leonardo,* Vol. 8, pp. 13–19, Pergammon Press, England, 1975.
7) B. Hero, "Drawings Based on Laser Lissajous Figures and the Lambdoma Diagram," *Leonardo,* Vol. 11, pp. 301–303, 1978.
8) B. Hero, "The Mathematical Laws of Sound (Relationshio of Sound to Gravity)," *Energy Unlimited* #12, Box 288, Los Lunas, New Mexico 80731.

Figure 16. Table of Frequencies and Musical Notes Relative to Miles in Air.

This table allows one to easily find the distance correlation in miles with musical notes and frequencies.

(SCALE BASED ON C = 256 AND INTERVALS = THE 12th ROOT OF 2. DATE = 6/30/85)

10 MI 350 CPS F	20 MI 350 CPS F	30 MI 467 CPS Bb	40 MI 350 CPS F
50 MI 280 CPS D	60 MI 467 CPS Bb	70 MI 400 CPS Ab	80 MI 350 CPS F
90 MI 311 CPS Eb	100 MI 280 CPS D	110 MI 255 CPS C	120 MI 467 CPS Bb
130 MI 431 CPS A	140 MI 400 CPS Ab	150 MI 374 CPS G	160 MI 350 CPS F
170 MI 330 CPS E	180 MI 311 CPS Eb	190 MI 295 CPS D	200 MI 280 CPS D
210 MI 267 CPS C#	220 MI 255 CPS C	230 MI 487 CPS B	240 MI 467 CPS Bb
250 MI 448 CPS Bb	260 MI 431 CPS A	270 MI 415 CPS Ab	280 MI 400 CPS Ab
290 MI 386 CPS G	300 MI 374 CPS G	310 MI 361 CPS F#	320 MI 350 CPS P
330 MI 340 CPS F	340 MI 330 CPS E	350 MI 320 CPS Eb	360 MI 311 CPS Eb
370 MI 303 CPS Eb	380 MI 295 CPS D	390 MI 287 CPS D	400 MI 280 CPS D
410 MI 273 CPS C#	420 MI 267 CPS C#	430 MI 260 CPS C	440 MI 255 CPS C
450 MI 249 CPS C	460 MI 487 CPS B	470 MI 477 CPS B	480 MI 467 CPS Bb
490 MI 457 CPS Bb	500 MI 448 CPS Bb	510 MI 440 CPS A	520 MI 431 CPS A
530 MI 423 CPS A	540 MI 415 CPS Ab	550 MI 408 CPS Ab	560 MI 400 CPS Ab
570 MI 393 CPS G	580 MI 386 CPS G	590 MI 380 CPS G	600 MI 374 CPS G
610 MI 367 CPS F#	620 MI 361 CPS F#	630 MI 356 CPS F#	640 MI 350 CPS F
650 MI 345 CPS F	660 MI 340 CPS F	670 MI 334 CPS E	680 MI 330 CPS E
690 MI 325 CPS E	700 MI 320 CPS Eb	710 MI 316 CPS Eb	720 MI 311 CPS Eb
730 MI 307 CPS Eb	740 MI 303 CPS Eb	750 MI 299 CPS D	760 MI 295 CPS D
770 MI 291 CPS D	780 MI 287 CPS D	790 MI 284 CPS D	800 MI 280 CPS D
810 MI 277 CPS C#	820 MI 273 CPS C#	830 MI 270 CPS C#	840 MI 267 CPS C#
850 MI 264 CPS C#	860 MI 260 CPS C	870 MI 257 CPS C	880 MI 255 CPS C
890 MI 252 CPS C	900 MI 249 CPS C	910 MI 493 CPS B	920 MI 487 CPS B
930 MI 482 CPS B	940 MI 477 CPS B	950 MI 472 CPS B	960 MI 467 CPS Bb
970 MI 462 CPS Bb	980 MI 457 CPS Bb	990 MI 453 CPS Bb	1000 MI 448 CPS Bb

```
1010 MI 444 CPS Bb   1020 MI 440 CPS A    1030 MI 435 CPS A    1040 MI 431 CPS A
1050 MI 427 CPS A    1060 MI 423 CPS A    1070 MI 419 CPS A    1080 MI 415 CPS Ab
1090 MI 411 CPS Ab   1100 MI 408 CPS Ab   1110 MI 404 CPS Ab   1120 MI 400 CPS Ab
1130 MI 397 CPS Ab   1140 MI 393 CPS G    1150 MI 390 CPS G    1160 MI 386 CPS G
1170 MI 383 CPS G    1180 MI 380 CPS G    1190 MI 377 CPS G    1200 MI 374 CPS G
1210 MI 370 CPS F#   1220 MI 367 CPS F#   1230 MI 364 CPS F#   1240 MI 361 CPS F#
1250 MI 359 CPS F#   1260 MI 356 CPS F#   1270 MI 353 CPS F#   1280 MI 350 CPS F
1290 MI 347 CPS F    1300 MI 345 CPS F    1310 MI 342 CPS F    1320 MI 340 CPS F
1330 MI 337 CPS F    1340 MI 334 CPS E    1350 MI 332 CPS E    1360 MI 330 CPS E
1370 MI 327 CPS E    1380 MI 325 CPS E    1390 MI 322 CPS E    1400 MI 320 CPS Eb
1410 MI 318 CPS Eb   1420 MI 316 CPS Eb   1430 MI 313 CPS Eb   1440 MI 311 CPS Eb
1450 MI 309 CPS Eb   1460 MI 307 CPS Eb   1470 MI 305 CPS Eb   1480 MI 303 CPS Eb
1490 MI 301 CPS Eb   1500 MI 299 CPS D    1510 MI 297 CPS D    1520 MI 295 CPS D
1530 MI 293 CPS D    1540 MI 291 CPS D    1550 MI 289 CPS D    1560 MI 287 CPS D
1570 MI 285 CPS D    1580 MI 284 CPS D    1590 MI 282 CPS D    1600 MI 280 CPS D
1610 MI 278 CPS C#   1620 MI 277 CPS C#   1630 MI 275 CPS C#   1640 MI 273 CPS C#
1650 MI 272 CPS C#   1660 MI 270 CPS C#   1670 MI 268 CPS C#   1680 MI 267 CPS C#
1690 MI 265 CPS C#   1700 MI 264 CPS C#   1710 MI 262 CPS C    1720 MI 260 CPS C
1730 MI 259 CPS C    1740 MI 257 CPS C    1750 MI 256 CPS C    1760 MI 255 CPS C
1770 MI 253 CPS C    1780 MI 252 CPS C    1790 MI 250 CPS C    1800 MI 249 CPS C
1810 MI 495 CPS B    1820 MI 493 CPS B    1830 MI 490 CPS B    1840 MI 487 CPS B
1850 MI 485 CPS B    1860 MI 482 CPS B    1870 MI 480 CPS B    1880 MI 477 CPS B
1890 MI 474 CPS B    1900 MI 472 CPS B    1910 MI 469 CPS B    1920 MI 467 CPS Bb
1930 MI 465 CPS Bb   1940 MI 462 CPS Bb   1950 MI 460 CPS Bb   1960 MI 457 CPS Bb
1970 MI 455 CPS Bb   1980 MI 453 CPS Bb   1990 MI 451 CPS Bb   2000 MI 448 CPS Bb
2010 MI 446 CPS Bb   2020 MI 444 CPS Bb   2030 MI 442 CPS A    2040 MI 440 CPS A
2050 MI 437 CPS A    2060 MI 435 CPS A    2070 MI 433 CPS A    2080 MI 431 CPS A
2090 MI 429 CPS A    2100 MI 427 CPS A    2110 MI 425 CPS A    2120 MI 423 CPS A
2130 MI 421 CPS A    2140 MI 419 CPS A    2150 MI 417 CPS Ab   2160 MI 415 CPS Ab
2170 MI 413 CPS Ab   2180 MI 411 CPS Ab   2190 MI 409 CPS Ab   2200 MI 408 CPS Ab
2210 MI 406 CPS Ab   2220 MI 404 CPS Ab   2230 MI 402 CPS Ab   2240 MI 400 CPS Ab
2250 MI 398 CPS Ab   2260 MI 397 CPS Ab   2270 MI 395 CPS Ab   2280 MI 393 CPS G
2290 MI 391 CPS G    2300 MI 390 CPS G    2310 MI 388 CPS G    2320 MI 386 CPS G
2330 MI 385 CPS G    2340 MI 383 CPS G    2350 MI 381 CPS G    2360 MI 380 CPS G
2370 MI 378 CPS G    2380 MI 377 CPS G    2390 MI 375 CPS G    2400 MI 374 CPS G
2410 MI 372 CPS G    2420 MI 370 CPS F#   2430 MI 369 CPS F#   2440 MI 367 CPS F#
2450 MI 366 CPS F#   2460 MI 364 CPS F#   2470 MI 363 CPS F#   2480 MI 361 CPS F#
2490 MI 360 CPS F#   2500 MI 359 CPS F#   2510 MI 357 CPS F#   2520 MI 356 CPS F#
2530 MI 354 CPS F#   2540 MI 353 CPS F#   2550 MI 352 CPS F#   2560 MI 350 CPS F
2570 MI 349 CPS F    2580 MI 347 CPS F    2590 MI 346 CPS F    2600 MI 345 CPS F
2610 MI 343 CPS F    2620 MI 342 CPS F    2630 MI 341 CPS F    2640 MI 340 CPS F
2650 MI 338 CPS F    2660 MI 337 CPS F    2670 MI 336 CPS F    2680 MI 334 CPS E
2690 MI 333 CPS E    2700 MI 332 CPS E    2710 MI 331 CPS E    2720 MI 330 CPS E
2730 MI 328 CPS E    2740 MI 327 CPS E    2750 MI 326 CPS E    2760 MI 325 CPS E
2770 MI 324 CPS E    2780 MI 322 CPS E    2790 MI 321 CPS Eb   2800 MI 320 CPS Eb
2810 MI 319 CPS Eb   2820 MI 318 CPS Eb   2830 MI 317 CPS Eb   2840 MI 316 CPS Eb
2850 MI 314 CPS Eb   2860 MI 313 CPS Eb   2870 MI 312 CPS Eb   2880 MI 311 CPS Eb
2890 MI 310 CPS Eb   2900 MI 309 CPS Eb   2910 MI 308 CPS Eb   2920 MI 307 CPS Eb
2930 MI 306 CPS Eb   2940 MI 305 CPS Eb   2950 MI 304 CPS Eb   2960 MI 303 CPS Eb
2970 MI 302 CPS Eb   2980 MI 301 CPS Eb   2990 MI 300 CPS Eb   3000 MI 299 CPS D
3010 MI 298 CPS D    3020 MI 297 CPS D    3030 MI 296 CPS D    3040 MI 295 CPS D
3050 MI 294 CPS D    3060 MI 293 CPS D    3070 MI 292 CPS D    3080 MI 291 CPS D
3090 MI 290 CPS D    3100 MI 289 CPS D    3110 MI 288 CPS D    3120 MI 287 CPS D
3130 MI 286 CPS D    3140 MI 285 CPS D    3150 MI 284 CPS D    3160 MI 284 CPS D
3170 MI 283 CPS D    3180 MI 282 CPS D    3190 MI 281 CPS D    3200 MI 280 CPS D
3210 MI 279 CPS D    3220 MI 278 CPS C#   3230 MI 277 CPS C#   3240 MI 277 CPS C#
3250 MI 276 CPS C#   3260 MI 275 CPS C#   3270 MI 274 CPS C#   3280 MI 273 CPS C#
3290 MI 272 CPS C#   3300 MI 272 CPS C#   3310 MI 271 CPS C#   3320 MI 270 CPS C#
3330 MI 269 CPS C#   3340 MI 268 CPS C#   3350 MI 267 CPS C#   3360 MI 267 CPS C#
3370 MI 266 CPS C#   3380 MI 265 CPS C#   3390 MI 264 CPS C#   3400 MI 264 CPS C#
3410 MI 263 CPS C    3420 MI 262 CPS C    3430 MI 261 CPS C    3440 MI 260 CPS C
3450 MI 260 CPS C    3460 MI 259 CPS C    3470 MI 258 CPS C    3480 MI 257 CPS C
3490 MI 257 CPS C    3500 MI 256 CPS C    3510 MI 255 CPS C    3520 MI 255 CPS C
3530 MI 254 CPS C    3540 MI 253 CPS C    3550 MI 252 CPS C    3560 MI 252 CPS C
3570 MI 251 CPS C    3580 MI 250 CPS C    3590 MI 250 CPS C    3600 MI 249 CPS C
3610 MI 248 CPS C    3620 MI 495 CPS B    3630 MI 494 CPS B    3640 MI 493 CPS B
3650 MI 491 CPS B    3660 MI 490 CPS B    3670 MI 489 CPS B    3680 MI 487 CPS B
3690 MI 486 CPS B    3700 MI 485 CPS B    3710 MI 483 CPS B    3720 MI 482 CPS B
3730 MI 481 CPS B    3740 MI 480 CPS B    3750 MI 478 CPS B    3760 MI 477 CPS B
```

3770 MI 476 CPS B 3780 MI 474 CPS B 3790 MI 473 CPS B 3800 MI 472 CPS B
3810 MI 471 CPS B 3820 MI 469 CPS B 3830 MI 468 CPS Bb 3840 MI 467 CPS Bb
3850 MI 466 CPS Bb 3860 MI 465 CPS Bb 3870 MI 463 CPS Bb 3880 MI 462 CPS Bb
3890 MI 461 CPS Bb 3900 MI 460 CPS Bb 3910 MI 459 CPS Bb 3920 MI 457 CPS Bb
3930 MI 456 CPS Bb 3940 MI 455 CPS Bb 3950 MI 454 CPS Bb 3960 MI 453 CPS Bb
3970 MI 452 CPS Bb 3980 MI 451 CPS Bb 3990 MI 449 CPS Bb 4000 MI 448 CPS Bb
4010 MI 447 CPS Bb 4020 MI 446 CPS Bb 4030 MI 445 CPS Bb 4040 MI 444 CPS Bb
4050 MI 443 CPS Bb 4060 MI 442 CPS A 4070 MI 441 CPS A 4080 MI 440 CPS A
4090 MI 438 CPS A 4100 MI 437 CPS A 4110 MI 436 CPS A 4120 MI 435 CPS A
4130 MI 434 CPS A 4140 MI 433 CPS A 4150 MI 432 CPS A 4160 MI 431 CPS A
4170 MI 430 CPS A 4180 MI 429 CPS A 4190 MI 428 CPS A 4200 MI 427 CPS A
4210 MI 426 CPS A 4220 MI 425 CPS A 4230 MI 424 CPS A 4240 MI 423 CPS A
4250 MI 422 CPS A 4260 MI 421 CPS A 4270 MI 420 CPS A 4280 MI 419 CPS A
4290 MI 418 CPS A 4300 MI 417 CPS Ab 4310 MI 416 CPS Ab 4320 MI 415 CPS Ab
4330 MI 414 CPS Ab 4340 MI 413 CPS Ab 4350 MI 412 CPS Ab 4360 MI 411 CPS Ab
4370 MI 410 CPS Ab 4380 MI 409 CPS Ab 4390 MI 408 CPS Ab 4400 MI 408 CPS Ab
4410 MI 407 CPS Ab 4420 MI 406 CPS Ab 4430 MI 405 CPS Ab 4440 MI 404 CPS Ab
4450 MI 403 CPS Ab 4460 MI 402 CPS Ab 4470 MI 401 CPS Ab 4480 MI 400 CPS Ab
4490 MI 399 CPS Ab 4500 MI 398 CPS Ab 4510 MI 398 CPS Ab 4520 MI 397 CPS Ab
4530 MI 396 CPS Ab 4540 MI 395 CPS Ab 4550 MI 394 CPS G 4560 MI 393 CPS G
4570 MI 392 CPS G 4580 MI 391 CPS G 4590 MI 391 CPS G 4600 MI 390 CPS G
4610 MI 389 CPS G 4620 MI 388 CPS G 4630 MI 387 CPS G 4640 MI 386 CPS G
4650 MI 386 CPS G 4660 MI 385 CPS G 4670 MI 384 CPS G 4680 MI 383 CPS G
4690 MI 382 CPS G 4700 MI 381 CPS G 4710 MI 381 CPS G 4720 MI 380 CPS G
4730 MI 379 CPS G 4740 MI 378 CPS G 4750 MI 377 CPS G 4760 MI 377 CPS G
4770 MI 376 CPS G 4780 MI 375 CPS G 4790 MI 374 CPS G 4800 MI 374 CPS G
4810 MI 373 CPS G 4820 MI 372 CPS G 4830 MI 371 CPS F# 4840 MI 370 CPS F#
4850 MI 370 CPS F# 4860 MI 369 CPS F# 4870 MI 368 CPS F# 4880 MI 367 CPS F#
4890 MI 367 CPS F# 4900 MI 366 CPS F# 4910 MI 365 CPS F# 4920 MI 364 CPS F#
4930 MI 364 CPS F# 4940 MI 363 CPS F# 4950 MI 362 CPS F# 4960 MI 361 CPS F#
4970 MI 361 CPS F# 4980 MI 360 CPS F# 4990 MI 359 CPS F# 5000 MI 359 CPS F#
5010 MI 358 CPS F# 5020 MI 357 CPS F# 5030 MI 356 CPS F# 5040 MI 356 CPS F#
5050 MI 355 CPS F# 5060 MI 354 CPS F# 5070 MI 354 CPS F# 5080 MI 353 CPS F#
5090 MI 352 CPS F# 5100 MI 352 CPS F# 5110 MI 351 CPS F 5120 MI 350 CPS F
5130 MI 349 CPS F 5140 MI 349 CPS F 5150 MI 348 CPS F 5160 MI 347 CPS F
5170 MI 347 CPS F 5180 MI 346 CPS F 5190 MI 345 CPS F 5200 MI 345 CPS F
5210 MI 344 CPS F 5220 MI 343 CPS F 5230 MI 343 CPS F 5240 MI 342 CPS F
5250 MI 341 CPS F 5260 MI 341 CPS F 5270 MI 340 CPS F 5280 MI 340 CPS F
5290 MI 339 CPS F 5300 MI 338 CPS F 5310 MI 338 CPS F 5320 MI 337 CPS F
5330 MI 336 CPS F 5340 MI 336 CPS F 5350 MI 335 CPS E 5360 MI 334 CPS E
5370 MI 334 CPS E 5380 MI 333 CPS E 5390 MI 333 CPS E 5400 MI 332 CPS E
5410 MI 331 CPS E 5420 MI 331 CPS E 5430 MI 330 CPS E 5440 MI 330 CPS E
5450 MI 329 CPS E 5460 MI 328 CPS E 5470 MI 328 CPS E 5480 MI 327 CPS E
5490 MI 327 CPS E 5500 MI 326 CPS E 5510 MI 325 CPS E 5520 MI 325 CPS E
5530 MI 324 CPS E 5540 MI 324 CPS E 5550 MI 323 CPS E 5560 MI 322 CPS E
5570 MI 322 CPS E 5580 MI 321 CPS Eb 5590 MI 321 CPS Eb 5600 MI 320 CPS Eb
5610 MI 320 CPS Eb 5620 MI 319 CPS Eb 5630 MI 318 CPS Eb 5640 MI 318 CPS Eb
5650 MI 317 CPS Eb 5660 MI 317 CPS Eb 5670 MI 316 CPS Eb 5680 MI 316 CPS Eb
5690 MI 315 CPS Eb 5700 MI 314 CPS Eb 5710 MI 314 CPS Eb 5720 MI 313 CPS Eb
5730 MI 313 CPS Eb 5740 MI 312 CPS Eb 5750 MI 312 CPS Eb 5760 MI 311 CPS Eb
5770 MI 311 CPS Eb 5780 MI 310 CPS Eb 5790 MI 310 CPS Eb 5800 MI 309 CPS Eb
5810 MI 308 CPS Eb 5820 MI 308 CPS Eb 5830 MI 307 CPS Eb 5840 MI 307 CPS Eb
5850 MI 306 CPS Eb 5860 MI 306 CPS Eb 5870 MI 305 CPS Eb 5880 MI 305 CPS Eb
5890 MI 304 CPS Eb 5900 MI 304 CPS Eb 5910 MI 303 CPS Eb 5920 MI 303 CPS Eb
5930 MI 302 CPS Eb 5940 MI 302 CPS Eb 5950 MI 301 CPS Eb 5960 MI 301 CPS Eb
5970 MI 300 CPS Eb 5980 MI 300 CPS Eb 5990 MI 299 CPS D 6000 MI 299 CPS D
6010 MI 298 CPS D 6020 MI 298 CPS D 6030 MI 297 CPS D 6040 MI 297 CPS D
6050 MI 296 CPS D 6060 MI 296 CPS D 6070 MI 295 CPS D 6080 MI 295 CPS D
6090 MI 294 CPS D 6100 MI 294 CPS D 6110 MI 293 CPS D 6120 MI 293 CPS D
6130 MI 292 CPS D 6140 MI 292 CPS D 6150 MI 291 CPS D 6160 MI 291 CPS D
6170 MI 290 CPS D 6180 MI 290 CPS D 6190 MI 290 CPS D 6200 MI 289 CPS D
6210 MI 289 CPS D 6220 MI 288 CPS D 6230 MI 288 CPS D 6240 MI 287 CPS D
6250 MI 287 CPS D 6260 MI 286 CPS D 6270 MI 286 CPS D 6280 MI 285 CPS D
6290 MI 285 CPS D 6300 MI 284 CPS D 6310 MI 284 CPS D 6320 MI 284 CPS D
6330 MI 283 CPS D 6340 MI 283 CPS D 6350 MI 282 CPS D 6360 MI 282 CPS D
6370 MI 281 CPS D 6380 MI 281 CPS D 6390 MI 280 CPS D 6400 MI 280 CPS D
6410 MI 280 CPS D 6420 MI 279 CPS D 6430 MI 279 CPS D 6440 MI 278 CPS C#
6450 MI 278 CPS C# 6460 MI 277 CPS C# 6470 MI 277 CPS C# 6480 MI 277 CPS C#
6490 MI 276 CPS C# 6500 MI 276 CPS C# 6510 MI 275 CPS C# 6520 MI 275 CPS C#

```
6530 MI 274 CPS C#   6540 MI 274 CPS C#   6550 MI 274 CPS C#   6560 MI 273 CPS C#
6570 MI 273 CPS C#   6580 MI 272 CPS C#   6590 MI 272 CPS C#   6600 MI 272 CPS C#
6610 MI 271 CPS C#   6620 MI 271 CPS C#   6630 MI 270 CPS C#   6640 MI 270 CPS C#
6650 MI 269 CPS C#   6660 MI 269 CPS C#   6670 MI 269 CPS C#   6680 MI 268 CPS C#
6690 MI 268 CPS C#   6700 MI 267 CPS C#   6710 MI 267 CPS C#   6720 MI 267 CPS C#
6730 MI 266 CPS C#   6740 MI 266 CPS C#   6750 MI 265 CPS C#   6760 MI 265 CPS C#
6770 MI 265 CPS C#   6780 MI 264 CPS C#   6790 MI 264 CPS C#   6800 MI 264 CPS C#
6810 MI 263 CPS C    6820 MI 263 CPS C    6830 MI 262 CPS C    6840 MI 262 CPS C
6850 MI 262 CPS C    6860 MI 261 CPS C    6870 MI 261 CPS C    6880 MI 260 CPS C
6890 MI 260 CPS C    6900 MI 260 CPS C    6910 MI 259 CPS C    6920 MI 259 CPS C
6930 MI 259 CPS C    6940 MI 258 CPS C    6950 MI 258 CPS C    6960 MI 257 CPS C
6970 MI 257 CPS C    6980 MI 257 CPS C    6990 MI 256 CPS C    7000 MI 256 CPS C
7010 MI 256 CPS C    7020 MI 255 CPS C    7030 MI 255 CPS C    7040 MI 255 CPS C
7050 MI 254 CPS C    7060 MI 254 CPS C    7070 MI 253 CPS C    7080 MI 253 CPS C
7090 MI 253 CPS C    7100 MI 252 CPS C    7110 MI 252 CPS C    7120 MI 252 CPS C
7130 MI 251 CPS C    7140 MI 251 CPS C    7150 MI 251 CPS C    7160 MI 250 CPS C
7170 MI 250 CPS C    7180 MI 250 CPS C    7190 MI 249 CPS C    7200 MI 249 CPS C
7210 MI 248 CPS C    7220 MI 248 CPS C    7230 MI 496 CPS B    7240 MI 495 CPS B
7250 MI 495 CPS B    7260 MI 494 CPS B    7270 MI 493 CPS B    7280 MI 493 CPS B
7290 MI 492 CPS B    7300 MI 491 CPS B    7310 MI 491 CPS B    7320 MI 490 CPS B
7330 MI 489 CPS B    7340 MI 489 CPS B    7350 MI 488 CPS B    7360 MI 487 CPS B
7370 MI 487 CPS B    7380 MI 486 CPS B    7390 MI 485 CPS B    7400 MI 485 CPS B
7410 MI 484 CPS B    7420 MI 483 CPS B    7430 MI 483 CPS B    7440 MI 482 CPS B
7450 MI 481 CPS B    7460 MI 481 CPS B    7470 MI 480 CPS B    7480 MI 480 CPS B
7490 MI 479 CPS B    7500 MI 478 CPS B
```

Published 1986 by
The United States Psychotronics Association
3459 Montrose Avenue, Chicago, Illinois 60618

ACOUSTIC LEVITATION OF STONES

By

Bruce L. Cathie

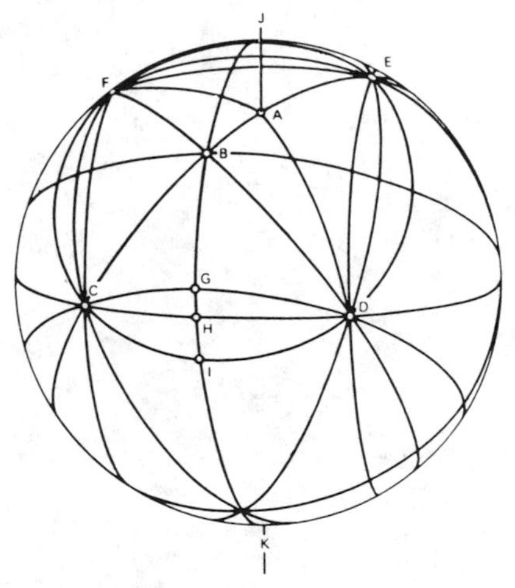

A New Zealand scientist recently gave me an intriguing extract from an article published in a German magazine, relating to a demonstration of levitation in Tibet. After obtaining a translation by a German journalist, in English, I was amazed at the information contained in the story, and was surprised that the article had slipped through the suppression net which tends to keep such knowledge from leaking out to the public. All the similar types of stories that I had read up until now were generally devoid of specific information necessary to prove the veracity of the account. In this case a full set of geometric measurements were taken, and I discovered, to my great delight, that when they were converted into their equivalent geodetic measures, relating to grid harmonics the values gave a direct association with those in the unified harmonic equations published in my earlier works.

The following extracts are translations taken from the German article: 'We know from the priests of the far east that they were able to lift heavy boulders up high mountains with the help of groups of various sounds ... the knowledge of the various vibrations in the audio range demonstrates to a scientist of physics that a vibrating and condensed sound field can nullify the power of gravitation. Swedish engineer Olaf Alexanderson wrote about this phenomenon in the publication, Implosion No. 13.

The following report is based on observations which were made only 20 years ago in Tibet. I have this report from civil engineer and flight manager, Henry Kjelson, a friend of mine. He later on included this report in his book, The Lost Techniques. This is his report:

A Swedish doctor, Dr Jarl, a friend of Kjelsons, studied at Oxford. During those times he became friends with a young Tibetan student. A couple of years later, it was 1939, Dr Jarl made a journey to Egypt for the English Scientific Society. There he was seen by a messenger of his Tibetan friend, and urgently requested to come to Tibet to treat a high Lama.

After Dr Jarl got the leave he followed the messenger and arrived after a long journey by plane and Yak caravans, at the monastery, where the old Lama and his friend who was now holding a high position were now living.

Dr Jarl stayed there for some time, and because of his friendship with the Tibetans he learned a lot of things that other foreigners had no chance to hear about, or observe.

One day his friend took him to a place in the neighbourhood of the monastery and showed him a sloping meadow which was surrounded in the north west by high cliffs. In one of the rock walls, at a height of about 250 metres was a big hole which looked like the entrance to a cave. In front of this hole there was a platform on which the monks were building a rock wall. The only access to this platform was from the top of the cliff and the monks lowered themselves down with the help of ropes.

In the middle of the meadow, about 250 metres from the cliff, was a polished slab of rock with a bowl like cavity in the centre. The bowl had a diameter of one metre and a depth of 15 centimetres. A block of stone was manoeuvred into this cavity by Yak oxen. The block was one metre wide and one and one-half metres long. Then 19 musical instruments were set in an arc of 90 degrees at a distance of 63 metres from the stone slab. The radius of 63 metres was measured out accurately. The musical instruments consisted of 13 drums and six trumpets. (Ragdons).

Eight drums had a cross-section of one metre, and a length of one and one-half metres. Four drums were medium size with a cross-secion of 0.7 metre and a length of one metre. The only small drum had a cross-section of 0.2 metres and a length of 0.3 metres. All the trumpets were the same size. They had a length of 3.12 metres and an opening of 0.3 metres. The big drums and all the trumpets were fixed on mounts which could be adjusted with staffs in the direction of the slab of stone. The big drums were made of 3mm thick sheet iron, and had a weight of 150 kg. They were built in five sections. All the drums were open at one end, while the other end had a bottom of metal, on which the monks beat with big leather clubs. Behind each instrument was a row of monks. The situation is demonstrated in the following diagram:

DIAGRAM 21

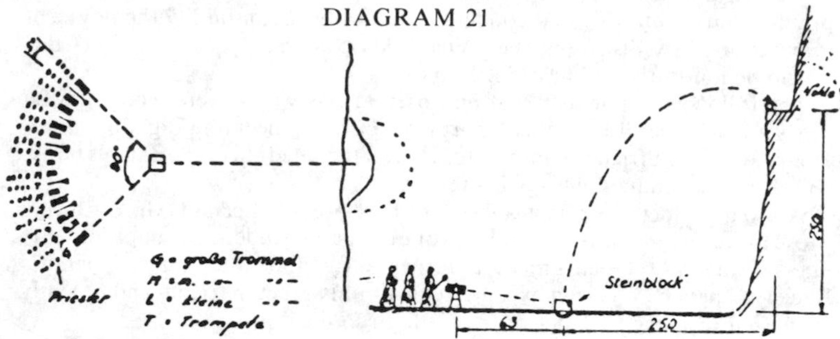

When the stone was in position the monk behind the small drum gave a signal to start the concert. The small drum had a very sharp sound, and could be heard even with the other instruments making a terrible din. All the monks were singing and chanting a prayer, slowly increasing the tempo of this unbelievable noise. During the first four minutes nothing happened, then as the speed of the drumming, and the noise, increased, the big stone block started to rock and sway, and suddenly it took off into the air with an increasing speed in the direction of the platform in front of the cave hole 250 metres high. After three minutes of ascent it landed on the platform.

Continuously they brought new blocks to the meadow, and the monks using this method, transported 5 to 6 blocks per hour on a parabolic flight track approximately 500 metres long and 250 metres high. From time to time a stone split, and the monks moved the split stones away. Quite an unbelievable task.

Dr Jarl knew about the hurling of the stones. Tibetan experts like Linaver, Spalding and Huc had spoken about it, but they had never seen it. So Dr Jarl was the first foreigner who had the opportunity to see this remarkable spectacle. Because he had the opinion in the beginning that he was the victim of mass-psychosis he made two films of the incident. The films showed exactly the same things that he had witnessed.

The English Society for which Dr Jarl was working confiscated the two films and declared them classified. They will not be released until 1990. This action is rather hard to explain, or understand. : End of trans.'

The fact that the films were immediately classified is not very hard to understand once the given measurements are transposed into their geometric equivalents. It then becomes evident that the monks in Tibet are fully conversant with the laws governing the structure of matter, which the scientists in the modern day western world are now frantically exploring. It appears, from the calculations, that the prayers being chanted by the monks did not have any direct bearing on the fact that the stones were levitated from the ground.The reaction was not initiated by the religious fervour of the group, but by the superior scientific knowledge held by the high priests. The secret is in the geometric placement of the musical instruments in relation to the stones to be levitated, and the harmonic tuning of the drums and trumpets. The combined loud chanting of the priests, using their voices at a certain pitch and rhythm most probably adds to the combined effect, but the subject matter of the chant, I believe, would be of no consequence.

The sound waves being generated by the combination were directed in such a way that an anti-gravitational effect was created at the centre of focus (position of the stones) and around the periphery, or the arc, of a third of a circle through which the stones moved.

If we analyse the diagram published with the original article, then compare it with the modified diagram, we become aware of the following coordinates, and the implications, when compared with my previously published works.

The distance between the stone block and the central pivot of the drum supports is shown as 63 metres. The large drums were said to be one and one half metres long, so the distance from the block to the rear face of each drum could be close to 63.75 metres considering that the pivot point would be near the centre of balance. My theoretical analysis, by calculator, indicates that the exact distance would be 63.7079 metres for the optimum harmonic reaction. By mathematical conversion we find that this value is equal to 206.2648062 geodetic feet, which is harmonically equal to the length of the earth's radius in seconds of arc (relative to the earth's surface) 206264.8062. This also leads us to the following associations:

(206.2648062 x 2)

= 412.5296124

This number squared:

= 170180.68 which is the theoretical harmonic of mass at the earth's surface.

The four rows of monks standing behind the instruments in a quarter circle added to the production of sound by their loud chanting and must be taken in to account in regards to the geometric pattern. If we assume that they were standing approximately two feet apart, we can add a calculated value of 8.08865 geodetic feet to the radius of the complete group. This gives a maximum radius of:

214.3534583 geodetic feet.

The circumference of a complete circle with this radius would be:
1346.822499 geodetic feet.
Which is a half harmonic of:
2693.645 (unified field)
The distance from the stone block to a calculated point within the cliff face and the height of the ledge on the cliff face from ground level is given as 250 metres. If we can now imagine that the raised stone blocks pass through a quarter arc of a circle during their flight from ground level to the hole in the cliff face, then the pivot point of the radius would be coincident with this position. See diagram.
The theoretical radius was found to be:
249.8767262 metres which very closely approximates the estimate.
This converts to:
809.016999 geodetic feet.
The diameter of the full circle would therefore be:
1618.034 geodetic feet.

A circle with this diameter has a circumference of 5083.203728 units, which can be divided into three even lengths of 1694.4. It therefore appears that the levitated blocks, once resonated to a certain frequency, would tend to carry out a flight path that is coincident to one third of a circle. The spacial distance being equivalent to the mass harmonic at the centre of a light field, 1694443.

The instruments used by the group, in theory, would also have been tuned to produce harmonic wave forms associated with the unified fields. The given measurements are in rounded off parts of a metre but in practice some slight variations from these measurements would be expected in order to create the appropriate resonating cavities within the instruments. The geometric arrangement, and the number of instruments in the group would also be a most important factor.

If the given measurement for each type of drum is modified fractionally and converted to its geometric equivalent an interesting value for the cubic capacity is evident.
The large drums:
1.517201563 metres long, 1.000721361 metres wide
= 58.94627524 geodetic inches long, 38.88 geodetic inches wide.
= 69984 cubic geodetic inches capacity
= 40.5 cubic geodetic feet capacity.
Therefore the cubic capacity for eight drums:
= 324 cubic geodetic feet.
This harmonic value is built into the world grid and is equal to half the harmonic 648.
The medium sized drums:
1.000721361 metres long, 0.695189635 metres wide
= 38.88 geodetic inches long, 27.00948944 geodetic inches wide
= 22276.59899 cubic geodetic inches capacity
= 12.89155034 cubic geodetic feet capacity.
Therefore the cubic capacity for four drums:
= 51.56620136 cubic geodetic feet.

14.97414932 centimetres
= 5.895334377 inches
= 5.817764187 geodetic inches
= 0.484813682 geodetic feet.

As the dish-shape was focussed upwards towards the stone block to be levitated it would be expected that some type of reaction would take place which had an effect on the mass. The geometric shape of the cavity does seem to be engineered in such a way that the projected frequency vortex causes a reciprocal reaction to the mass harmonic of each block.
The reciprocal of:
0.484813682
= 2.062648055
Twice this value:
= 4.12529611
The square of this value:
= 17.018068 (the harmonic of mass at the earth's surface, 17018068)

I believe that there is not much doubt that the Tibetans had possession of the secrets relating to the geometric structure of matter, and the methods of manipulating the harmonic values, but if we can grasp the mathematical theory behind the incident, and extend the application, then an even more fascinating idea presents itself.

In my last book I mentioned the flying machines described in ancient records, that flew through the air with a melodious sound, and theorised that the sonic apparatus was tuned to the harmonic unified equations.

Now the Tibetans have given us a direct indication of how to construct a sonically propelled anti-gravitational flying machine. All that is necessary is to complete the circle of sonic generators, indicated by the drums, trumpets, etc., and we have a disc which creates an anti-gravitational lifting force at the centre. (see diagram 23).

To create this diagram I made four photo-copies of the original illustration showing the arrangement of drums, trumpets etc. and then cut out the 90 degree segments and fitted them together into a circular pattern. This was then photo-copied a second time in the relationship with a disc-shaped vehicle. When the circular pattern was formed it became evident that the Tibetans had placed the drums and trumpets on the arc of a quarter circle, but the placement of the Priests behind the drums tended to form a spiral. This conforms with the concept of the formation of matter due to the spiralling, vortexual, wave motions in space, discussed in my earlier works. Similar wave motions would have to be created in order to manipulate matter.

The inner diameter of the sonic generators in the theoretical vehicle would be 412.5296 geodetic feet, with the previously described harmonic associations. The outer diameter, estimated from the placement of the Tibetan priests, would be 428.7069166 geodetic feet. If we square the inner diameter we have the harmonic of mass 17018068 relative to the earth's surface, and the outer diameter would give a circumference tuned to the unified equation. The lift vectors through the centre would resonate at harmonic frequencies in opposition to the mass value at the centre of a unified, or light, field = 1694443.

From this it would appear that a vehicle could be constructed that would resonate at frequencies in sympathy with the unified fields demonstrated throughout this work.

It is my opinion that our own scientific establishments are far ahead in this type of research, and that many experimental vehicles have already been constructed. High frequency generators have probably taken the place of the low frequency sonic methods, and electronic systems produced which would allow complete control of movement.

With this type of research going on, I would say that the days of the conventional aeroplane are numbered.

DIAGRAM 22

Showing relationship of Priests, drums and stone blocks, to the hole in the cliff face.

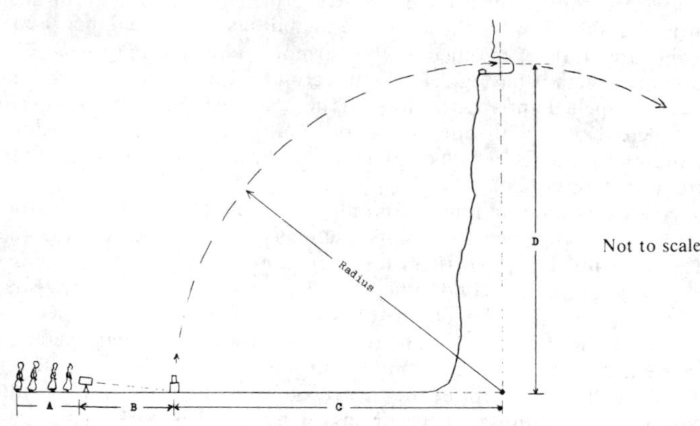

Distance
A = 8.08865 geo/ft.
B = 206.2648062 geo/ft.
C = 809.016999 geo/ft.
D = 809.016999 geo/ft.

DIAGRAM 23

Diagram showing how the geometric pattern of sonic generators created by the Tibetan Monks can be combined in a circular, or disc, shape. the resultant forces of the harmonic fields set up would combine into a doughnut shaped anti-gravitational field which would levitate the disc, or vehicle.

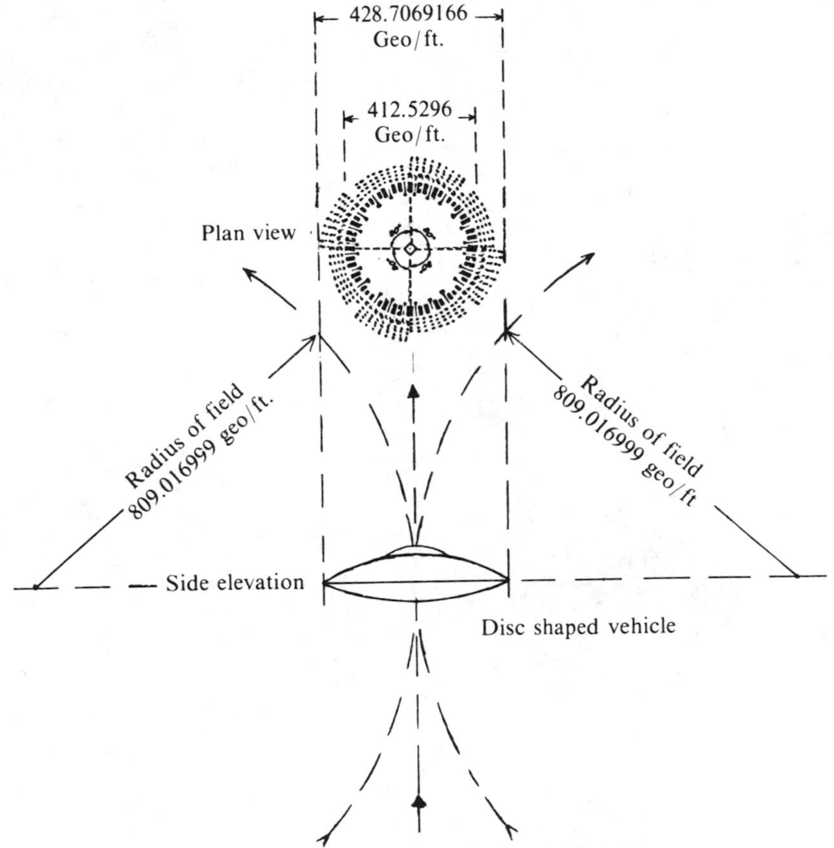

412.5296 squared = 170180.68 = mass harmonic
428.7069166 diameter = circumference of 1346.822499
= half harmonic of 2693.645 (unified equation)

SCALAR WAVES AND TESLA SHIELDS: NIKOLA TESLA--FATHER OF STAR WARS?

New York June 20 1896. Nikola Tesla

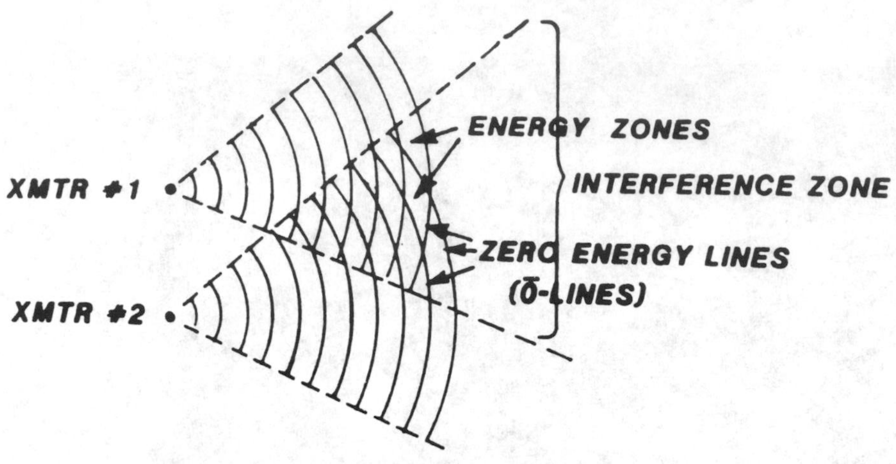

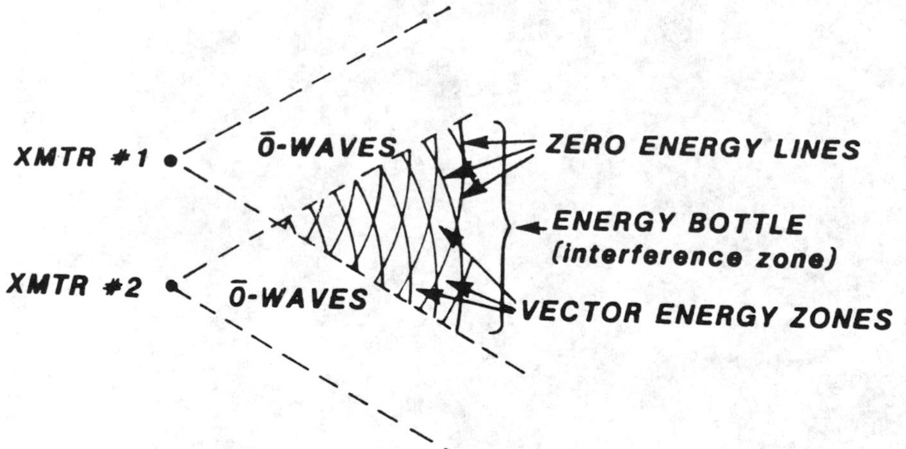

THOMAS BEARDEN'S DIAGRAMS OF LONGITUDINAL WAVE INTERFERENCE: ACCORDING TO BEARDEN, THESE RADIO WAVES, KNOWN AS SCALAR WAVES, ARE FAR MORE DISTRUCTIVE, AND EASY TO USE THAN LASERS. IS THIS THE REAL SYSTEM THAT THE USA PLANS TO PUT IN SPACE?

In recent years the proposal of a "Star Wars" system in space has gained a great deal of momentum and controversy. This proposed system is said to be the ultimate system to insure the security of the United States--and the world, at least by those who propose it. Those fighting against it maintain that it is not technically feasible.

Supporters in the Reagan Administration propose a system that would work like this: when Soviet ICBM missles, loaded with their nuclear payloads, are launched at the U.S., the "Star Wars" system, hovering in space, would fire super-high powered Lasers at the missiles while they are still in the air, thereby disabling them. These super-high powered Lasers would be powered by small atomic explosions within the "Star Wars" satellites themselves.

Critics charge that Laser technology has not advanced enough to enable the United States, or any country, to pull off such a feat. Yet another alternative rarely discussed in the media is available, and it is a technology fifty years old, invented by Nikola Tesla, the electrical genius who lit the world: Scalar Waves!

Scalar Waves are a form of radio waves creating what is known as Longitudinal Wave Interference. Where two Scalar Waves meet, an energy bottle is created which disintegrates all matter within that bottle, producing what is in effect a miniature atomic explosion but without any resulting radiation.

Thomas Bearden, a retired Pentagon war games expert and active consulting engineer to the Defense Department, has written a number of papers on Scalar Wave systems and often lectures on Scalar Waves at Alternative Energy conferences. According to Bearden, the Soviets are way ahead of the U.S. in Scalar Wave technology and are already using it against the U.S.

Scalar Wave technology is apparently very real and deadly. Furthermore, it is a great deal more simple to use than Lasers, far more effective, and does not require mini-atomic explosions to power it. Is it possible that Scalar "Howitzers," as Bearden calls them, is the real system that the Pentagon would like to put into space? What applications might such a system have?

The Pentagon has insisted so far that their proposed "Star Wars" program is entirely defensive, designed to protect the U.S. from a nuclear attack. Incredibly, Ronald Reagan even said in a press conference once that after the United States had built their "Star Wars" system, they would give it to the Russians, who would then build their own system in space, so the world would be theoretically safe from nuclear war for ever more! Reagan later said in another news conference that maybe this

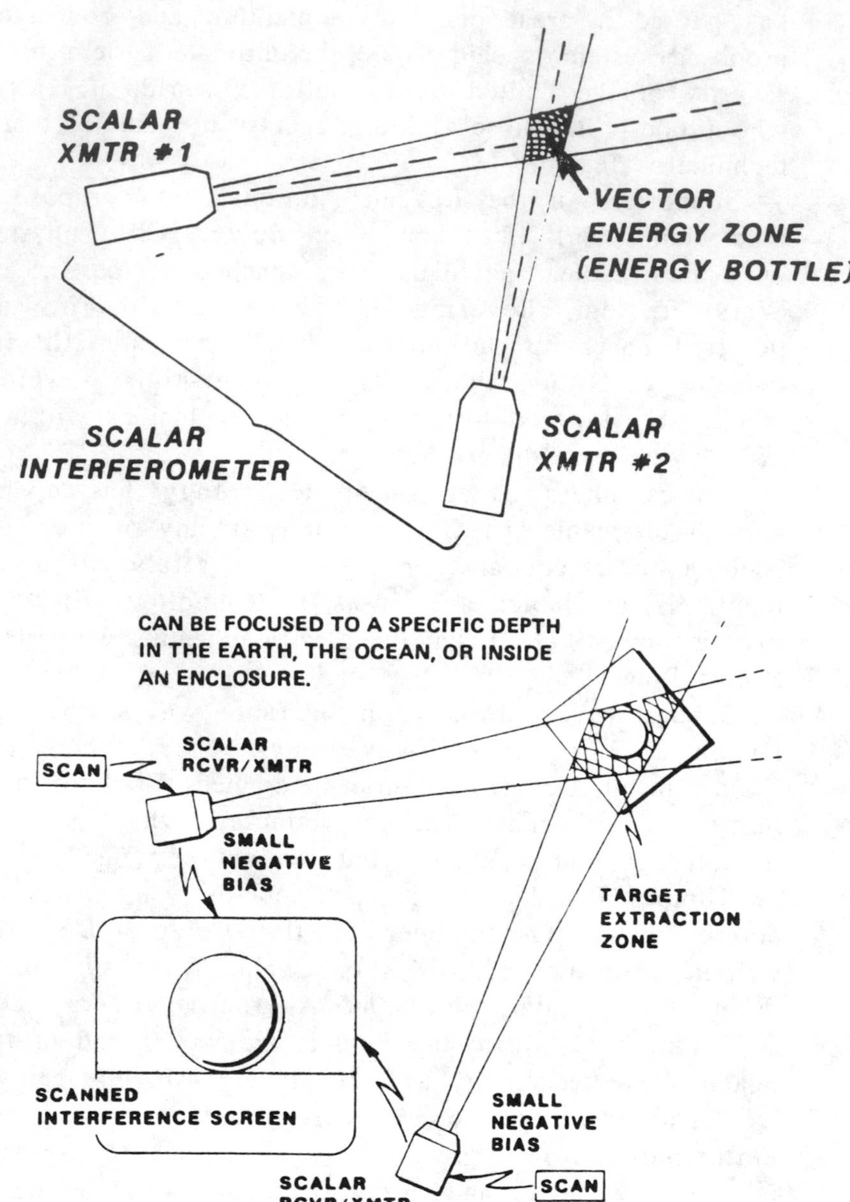

WHERE TWO SCALAR WAVES MEET, AN ENERGY BOTTLE IS CREATED, AND ALL MATTER WITHIN THAT BOTTLE IS DISINTIGRATED. MORE EFFECTIVE THAN LASERS? WHAT IS THE REAL PURPOSE BEHIND STAR WARS?

wasn't such a good idea afterall.

When a "Stars Wars" system using Scalar Wave technology is activated, its uses are in fact more "offensive" than "defensive." If Scalar Wave weapons are real, they are a weapon of such incredible power and versatility, then no one on our planet would be safe from them. Given the proper coordinates, the Scalar transmitters located on satellites in space could disintegrate any target on the planet, be it a missile, enemy base, rioting city district, farm house or persons gathering in a park. Such a "Star Wars" system would be a literal "Death Star" in space! Its uses could be population control, extermination, and military domination of an entire planet. George Lucas may be more of a prophet than he realizes.

On the brighter side, Scalar Waves can be warped into a dome around objects, such as cities or houses (publishing companies included). Such a Scalar Wave force field is generally known as a Tesla Shield, and it would be analogous to the "shields" referred to in the popular "Star Trek" series. Tesla Shields have a definite defensive application, and could not in any way be used for offensive purposes (although a platoon of soldiers charging into a Tesla Shield would be instantly disintegrated). The only defense from a blast of a Scalar Wave Howitzer would be a Tesla Shield. Therefore, those persons wishing to use Scalar Waves on an unsuspecting population would rather that they were unaware of this technology, and thereby unable to protect themselves by use of the same technology. Is this the reason that the Pentagon does not discuss Scalar Wave technology, but rather maintains that they are going to use impractical Laser technology instead?

Scalar Wave Technology is straight out of science-fiction, yet it *was invented more than fifty years ago by Nikola Tesla* (see the article by Nikola Tesla in **The Anti-Gravity Handbook**). Another interesting application of Scalar Wave technology is its use in "Light Sabers." If a Scalar Wave emanates from a gripable handle and then is bent back on itself, it would become exactly like a "Light Saber" as depicted in the "Star Wars" movies featuring Jedi Knights (written and produced by George Lucas).

Are Scalar Waves a real technology? Do the Soviets have this technology? Assuredly so. The Americans do as well. The secret American base at Pine Gap in Central Australia is said to have two Scalar Wave towers in it already. We urge readers to read some of the biographies of Nikola Tesla. Does the Pentagon really plan to put Scalar Wave Howitzers into space? If so, is it purely for defensive purposes? In the following articles and diagrams, the reality of Scalar Waves will be demonstrated.

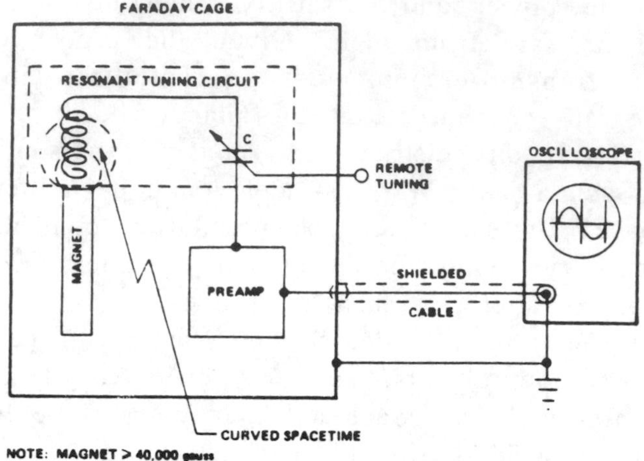

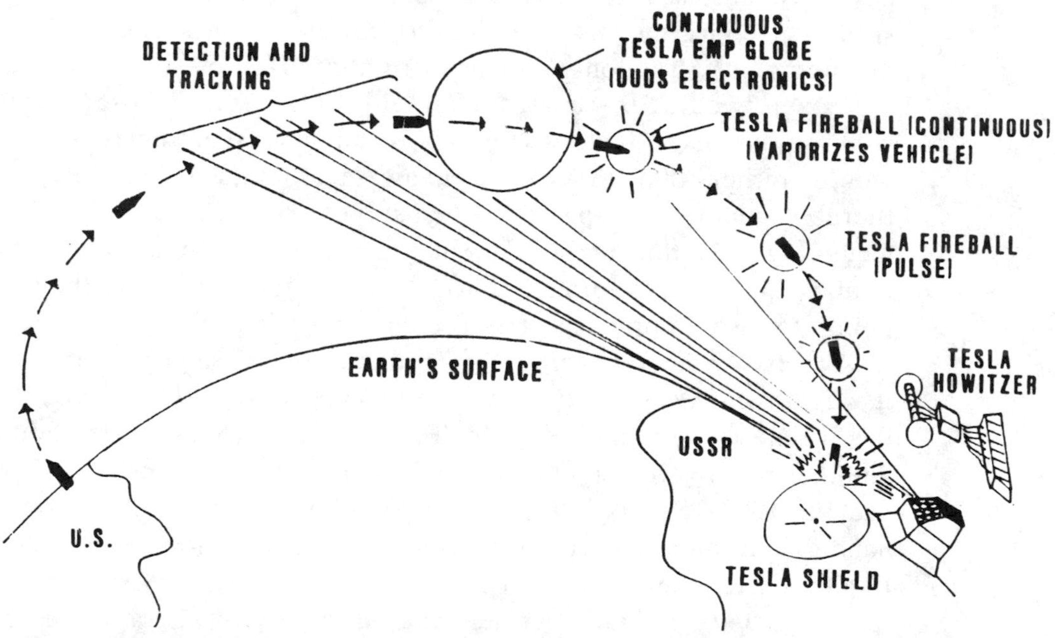

BEARDEN'S IDEA OF A SCALAR WAVE-TESLA HOWITZER IN ACTION. IMAGINE THIS SYSTEM HOVERING ABOVE OUR PLANET IN SPACE--THE U.S. MILITARY WOULD RATHER THAT YOU DIDN'T. NOTE THE TESLA SHIELD AT THE BOTTOM OF THE DRAWING. A TESLA SHIELD IS A ESSENTIALLY A SCALAR ENERGY BOTTLE WARPED AROUND AN OBJECT, SUCH AS THE SCALAR HOWITZER ITSELF OR EVEN A CITY, CREATING AN INPENETRABLE FORCE FIELD.

Was Edison adversary father of 'Star Wars'?

By James Coates
Chicago Tribune

COLORADO SPRINGS, Colo.—Giants have trod the ground here. Zebulon Pike, legendary explorer of the unknown West, gave his name to the majestic white- capped peak just outside of town.

President Dwight Eisenhower came here to carve America's ultimate nuclear war command center, the awesome North American Aerospace Defense Command [NORAD] bunker, into the granite underneath Pike's Peak's neighboring summit, Cheyenne Mountain.

Most impressive of all, the man who invented radio and who discovered the way that the world transmits its electrical power did much of his creative work here.

But, wait. Weren't we taught that radio was invented by an Italian named Guglielmo Marconi? And that the legendary Thomas Alva Edison devised today's electrical power system in his New Jersey laboratories?

"We were taught wrong," said Toby Grotz, president of the International Tesla Society based here in honor of a little-known flamboyant genius named Nikola Tesla.

Two years before Marconi demonstrated his wireless radio transmission, Tesla, a naturalized Yugoslavian immigrant, performed an identical feat at the 1893 World's Fair in Chicago.

On June 21, 1943, in the case of Marconi Wireless Telegraph Co. vs. the United States the Supreme Court ruled that that Tesla's radio patents had predated those of the Italian genius.

To be sure, Edison invented the incandesent light bulb. But he powered it and all of his other projects with inefficient direct current [DC] electricity.

It was Tesla who discovered how to use the far more powerful phased form of alternating current [AC] electricity that is virtually the universal type of electricity employed by modern civilization.

And now, there are indications that Tesla also discovered many of the devices which the United States military-industrial complex is seeking to develop and build for the Pentagon's controversial Star Wars antimissile defense system.

Grotz and other Tesla experts speculate that recent puzzling reports of immense clouds forming within minutes over Soviet arctic territory are indications that the Soviet Union is testing devices for transmitting energy over large distances developed nearly a century ago by Tesla.

Of particular interest to Tesla researchers, said Grotz, is a widely reported April 9, 1984, event in which at least four airline pilots reported seeing an eruption near Japan that appeared to be a nuclear explosion cloud that billowed to a height of 60,000 feet and a width of 200 miles within just two minutes and enveloped their aircraft.

In late July the Cox News Service reported that all four of these planes had been examined by the U.S. Air Force at Anchorage, Alaska, and were found to be free of radiation despite the fact they had flown through the mysterious cloud in question.

Grotz said that such clouds could form if someone were attempting to implement Tesla's plans for broadcasting energy by "creating resonances inside the earth's ionospheric cavity" calculated in Colorado Springs during 1899 experiments by the electrical genius.

Nikola Tesla: Is his research helping the Soviet Union build the ultimate weapon?

Each year about 400 members of the Tesla Society, sanctioned by the prestigous International Institute of Electric Engineering [IIEE], meet here where the wizard of electricity carried out his most startling lightning-crackling experiments to discuss one of the strangest stories in the annals of American science.

It is a story of tormented genius. It also is the story of a little-known but intensely bitter feud that pitted Edison and the fabulously wealthy financier J.P. Morgan on one side and Tesla and his ally, the equally powerful George Westinghouse on the other. And, finally, it is a spy story.

Many in the Tesla Society are convinced

that foolish U.S. bureaucrats shipped the secrets needed to build Star Wars that Tesla discovered to communist-controlled Yugoslavia shortly after World War II, thereby allowing the Soviets an enormous head start in the quest for a particle beam weapon that is deemed essential to building any missile shield.

In an interview between sessions at this August's Tesla symposium, Grotz explained that Tesla was drawn to Colorado Springs because he needed both the dry climate and the furiously powerful lightning storms that so often come tumbling down the sides of Pikes Peak and Cheyenne Mountain.

"Tesla dreamed of supplying limitless amounts of power freely and equally available to all persons on Earth," said Grotz.

And he was convinced he could do so by broadcasting electrical power across large distances just as radio transmits far smaller amounts of energy, explained Grotz.

The same energy beams, of course, could be directed at the speed of light to destroy enemy planes and missiles as well as to supply electricity, he noted.

Such investigations take one into the realm of the most complicated question facing science today, the so-called Unified Field Theory that Albert Einstein himself confessed was beyond his abilities, acknowledged Grotz, an engineer for the Martin Marietta Aerospace company in Denver.

Tesla believed that he could broadcast power by producing vibrations in the atmosphere that were perfectly in phase with the natural vibrations that exist in thunderstorms, said Grotz.

Then, anyone with a receiver could simply tap into broadcasts and acquire elecricity just as they receive radio or TV broadcasts.

On a hilltop just where the prairies sweep up to the foot of the Rockies, Tesla erected a gigantic version of what is known as the Tesla Coil, a device that produces dramatic arcs of electricity by rapidly changing its resistance.

Nearly every natural history museum and high school physics lab in the world sports a Tesla Coil capable of making delighted students' hair stand on end or of arcing dramatic sparks from the fingertips of someone who, standing firmly on a rubber mat, holds the other hand over the coil's top.

At the corner of Foote and Kowia streets in Colorado Springs, Tesla erected a coil 122 feet high. Tapping into the entire city electric system, the electricial genius sent millions of volts of current into the structure and bolts of man-made lightning leaped as much as 135 feet into the brooding sky to mingle with other bolts created in nature.

The first time he threw the switch, the entire city was blacked, tests created artificial clouds around his installation and caused lights to burn as much as 26 miles away, according to news reports of the time.

The Colorado Springs artificial lightning bolts created during the single year that Tesla lived here, 1899-1900, have never been duplicated, said Grotz.

The experiments established that lightning storms as they swooped down the Rockies and then rumbled across the plains into Kansas were resonating at a frequency of 7.68 cycles per second.

This natural phenomenon was rediscovered in the 1960s by researcher W.O. Schumann while working for the Navy on ways to broadcast nuclear war orders to submerged submarines, said Grotz.

A paper widely circulated at the Tesla symposium called "Star Wars Now! The Bohm-Aharonov Effect, Scalar Interferometry and Soviet Weaponization" speculates that the mysterious clouds that frightened airline pilots were created when energy was drained from one area and transmitted to another using Tesla principles.

The paper's author, T.E. Beaden, a retired Pentagon war games expert and active consulting engineer to the Defense Department, said the result of such energy transmissions is a "cold explosion" that could be enormously destructive.

Noting that the cloud covered 150 miles, Beaden wrote, "A single shot of such a weapon could almost instantly freeze every NATO soldier in that area into a block of ice."

Grotz acknowledged that much of the world's mainstream scientific community doubts the claims made by Tesla fans like himself and Beaden.

"But," he added, "Tesla always was rejected by the establishment."

After Tesla began building AC dynamos, motors and other devices with financial backing from Westinghouse, Edison and his General Electric Company waged a campaign to discredit AC by emphasizing its dangers, according to Tesla biographer Margaret Cheney in her "Tesla, Man Out of Time."

Edison would force dogs and cats to stand on steel plates energized by AC current and then throw a switch, electrocuting them. He called the process "Westinghousing," Cheney wrote.

Ultimately Tesla lost out to Edison and other foes, even though his AC power system prevailed.

The visionary died in 1943 in a New York hotel room he shared with several pigeons that he considered his only friends, the biographer said.

After the war, Tesla's relatives in Yugoslavia petitioned Washington to receive 17 trunks of papers and laboratory equipment that he had stored in a New York garage.

In 1952 these items were sent to Belgrade where they are housed in a Tesla museum.

But, said Grotz, "What do you suppose are the chances that everything was first copied by the KGB?"

"In the USA we don't even give him credit for inventing the radio and the Soviet bloc is building Tesla museums," said the engineer.

"Why do they respect him so much?"

Artist's conception of "cosmic ray" guns planned by U.S. scientists. Unless we can come up with weapons more advanced even than the Russian N-bomb, we can be subjected to "atomic blackmail" and subjugated by the communists.

TESLA SHIELDS AND SCALAR WAVE BEAM WEAPONS ARE NOTHING NEW. THIS DRAWING IS REPRINTED FROM AN ARTICLE IN THE NOVEMBER, 1961 ISSUE OF POLICE GAZETTE ENTITLED, "WHY U.S. MUST BEAT RUSSIA'S DEATH RAY BOMB." (The article was infact about Neutron Bombs, a topic that was to surface again more than fifteen years later! Is our technology really that far behind, or is this just what the government would have us believe?

TESLA SCALAR WAVE SYSTEMS: THE EARTH AS A CAPACITOR

by Richard L. Clark

Nikola Tesla engineered his communications and power broadcast systems based on the Earth as a spherical capacitor plate with the ionosphere as the other plate. The frequencies that work best with this system are 12 Hz and its harmonics and the "storm" frequency around 500 KHz. The basic Earth electrostatic system and the basic Tesla designs are shown in the figure below. All lengths or circuits must be one-quarter wavelength or some odd multiple of it.

The elevated capacitor has really two functions, Capacity to Ground (Cg) and Capacity to Ionosphere (Ci). The bottom plate only to ground is Cg, and both plates are Ci. L2 and C3 are a resonant stepdown air core coupling system at the desired frequency. Simple calculations will allow resonant frequency values to be determined from the Tesla Equivalent Circuit diagram. Be extemely careful of the high voltages in this system. ###

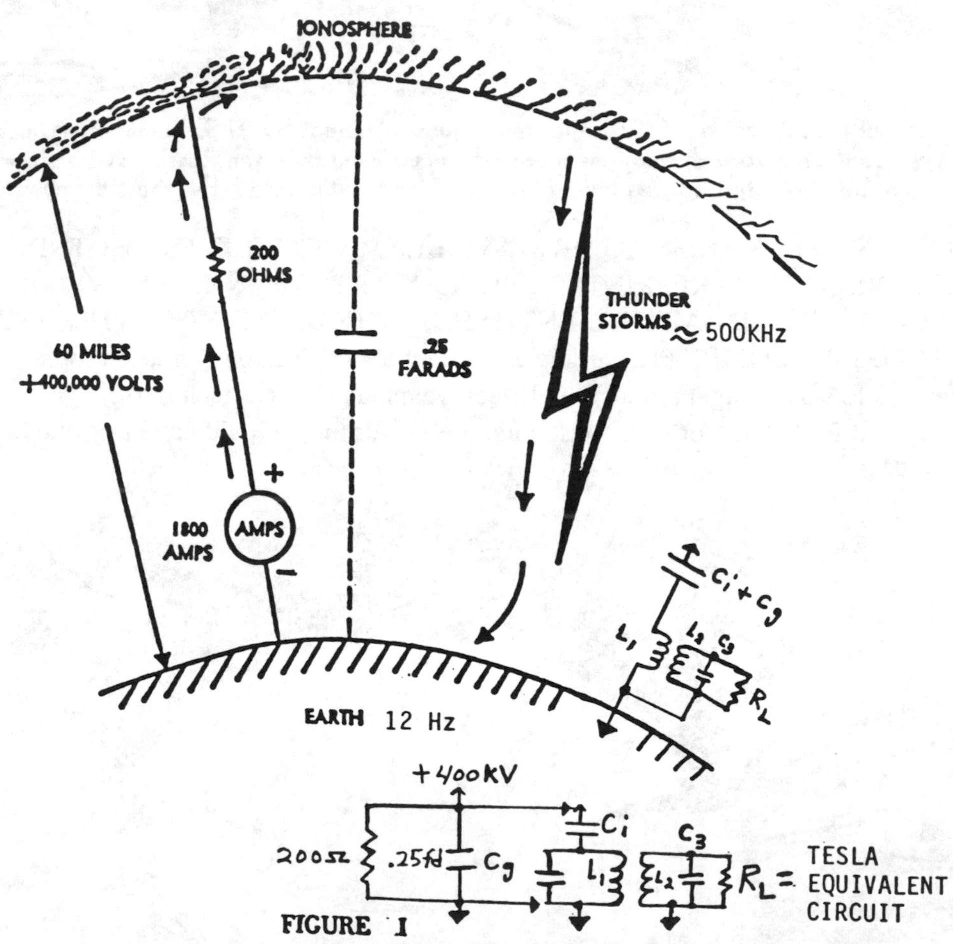

FIGURE I

Equivalent circuit of earth's electrostatic voltage field.

TESLA SYSTEM

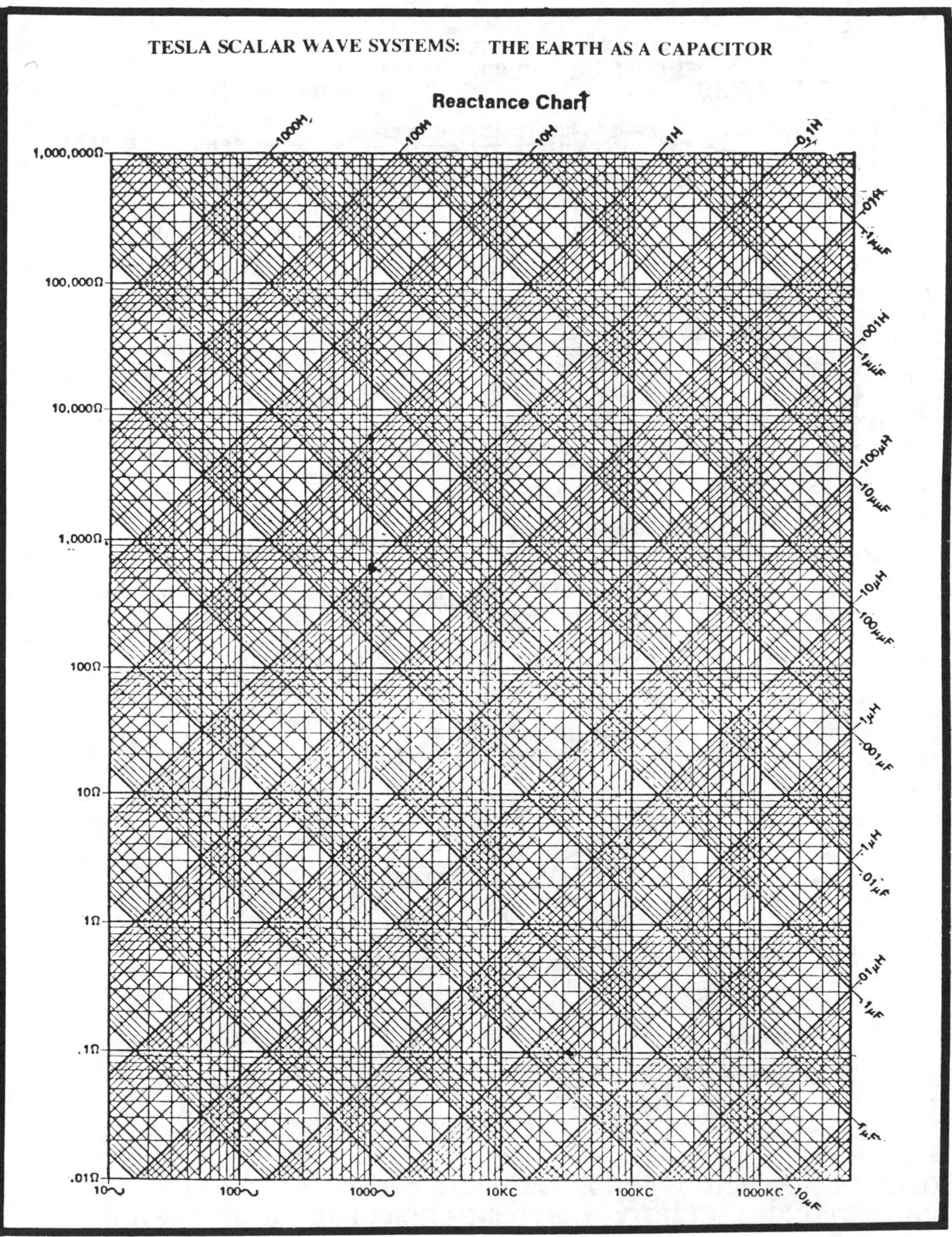
TESLA SCALAR WAVE SYSTEMS: THE EARTH AS A CAPACITOR
Reactance Chart
1000H
100H
10H
1H
0.1H
1,000,000Ω
100,000Ω
10,000Ω
1,000Ω
100Ω
10Ω
1Ω
.1Ω
.01Ω
10~
100~
1000~
10KC
100KC
1000KC
.01H
.1μF
.001H
1μF
100μH
10μF
10μH
100μF
1μH
.001μF
.1μH
.01μF
.01μH
.1μF
1μF
10μF

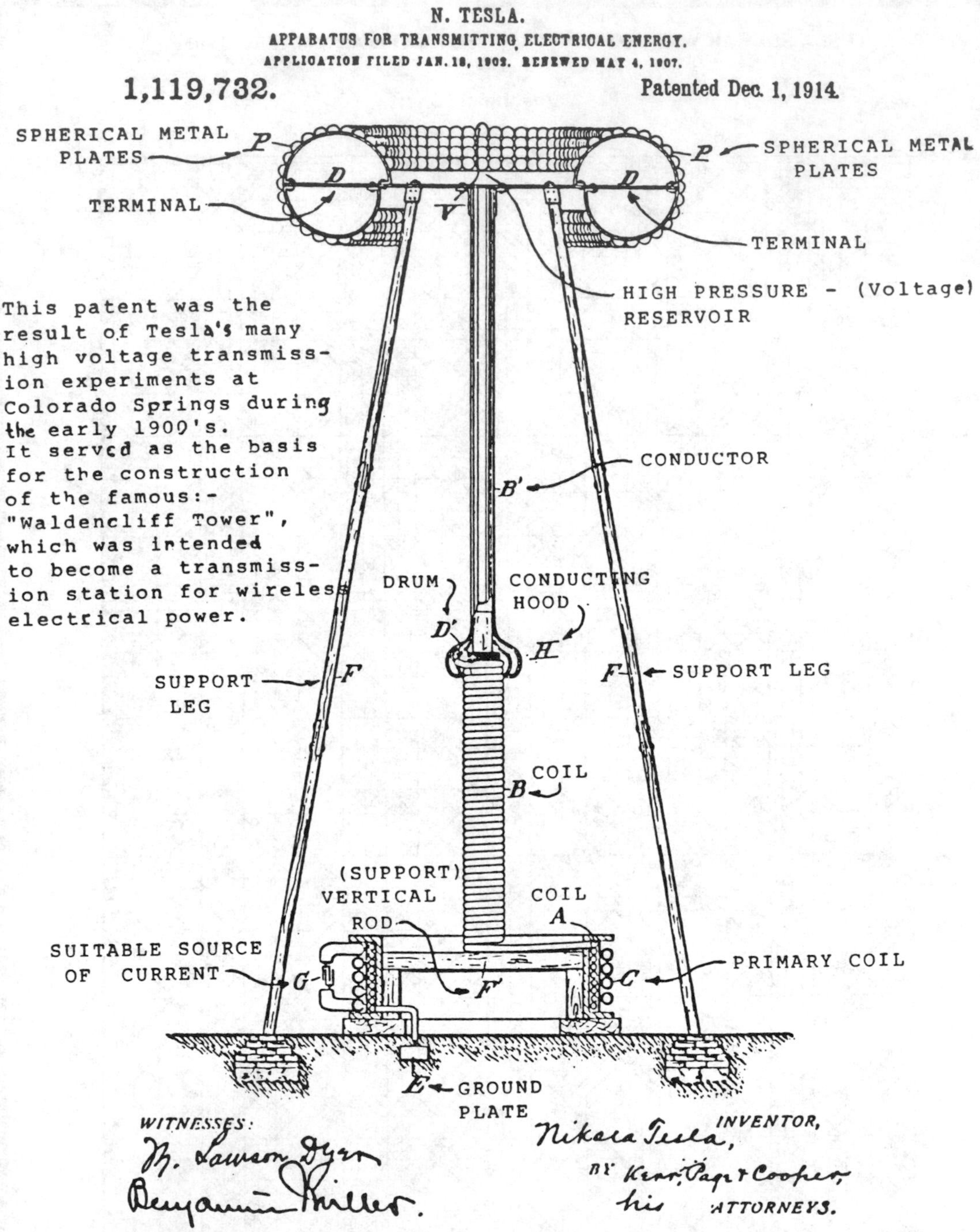

N. TESLA.

APPARATUS FOR TRANSMITTING ELECTRICAL ENERGY.

APPLICATION FILED JAN. 18, 1902. RENEWED MAY 4, 1907.

1,119,732. Patented Dec. 1, 1914.

SPHERICAL METAL PLATES — P
TERMINAL — D
V
SPHERICAL METAL PLATES — P
TERMINAL — D
HIGH PRESSURE - (Voltage) RESERVOIR

This patent was the result of Tesla's many high voltage transmission experiments at Colorado Springs during the early 1900's. It servcd as the basis for the construction of the famous:- "Waldencliff Tower", which was intended to become a transmission station for wireless electrical power.

CONDUCTOR — B'
DRUM — D'
CONDUCTING HOOD — H
SUPPORT LEG — F
SUPPORT LEG — F
COIL — B
(SUPPORT) VERTICAL ROD — F'
COIL — A
SUITABLE SOURCE OF CURRENT — G
PRIMARY COIL — C
GROUND PLATE — E

WITNESSES:
M. Lawson Dyer
Benjamin Miller.

INVENTOR,
Nikola Tesla,
BY Kerr, Page & Cooper,
his ATTORNEYS.

SOME TESLA PATENTS FOR THE ELECTRICAL APPARATUS FOR TRANSMITTING ELECTRICTY--THE FOUNDATION OF TESLA SHEILDS AND SCALAR WAVES.

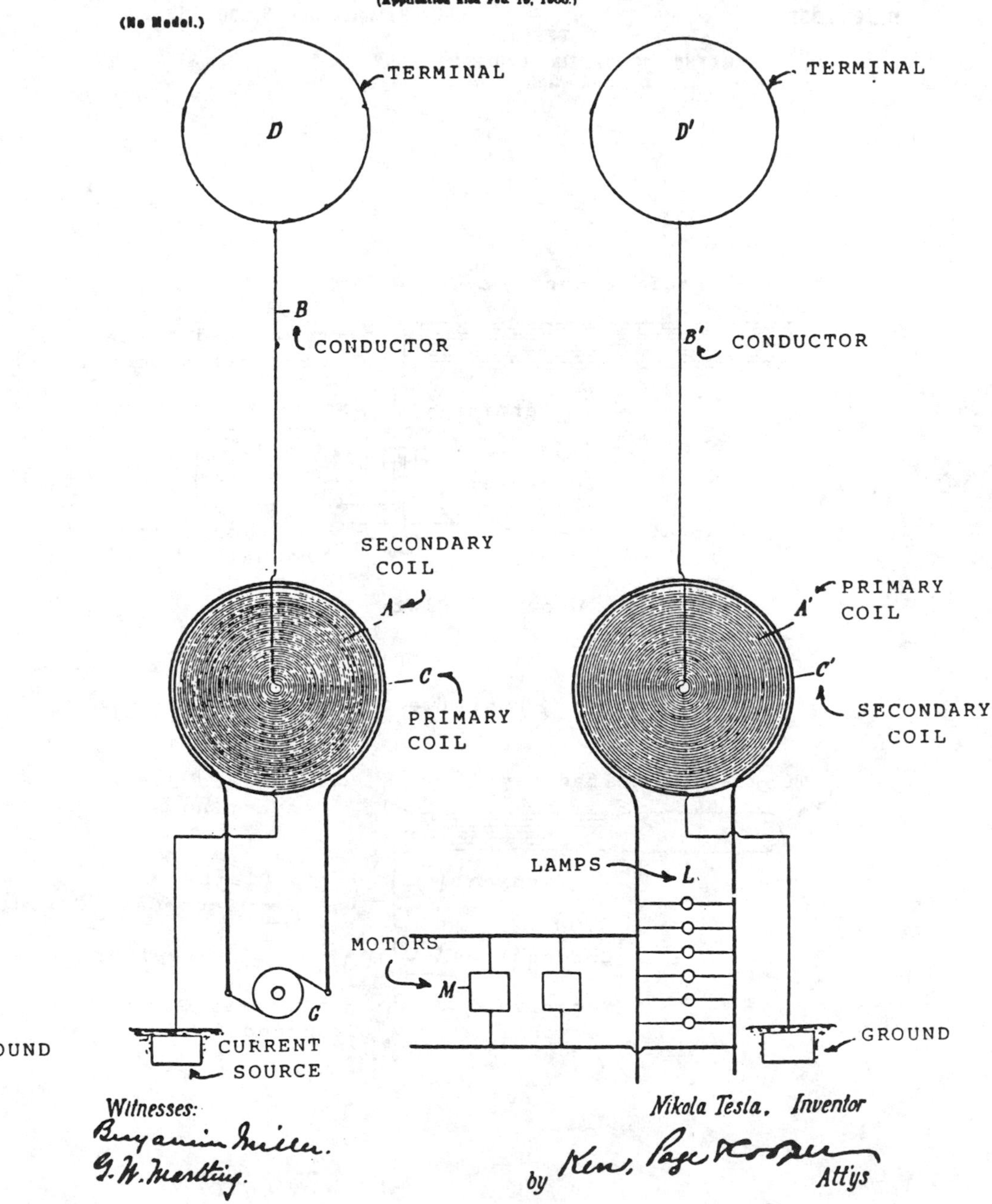
No. 649,621.
Patented May 15, 1900.
N. TESLA.
APPARATUS FOR TRANSMISSION OF ELECTRICAL ENERGY.
(Application filed Feb. 19, 1900.)
(No Model.)
TERMINAL
D
TERMINAL
D'
B
CONDUCTOR
B'
CONDUCTOR
SECONDARY COIL
A
C
PRIMARY COIL
PRIMARY COIL
A'
C'
SECONDARY COIL
LAMPS
L
MOTORS
M
G
GROUND
CURRENT SOURCE
GROUND
Witnesses:
Nikola Tesla, Inventor
Att'ys

No. 685,958. Patented Nov. 5, 1901.

N. TESLA.

METHOD OF UTILIZING RADIANT ENERGY.

(Application filed Mar. 21, 1901.)

(No Model.)

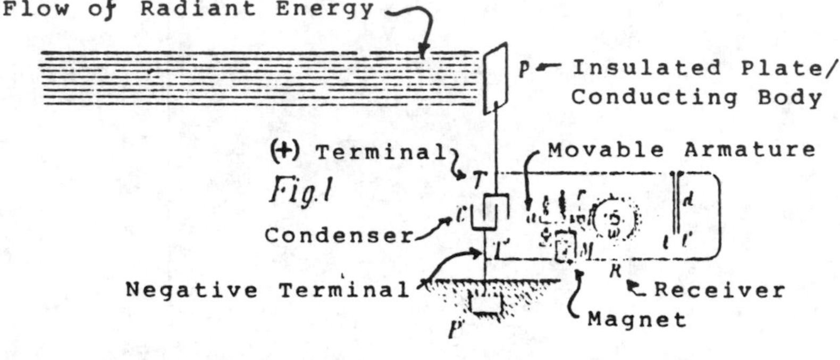

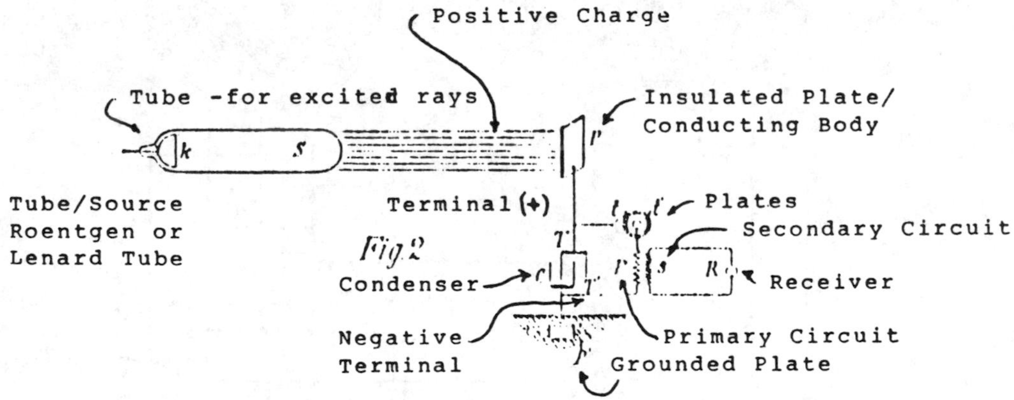

Witnesses:
Raphaël Netter
M. Lawson Dyer

Nikola Tesla, Inventor

by Kerr, Page & Cooper Att'ys

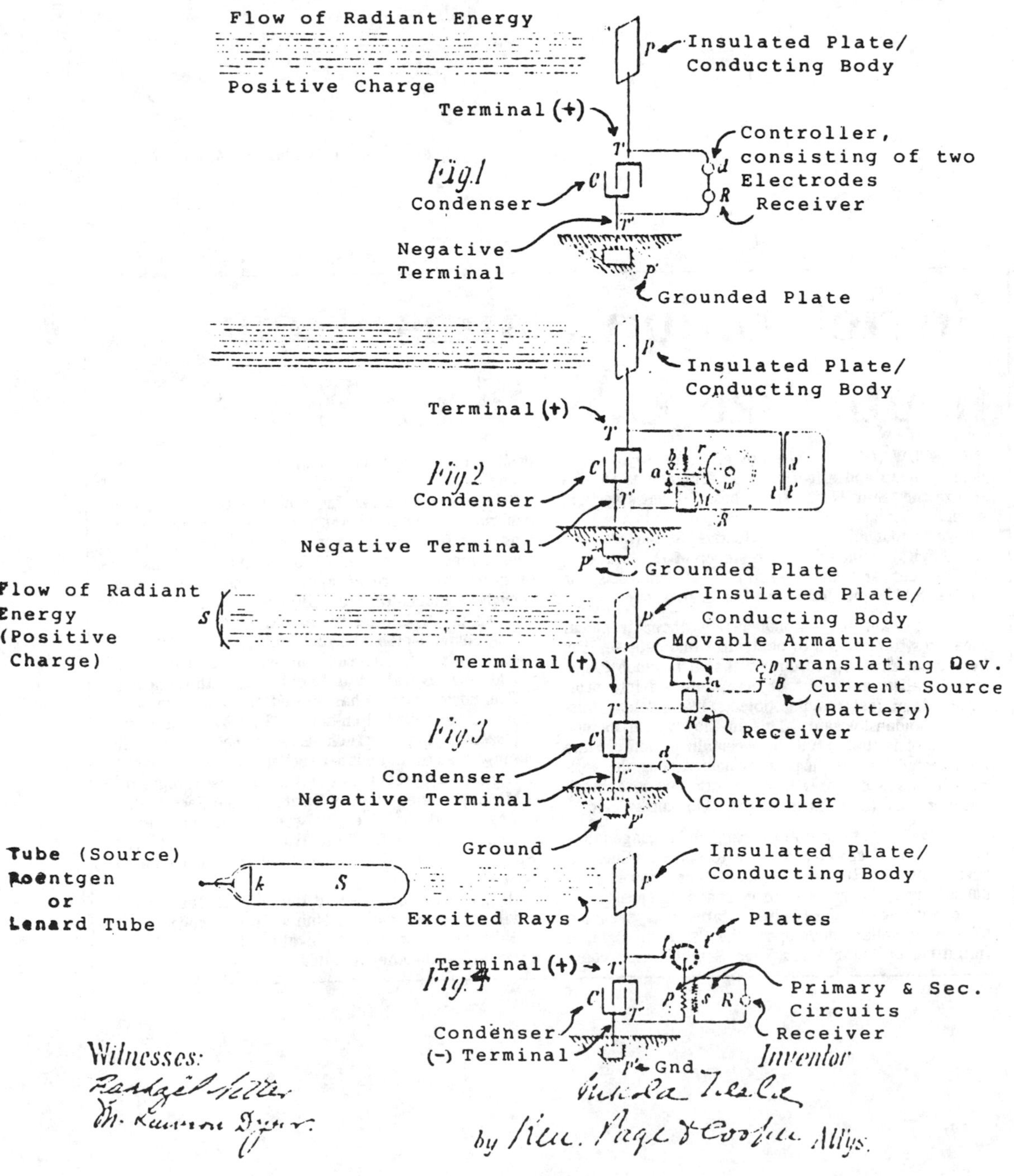
No. 685,957.
Patented Nov. 5, 1901.
N. TESLA.
APPARATUS FOR THE UTILIZATION OF RADIANT ENERGY.
(Application filed Mar. 21, 1901.)
(No Model.)
Flow of Radiant Energy
Positive Charge
Insulated Plate/ Conducting Body
Terminal (+)
Controller, consisting of two Electrodes
Receiver
Fig.1
Condenser
Negative Terminal
Grounded Plate
Insulated Plate/ Conducting Body
Terminal (+)
Fig.2
Condenser
Negative Terminal
Grounded Plate
Flow of Radiant Energy (Positive Charge)
Insulated Plate/ Conducting Body
Movable Armature
Translating Dev.
Current Source (Battery)
Terminal (+)
Receiver
Fig.3
Condenser
Negative Terminal
Controller
Ground
Tube (Source) Roentgen or Lenard Tube
Insulated Plate/ Conducting Body
Excited Rays
Plates
Terminal (+)
Fig.4
Primary & Sec. Circuits
Condenser
Receiver
(-) Terminal
Gnd
Witnesses:
Inventor
Nikola Tesla
by Kerr, Page & Cooper Attys.

The Daily Journal, Kankakee, Ill., Wednesday, August 27, 1986

Soviet Union claims it can neutralize U.S. 'Star Wars'

MOSCOW (UPI) — The Soviet Union says it can deploy cheap and effective countermeasures to neutralize the "Star Wars" space-based defense system, a senior Soviet nuclear scientist said today.

"We cannot allow it (an effective 'Star Wars' system)," Vitaly Goldanksy, a member of the Academy of Sciences and the Committee of Scientists for Peace, told a Moscow news conference.

"If we want to talk concretely about technical measures to be taken to neutralize this defense, it is very clear first and foremost, that it is much easier to neutralize stationary objects launched into orbit rather than fast moving objects like nuclear missiles," Goldansky said. "This method would include space means that would in a certain period of time be directed for the purpose of neutralizing the anti-missile space defense. I would say this is a much cheaper way (than 'Star Wars')," Goldansky said.

Although it appeared in the English language interpretation as a direct reference to space "mines," a review of the Russian language tape showed Goldansky used the general term space "means."

He said while the United States was spending billions of dollars developing the Strategic Defense Initiative, or "Star Wars," the Soviet Union could easily counter without causing any damage to its economy.

"U.S. hopes to make the Soviet national economy bankrupt due to the arms race and anti-missile defense are futile because it is easy to find effective countermeasures to an ABM (antiballistic missile) program, which are cheaper ... without the serious economic expenditure of billions of dollars that is planned in the United States," Goldansky said.

The Soviet Union already deploys what U.S. officials have termed a crude anti-satellite device that would take several orbits to catch up with its target.

The Soviet Union has hinted at other ways of reducing the multibillion-dollar "Star Wars" program to "useless junk" — such as overwhelming it with dummy missles and coated rockets at a cost of just 1 percent to 2 percent of the U.S. defense program.

Monday, Soviet Chief of Staff Marshal Sergei Akhromeyev said the Kremlin would come up with a surprise response to "Star Wars" that would send Washington scurrying to find another space-based system.

"If it is necessary we will find a quick answer and it will not be the way the United States expects it. It will be an answer that devalues the 'Star Wars' program," Akhromeyev said.

MORE ANTI-GRAVITY PATENTS

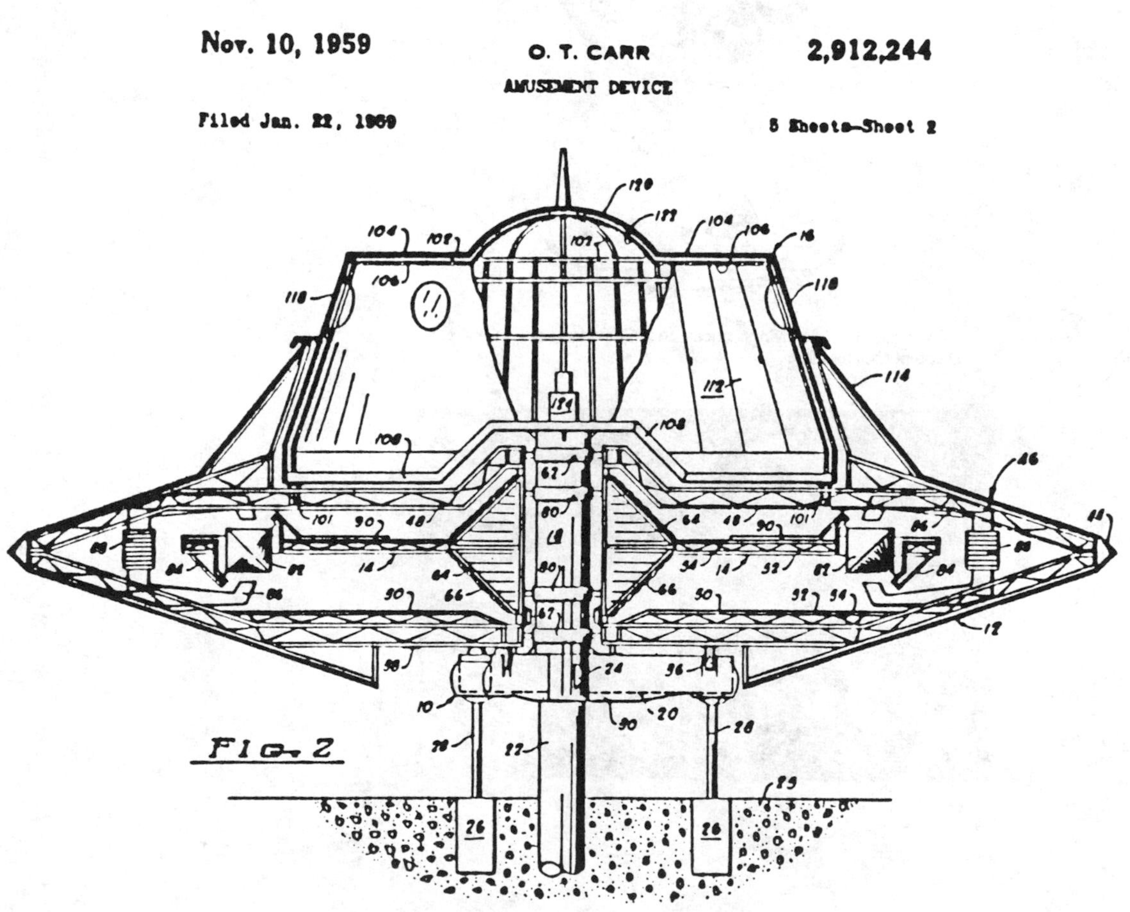

United States Patent — **Des. 238,938**
Patented Feb. 24, 1976

238,938

AIRCRAFT

Paul S. Moller, Dixon, Calif., assignor to Discojet Corporation, Davis, Calif.

Filed Mar. 24, 1975, Ser. No. 561,234

Term of patent 14 years

Int. Cl. D12—07

U.S. Cl. D12—79

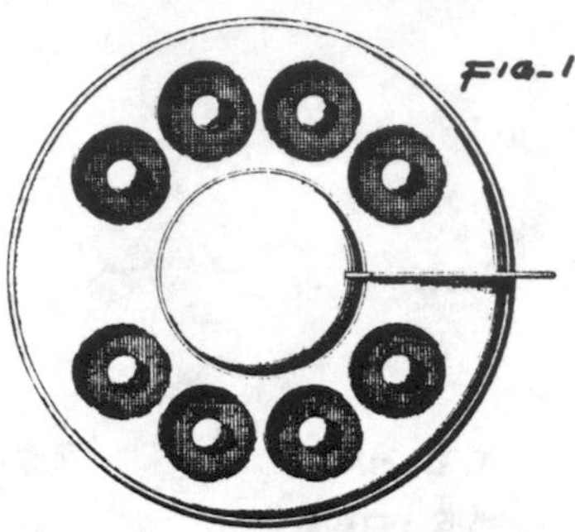

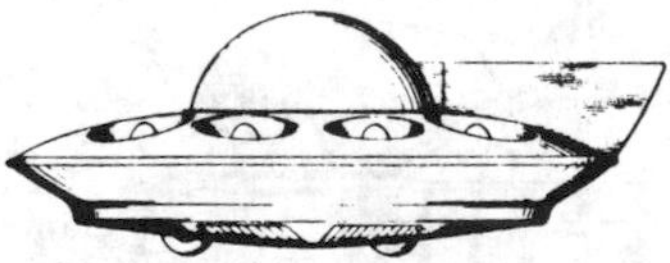

Patent design for a flying saucer under development at the Discojet Corporation.

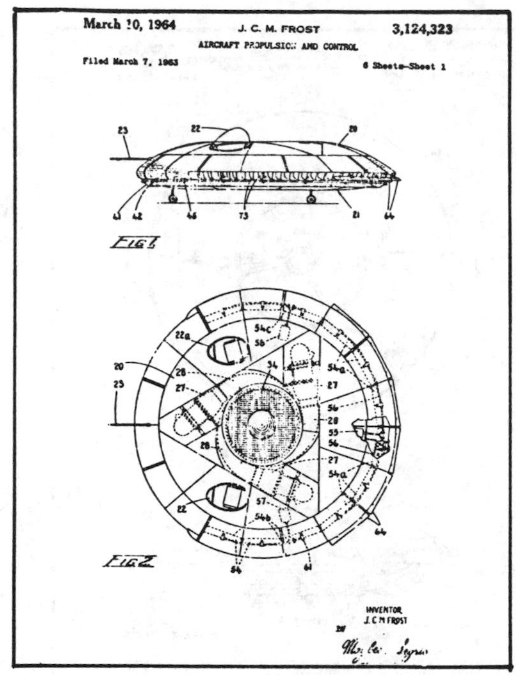

Patented design for J. C. M. Frost's circular aircraft.

First of two patented designs by Leonor Zalles for a circular airship.

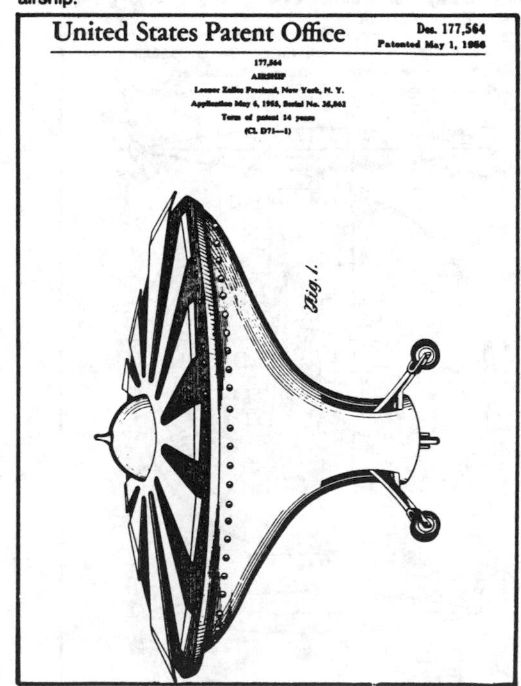

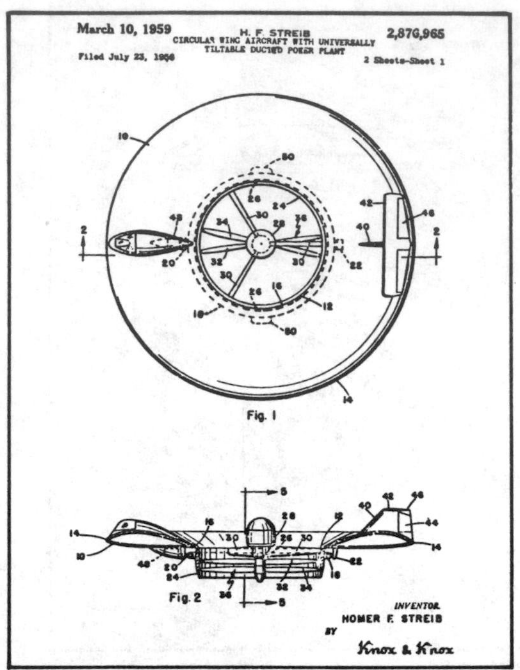

Patented design for Homer Streib's circular wing aircraft, with tiltable ducted power plant, capable of vertical and lateral flight.

Patented design for Nathan Price's "High Velocity High Altitude V.T.O.L. Aircraft."

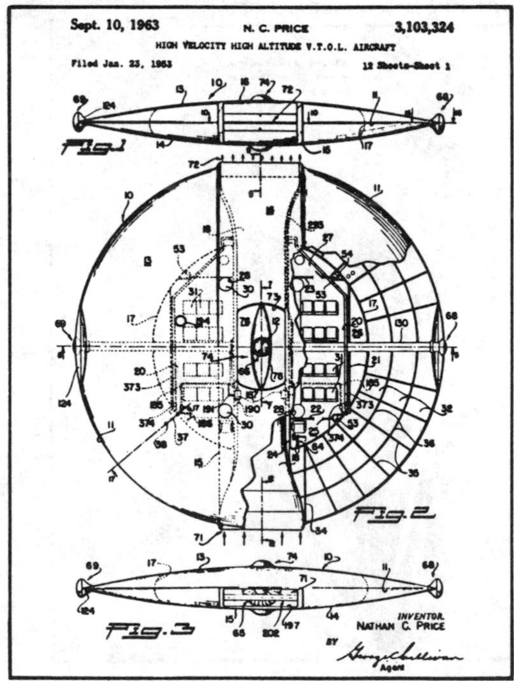

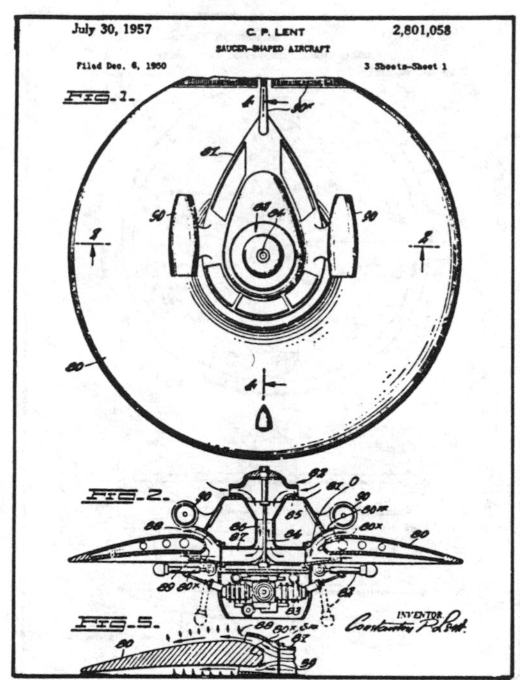

Patented design for Constantin Lent's flying saucer.

Patented design for Irwin Barr's rotating "Flying Machine."

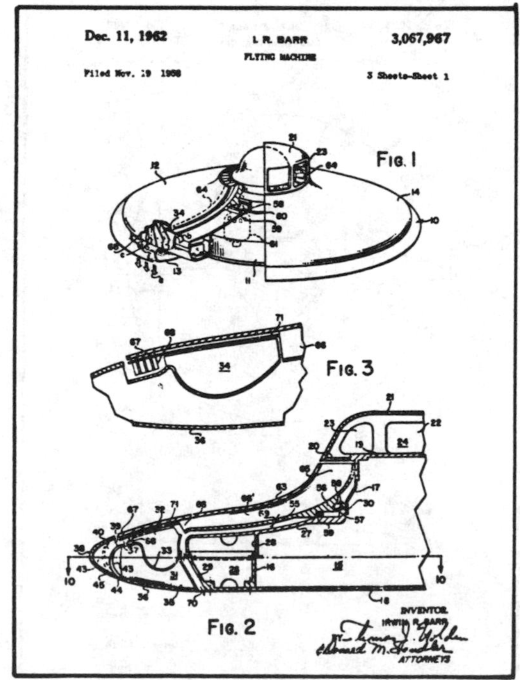

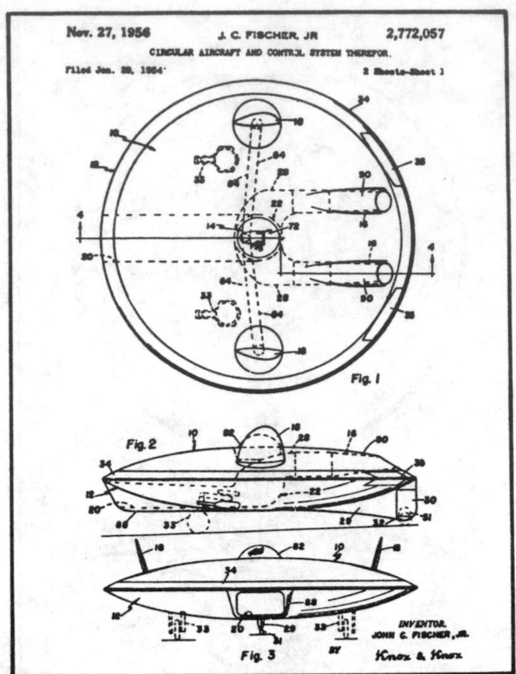

Patented design for John Fischer's rotating circular aircraft.

Patented design for Homer Streib's circular wing aircraft capable of vertical and lateral flight.

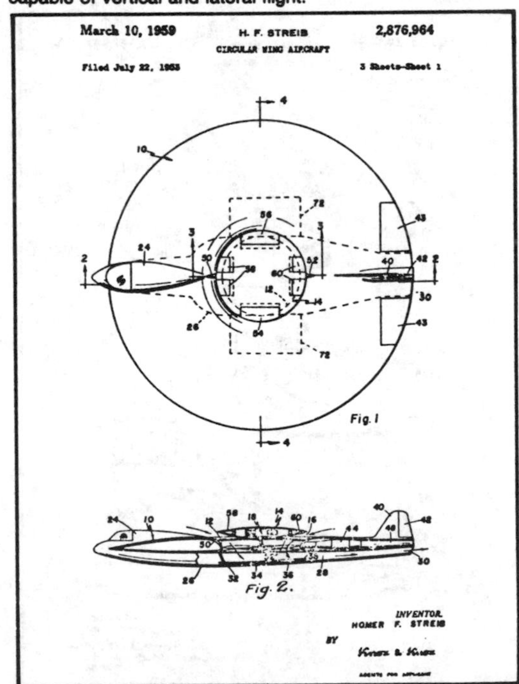

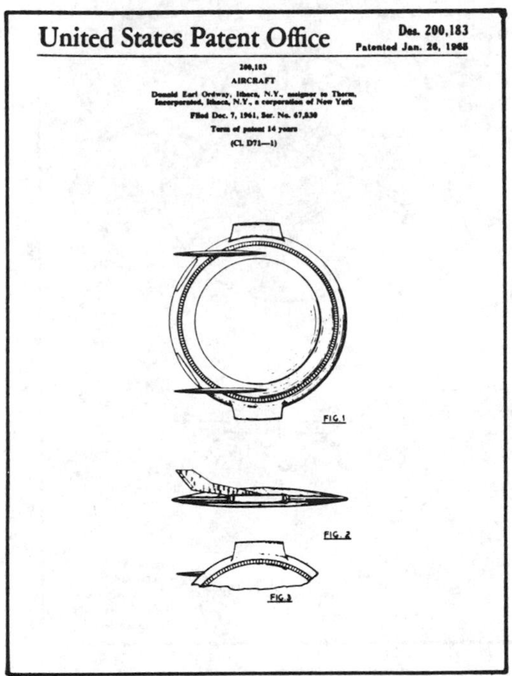

United States Patent Office

Des. 200,183
Patented Jan. 26, 1965

200,183
AIRCRAFT
Donald Earl Ordway, Ithaca, N.Y., assignor to Therm, Incorporated, Ithaca, N.Y., a corporation of New York
Filed Dec. 7, 1961, Ser. No. 67,830
Term of patent 14 years
(Cl. D71—1)

FIG. 1

FIG. 2

FIG. 3

Patented design for Donald Ordway's circular aircraft.

Patented design for John Sherwood's "Vertical Lift Flying Machine."

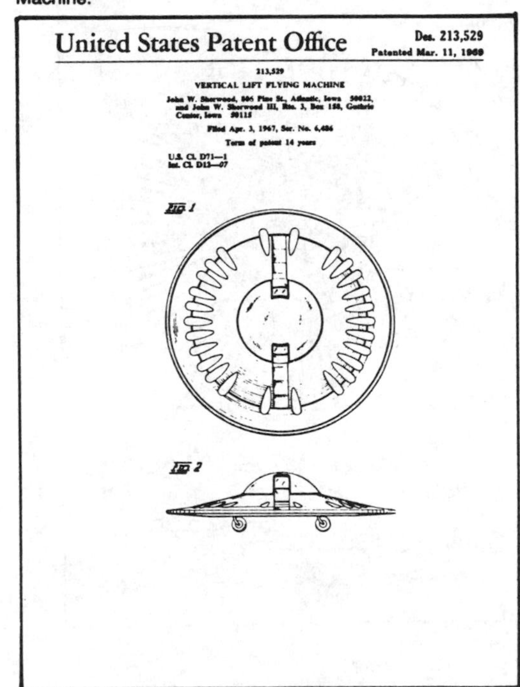

United States Patent Office

Des. 213,529
Patented Mar. 11, 1969

213,529
VERTICAL LIFT FLYING MACHINE
John W. Sherwood, 806 Pine St., Atlantic, Iowa 50022, and John W. Sherwood III, Rte. 3, Box 158, Guthrie Center, Iowa 50115
Filed Apr. 3, 1967, Ser. No. 6,486
Term of patent 14 years
U.S. Cl. D71—1
Int. Cl. D12—07

FIG. 1

FIG. 2

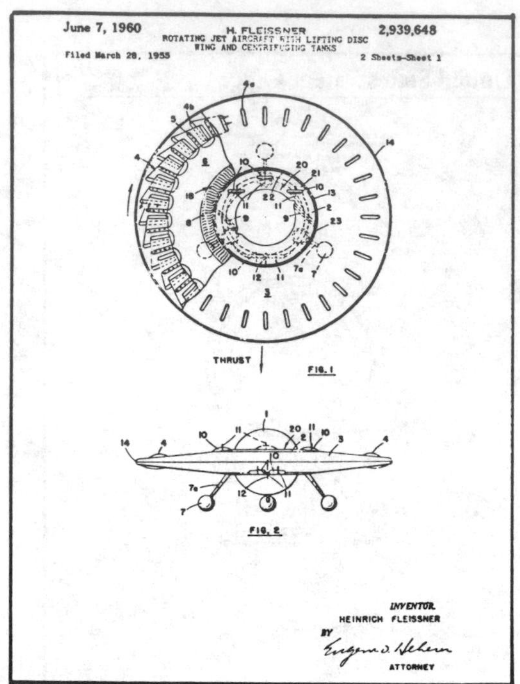

Patented design for Archie Leggett's interplanetary craft.

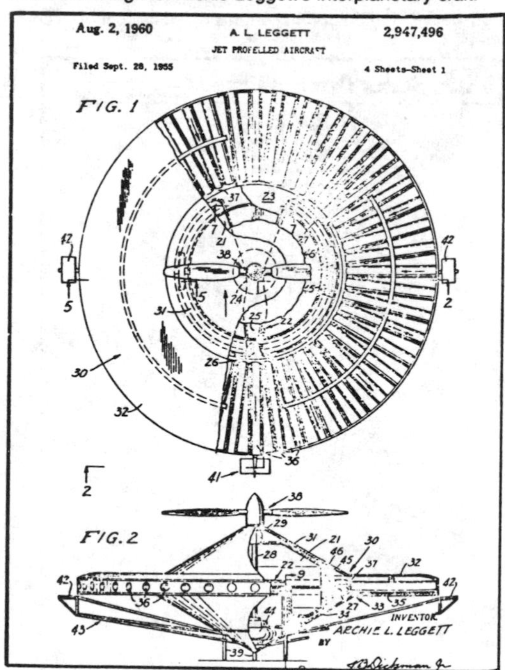

MORE HEADLINES OF THE PAST, PRESENT & FUTURE: OR "I MARRIED AN ALIEN"

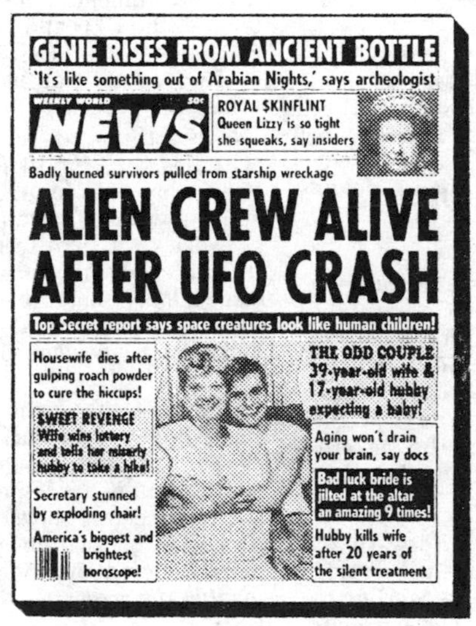

GENIE RISES FROM ANCIENT BOTTLE

'It's like something out of Arabian Nights,' says archeologist

WEEKLY WORLD NEWS 50¢

ROYAL $KINFLINT
Queen Lizzy is so tight she squeaks, say insiders

Badly burned survivors pulled from starship wreckage

ALIEN CREW ALIVE AFTER UFO CRASH

Top Secret report says space creatures look like human children!

Housewife dies after gulping roach powder to cure the hiccups!

SWEET REVENGE
Wife wins lottery and tells her miserly hubby to take a hike!

Secretary stunned by exploding chair!

America's biggest and brightest horoscope!

THE ODD COUPLE
39-year-old wife & 17-year-old hubby expecting a baby!

Aging won't drain your brain, say docs

Bad luck bride is jilted at the altar an amazing 9 times!

Hubby kills wife after 20 years of the silent treatment

San Francisco Chronicle Monday, September 16, 1985

U.S. Contesting Lawsuit Over UFO Radiation

Houston

Three people suing the federal government for $20 million say they do not know to this day what it was that hovered far over their heads and zapped them with radiation almost five years ago.

They claim it was an unidentified flying object that was escorted away by military helicopters. They say they suspect it was a secret U.S. military experiment. In any event, they say, the government should have warned residents that a UFO was in their area.

The military says it had nothing to do with the alleged occurrence Dec. 29, 1980, on a rural road northeast of Houston. Even if there were UFOs, a U.S. attorney says, the government has no duty to warn people about them because the government does not know whether they are dangerous.

With such straightforward arguments, the government is urging U.S. District Judge Ross Sterling to throw out a lawsuit filed here last year by former Dayton, Texas, cafe owner Betty Cash, 56, former waitress Vickie Landrum, 61, and Landrum's grandson, Colby Landrum, 11.

The suit claims that about 9 p.m. on Dec. 29, 1980, while headed for their homes in Dayton along a two-lane road about 30 miles northeast of Houston, the three encountered a brightly glowing craft the size of a city water tower. It hovered at treetop level, had red and orange flames flowing from its bottom, and bathed them in intense heat for several minutes before it was escorted away by at least 23 helicopters, they assert.

Their lawsuit, filed under the Federal Tort Claims Act, claims that the government failed to warn them of the UFO and "negligently, carelessly and recklessly" allowed it "to fly over a publicly used road and come in contact with the plaintiffs."

As a result, all suffered stomach pains, vomiting, diarrhea, radiation burns, deteriorating eyesight, and the women's hair fell out and grew back with a different texture, the suit claims. It also says they became highly sensitive to sunlight, suffered blisters and headaches, and that Cash developed breast cancer.

Despite the plaintiffs' report that there were no markings on the "large, unconventional aerial object" or on the helicopters, the lawsuit has recently moved from simply suggesting that the government merely knew about the UFO to saying that the government owned the UFO.

The government has offered affidavits from high-ranking officials that it had nothing to do with the UFO.

Dallas Times Herald

The Incredible Story They Tried to Hide for 28 Years

Ike Met Space Aliens

EISENHOWER met with space aliens in 1954 and saw their advanced UFOs operate.

President Dwight D. Eisenhower met with beings from outer space almost 30 years ago, a British high government official reveals.

According to the Earl of Clancarty, a member of Parliament and the author of seven UFO books, the top secret meeting took place in 1954 at Edwards Air Force Base in California.

The awestruck Ike watched as the aliens demonstrated how their spacecraft worked — and he convinced them not to make widespread contact with the people of Earth, to avoid panic.

And world-famous UFO expert Charles Berlitz confirms the astonishing story!

Lord Clancarty, who heads a group in the House of Lords demanding the British government release classified UFO information, says he was told of the incredible encounter by a former top U.S. test pilot. "The pilot said he was one of six people at Eisenhower's meeting with the beings," Lord Clancarty disclosed. "He had been called in as a technical adviser because of his reputation and abilities as a test pilot."

The test pilot told Lord Clancarty, "Five different alien craft landed at the base. Three were saucer-shaped and two were cigar-shaped. Eisenhower, who was vacationing in nearby Palm Springs at the time, was apparently summoned to the base by military officials. As Eisenhower and his small group watched, the aliens first disembarked and then approached them.

"The aliens looked something like humans, but not exactly," the pilot said.

He described the aliens as having humanlike features, although misshapen. They were about the same height and build as an average man and able to breathe air without a helmet. The aliens spoke English and told Eisenhower they wanted to begin "an education program for the people of Earth" to make mankind aware of their presence.

"Eisenhower told them he didn't think the world was ready for that, and was concerned this revelation would cause panic," according to the pilot.

"The aliens seemed to understand and agree, and then said they would continue to make contact with isolated individuals, until Earth people got used to them," the pilot said. "Eisenhower said that he thought this was all right, as long as the aliens didn't create panic and confusion."

UFO EXPERT Lord Clancarty

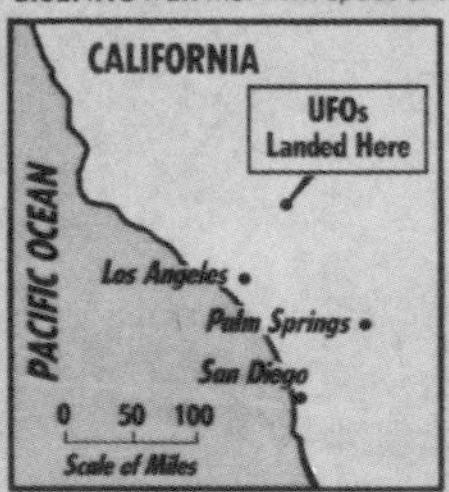

MAP shows area of California where UFOs landed. Ike was in Palm Springs in February 1954, and mysteriously disappeared at time of UFO visit.

He Inspected Their UFOs & Told Them Not to Panic Earth

Then, before the stunned President and his companions, the aliens displayed their awesome technical advances.

"They demonstrated their spacecraft for the President," the pilot said. "They showed him their ability to make themselves invisible.

"This really caused the President a lot of discomfort because none of us could see them even though we knew they were there. The aliens then boarded their ships and departed. All of us were sworn to complete secrecy."

Said Lord Clancarty, "The pilot said he'd never spoken to another person about this, but now everyone involved except him was dead."

Rumors of the Eisenhower meeting have circulated for decades. In fact, during the mid-1950s a sergeant told Los Angeles UFO expert Gabe Green about the aliens' awe-inspiring arrival at Edwards.

"I was at gunnery practice, under the command of a general," the sergeant wrote to Green. "We were shooting live ammo at targets when all of a sudden five UFOs flew right over us.

"The general ordered all batteries to open fire on the craft. We did, but our shells had no effect whatsoever.

"We all stopped firing and watched the UFOs land at one of the large hangars."

In his book "The Roswell Incident," the UFO expert Charles Berlitz reveals another witness to the astonishing close encounter. A man named Gerald Light told about the incident in a letter dated April 16, 1954.

"In his letter, Light stated he had seen five spacecraft that had been delivered by the aliens at the base," Berlitz wrote.

"Light wrote, 'I had the distinct feeling that the world as I knew it had come to an end. It has finally happened — we have seen and met aliens from another world.' "

Incredibly, Berlitz says, Eisenhower mysteriously disappeared from his Palm Springs retreat — not far from Muroc — on Feb. 20, 1954, the date of the reported meeting.

"The President had a press conference scheduled but never showed up," Berlitz wrote. "He disappeared.

"There were wild rumors that the President was ill. The official explanation was that Eisenhower had visited a local dentist, but inquiries by the press failed to discover which dentist treated the President."

Now, Lord Clancarty's new revelations could blow the lid off the mystery.

"I have heard the Eisenhower meeting story many times but have never been able to confirm it," said J. Allen Hyneck, director of the Center for UFO Studies.

"With this additional information, we'll investigate the incident further."

— DARY MATERA

HANGARS at Edwards Air Force Base. UFOs reportedly landed near this site.

• ARTIST's SKETCH, above, made from descriptions of the strange-looking space alien baby, shown here with its mother, who refuses to allow photographs to be taken of her green-skinned infant.

16-year-old's own story:

I gave birth to a space alien baby

SIXTEEN-YEAR-OLD Magdelena Munoz insisted all along the father of her baby was a monstrous space alien. But only her parents believed her, until she gave birth to a strange-looking green baby with pointed ears that was not of this world.

Family shocked by its pointed ears & claw-like hands

The high school junior from Mexico City told police nine months ago that a horrible looking creature attacked her while she was walking home from the library at about 10 p.m.

The heartless police officers thought the young girl was making up the story so she wouldn't get in trouble with her parents, and the police never followed through on their investigation of the incident.

Then last week, the tormented teen gave birth to a 7-lb. 3-oz. boy.

The baby was born with pointed ears, greenish skin and claw-like hands and feet.

"We don't know what to do about this baby," says the doctor who delivered the infant.

"The girl wants to keep it, but the girl's parents and I agree it would be too difficult to explain to the community.

"Also, we want to keep the baby here where we can study it," he adds.

Magdelena, who attends a Mexico City public high school, says she was studying late at the library to finish a term paper when the incident happened.

Landed

"I decided to cut through the park on my way home," she says.

"I saw this strange looking light in the sky," she recalls.

"It seemed to float back and forth over the trees, and then it landed about 100 yards in front of me.

"It was a domed space vehicle.

"A door opened, and four creatures came out. They sprayed me with something, and I was paralyzed," recalls Magdelena.

"They carried me into their spaceship, and then they did all sorts of terrible things to me."

When Magdelena got home, she says she was afraid to tell her parents about her bizarre experience.

• SPACE BABY's mom says she wants to raise her child as a human

"Mom could tell there was something wrong, so I finally told her," Magdelena remembers.

"I thought Dad was going to kill somebody when he heard what had happened," says the girl.

Convictions

When Magdelena discovered she was pregnant, she decided to have the baby.

She reached this decision in spite of the incident, claiming her religious convictions made it impossible for her to have an abortion.

"I don't care what the doctors say," says Magdelena.

"I want to raise my child and make a human being out of him."

— BARBARA GILBERT

Anti-gravity motor idea

LONDON, Sunday (AAP). — A British scientist said yesterday that he was on the threshold of inventing an anti-gravity motor that could make short work of projecting a spaceship from the earth's gravitational field.

Professor Eric Laithwaite, 53, professor of heavy electrical engineering at London's Imperial College of Science and Technology, said the motor is based on the gyroscope, a rapidly spinning top that defied gravity.

Although Professor Laithwaite is far from production stage, he demonstrated the motor's principle at the Royal Institution in London on Friday.

Inside a box he brought before his audience were two electrically driven gyroscopes, each placed on a hinged metal arm fixed to a central pivot.

He made the gyroscopes rotate at high speed, and they rose into the air on the arms until they reached a curved rail that pushed them down again. The process then repeated itself.

With the two gyroscopes motionless, the box weighed about 10 kilograms, with the gyroscopes spinning, the contraption weighed 7½ kilograms.

Professor Laithwaite said the loss of weight corresponded to the gravity loss produced by the spinning gyroscopes. Theoretically, the machine could produce weightlessness.

"A spaceship with this device could be blasted from the earth's gravitational field with conventional rocket fuel", he said.

UFO alien is captured alive & docs say he's human

AN ALIEN being captured alive from a flying saucer has astounded scientists who say the space creature is human.

According to reports from the UFO Research Center outside Sao Paulo, Brazil, the alien has been examined by a battery of doctors from around the world who swear it has all the characteristics of a humanoid.

Dr. Roland Glenn, a noted British genetic researcher, says, "medically, scientifically and physiologically, the being is human.

"The only difference between it and the rest of us is it came from another planet," he adds.

Roots

Other experts say that might not be a difference at all.

"The fact that this creature is human raises the distinct possibility that all earthlings have their roots in outer space," says South African scientist Dr. Philip Crane.

"Perhaps we are all descendants of a race from another solar system," Dr. Crane adds. "Frankly, I can think of no other explanation."

"Various psychics and UFO experts have been saying Earth was originally populated by space visitors," says Dr. Glenn. "Now we have reason to believe they may be right.

"At the very least, this development will change the way we view evolution on this planet," Dr. Glenn adds.

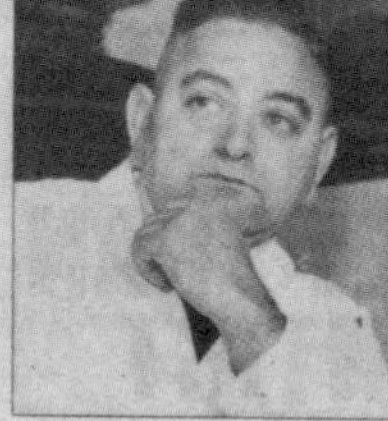

• LAURA FREEMAN communicates with alien using mental telepathy

• GENETIC RESEARCHER Dr. Roland Glenn says space creature is just like a human being

SPECIAL SUN STORY by CHRIS LUKE

The bizarre circumstances surrounding the alien's capture suggest it came here to teach us something, the scientists say.

"UFO sightings are not uncommon here," notes Research Center caretaker Jose Cabral. "But this one landed outside the center, not more than 100 feet from the main building.

Struggle

"The alien exited the spacecraft and walked right to the back door," Cabral adds. "We let him inside, and he lay down on the examination table without the least bit of struggle."

For now, the alien being is held under tight security at the Center as experiments continue.

Dr. Crane does report, however, that the visitor stands just under six feet tall and weighs 165 pounds.

"Except for its blue-colored skin, it looks just like any normal human," he says.

The scientists have even brought in a psychic who claims she can talk with the creature.

"This being obviously exists on a higher vibrational frequency than most humans," says psychic Laura Freeman. "But, through mental telepathy, I have been able to communicate with it.

"It says it came from the planet Kronar in a faraway galaxy," Freeman adds. "It says it has come here by order of its 'Supreme Commander' to show earthlings we are all the same and that we must all learn to live together peacefully if we are to survive."

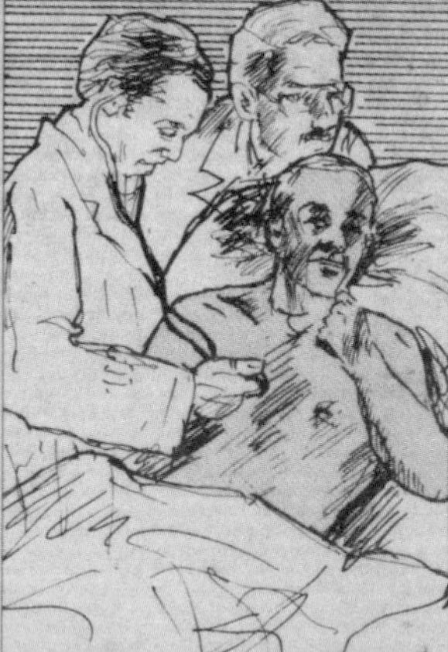

• A TEAM OF doctors and scientists have carefully examined the alien being, who tells a psychic he's come to promote universal peace.

26 — SUN — November 4, 1986

Ruins of an ancient city found on Jupiter moon!

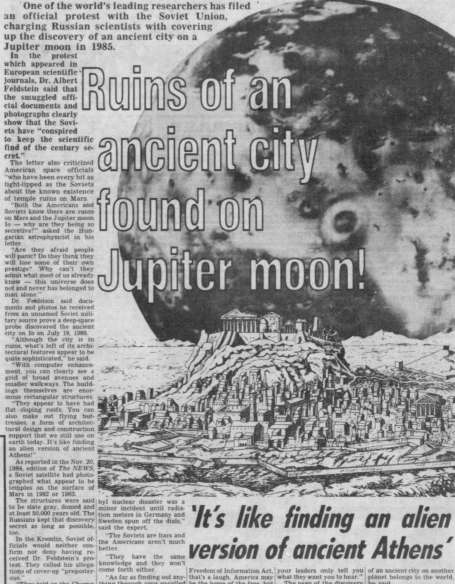

One of the world's leading researchers has filed an official protest with the Soviet Union, charging Russian scientists with covering up the discovery of an ancient city on a Jupiter moon in 1985.

In the protest which appeared in European scientific journals, Dr. Albert Feldstein said that the smuggled official documents and photographs clearly show that the Soviets have "conspired to keep the scientific find of the century secret."

The letter also criticized American space officials "who have been every bit as tight-lipped as the Soviets about the known existence of temple ruins on Mars.

"Both the Americans and Soviets know there are ruins on Mars and the Jupiter moon Io — why are they being so secretive?" asked the Hungarian astrophysicist in his letter.

"Are they afraid people will panic? Do they think they will lose some of their own prestige? Why can't they admit what most of us already know — this universe does not and never has belonged to man alone."

Dr. Feldstein said documents and photos he received from an unnamed Soviet military source prove a deep-space probe discovered the ancient city on Io on July 19, 1985.

"Although the city is in ruins, what's left of its architectural features appear to be quite sophisticated," he said.

"With computer enhancement, you can clearly see a grid of broad avenues and smaller walkways. The buildings themselves are enormous rectangular structures.

"They appear to have had flat sloping roofs. You can also make out flying buttresses, a form of architectural design and construction support that we still use on earth today. It's like finding an alien version of ancient Athens!"

As reported in the Nov. 20, 1984, edition of *The NEWS*, a Soviet satellite had photographed what appear to be temples on the surface of Mars in 1982 or 1983.

The structures were said to be slate gray, domed and at least 50,000 years old. The Russians kept that discovery secret as long as possible, too.

In the Kremlin, Soviet officials would neither confirm nor deny having received Dr. Feldstein's protest. They called his allegations of cover-up "preposterous."

"They told us the Chernobyl nuclear disaster was a minor incident until radiation meters in Germany and Sweden spun off the dials," said the expert.

"The Soviets are liars and the Americans aren't much better.

"They have the same knowledge and they won't come forth either.

'It's like finding an alien version of ancient Athens'

"As far as finding out anything through your so-called Freedom of Information Act, that's a laugh. America may be the home of the free, but your leaders only tell you what they want you to hear."

The news of the discovery of an ancient city on another planet belongs to the world, he said.

WEEKLY WORLD NEWS
October 28, 1986

UFO SHOCKER IN THE DEVIL'S TRIANGLE!

Bahamian researchers are investigating reports that a UFO saved a family from drowning after their pleasure boat sank in the Devil's Triangle.

Dr. Leopold Stinson told a symposium in Caracas, Venezuela, that the May 5 incident appeared to have all the indications of a verifiable alien encounter.

Stinson quoted the family as having said the UFO rose out of the sea just seconds before their 32-foot boat went under.

Incredibly, they claim the starship rescued them by air-dropping a life raft that bore the insignia of the U.S. Air Force.

And it is that raft, said Stinson, that might prove once and for all that an alien intelligence is operating in the Devil's Triangle.

"The raft is a type that was commonly used in the 1950s," he said.

"If we can match the numbers on its side to any plane known to have disappeared in the Triangle in that era, it would suggest that it had been hijacked and stored, perhaps by beings that are not of this world."

Stinson said that the quest to match the numbers could take weeks, months or years owing to the large number of planes that have vanished in the Triangle.

Meanwhile, the investigation will focus on accounts from the rescued family, he said.

"These are very articulate people and they have been quite cooperative," he continued.

"The husband and wife are medical doctors from Brazil.

"They have two children, both in college."

According to Stinson, the family had been island-hopping in the Caribbean for several months.

They were reportedly on their way to the Bahamas when their boat started taking on water.

"Their own life raft was in an interior compartment and the boat was sinking so fast they couldn't get to it," said Stinson.

"They told me they sent out an SOS over the radio but were certain they were going to die."

The UFO — golden-colored and shaped like a star — rose out of the water about 75 yards away, the family said.

"By this time, they were almost out of their minds with fear," said Stinson.

"But they did recall that the UFO crackled and hummed as it cleared the surface and moved toward them. They said the craft came to within 20 or 30 feet of where their boat was sinking and dropped the Air Force raft from its belly.

"They told me the craft hovered overhead for a few seconds, then it vanished in the sky.

"The stunned but grateful family swam to the raft and climbed aboard. Shaken by their terrifying ordeal, they huddled together in the darkness of the vast nighttime sea," added Stinson.

"Their capsized boat slipped noiselessly beneath the ocean's swells and a bizarre silence settled in around the frightened family. They joined hands and prayed. And waited."

About 20 minutes later, the crew of a Bahamian-based sportfishing boat found the family afloat in the raft and took them ashore, said Stinson.

They reported the incident to authorities, who alerted Stinson's UFO/Devil's Triangle research group.

Carlos Garcia, a science reporter in Caracas, said the reaction of Stinson's colleagues at the symposium was mixed.

"They are anxious to see his report in the journals so they can weigh all the evidence for themselves," he said.

— RIKI MOSS

UFO lowered a life raft to drowning family in bizarre Devil's Triangle incident.

Alien spacecraft rises from sea to save a drowning family

Outer-space rocks found on Earth

They burn & explode if handled

• DR. HARVEY BUXTRAM, UFO investigator, warns against touching red space rocks, right

RED, GLOWING ROCKS, which catch fire and disintegrate after being touched by human hands, are being found in abundance in Russia, China and Ethopia, and officials are saying these rocks are not from this world.

"In all locations where the rocks have been discovered, a UFO has been sighted several days before," says UFO investigator Dr. Harvey Buxtram.

"We believe, for some unknown reason, our alien visitors are leaving these rocks behind."

Buxtram states that several days after the rocks catch fire and disintegrate, an eerie green glow begins radiating from the ashes.

Ashes

"One man in Ethopia picked up one of these alien rocks, threw it in the trunk of his car and started driving away. The back of his car exploded shortly after," reports Buxtram.

"All that remained of the rock was a pile of hot ashes."

Several days later, as a laboratory examined the ashes, they began giving off a strange, green glow.

"The glow lasted for most of the day before it faded," says Buxtram. "After that, the remaining ashes just vanished."

Over 100 of these strange rocks have been found throughout the world. In each case, they catch fire and disintegrate one to three minutes after being handled by a human.

"The rocks do not seem to be toxic or radioactive and contain no signs of life such as bacteria," says Buxtram. "There seems to be no reason for them to be dropped off on earth."

Still, the UFO investigator believes that's exactly what the aliens are doing.

"It's more than just a coincidence that each time a UFO is sighted, these rocks are discovered at the spot within several days," he declares.

Contact

"Our visitors from another world are trying to tell us something, but we have no idea what it could be."

Buxtram warns that anybody coming into contact with the red rocks should not handle them.

June 17, 1986 — SUN — 37

Nude beer back on shelves

Beer drinkers may be tempted to start collecting their empties because of a new brew with labels featuring bikini-clad models who can be scratched topless.

Nude Beer, which went bust when introduced in 1983, is back on the shelves in Southern California despite critics' claims that it's labels are too racy. "The definition of obscenity certainly isn't a scratch-off bikini top," said Eugene Pace, president of Golden Beverage Co. of Irvine, Calif.

Pace took over the beer after its predecessor, Nude Products Inc., went out of business.

Pace, who is an attorney, said six-packs of Nude Beer will sell for about $4 and models featured on the labels will change frequently.

ANTI-GRAVITY COMIX

Einstein discovers that time is actually money.

FINAL SCENE OF "THE LATTER DAYS"
AND THE OPENING SCENE OF "THE MIGHTY MILLENNIUM"

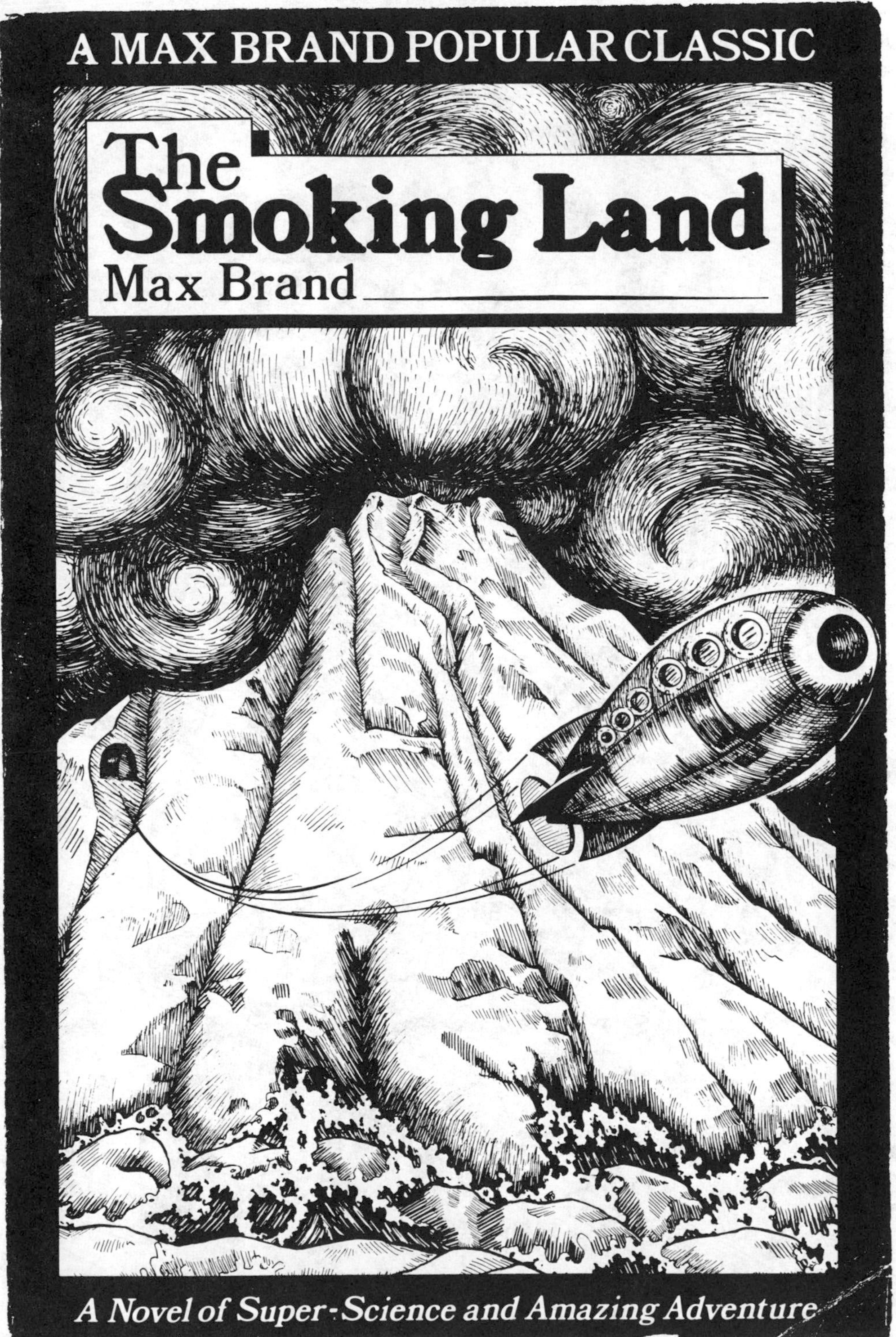

A MAX BRAND POPULAR CLASSIC
The Smoking Land
Max Brand
A Novel of Super-Science and Amazing Adventure

Back in the twenties, the idea of aircraft and space ships being powered by Anti-Gravity was quite popular. Yet, sixty years later this technology has failed to emerge--or has it?

Traders in the Lost Art
by R.H. AYANI
OH, BY THE WAY, I'M O'BRIAN OF THE T.P...
THIS WAY, BOSS!
TREE PLANTERS, PERHAPS? WHERE ARE WE?
AND HERE COMES ALTERNATIVE ONE!
ALTERNATIVE WHAT?
HEY, MY NAME'S BRAIN!
WE'RE SQUATTERS! ANY GOOD SQUATS DOWN HERE?
HEY, MAN! HE'S WITH THE THOUGHT POLICE! SSH!
THIS WAS HOW THE ELECT THOUGHT THEY'D SURVIVE IT ALL; NOW IT'S AN ILLUMINATI RETIREMENT VILLAGE!
AN EARLY EXPERIMENT IN POST-HOLOCAUST SURVIVAL; THESE DAYS IT'S JUST A MANAGERIAL SUPERANNUATION OPTION!
MDCCLXXVI
FUNERALS
MEDICARE
Restaurant
NORMAL
WHAT ARE THOSE DOING HERE?
NUGAN HAD A HAND IN IT; OLD UNDERGROUND PUBLIC TOILETS ARE STILL CONNECTED TO WATER + POWER — EASILY TAPPED!
WHOSE SURVIVAL?
AND THEY'RE CLOSE TO THE SUBWAY! THEY USED TO CALL THEM ARKS.
WOW! SOME ALTERNATIVE! BUT WHO COULD BUILD IT HERE UNDER THE CITY?
AND THE PAPERS BLAME ITALIANS!
WHO ARE THE ELECT?
THE FOUR SQUATTERS CONTINUE THEIR LABYRINTHINE TREK IN THE FOOTSTEPS OF O'BRIAN OF THE T.P., WENDING THEIR WAY EVER DOWNWARD......
A REST BREAK...
LISTEN, BRAIN, I RECKON WE SHOULD FIND OUR WAY OUT OF HERE AND TELL PEOPLE WHAT WE'VE SEEN!
LIKE WHO? THIS IS WHERE I SAY NO-ONE'D BELIEVE US! BESIDES, WE DON'T KNOW THE WAY OUT YET, NAMASHI-GLUB-
GREAT.
WE'RE STUCK WITH THE THOUGHT POLICE!
TIME PATROL, ACTUALLY.
I'M BEGINNING TO WONDER WHY WE'RE FOLLOWING YOU, MAN!
WHO ARE THE "ELECT," HUH?
WHO ELECTED THEM?
THEIR GOD, APPARENTLY.
JUST AHEAD WE HAVE ALTERNATIVE 1A. IT'S WHY ALL THE CATTLE ARE TAKEN BY THE AIR FORCE....
LOOK, MASTER! SALT WATER!
YOU SEE, THEY USE THE BLOOD FOR HAEMOGLOBIN SPONGES.
THIS IS GETTING WEIRDER...
THESE TERRESTRIAL SOLUTIONS ARE USELESS IF ANYTHING REALLY GOES WRONG!
BUT UNDERWATER?
THEY ALL SEEM LIKE GOOD IDEAS AT THE TIME.
WHO'D BUILD IT ALL?
WHEN YOU'RE IMMORTAL YOU GAIN A LITTLE PERSPECTIVE!
LOOK OUT!
SSH!
HUMANS HAVE A GAS INSECURITY!
R.A. 3/85
WHAT ARE THEY, ALIENS?
NO, STRAIGHT GENE-SPLICE WORK — THE "ALIENS" ARE DOWNSTAIRS. COME ON!
DO NOT FEED
THE STORY OF FOUR SQUATTERS IN SEARCH OF A HOME BENEATH A MAJOR CITY IN THE NEW REPRESSION.
CONTINUED NEXT ISSUE: ALTERNATIVE TWO!

DEEP BENEATH A GREAT CITY OF OZ
EPISODE FOUR OF
Traders in the Lost Art
BY R. HEPU AYANI
'STRUTH! WHAT'S THAT?
NOS! HE LOOKS LIKE THE DEVIL!
WHAT A CUTE LEETLE THING!
IS THAT AN ALIEN, O'BRIAN?
SSH! WE'RE BORROWING HER VEHICLE!
HER?
IF YOU'RE ALL UN-CONSCIOUS RACISTS, HOW WILL YOU REACT TO THE UNHUMAN?
HEY, I'M NO RACIST!
YOU'RE NOT PROGRAMMED FOR THE TRULY ALIEN; RACISM'S A REDUNDANT SURVIVAL TRAIT.
ALL CLEAR, MASTER!
A FLYING SAUCER!
HMPH! IT'S A PLANAR GEOID!
AS YOUR JUNG SAID,* IF THEY DIDN'T EXIST IT'D BE NECESSARY TO CREATE THEM, HA HA!
I DON'T BELIEVE IT!
GOOD. RARELY BELIEVE ANYTHING.
* PARAPHRASING SARTRE
RA. 6/85
THE 4 SQUATTERS FOLLOW O'BRIAN OF THE T.P. THROUGH STRANGE SUBTERRANEAN CHAMBERS UNTIL...
A NONCE LATER....
HEY, A MAP OF ANTARCTICA!
NO, REALTIME. WE'RE IN ORBIT NOW.
I DIDN'T FEEL A THING!
?
WHAT'S THAT ON THE DARK SIDE OF THE MOON?
JOINT U.S./U.S.S.R.* BASE. BUT ALTERNATIVE 2'S THE COLONY ORBITING HERE...
WHERE DO THEY GET ALL THE PEOPLE?
WHAT'S DIS?
2 SIDES OF THE SAME SPHERE
FNORD
¡OMO! THEY'VE SEEN US.
ALIENS?
NO, THE YANKEES!
EYE'LL TELL YOU ON THE WAY TO MARS!
HOW COULD WE BUILD THOSE?!
WHO'S 'WE', WHITE MAN?
NEXT ISSUE: ALTERNATIVE THREE!

EPISODE V
Traders in the Lost Art
R. HERU AYANI
THE YANKS ARE STILL AFTER US!
WHAT THE..
The four young squatters are en route to Mars in a hijacked geoid..
'TIS A DREAM-BODY FROM OZ.
YOU MEAN IT'S NOT REAL?
NO—'TIS UNREAL.
CRIPES, IT'S TURNING THEM BACK!
AS O'BRIAN OF THE TIME PATROL BRINGS IN THE CRAFT..
HM..LOOKS LIKE COMPANY!
ALIEN RUINS!?
WE'RE THE ALIENS HERE.
AH...HERE'S MERU.
YOU MEAN MARS, O'BRIAN!
WE CAN LAND BY THE PYRE AMID THE RUINS...
WHERE ARE D'ER SPACESUITS?
JUST WEAR THIS DISK.
IT'S A SUIT IN ITSELF.
RA 25/11/85
MOMENTS LATER...
THESE ARE YOUR RUINS, WE'RE HERE T' SAVE YER MEMORY.
?
WATCH IT, IVAN, YOU BROKE THAT STATUE!
SO? VE JUS'SAY VE FOUND IT LIKE THAT!
THEY HAVE T' MAKE IT PAY, Y'SEE.
WHO?
O.K. WHO'S TO KNOW?
USSA
WE HAVE T'GO—'TIS RADIOACTIVE HERE!
WHAT ABOUT THEM?
'TIS BELOW THEIR ACCEPTED SAFETY LEVEL.
O'BRIAN LEADS THE SQUATTERS TO...
..A PIVOTING STONE BLOCK!
DON'T TOUCH ANYTHING!
WHY NOT?
NOW YOU'VE DONE IT.
Eternity
O'BRIAN! WHAT'RE YOU DOING IN THIS TIME ZONE?
-B'DINK-
-KLIK-

THE ANTI-GRAVITY FILE

Including:
Nazi Flying Saucers
Anti-Gravity and Superconductors
Captured Aliens
Secret Goverment Research
Homemade Saucers
and more.

SUPERCONDUCTORS, MAGNETISM AND ANTIGRAVITY

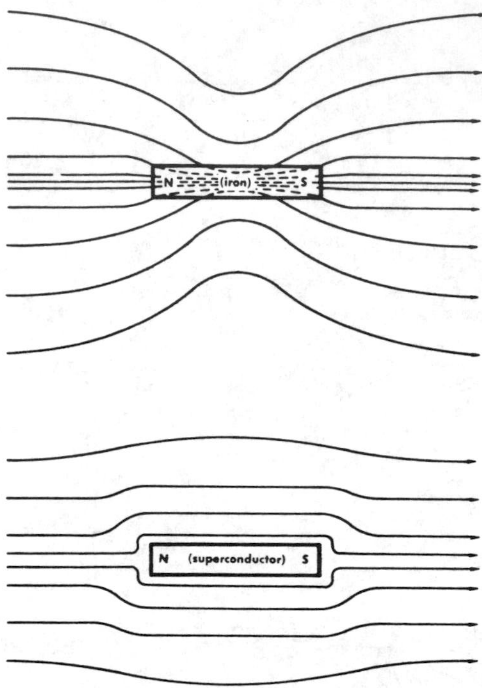

Contrasting effects of iron and superconductor in a field of magnetic lines of force. Top: A ferromagnetic material in a magnetic field concentrates the lines of force. Bottom: A superconductor in a magnetic field forces the lines of force to diverge and bypass.

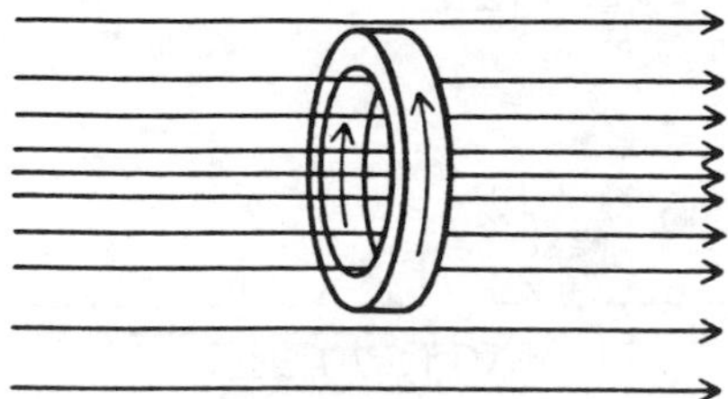

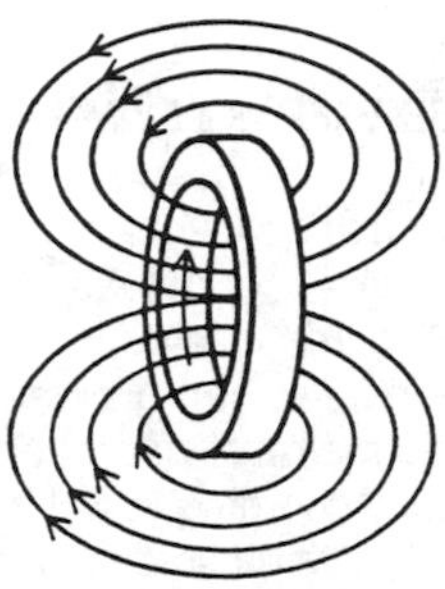

Magnetic memory effect on superconductor in external magnetic field. Top: A ring is made superconducting while resting stationary in an external magnetic field. Bottom: The external magnetic field is removed while ring remains superconducting. Only the outer surface current stops.

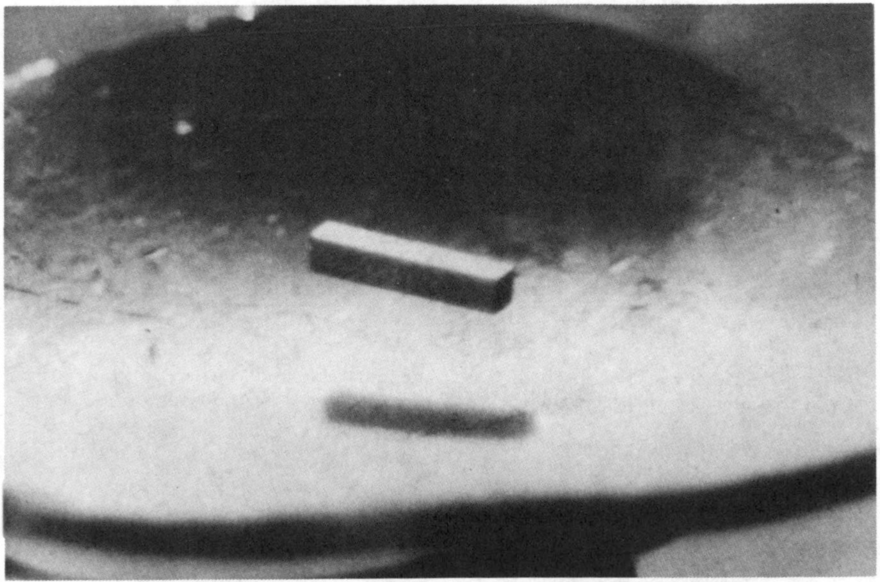

Michigan State University

A bar magnet "levitates" over a superconducting lead dish. A "mirror image" of magnetic lines of force exists invisibly in the lead surface at just about the position of the shadow. The "mirror image" is of equal strength to the bar magnet.

NAZI FLYING SAUCERS

The 'Schriever-Habermohl' flying disc developed between 1943 and 1945. In 1944, climbing vertically, it reached a height of 12 km in 3.12 minutes and a horizontal flying speed of 2000 km/h.

VICTOR SCHAUBERGER' S FLYING SAUCERS

Victor Schauberger (1885-1958), an Austrian inventor who was involved with Hitler's Third Riech, invented a number of "flying disks" for the Nazis between 1938 and 1945. Based on "liquid vortex propulsion" many of them, according to records, actually flew. One "flying saucer" reputedly destroyed at Leonstein, had a diameter of 1.5 meters, weighed 135 kilos, and was started by an electric motor of one twentieth horsepower. It had a trout turbine to supply the energy for lift-off. According to Schauberger, "If water or air is rotated into a twisting form of oscillation known as 'colloidal', a build up of energy results, which, with immense power, can cause levitation." On one attempt the apparatus "rose upwards, trailing a blue-green, and then a silver colored glow." The Russians blew up Schauberger's apartment in Leonstein, after taking what remained that the American's hadn't taken first. Schauberger supposedly worked on a top secret project in Texas for the U.S. Goverment and died shortly afterward of ill health. On his deathbed, Schauberger repeated over and over, "They took everything from me. Everything. I don't even own myself."

The first test-model developed between 1941 and 1942. This had the same flight properties as that in fig. (a), but something was wrong with the controls.

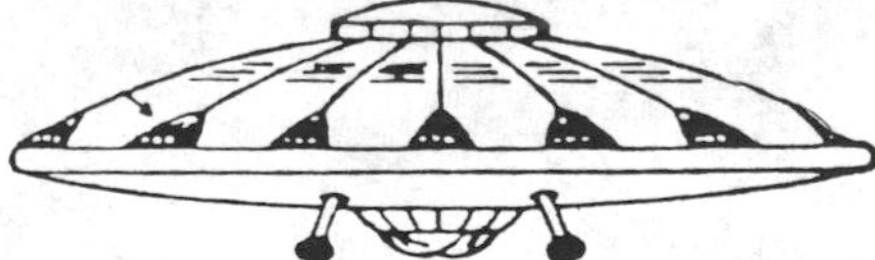

The 'Ballenzo-Schriever-Miethe Disc'. The retractable undercarriage legs terminated in inflatable rubber cushions. It carried a crew of three.

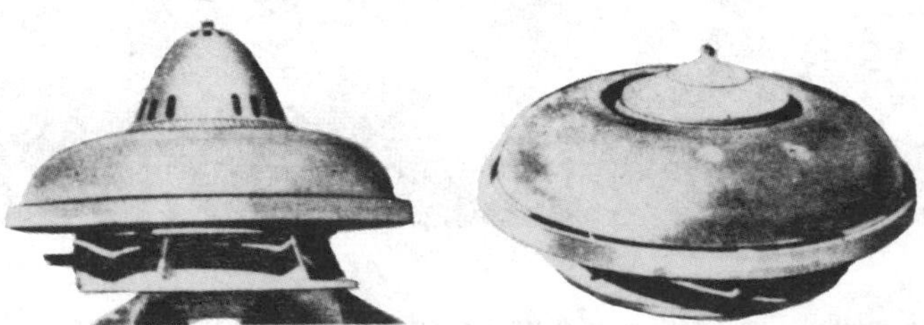

Schauberger's models of 'flying saucers'.

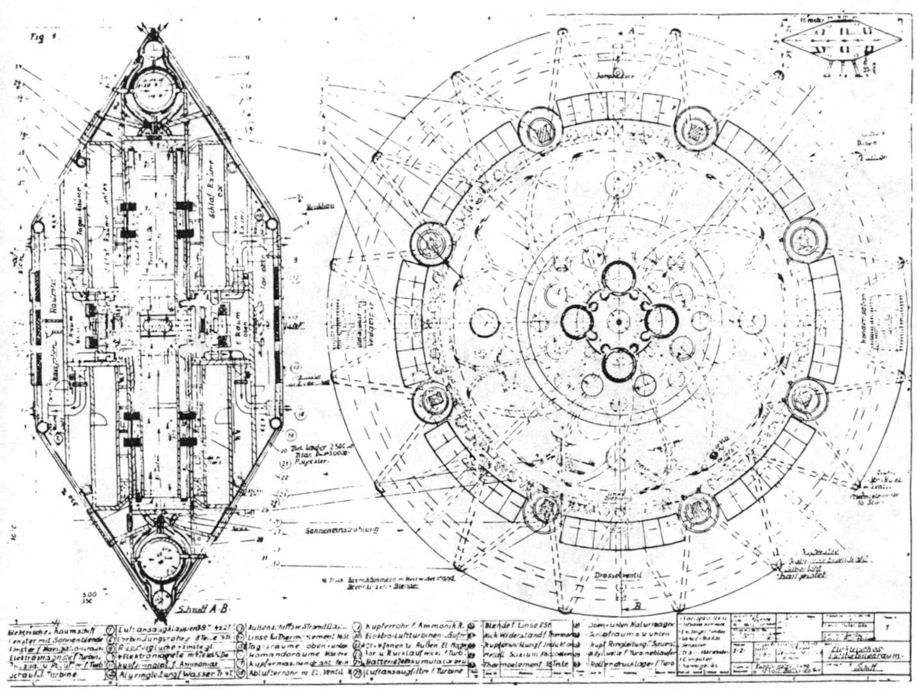

Left: blueprints for a flying saucer. According to the obscure single-issue publication *Brisant*, in which these diagrams appeared in 1978, they are plans for a disc-shaped spaceship, modified by the West German government to make them 'safe' for publication. Although 'electromagnetic turbines', 'laser-radar' and computers are indicated, the design is not a practical one. The diagrams appear in an article on Rudolf Schriever's Second World War designs, and may have been inspired by them

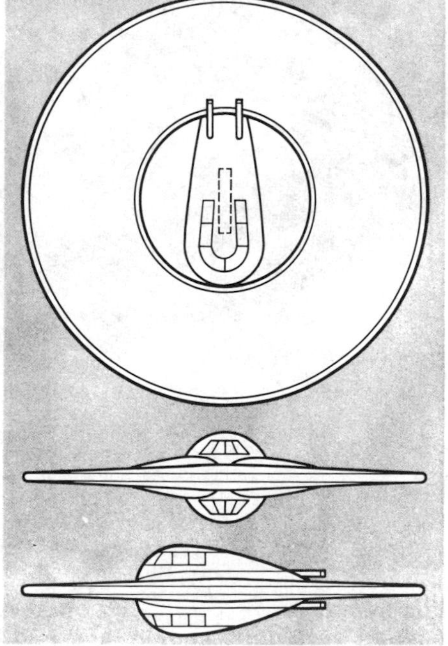

Right: a flying disc designed by Dr Miethe, one of the team of brilliant engineers working on unconventional aircraft designs for the Nazi war effort. This 'saucer' was almost ready for operational use in 1945, when the factories in Prague were overrun by the Allies

the Avro Car, built for the US Air Force and US Army by the Avro-Canada company. It was designed by an English engineer, John Frost. Officially, work on it was dropped in 1960 – despite the early claim that the machine would reach twice the speed of sound

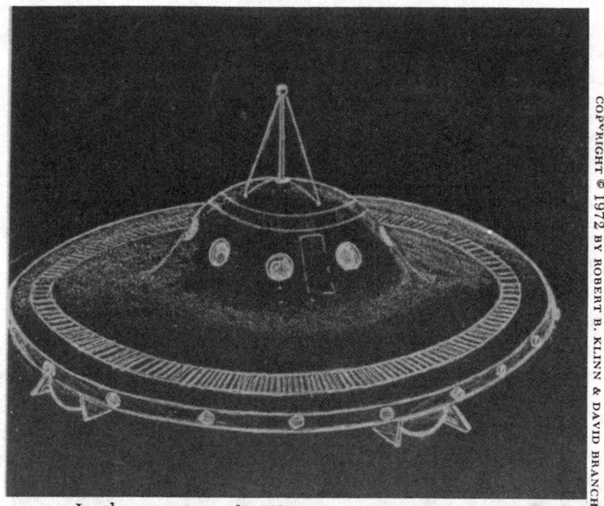

In the summer of 1958, a mechanic made this drawing of the UFO he saw hovering over a runway at Holloman Air Force Base.

OPERATIONAL PROTOTYPE of a "Neg. -G" or ANTI-GRAVITY DEVICE

ABOVE: WHY IS IT THAT FLYING SAUCERS ARE OFTEN SEEN HOVERING AROUND MILITARY BASES?
BELOW: A SO-CALLED SEARLE DISC IN ACTION.

Nobody has yet captured and inspected a Flying Saucer. But, according to the latest scientific theories known to Earthmen, if Flying Saucers exist, this is what they would look like.

Method of operation? From a sophisticated power source they would create their own gravitational field and move by 'falling' into it. Changing direction is simply a matter of changing the field.

The center of the gravitational field would be so close to the spacecraft that small auxiliary generators would have to be placed strategically to avoid distortion of normal gravity effect.

At high velocities, the high intensity field produced by the craft moves the surrounding air molecules along with it. Thus the Flying Saucer behaves exactly the same in the atmosphere as it does in airless space—it is both supported and propelled by its own gravitational field.

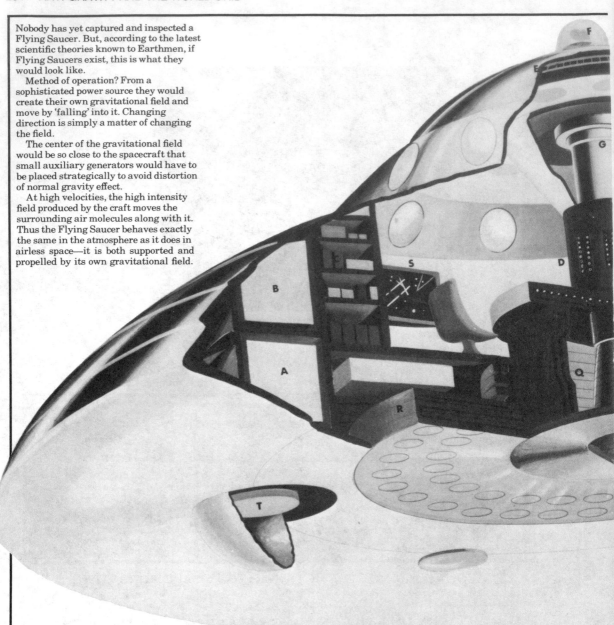

Gravitic propulsion—a theory which science-author Leonard G. Cramp expands in his book *Piece for a Jigsaw*—is simple and efficient. The diagram on the right shows the sort of propulsion we are familiar with in a car or jet plane: the force is applied to the first truck and conveyed to the others by impact. The car driver, for instance, is pushed along by the seat of his pants. Gravitic propulsion, however, is applied *uniformly* to a spacecraft and everyone in it. Just as an electro-magnet attracts iron filings.

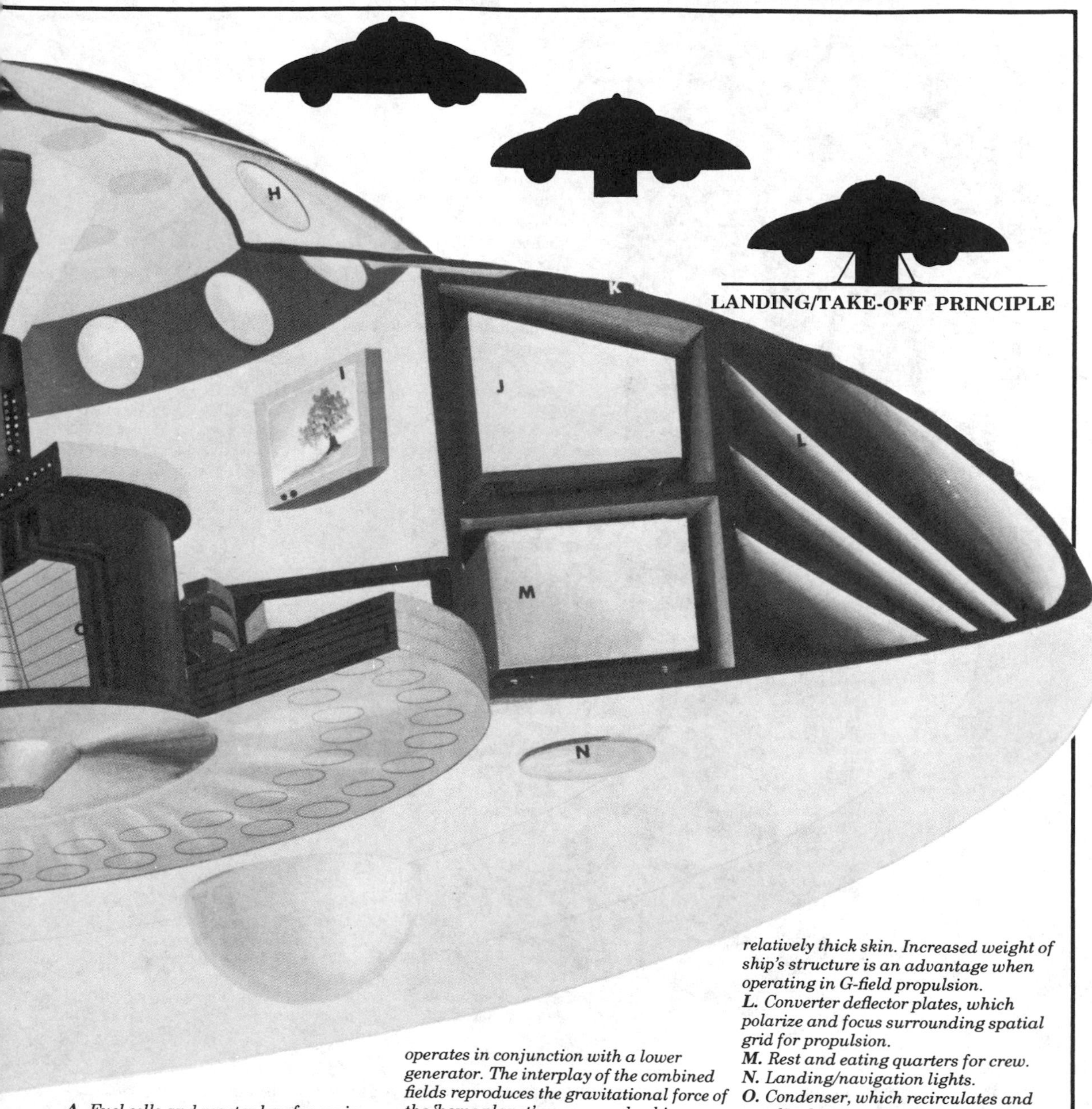

A. Fuel cells and reactor bay for main energy source.
B. Water tanks for reactor coolant, etc.
C. Store room for spares and maintenance.
D. Instrument console for in-flight control.
E. Cabin environment condition unit to maintain 1G atmospheric pressure, oxygen content and temperature control.
F. Automatic navigation and homing radar device which takes plots on special co-ordinates, using star readings.
G. Upper crew protection generator, which operates in conjunction with a lower generator. The interplay of the combined fields reproduces the gravitational force of the 'home planet' on crew and cabin content, regardless of ship's acceleration.
H. Special steel portholes for direct visual observation. They can be made transparent by electrical means.
I. One of several TV screens which can display exterior long-range, or close-up telephoto views.
J. Main electrical bay, housing main radio units and main computer.
K. Outer skin of free rotatable flange is stepped to help dissipate large electro-static charge build-up. Note relatively thick skin. Increased weight of ship's structure is an advantage when operating in G-field propulsion.
L. Converter deflector plates, which polarize and focus surrounding spatial grid for propulsion.
M. Rest and eating quarters for crew.
N. Landing/navigation lights.
O. Condenser, which recirculates and supplies hot water for services.
P. Heat dispersal cone and crew lower field generator.
Q. Main propulsion generator, which supplies high-voltage pulsed electricity to energize converter plates.
R. Generator plates, which work together with propulsion generator.
S. TV screen showing computerized video navigation chart.
T. Auxiliary propulsion and stabilizing units which can be swiveled in any direction to turn or tilt craft.

Illustration by John Batchelor

CAPTURED ALIENS

this controversial picture is said to show a dead crew member from a crashed UFO found near Mexico City in the 1950s. The creature was apparently taken to Germany for examination – never to be heard of again

The above photocopy (unfortunately of poor quality) purportedly shows a captured alien in the hands of the American military. On May 22, 1950, an unnamed informant turned the original of this photograph over to agent John Quinn of the New Orleans FBI Field Office claiming he had purchased the photograph from another individual for the sum of $1.00 and was "placing it in the hands of the goverment" because it pictured "a man from Mars in the United States". The picture, supposedly showing an alien survivor of a UFO crash in the custody of two U.S. military policemen, reportedly first surfaced in Wiesbaden, Germany, in the late 1940s allegedly in the possession of a U.S. GI stationed there at the time. How he came into possession of such a picture remains unclear, as do the identities of the two soldiers portrayed, the location of the military base and the nature of the portable respiratory apparatus that is obviously being used to assist the alien's breathing. Receiving some limited publicity in Germany during the late 40s, the photo and story was naturally regarded with skepticism by U.S. officials.

This derelict manmade "flying saucer" was found in a Maryland barn on August 17, 1949. Courtesy of the Modern Military Branch, National Archives, Washington, D.C.

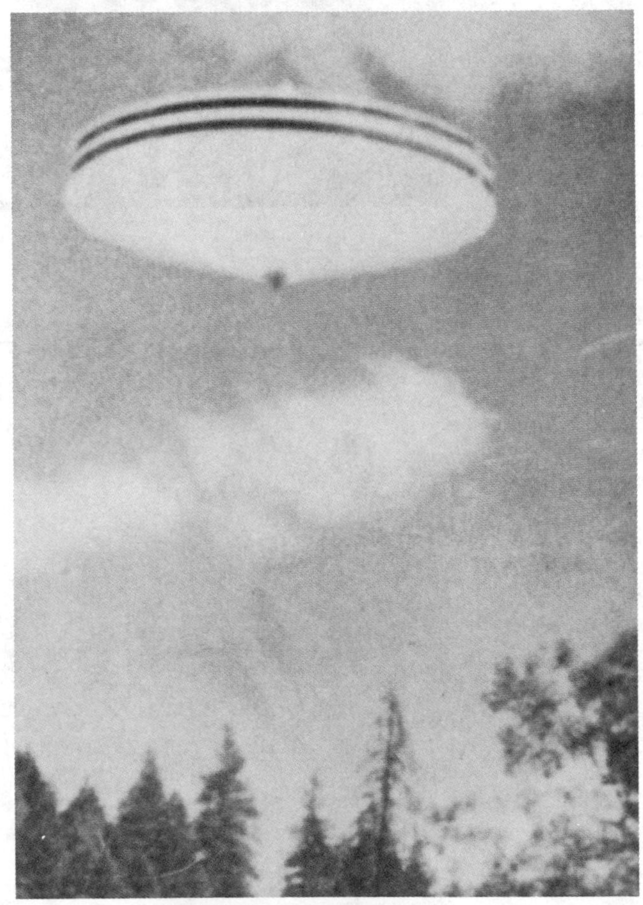

A classic flying saucer photograph purportedly depicting an extraterrestial vehicle. Courtesy of Daniel W. Fry.

ANTI - GRAVITY & THE UNIFIED FIELD

EDITED BY DAVID HATCHER CHILDRESS

Is Einstein's Unified Field the answer to all of our energy problems? Explored in this compilation of material is how gravity, electricity and magnetism manifest from a unified field around us. Why artificial gravity is possible; Secrets of UFO propulsion; free energy; Nikola Tesla and anti-gravity airships of the 20's and 30's; Flying saucers as superconducting whirls of plasma; anti-mass generators; vortex propulsion; suppressed technology; government coverups; gravitational pulse spacecraft & more. 240 pages, 7x10 paperback, 130 rare photographs, diagrams and drawings, ISBN 0-932813-10-0. $14.95 (code: AGU).

ANTI - GRAVITY & THE WORLD GRID

EDITED BY DAVID HATCHER CHILDRESS

Is the earth surrounded by an intricate electromagnetic grid network offering free energy? This compilation of material on the earth grid, ley lines, and world power points contains chapters on the geography, mathematics, and light harmonics of the earth grid. Learn the purpose of ley lines and ancient megalithic structures located on the grid. Discover how the grid made the Philadelphia Experiment possible. Explore Coral Castle and many other mysteries. Including, acoustic levitation, Tesla Shields and Scalar Wave weaponry. Browse through the section on anti-gravity patents, and research resources. 274 pages, 150 rare photographs, diagrams and drawings, 7x10 paperback, ISBN 0-932813-03-8, $12.95. (code: AGW)

THE ANTI - GRAVITY HANDBOOK

EDITED BY DAVID HATCHER CHILDRESS

An astounding and revolutionary work! Find out how to build a flying saucer, learn about crystals and their role in Anti-gravity theory. Read Arthur C. Clarke on gravity control, Nikola Tesla and free energy, NASA and gravity research, the mysterious technology of the RAMA empire and Bruce Cathie's anti-gravity equation. Discover Searle discs and all about the moon and more. Browse through the section on anti-gravity patents, and research resources. 210 pages, 140 rare photographs, diagrams and drawings, 7x10 paperback, ISBN 0-932813-01-1. $12.95. (code: AGH)

TAPPING THE ZERO POINT ENERGY

MORAY B. KING

The author, a well-known researcher, explains how free energy and anti-gravity are possible with today's physics. The theories of the zero point energy show there are tremendous fluctuations of electrical field energy imbedded within the fabric of space. This book shows how in the 1930s inventor T. Henry Moray could produce a fifty kilowatt "free energy" machine; how an electrified vortex plasma creates anti-gravity; how the Pons/Fleischmann "cold fusion" experiment could produce tremendous heat without fusion; and how certain experiments might produce a gravitational anomaly. 170 pages, 6x9 paperback, 60 diagrams and drawings. $9.95. (code: TAP)

INTERNATIONAL TESLA SYMPOSIUM PROCEEDINGS

EDITED BY STEVEN R. ELSWICK

The best collection of Tesla material currently in print, it includes papers on the transmission of electricity through the earth without wires, Tesla and particle beam weapons, advanced gravitics, levitation, Maxwell's lost Unified Field theory, radiant energy, Tesla Coils and much more. 21 articles in all, a must for any serious Tesla studentl 304 pages, 9x11 hardback, illustrated with rare photographs & diagrams. $49.95. (code: ITS)

TESLA TECHNOLOGY SERIES VOL. 1:

The Problem of Increasing Human Energy & the Wireless Transmission of Power.

NIKOLA TESLA

Orignially published in June, 1900 in Century Magazine, this small book outlines Tesla's master blueprint for the world. It includes chapters on the transmission of electricity through the earth without wires, the secret of tuning the electrical oscillator, unexpected properties of the atmosphere, and some strange experiments. 92 pages, 6x9 paperback, illustrated with rare photographs & diagrams. $9.95. (code: TESL)

TESLA TECHNOLOGY SERIES VOL. 2:

Boundary Layer Breakthrough: The Bladeless Tesla Turbine

JEFFREY HAYES

The amazing Tesla turbine is the world's most efficient engine. This book traces the history and developement of the bladeless turbine by Nikola Tesla and Jake Possell. Though these are 20 times more efficient than conventional turbine, they are barely known to the scientific world, This advanced technology is 90 years old!. 184 pages, 6x9 paperback, illustrated with rare photographs & diagrams. $19.95. (code: BLB)

ETHER TECHNOLOGY

A Rational Approach to Gravity Control

RHO SIGMA

Before the term "Quantum Field" there was the "Ether". Written by a well-known American scientist under the pseudonym of Rho Sigma, this brief book discusses in detail international efforts at gravity control and discoid craft propulsion. Includes chapters on Searle discs, T. Townsend Brown, Ether-Vortex-Turbines, and more. Forward by former NASA astronaut Edgar Mitchell. 108 pages, 6x9 paperback, illustrated with photographs & diagrams. $9.95. (code: ETT)

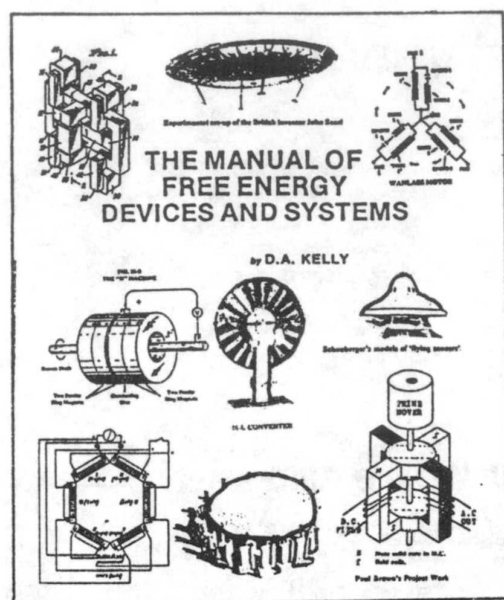

THE MANUAL OF FREE ENERGY DEVICES

DON KELLY

Combining Vol. One and Two, Kelly descibes the viability and progress of each device from Nikola Tesla to the present. Also mentioned are various spin-off inventions as a result of free energy research. Included are chapters on Joseph Newman, "N" Field Machines, Victor Schauberger, John Searle, Wilhelm Reich, and Rudolf Steiner. 123 pages, 9x11 paperback, illustrated with rare photographs, patents & diagrams. ISBN 0-932298-59-5. $12.95. (code: FED)

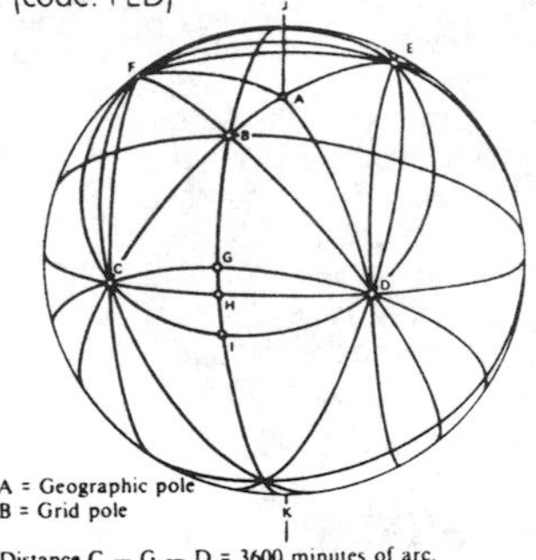

A = Geographic pole
B = Grid pole

Distance C — G — D = 3600 minutes of arc.
Distance C — H — D = 3418.6069 minutes of arc
Distance C — I — D = 3643.2 minutes of arc

THE AWESOME LIFE FORCE

JOSEPH CATER

Here is a book that purports to solve all of the mysteries of life, including: UFO phenomenon, gravity, Wilhelm Reich and orgone energy, teleportation, time travel, materializations, and just about every other strange occurrence. A must for anyone exploring the strange nature of reality. 472 pages, 5x8 paperback, 30 diagrams and line drawings, ISBN 0-86540-374-0. $15.95 (code: ALF)

THE BRIDGE TO INFINITY

Harmonic 371244

CAPTAIN BRUCE CATHIE

This book is Air New Zealand Captain Bruce Cathie's fourth on the controversial subject of Light Harmonics and the fabric of the universe. Cathie has popularized the concept that the earth is criss-crossed by an electromagnetic grid system that can be used for anti-gravity, free energy, levitation and more. The book includes a new analysis of the harmonic nature of reality, acoustic levitation, pyramid power, harmonic receiver towers, and UFO propulsion. It concludes that today's scientists have at their command a fantastic store of knowledge with which to advance the welfare of the human race. 200 pages, 6x9 paperback, illustrated with photographs & diagrams. $11.95. (code: BTF)

THE BRIDGE TO INFINITY

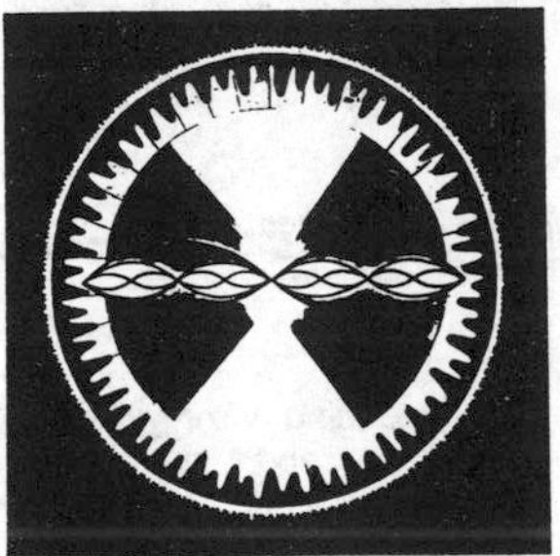

HARMONIC 371244

NEW

PULSE OF THE PLANET

EDITED BY JAMES DE MEO, PH.D.
FORWARD BY EVA REICH

An anthology of material on orgone energy and related subjects. Find out about cloud busting in Arizona and California to end the drought, orgone accumulator therapy, Orgonotic Devices, evidence of a worldwide climate-linked geographical pattern to human behavior, and more. 144 pages, 10x11 paperback, with diagrams, maps & photographs. $20.00. (code: PUP)

THE DEATH OF ROCKETRY

DICKINSON AND COOK

A large and heavily illustrated book on reactionless spacedrives. Full of patents, diagrams, photos and drawings, it clearly explains the principles behind such patents as the Dean Drive, the Cook Drive, the Laskowitz Drive, the Nowlin Drive, the Matyas Drive and much more. One of the best books we have seen on the subject, and not to be missed by serious researchers. The Jet Propulsion Laboratory (JPL) has recently confirmed that these drives work! 122 pages, 9x12 paperback, illustrated with photographs & diagrams. ISBN 0-9604584-0-9 $23.95. (code: DOR)

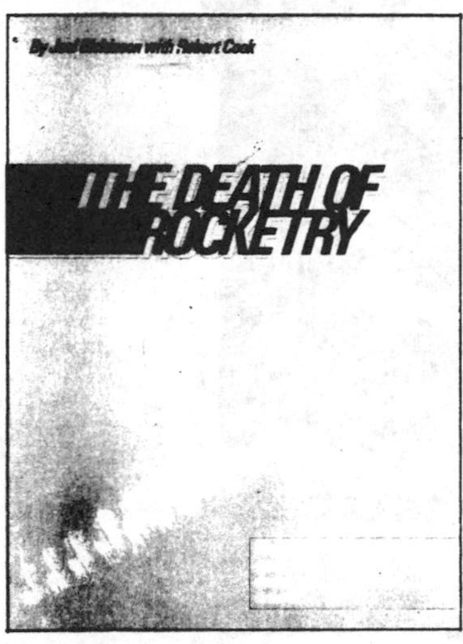

THE ENERGY GRID

Harmonic 695 The Pulse of the Universe

CAPTAIN BRUCE CATHIE

This is a compilation (updated and corrected) of Air New Zealand Captain Bruce Cathie's first three books. They are all rare, suppressed and out of print. Exploring the energy grid in great detail, there are chapters on Unified Equations, the mysterious aerials, Pythagoras & the Grid, Nikola Tesla, nuclear detonation & the grid, maps of the ancients, an Australian Stonehenge, & much more. Cathie's books are a must for the serious student of Anti-Gravity and lost science. 255 pages, 6x9 paperback, illustrated with photographs & diagrams. ISBN 0-922-356-20-3. $13.95. (code: TEG)

CROP CIRCLE SECRETS

EDITED BY DONALD CYR

This exciting book is a large format, highly illustrated compilation on crop circles and their related phenomenon. Includes a number of discussions on the relationships to ancient megaliths, ancient crop circles, the importance of magnetic field lines, King Arthur's crop circle, the Jupiter Canopy model, and other strange vortex effects. 80 pages, 8x10 paperback, 100 photos, illustrations and maps. $9.95. (code: CCS)

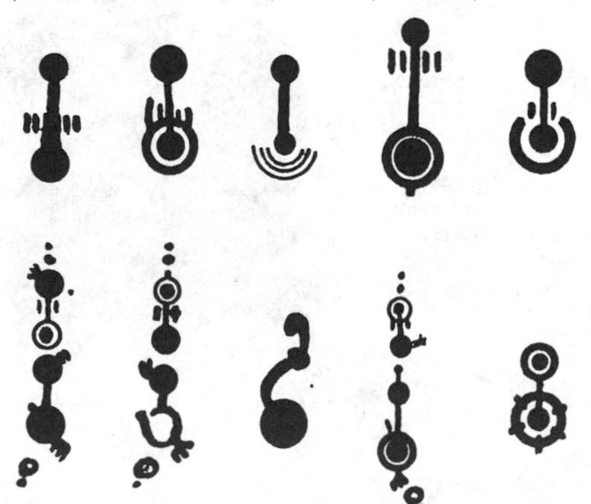

THE STONES CRY OUT

God's Best Kept Secrets Hidden in Stone

BONNIE GAUNT

Stones have been the most permanent and time-enduring objects used by man to record his existence on the planet. Ancient structures such as the Great Pyramid and Stonehenge have endured through more than 4,000 years, hiding their secrets of ancient wisdom. Those stones now cry out to be heard. Their message reveals an insight into the awesome and majestic laws of the universe, and an intimate knowledge of the Creator. 144 pages, 5x8 paperback., 87 diagrams, maps & photographs. $9.95 (code: SCO)

THE ORGONE ACCUMULATOR HANDBOOK

JAMES DE MEO, PH.D.

Forward by Eva Reich

In 1957 all books dealing with orgone were banned and burnt by the U.S. government and its inventor was jailed and assassinated. But today, you can build and experiment with an orgone accumulator of your own. This book presents construction plans and ideas on how to use this simple device for collecting orgone energy and helping to heal plants and animals. In addition, there are suggestions for protecting yourself against toxic energy. 155 pages, 6x9 paperback, with diagrams, maps & photographs. $12.95. (code: OAH)

LOST CITIES OF NORTH & CENTRAL AMERICA

DAVID HATCHER CHILDRESS

The fifth book in the Lost Cities Series.

We have been getting orders for this book for the last three years, and finally we are going to get it into print. So hold onto your armchairs, for the adventure isn't over yet, and those that can't get enough of lost cities and ancient mysteries can sink their teeth into another volume... Maverick archaeologist Childress continues his world-wide odyssey in quest of the fantastic mysteries of the past. In this exciting book, discover a sunken city in Guatemala, Sumerians in Nicaragua, secret Mayan cities in Mexico, tunnel systems in Arizona, gigantic pyramids in Illinois and even sunken structures in Wisconsin. Join him in search of legendary cities, vast gold treasure, jungle pyramids, ancient seafarers, and living dinosaurs. Soon to be an international television show. 416 pages, 6x9 paperback, illustrated, ISBN 0-932813-09-7, $14.95 (code: NCA)

STONE FRIEZE FROM MAYA RUINS AT TIKAL, GUATEMALA.

MEN AND GODS IN MONGOLIA

HENNING HASLUND

The third book in our Mystic Traveller Series

First published in 1935 by Kegan Paul of London, this rare and unusual travel book takes us into the virtually unknown world of Mongolia, a country that only now, after seventy years, is finally opening up to the west. Haslund, a Swedish explorer, takes us to the lost city of Karakota in the Gobi desert. We meet the Bodgo Gegen, a God-king in Mongolia similar to the Dalai Lama of Tibet. We meet Dambin Jansang, the dreaded warlord of the "Black Gobi". There is even material in this incredible book on the Hi-mori, an "airhorse" that flies through the air (similar to a Vimana) and carries with it the sacred stone of Chintamani. Aside from the esoteric and mystical material, there is plenty of just plain adventure: caravans across the Gobi desert, kidnapped and held for ransom, initiation into shamanic societies, warlords and the violent birth of a new nation. 358 pages, 6x9 paperback, illustrated, 57 photos, illustrations and maps, $15.95. (code: MGM)

IN SECRET TIBET

THEODORE ILLION

Reprint of a rare 30's travel book. Illion was a German traveller who not only spoke fluent Tibetan, but travelled in disguise through forbidden Tibet when it was off-limits to all outsiders. His incredible adventures make this one of the most exciting travel books ever published. Includes illustrations of Tibetan monks levitating stones by accoustics. 210 pages, 6x9 paperback, illustrated, ISBN 0-932813-13-5. $15.95 (code: IST)

DARKNESS OVER TIBET

THEODORE ILLION

In this second reprint of the rare 30's travel books by Illion, the German traveller continues his travels through Tibet and is given the directions to a strange underground city. As the original publisher's remarks said, this is a rare account of an underground city in Tibet by the only westerner ever to enter it and escape alive! 210 pages, 6x9 paperback, illustrated, ISBN 0-932813-14-3. $15.95. (code: DOT)

NU SUN

Asian American Voyages 500 BC

GUNNAR THOMPSON.

This large and attractive book tells the true story of ancient Chinese voyages to North America and the amazing account of their colonial settlements. Incredible revelations about the mysterious origins of the Mayans and the Taoist source of Chinese & Mayan religious symbolism. Similarities between ancient Asian sculptures, pyramids and temples and those of ancient Meso-America are explored in great detail. The startling parallels between ancient Taoist motifs and those used by the Mayans are enough to convince even the most die-hard sceptic. More than 500 illustrations of actual artifacts. 240 pages, 8x11 hardback, Profusely illustrated, bibliography & index. $24.95. (code: NUS)

VIMANA AIRCRAFT OF ANCIENT INDIA & ATLANTIS

DAVID HATCHER CHILDRESS

INTRODUCTION BY IVAN T. SANDERSON

Did the ancients have the technology of flight? In this incredible volume on ancient India, authentic Indian texts such as the Ramayana and the Mahabharata, are used to prove that ancient aircraft were in use more than four thousand years ago. Included in this book is the entire Fourth Century BC manuscript Vimaanika Shastra by the ancient author Maharishi Bharadwaaja, translated into English by the Mysore Sanskrit professor G.R. Josyer. Also included are chapters on Atlantean technology, the incredible Rama Empire of India and the devastating wars that destroyed it. Also an entire chapter on mercury vortex propulsion and mercury gyros, the power source described in the ancient Indian texts. Not to be missed by those interested in ancient civilizations or the UFO enigma. 334 pages, 6x9 paperback, 104 rare photographs, maps and drawings. $15.95. (code: VAA)

ORDERING INSTRUCTIONS

- Please Print All Information
- Please Do Not Send Cash
- Remit By Check ▪ MO ▪ Credit Card
- Telephone/FAX Credit Card Orders
- Call Anytime
- 10% Discount for 3 Or More Books

BACKORDERS:
We will backorder all out-of-stock books unless otherwise requested

RETAILERS:
Standard Discounts Available
Call ▪ Write ▪ FAX for Information

SHIPPING CHARGES

UNITED STATES:

- Postal Bookrate
  $1.50 First Item
  50¢ Each additional Item
- Postal Airmail
  $5.00 Each Item
- United Parcel Service (UPS)
  $3.00 First Item
  50¢ Each additional Item

CANADA:

- Postal Bookrate
  $2.00 First Item
  50¢ Each additional Item
- Postal Airmail
  $6.00 Each Item

SPECIAL PAYMENT NOTICE: FOR CANADIAN ORDERS:

- Payment MUST BE USD$
- Canadian Postal Money Orders OK
- NO Personal Checks
- Other checks MUST BE drawn on a US Bank

ALL OTHER COUNTRIES:

- Surface Delivery
  $4.00 First Item
  $1.00 Each additional Item
- Airmail
  $10.00 Each Item

SPECIAL PAYMENT NOTICE: FOR INTERNATIONAL ORDERS:

AVOID DELAY ▪ PLEASE NOTE

- Payment must be USD$
- Checks must be drawn on US Bank
- Add $5.00 for Airmail Subscription To Future Catalogs

Adventures Unlimited Press

Publishers Network
Post Office Box 22
Stelle, IL 60919-9989
Phone: 815 253 6390
FAX: 815 256 2299

My first order ☐
I have ordered before ☐
This is a new address ☐

Name ____________
Address ____________
City ____________ State/Province ____________
ZIP/Postal Code ____________
Tel. (Home) ____________ (Work) ____________

Title Code	Item Description	Price	Qty	Amount
Please Use Title Codes		Item Totals		
	10% for 3 or more items	Less Discount		
		Previous Credit		
	Illinois Residents add 7%	Sales Tax		
	Postal ☐ UPS ☐ Airmail ☐	Shipping		
	☐ Check/MO Enclosed (USD$)	Total Remit		

☐ Please charge this to my MasterCard / Visa

Card Number ____________ Expire Date ____________
Signature ____________

SEND A CATALOG TO MY FRIENDS

Name
Address

Name
Address